P9-AQK-957

THE SOLITARY SELF

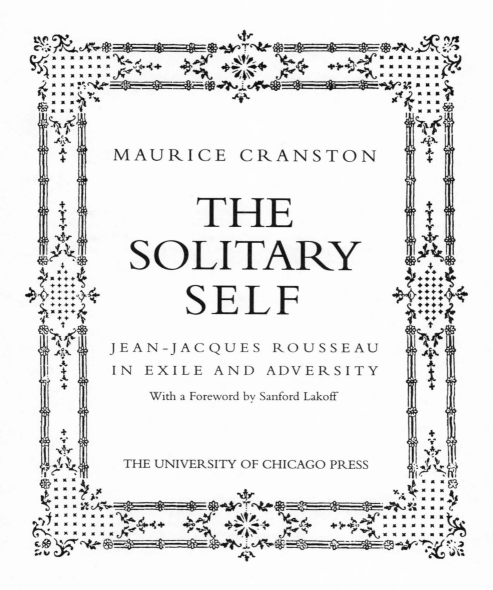

MAURICE CRANSTON

THE
SOLITARY
SELF

JEAN-JACQUES ROUSSEAU
IN EXILE AND ADVERSITY

With a Foreword by Sanford Lakoff

THE UNIVERSITY OF CHICAGO PRESS

MAURICE CRANSTON, former president of the Institut Internationale de Philosophie Politique, taught political science at the London School of Economics from 1959 until his death in November 1993. His works include *Jean-Jacques: The Early Life and Work of Jean-Jacques Rousseau, 1712–1754*, and *The Noble Savage: Jean-Jacques Rousseau, 1754–1764* (the first two volumes of his biography of Rousseau), both published by the University of Chicago Press.

The University of Chicago Press, Chicago 60637
Viking/Penguin, Ltd., London
© 1997 by Maximiliana Cranston
Foreword © 1997 by The University of Chicago
All rights reserved. Published 1997
Printed in the United States of America
06 05 04 03 02 01 00 99 98 97   1 2 3 4 5

ISBN: 0-226-11865-7 (cloth)

Library of Congress Cataloging-in-Publication Data

Cranston, Maurice William, 1920–1993
    The solitary self : Jean-Jacques Rousseau in exile and adversity /
Maurice Cranston ; with a foreword by Sanford Lakoff.
        p.   cm.
    Includes bibliographical references (p.   ) and index.
    ISBN 0-226-11865-7 (cloth)
    1. Rousseau, Jean-Jacques, 1712–1778—Biography.   2. Authors, French—18th century—
Biography.   3. Philosophers—France—Biography.   I. Title.
PQ2047.C73   1997
848'.509—dc20
[B]   96-12922
                                                                                          CIP

CONTENTS

PLATES

Rousseau's tomb on the Isle des Peupliers, *eighteenth-century engraving by J.-M. Moreau Le Jeune*

FOREWORD

Maurice Cranston had completed the first seven chapters of this third and concluding volume of his biography of Jean-Jacques Rousseau before his sudden death in November 1993. The eighth chapter has been composed from his notes and from a prepared lecture, supplemented by material from other sources. The epilogue, except for a few added pages, is drawn from three of his analytical studies: *The Romantic Movement* (Blackwell 1994); *Philosophers and Pamphleteers: Political Theorists of the Enlightenment* (Oxford University Press 1986), first presented as the Carlyle Lectures at Oxford; and 'Jean-Jacques Rousseau and the Fusion of Democratic Sovereignty with Aristocratic Government' (*The History of European Ideas*, Elsevier Science Ltd., 1989). The kind permission of the publishers for the use of these materials is gratefully acknowledged.

Professor Cranston spent the better part of two decades on the research—much of it devoted to examining archival records and tracing Rousseau's wanderings—which led to this magisterial work. He was a cherished friend of mine and of many academics and writers throughout Europe, North America, and Australia, admired as much for his wit and lucidity as for the depth of his scholarship. It has therefore been a privilege and a consolation to help bring this final volume to publication. I wish to thank the Suntory and Toyota Centres at the London School of Economics for research support and, for their invaluble cooperation, Professor Cranston's elder son, Nicholas Cranston; John Tryneski, Leslie Keros, and Randy Petilos of the University of Chicago Press; and two distinguished Rousseau scholars, Christopher Kelly of the University of Maryland, Baltimore County, and Robert Wokler of the University of Manchester.

Sanford Lakoff
University of California, San Diego

INTRODUCTION

In Rousseau's life there were three phases. The first was picaresque. He was born in Geneva in 1712 in the patrician home of a mother who died giving him birth, and his early childhood was spent in the company of a profligate artisan father. A gentleman's education in the house of a private tutor was followed by a plebeian apprenticeship in an engraver's workshop, from which Rousseau fled at the age of sixteen. After converting to Catholicism in pursuit of the patronage of Savoyard nobility, he worked variously as a footman in Turin, the steward and lover of a Swiss baroness in Chambéry, a music teacher in Lausanne, and an interpreter for a Levantine mountebank. A teaching job in the household of the police chief of Lyons, whose brothers were the philosophers Condillac and Mably, introduced him to the France of the Enlightenment; and at the age of thirty, he set out with another young man from the provinces, Denis Diderot, to conquer the literary and music worlds of Paris. Much to their surprise, both succeeded—Diderot with his *Encyclopédie*, Rousseau, after a hectic interlude as secretary to the French ambassador in Venice, with his *Discourse on the Sciences and the Arts*, his pamphlets in defence of Italian music, and his opera *Le Devin du village*.

The second phase of Rousseau's life was marked by his retreat from Paris and his renunciation of the standard rewards of fame. Recovering his rights as a citizen of Geneva and as a communicant of the Calvinist church, he withdrew to what was then the rustic seclusion of Montmorency, living frugally with a semiliterate mistress and working hard. Although increasingly afflicted with a urinary disorder, he produced within nine years several of his most substantial books, including *The Social Contract*, *Julie, ou la Nouvelle Héloïse*, and *Émile*.

His solitude was interrupted by an ill-fated love affair in one summer and a busy social life among the noble and princely at the Château de Montmorency in other summers. The prodigious success of *Julie*, an epistolary novel, transformed the author from a literary celebrity into a cult figure.

Émile was less fortunate. The efforts of Rousseau's exalted friends to secure its publication on French soil drew the attention of the Paris *parlement*, a judicial council, which promptly ordered the burning of the book and the arrest of the author.

A swift escape to Switzerland ended this second phase of Rousseau's life, which had been a relatively happy one. The third and last phase was to prove as unsettled as the first, but 'romantic' only in the darker sense of *Sturm und Drang*. Condemned to wander the earth in search of asylum, he felt befriended one moment, betrayed the next. Obsessed by feelings of persecution, not all unwarranted, he came to see himself as a social outcast and concentrated on writing autobiographical works aimed at revealing his essential innocence and truthfulness. Through this introspection, he was to transform his misery and solitude into enduring works of literature—the most notable his *Confessions*.

1

A MIXED WELCOME

On 14 June 1762, a few days before his fiftieth birthday, Jean-Jacques Rousseau arrived as a refugee at Yverdon in Switzerland. The welcome he received helped him soon to overcome the ordeal of his flight from Montmorency. His old friend Daniel Roguin, a retired Swiss banker from Paris, embraced him and installed him in his villa on the shores of Lake Neuchâtel. It was a house packed with Roguin's nieces and great-nieces, all of whom greeted Rousseau with warmth and excitement.

'Oh why did Providence have me born among men, and make me of a different species?' Rousseau wrote[1] soon after his arrival. He was nevertheless delighted to be surrounded by the attentive and affectionate members of the 'Roguinerie', as his host called his numerous relations. With his *gouvernante*, Thérèse Levasseur, left behind at his cottage in Montmorency, Rousseau needed to be looked after. His enjoyment—and approval—of solitude notwithstanding, he had never lived entirely alone; without a nurse, cook, housekeeper, and mistress, without Thérèse to perform all these roles in turn, he was lost. Thus he had no reason for displeasure in Roguin's crowded villa, where the family and staff vied with one another to be of service to him.

'I feel much better now,' Rousseau reported[2] to the Maréchale de Luxembourg on 17 June, three days after his arrival; 'the air of my native country, the warmth of friendship, the beauty of the neighbourhood and the summer weather, all concur to cure the fatigues of that most wretched journey.'

Everyone at the Villa Roguin wanted Rousseau to settle among them. His host's cousin George-Augustin Roguin, a colonel retired from service in the Sardinian army, offered him a *pavillon* on the estate. Roguin's niece Julianne, widow of Pierre Boy de La Tour, a merchant in Lyons whose business she had taken over, undertook to reorganise his modest finances. Her three daughters hugged him as he sat on the terrace of the villa in the summer sunshine. His favourite among the girls was Madeleine-Catherine, then aged fifteen; it was to her that he wrote some years later his celebrated *Lettres sur la botanique*.

Rousseau told Mme de Luxembourg that he hoped to keep his presence in Yverdon a secret, but he cannot seriously have expected to do so. Yverdon was a town of some 22,000 inhabitants, with a history dating back to a Roman foundation around a mineral spa and baths that still existed and that, despite his profound scepticism concerning all medical treatments and cures, Rousseau politely agreed to try. In such a small place his presence could hardly pass unnoticed. Even though he had not yet started to wear his Armenian caftan, he cut a striking figure. In his memoirs,[3] Bonstetten speaks of being startled to meet as a boy in Yverdon a stranger with eyes so fiery and lively—*so feurig und lebhaft*—as he had never seen before, only to learn later that the stranger was Rousseau. A local matron, seeing an unfamiliar, dapper figure emerging from the prefectorial château, observed[4] that the prefect's wife had acquired a new *perruquier*—a remark it is fortunate the philosopher did not hear, for *perruquier* was the despised profession of Wintzenried, Rousseau's erstwhile rival for the favours of Mme de Warens.

The stranger's identity soon became public knowledge. Daniel Roguin had too many relations among the inhabitants of Yverdon for the secret to be kept. Besides, Rousseau had to make his presence known to the authorities. Although Yverdon was situated on Lake Neuchâtel, it was part of the Pays de Vaud, a French-speaking province of the republic of Berne. That government was represented by a prefect, or *bailli*, whose château was, besides the church, the most prominent building in the town. The prefect at the time, Victor de Gingins, Seigneur de Moiry, received Rousseau on behalf of the republic with cordial and genuine friendship. His welcome was in part that of a fellow author, for the prefect had lately published a novel entitled *Pacha de Bude*.[5] He invited Rousseau several times to dine at the château and acted as best he could as his protector. On behalf of the town, the mayor (or *banneret*), Georges-François Roguin, a distant cousin of Rousseau's host, also embraced Rousseau with great ostentation; but his gesture, as it turned out later, was the kiss of Judas.

A letter from Rousseau's best friend in Geneva, Paul-Claude Moultou, dated 16 June,[6] brought the first warning of trouble brewing in that city. The Petit Conseil, Moultou reported, 'has banned your *Social Contract* and sealed all copies of *Émile* for examination'. Moultou also informed Rousseau that crowds of well-wishers had called at his house for news of him: 'a multitude of citizens admires your *Social Contract* as the arsenal of liberty.' He added, however, that 'a small number throws the book on the fire.' Moultou went on to suggest that Rousseau come to Geneva to defend himself and his writings.

From Paris, d'Alembert wrote[7] to assure Rousseau that the majority of the

public was on his side in France. People there, he told him, 'are against the
fanatics who are persecuting you for being right'. As for the men of letters
in France, d'Alembert declared that they looked on Rousseau as their
leader:★ 'if you came back to France you would find a thousand arms open
to receive you.' Unlike Moultou, however, d'Alembert stopped short of
proposing that Rousseau actually put his popularity to the test. Instead,
d'Alembert suggested that Rousseau seek asylum not far from Yverdon in
the principality of Neuchâtel; its sovereign, King Frederick II of Prussia, and
its governor, the Earl Marischal Keith, would, d'Alembert believed, be delighted to shelter him.

D'Alembert included in his letter some lavish praise of *Émile*, which
Rousseau read with a certain scepticism. His suspicions increased when he
observed that the letter was unsigned.[8] The letter was, moreover, dated from
the Château de Montmorency, a detail that fortified Rousseau's belief that
d'Alembert was out, as he wrote in the *Confessions*, 'to succeed me in the
affections of Mme de Luxembourg'.[9] There is, however, no sign of a cool-
ing of affection on the part of the Maréchale toward Rousseau at this time
or of any constraint on Rousseau's side. Both the Luxembourgs wrote frequently to him, begging for news of his situation and his health—which, at
first, was surprisingly good.

In one of his letters to M. de Luxembourg, Rousseau explained[10] that his
future plans depended on whether Thérèse decided to stay at Montlouis or
to join him in Switzerland. He insisted that he did not want to press her into
joining him if she felt the least reluctance; he would like her to come, but
his first desire, he said, was for her to be happy. By the same post, Rousseau
wrote[11] to Thérèse herself, putting the choice to her, urging her to consider
carefully whether she could endure a life of exile with him or would prefer
to stay in France. In either case, he asked her to seek advice about his possessions at Montlouis. If everything had not been confiscated by the officers
of the Paris *parlement*, he would like at least to have a trunk sent with clothes
and personal belongings 'of which I have a very great need'. He told her
where to find the *écus* with which to pay small debts and explained that he
had left a larger sum of money with M. de La Roche—the Luxembourgs'
steward—that would serve to pay for her journey if she elected to join him:
'I have not yet made up my mind where I shall settle in this country. I await
your reply before deciding, and I will arrange things differently if you do not
come.'

In the *Confessions*[12] Rousseau says he was by no means sure that Thérèse
would wish to join him. He had for some time noticed her growing more
distant from him, although he claimed that his fondness for her was the same

---

★This was grotesque flattery. Besides d'Alembert, the only man of letters who wrote to Rousseau
to express support in this time of trouble was Charles Duclos.

as ever. He attributed this change in her to the fact that he had ceased to
sleep with her, on health grounds ('I noticed that sexual intercourse with
women aggravated my complaint'), and also because he was afraid of making her pregnant again; although she remained attached to him, he assumed
that she was motivated 'by duty and not by love'.

He was mistaken. As soon as she was given the chance, Thérèse declared
her unfailing devotion to him and her impatience to join him in exile. Semiliterate as she was, she took up a pen at four o'clock in the morning and
wrote him a love letter.[13] She swore that her heart had always been his and
would never change as long as she lived; she told him she wished for nothing better than for them to share all their sorrows together: 'I cannot wait to
be with you and I embrace you with all my heart.' At the same time she sent
messages of goodwill from the Luxembourgs and other friends at Montmorency. She mentioned that she had been honoured and thrilled to receive
an invitation to meet the Prince de Conti, Rousseau's royal protector, into
whose presence she had been taken by Mme de Boufflers.* Given the
Prince's reputation for coldness and ungraciousness, the occasion was doubtless a noteworthy one. Mme de Boufflers herself sent Rousseau an account[15]
of Thérèse's audience, assuring him that his heart would have been warmed
by the kindness the Prince had showered upon his timid *gouvernante*,
'demonstrating at once the goodness of his nature and his esteem for you'.
She congratulated Rousseau on having earned by merit alone the friendship
of his Highness. Fortunately Rousseau had already remembered to write
to the Prince a letter[15] of thanks for making possible his escape from the
police of the Paris *parlement*.

Mme de Boufflers also found occasion in her letter to scold Rousseau. She
made it clear that she was distressed that he had not written any letters or
sent any messages to her. She said she had been to his bedroom at Montlouis
and, with tears in her eyes, had searched all the drawers in the hope of finding a note from him, only to be disappointed. She also told him she had
communicated with David Hume in order to secure an offer of refuge for
Rousseau in England, which she urged him to accept if it materialised. She
also demanded to be told what Rousseau intended to do to secure a livelihood since she could not imagine he had much money left.† Continuing in
this bossy vein, she implored Rousseau to moderate his indignation against
the Paris *parlementaires* since they were only doing their duty in enforcing a

---

*Since the Duchesse de Boufflers had by this time faded out of Rousseau's life, Marie-Charlotte
de Campet de Saujon, the Comtesse de Boufflers, will henceforth be referred to simply as Mme de
Boufflers.

†Other friends besides Mme de Boufflers were concerned about Rousseau's financial situation.
Charles Duclos wrote on 12 June to say he had '600 francs to offer you' (BPUN, MS 293, ff.79–80),
but Rousseau seems not to have accepted the offer.

law they did not make. She also advised him to stop trying to conceal the fact that he was in Switzerland but rather to publish it, so that people in France would stop suspecting that he was being hidden by the Maréchal de Luxembourg at Montmorency or by the Prince de Conti at l'Isle Adam. She was plainly afraid that either or both of these illustrious personages might be compromised by their association with Rousseau.

The letter ended with more reproaches from Mme de Boufflers for Rousseau's 'indifference' to her. We may feel sure that he was not unduly disturbed by this. Although they had never had the affair that Mme de Boufflers, with her singular liking for sleeping with philosophers, seems once to have hoped for, they behaved like former lovers—sparring, bickering, and quarrelling but still somehow concerned about each other's happiness. The one reproach in her letter that Rousseau was unwilling to swallow concerned his reaction to the proceedings of the Paris *parlementaires*. He declared in his reply[16] that he was amazed at her defence of those 'bigots of the Robe'. His grievance against them was not simply that they had banned *Émile* but that they had accepted, published, and printed a Judgement* of the book by the attorney-general Omer Joly de Fleury, whose comments, as Mme de Boufflers should have known since she read them, were a total calumny.

Rousseau's objection to the Judgement was surely justified. In it, *Émile* is described as

impugning the veracity of the Holy Scriptures, disputing the divinity of Jesus Christ and the existence of the Christian religion, asserting blasphemous, ungodly, and detestable principles, containing indecent material offensive to propriety and modesty, together with propositions subversive to sovereign authority, setting forth maxims of education which could only produce men devoted to scepticism and toleration, abandoned to their passions, men given over to the pleasures of the senses, dominated by pride and listening to no other voice than that of nature.

The Judgement concludes with the recommendation that since the author has not feared to put his name to the book, he should be promptly arrested, and the book itself lacerated and burned. Rousseau had the text of the Judgement before his eyes, since Mme de Luxembourg had sent him a copy of the printed version; and he could not fail to be distressed by its tenor. Unfortunately for him, it was widely circulated, and such was the force of the attorney-general's inelegant hyperbole that it led to the suppression of *Émile* in places other than France.

---

*Arrest de la Cour de Parlement, qui Condamne . . . Émile, Paris, 1762 (CC, XI, A254).

On 18 June—four days after Rousseau's arrival in Yverdon—*Émile* was discussed at a meeting of the Petit Conseil in Geneva. Copies, as Rousseau learned from Moultou, had already been seized. In Geneva, however, discussion of *Émile* was secondary to discussion of *The Social Contract*, and although the two books were put together on the agenda, *The Social Contract* was the one that really troubled the rulers of Geneva. In France, the *parlementaires* had been concerned with religious conformity; having lately penalised the Jesuits on the right, they were eager to prove their evenhandedness by punishing a Deist on the left. In Geneva, the preoccupations of the patrician government were firmly political. If *The Social Contract* disturbed them more than *Émile*, this was because it depicted a constitution, very similar to that of Geneva itself, being ruined by the magistrates' systematically taking sovereignty out of the hands of the people and transforming the state from a free republic into a despotism. Since this is precisely what the members of the Petit Conseil of Geneva—25 in all, drawn from a small group of patrician families—had been doing for years, they read *The Social Contract* as a direct challenge to their position and their policies. The indictment of *Émile* made it easier for them to act at the same time against *The Social Contract* and to claim that both books were being suppressed in the name of religion. As Moultou remarked, '*Émile* is the torch with which they set light to *The Social Contract*.'[17]

At their meeting on 18 June the members of the Petit Conseil did more than consign the two books to the flames. They decided also to deal harshly with the author. Although their meeting was secret, notes[18] taken by a member present indicate that there were three propositions before them. The first, to issue a warrant for the arrest of J.-J. Rousseau; the second, not to issue a warrant for his arrest; and the third, to resolve that should Rousseau ever come to Geneva he must be arrested and brought in judgement before them. The third proposal received the most votes. It was a compromise, and it allowed the spokesmen of the Conseil to engage thereafter in a good deal of equivocation. They could alternately deny that a warrant for Rousseau's arrest had been issued and intimate that the Conseil had resolved to arrest him.

The procurator-general, Robert Tronchin, had presented the case for suppressing *The Social Contract* and *Émile*; he also argued that Rousseau had no legal right to citizenship, on the grounds that his re-admission to the Church in 1754 had been irregular. Afterward Robert Tronchin claimed that he had done this to 'defend Rousseau', for if Rousseau was not a citizen he could not be indicted and arrested as a citizen; but only those who wanted to believe Robert Tronchin's claim believed it. The notes taken at the meeting of 18 June also show that it was resolved to 'write to Berne about the sale of *The Social Contract* and *Émile* in Nyon and Coppet', which would seem to substantiate Rousseau's belief that the Petit Conseil prompted the senators of the neighbouring republic to act against those books. This accusation, however, was squarely refuted by another member of the Tronchin family present at the meting, François Tronchin, who declared in a letter[19] to a friend that 'the idea that we could seek to indispose our neighbours against Rousseau surprises and distresses me; that would be an inhuman deed of which I believe no one capable.' For sheer humbug, the Tronchins of Geneva had no equal except Voltaire himself, around whom they gathered like worker bees around a queen. But at least one Tronchin revealed his true feelings about Rousseau: Dr Théodore Tronchin, in a letter[20] to Vernes, wrote, 'I wish that unfortunate man would die: or rather I wish he were dead, because his last two books will do no end of harm.' As for Voltaire himself, commenting to d'Alembert on Rousseau's condemnation by the Paris *parlement*, he maintained[21] that the 'monster' had brought all his troubles on himself with his pride and envy: 'Personally I regard him simply as the dog of Diogenes, or rather as a dog descended from a bastard of that dog.'

News of the decisions taken against him and his books in Geneva soon reached Rousseau in Yverdon. Not surprisingly it had a bad effect on his health. He informed Moultou on 22 June[22] that he had started to feel the pains that usually preceded a relapse: 'It is a great pity that I cannot be allowed to live peacefully in this very agreeable retreat. My good friend, how I enjoy being wanted and caressed as I am here. I no longer feel my misfortunes when I am loved.' He thanked Moultou for defending him in Geneva, but begged Moultou not to jeopardise his own position in that republic by being too openly Rousseau's champion. 'Keep quiet,' Rousseau urged. 'Respect the decisions of the magistrates and public opinion. Do not forsake me publicly, but speak little about me; do not write to me too often, and above all do not come to see me.'

Rousseau was anxious not to compromise his friend, but Moultou was really very capable of looking after himself. He was, in any case, no ordinary Genevese minister of religion; he was not even a citizen of Geneva by birth. He had been born in Montpellier and brought to Geneva as a child by his father, a very rich Protestant French émigré. Now aged 37, he had, besides his inherited wealth, consolidated his social position by marriage to Marianne Cayla, a member of a Genevese patrician family. Moultou moved in *mondain* circles, enjoying the company of such fashionable women as the Duchesse d'Anville and frequenting the sort of smart salons where more than once he came eye to eye with Voltaire. He possessed all the graces of privilege; for all his devotion to Rousseau, his sentiment as a latitudinarian and a Whig agreed more with Locke's.

Moultou regarded both the Petit Conseil's resolution to have Rousseau arrested if he came to Geneva, while not actually issuing a warrant for his arrest, and the procurator-general's claim that Rousseau was not legally a citizen, as evidence of an intention, as he suggested[23] to Rousseau, 'to keep you away from your homeland. They are afraid of you. You are too free, and they fear lest the rest of us should be as free as you are. They only wish you were not our fellow citizen. Be sure they will do all they can to rob you of the title. Only it remains to be seen if they will succeed.'

Moultou had not at this stage received Rousseau's injunction to cease defending him openly, and in any case would have refused to comply. He declared: 'I shall fight for you against the torrent as long as I have an ounce of strength and I shall do so more for the sake of virtue than of friendship.' He would not be alone in defending Rousseau.

For years a state of conflict had existed between the patrician families who dominated the Petit Conseil and a group of citizens who sought to preserve the legislative sovereignty of the Grand Conseil, to which every citizen belonged. Despite the French 'Mediation', which had ended a state of civil war between the two sides in 1737, the Petit Conseil had been unable to eliminate opposition to its hegemony. Just as the members of the Petit Conseil were alarmed by *The Social Contract* because it exposed their design, so the citizens of the opposition welcomed it because it justified their claims. *Émile* was of secondary importance. Even the liberal citizens tended to disagree with *Émile's* premise, believing that it carried criticism of Bible-based Christianity too far; but the patrician government's condemnation of *The Social Contract* prompted them to rally to Rousseau's defense.

Having learned of the measures being taken against him in Geneva, on 20 June Rousseau made a formal application[24] at Yverdon through the prefect, M. de Moiry, to be allowed to remain on Bernese territory. He addressed his plea in most respectful terms to 'Their Excellencies the Senators' in the hope that 'a defender of God's cause, of the laws and of virtue might find grace in their eyes.' He added, rather hopefully in the circumstances, that he desired not only their protection but their esteem.

The prefect supported Rousseau's position. He wrote[25] to Berne, saying that while Rousseau's principles 'were not of the most exact religious orthodoxy' they were 'of the most rigorous morality'. The philosopher's invariable rules were 'to worship God, love one's neighbour, respect the law, and submit to the government under which one lives'. M. de Moiry added that Rousseau was a man of the purest morals, of the most measured, chaste, and interesting conversation. 'His way of life is that of a hermit. His health is ruined. He prays to God in Church. I only ask that he be allowed to die in peace.'

Rousseau's prospects of being granted asylum in the Bernese republic were jeopardised, however, by the publication in the *Gazette de Berne* that month of the full text of the Paris *parlement's* libellous Judgement of *Émile*. Reading this threw Rousseau into a paroxysm of anger, as M. de Moiry told James Boswell sometime afterward:

[Rousseau] wished to insert an outrageous paragraph in the *Gazette de Berne* in which he compared Paris to Toulouse. I said to him: 'Do you realise the consequences? The French Ambassador [to the Swiss Confederation] at Soleure will lodge a complaint against you and you will be arrested. No, you will not insert it.' He replied: 'No I shall not do it. It may be that some day I shall feel that I am obliged to you; but now I do not feel it.' The decree of Geneva pierced his heart. He was terribly downcast.[26]

Rousseau was correct in thinking that the Paris indictment of *Émile* as blasphemous, indecent, ungodly, and so forth would prejudice his chances of a favourable response from the Senate. Unlike the rulers of Geneva, those in Berne had no reason to be alarmed by *The Social Contract*. An openly aristocratic constitution enabled their Excellencies to govern without making any pretence of having democratic authorisation; the few patrician families that ruled the state asserted only hereditary right, but they were strict in defence of religion, and even M. de Moiry did not expect them to tolerate *Émile*. 'Do what you will with the book,' he wrote in his letter, 'but I beg you to leave the author in peace.'

Messages of another kind reached Berne. Something like a campaign built up against Rousseau—a campaign seen to emanate from Geneva and especially from the clique around Voltaire. Rousseau was convinced that Voltaire fomented the agitation against him. 'It is at the instigation of M. de Voltaire that the Genevese have avenged the cause of God against me,' he wrote in his letter[27] to Mme de Boufflers. Rousseau was not alone in this belief. Julie von Bondeli reported[28] that 'the first blows were struck in Geneva by the cabal of Ferney'—Ferney being Voltaire's château just outside Geneva—and that 'the influence of the cabal reached as far as Berne.' She said she 'died of shame to think that the author of *La Pucelle* and *Candide* . . . should teach us to persecute a Rousseau'.

There is evidence enough of malice toward Rousseau. Charles Bonnet, for example, wrote from Geneva to the celebrated Bernese biologist Albrecht von Haller on 18 June,[29] reporting the indictment of Rousseau and adding: 'I do not doubt your Senate will follow our example and prove itself the avenger of Religion and Government.' In another letter[30] to Haller, Bonnet went so far as to say: 'Two hundred years ago, we would have roasted Rousseau: this time we have only roasted his books.'★

Reports of Voltaire's vendetta against Rousseau in Geneva reached even Paris, where people thought it strange that Voltaire—the great exponent of toleration, the tireless champion of Protestant victims of Catholic persecu-

★Geneva had indeed become less robust than Berne in dealing with its dissidents. Micheli du Crest, leader of the 1737 rebellion in Geneva, was serving a life sentence in a fortress, not as a prisoner of the Genevese but of the Bernese, after having played a small part in a rebellion in their republic.

tion in France—should himself promote the persecution of a fellow writer in Switzerland. When d'Alembert implored Voltaire to adopt a kindlier attitude, he simply denied any involvement in the persecution of Rousseau. He even pretended that he had offered the author of *Émile* refuge when the latter was indicted by the Paris *parlement*.[31] In truth, the only 'invitation' Voltaire ever addressed to Rousseau had been the suggestion, seven years earlier, that he settle in Geneva and 'join me in drinking the milk of our cows.'[32]

The Petit Conseil handled the case of Rousseau clumsily. When two of Rousseau's relations in Geneva asked for details of the warrant for his arrest, they were informed that there was no such warrant, and when they asked for a copy of the decree indicting him, they were told that the Petit Conseil's proceedings could not be made public. A group of fifteen citizens had no more success when they asked for details. Others challenged the legality of the suppression of the books on the grounds that the law of Geneva entrusted the identification and prosecution of heresy to the Consistory, not to the Petit Conseil. Then, on 22 June, one Charles Pictet—a leading citizen, the bearer of an illustrious Genevese name, a member of the Council of Two Hundred, and a retired colonel in the Sardinian army—wrote to the bookseller Duvillard, expressing certain criticisms of *The Social Contract* but protesting the unjust way in which the Petit Conseil had dealt with the author, a citizen who had brought honour to their republic. Colonel Pictet suggested that the 'infamous sentence passed on M. Rousseau' had three motives: to please Voltaire, to pay court to France, and to repair the damage done by the article in the *Encyclopédie*, which alleged that the Genevese clergy were Socinians—unitarians—in all but name. None of these motives, the colonel argued,[33] was creditable.

This letter fell into the hands of many people besides the bookseller to whom it was addressed, and Rousseau's friends had copies made, with the colonel's full knowledge, for circulation among his fellow citizens opposed to the patrician government. Pictet may have been wrong in his diagnosis of the government's motives, but he provoked an angry reaction. He was put on trial, censured, fined, and suspended for twelve months from his membership of the Council of Two Hundred. He offered only a feeble defence, but by putting him on trial the Petit Conseil in effect rekindled the embers of civil war between itself and the liberal element among the citizenry.

News of the colonel's letter reached as far away as Paris, where it was mentioned in the *Correspondance littéraire*,[34] the literary newsletter written by Rousseau's former friend turned enemy, Grimm, who added, with characteristic malice, that Rousseau had 'neither the courage nor the desire to take advantage of the fermentation the letter caused'.

It is hard to see what 'advantage' Rousseau could have taken. Moultou and other friends wanted him not only to provide a written statement, which could be used in his defence, but also to go to Geneva and defend himself in person. However, Rousseau informed Moultou on 6 July[35] that he had made up his mind to maintain silence: 'My book, dear Moultou, will speak for me.' Nevertheless it emerges from this letter that Rousseau was at least considering a visit to Geneva: 'Not only shall I await the month of September before coming to Geneva, but I am not even sure that the journey is really necessary since the Petit Conseil itself disavows the warrant . . . It would be madness in my situation to look for trouble when duty does not demand it. I shall always love my country, but I can no longer contemplate being there with any pleasure.'

Among the several friends in Geneva who wrote[36] to Rousseau, urging him to go there and face his accusers, was Capperonnier de Gauffecourt, who had lately returned to his native city from France; he reminded Rousseau that he had promised to support the author at the first sign of trouble, and hoped he would be allowed to help. The next day, Marc Chappuis, who had once incurred Rousseau's disapproval by usurping from Gauffecourt the salt monopoly in Geneva, wrote[37] to suggest that Rousseau would run no danger by coming to Geneva. 'Our religion is one of charity and tolerance,' he declared. 'So come and settle in the homeland which you ought to prefer to every other country and end your days peacefully amid your fellow citizens.'

Voltaire also suggested that Rousseau return. In a piece of advice coloured with his usual cynicism, Voltaire proposed that Rousseau go to the syndics of Geneva and promise to respect the religion of the country henceforth and, perhaps, state that the publisher had added the offensive pages to *The Social Contract*. Moultou, to whom Voltaire put forward this idea, told[38] Rousseau that he had replied to Voltaire: 'No, Monsieur, Jean-Jacques does not put his name to his writings in order to disavow them.'

Among the several friends who wrote to Rousseau from Paris was his favourite former pupil, the nobly born Mme de Chenonceaux. She was in poor health, indeed on the verge of a nervous breakdown, after months of unhappiness in her marriage to the wastrel son of the bourgeois Dupin family, but she was alert enough to realise, and to warn Rousseau in her letter,[39] that *The Social Contract* was likely to cause him more trouble than *Émile*; and she urged him to seek refuge in England.

This, as we have seen, was also the advice of Mme de Boufflers, but David Hume, whose help she sought in securing an offer of asylum in England, was in Scotland and consequently ill placed to do much for Rousseau at that time. Hume wrote[40] from Edinburgh—in English, a language the Comtesse knew well—to say 'there is no man in Europe of whom I have entertained a higher idea, and who I would be prouder to serve; and as I find his reputation very high in England, I hope everyone will endeavour to make him sensible of it by civilities and by services as far as he will accept of them. I revere his greatness of mind, which makes him fly obligations and dependence; and I have the vanity to think, that through the course of my life I have endeavoured to resemble him in those maxims.' In the same letter Hume held out the hope that Rousseau might receive a pension from George III, although he also expressed the fear that being unable to speak English Rousseau would 'find his abode in England not so agreeable as may be wished'.

On the same day[41] Hume wrote directly to Rousseau, again choosing to write in English despite his awareness that Rousseau did not understand the language. He expressed the most cordial sentiments: 'I will use the Freedom of telling you bluntly, without affecting the Finesse of a well-turned Compliment, that of all the men of letters in Europe, you are the Person I most revere.' Hume then went on to apologise for the fact that being far from London, he was unable to be of service to Rousseau in the manner he would have wished.

As an alternative to England, Mme de Boufflers had suggested[42] to Rousseau that he might find refuge in Germany with Mme de La Marck, who was willing to receive him at her château at Schleiden in the Rhineland. Moultou passed on a suggestion[43] from Leonhard Usteri for Rousseau to find 'safe refuge' in the 'wise republic' of Zürich. At the same time Frederick II of Prussia was being urged to offer Rousseau asylum in his principality of Neuchâtel.

Until the month of July, however, Rousseau had continued to hope that he might be allowed to remain on Bernese soil at Yverdon, surrounded by goodwill and, despite the return of poor health, happy in the knowledge that Thérèse would soon join him. Mme de Verdelin wrote[44] from Paris in the last week of June to say that Thérèse had packed her belongings and was ready to leave; she said she herself had taken charge of Rousseau's cat, Minette, and hoped it would 'soon be used to my caresses'. M. de Luxembourg wrote[45] saying that Rousseau's trunk with clothes and belongings was on its way to Yverdon and offering to undertake any other commissions Rousseau desired: 'I will never forgive the Genevese for what they have done about your book.'

Since Rousseau's presence in Yverdon was now widely known, he began to receive visitors. Among these was a doctor from Lausanne noted for his unorthodox views on hygiene and medicine, Samuel-André Tissot, who laid siege to Rousseau by going to Yverdon for a weekend with a friend and sending a note to Rousseau begging for half an hour of his time. Dr Tissot introduced himself as a fervent admirer of *Julie* as well as of *Émile*, the latter especially for its attacks on inoculation and conventional medical practice.

The interview seems to have passed off well, though Dr Tissot apparently did not discuss his own most celebrated book, since he drew it to Rousseau's attention only in the letter[46] he wrote after the visit. This book was *L'Onanisme*,[47] a best-seller translated into many languages and used to ter-rorise several generations of schoolboys by attributing to masturbation the effects that more scientific medicine ascribed to syphilis. Dr Tissot evidently found in Rousseau a supporter for his battle against the 'odious practice' since he had read the condemnation of it in *Émile*, where Rousseau warns 'once your pupil has learned to employ that dangerous supplement he is lost—he will carry to the grave the sad effects of this habit, the most harm-ful to which a young man may be subject.'[48] In his *Confessions*, Rousseau would admit to a lifelong indulgence in the 'supplement' and attribute its ap-peal to the fact that it enables a man with a powerful imagination to conquer in fantasy as many women as he pleases. Rousseau was soon congratulating Dr Tissot on his *L'Onanisme*, and they became firm friends.

On 1 July 1762 came the blow that Rousseau had been dreading ever since the publication of the Paris Judgement of *Émile* in the *Gazette de Berne*.[49] A meeting of the Bernese Senate resolved not only to forbid the sale of *Émile* but to expel the author from the territory of the republic.[50]

No mention was made of *The Social Contract*. Religion alone was being defended by the interdiction of *Émile* and the expulsion of its author. Reli-gion, however, possessed a political significance in the Republic of Berne, for it was by religion that the French-speaking Vaudois people were attached to the German-speaking régime in Berne; their Protestantism alone distin-guished them from the francophone Catholics of Fribourg, France, and Savoy and had impelled them to accept for more than two hundred years a government that was in most respects alien and imperialistic. Hence, if *Émile* was a threat to the Protestant religion, as it was said to be, it was a threat to Bernese ascendancy, so neither it nor its author could be tolerated in the Pays de Vaud. There was no question of judicial appeals or delays. The prefect of Yverdon was instructed to ensure that Rousseau departed within a few days.[51]

Rousseau was not entirely without friends in Berne. Vincent-Bernard Tscharner,* who had invited Rousseau while he was still at Montmorency to join the Société Economique de Berne,[52] intervened on his behalf; but although he belonged to a senatorial family, Tscharner was not a senator and his intervention was fruitless. Tscharner wrote[53] to the mayor of Yverdon, Georges-François Roguin—thinking he was the M. Roguin with whom Rousseau was staying—suggesting that Rousseau appeal to their Excellen-cies for the expulsion to be delayed for six or eight weeks. At the same time

---

*He should not be confused with Béat-Jacob Tscharner, a Senator who participated in the meet-ing of 1 July that ordered Rousseau's banishment.

Tscharner wrote[54] to the prefect, M. de Moiry, who was a cousin by marriage, urging him to make a similar appeal. In his reply[55] the prefect spoke of his high regard for Rousseau, describing him as 'a solitary philosopher with a clear and easy conscience, who worships God, loves mankind and respects the laws and who prays to God with us, albeit as a non-orthodox Christian'. He informed Tscharner that he was appealing for the delay of execution on the grounds of Rousseau's ill health, and he urged Tscharner to notify senators who might be well disposed that the appeal was on the way.

The mayor, responding[56] to Tscharner's suggestion that he intervene, explained that he was not the Roguin with whom Rousseau was staying. He expressed the opinion that whatever there was to fear from *Émile*, there was nothing to fear from the author, who led a life of retirement, preferring the solitude of the woods to commerce with other men. He suggested to Tscharner that two dignitaries from Berne, the commissioner-general Franz Ludwig Lerber and his son Professor Sigmund Ludwig Lerber, with whom Rousseau had dined at the prefectorial château, 'will be able to speak to you about him'.

It is unlikely that the mayor wrote to Berne in the terms that Tscharner proposed, for we learn from Rousseau's *Confessions*[57] that after the mayor's death, Daniel Roguin, as the mayor's kinsman, found among his papers 'proof that he had entered the plot to have [Rousseau] expelled from Yverdon and the Bernese republic'. As for the Lerbers with whom Rousseau dined, the son Sigmund Ludwig was a Scholarque who, on his return to Berne, promptly voted[58] for the suppression of *Émile*.

The prefect's appeal on Rousseau's behalf received a dusty answer from the Senate:[59]

Your representations to Their Excellencies in favour of J.-J. Rousseau do not merit consideration. Their Excellencies cannot modify their decision of 1 July, unless it be the case that J.-J. Rousseau is unable for health reasons to leave immediately. If so, they would allow him to prolong his stay at Yverdon for a week or a fortnight at the most; otherwise the Prefect must execute Their Excellencies' order and submit a report.

As soon as he received this communication on 9 July, M. de Moiry summoned Rousseau to the château. He had already warned the philosopher that there might be an order for the expulsion, although he did not say that he had already received one on 2 July. He gave an account[60] of the unhappy interview to James Boswell, when the Scots writer visited him two years later. According to this testimony, Rousseau did not need to be told that the order had come. The prefect tried to break the news gently by suggesting to Rousseau that he might be better off under the protection of Frederick II in

Neuchâtel: 'He fixed me with his fiery gaze,' the prefect told Boswell, ' "I believe I understand you." "Yes, you understand me." He left the same day. He came to take leave of us. There were tears in his eyes. He said, "They are tears of joy for having known you." '*

In the *Confessions*[62] Rousseau suggests that the prefect's pleas for toleration on his behalf 'far from calming the Senate's excitement only served to exasperate it'. Even before he realised that the order for his expulsion had actually arrived, he had decided to leave: 'The only difficulty was to decide where to go.'

The choice was limited. The offer from England had not materialised, the invitation to Zürich remained hypothetical, the château in the Rhineland, Rousseau felt, was too far away. The principality of Neuchâtel was near; its sovereign, Frederick II, was said to be well disposed. Roguin's niece, Mme Boy, offered to Rousseau an empty house she owned at Môtiers, although she warned him that it was ill equipped and in poor condition.

He says in the *Confessions*[63] that he hesitated to accept her offer for only one reason, namely, an aversion for Frederick II, whom he regarded as a warmonger and a tyrant. Rousseau recalls that he kept a framed portrait of the Prussian monarch in his study at Montlouis bearing an ungracious inscription,† which he did not doubt had been communicated to Frederick. In the end, however, he decided that he had 'the courage to put myself at the King's mercy'.[64] He said to himself, 'when Jean-Jacques lifts himself to the level of Coriolanus, will Frederick be inferior to the general of the Volsci?'[65] He agreed that if Mme Boy would allow him to pay rent, he would accept the house. A rent of thirty francs was settled.

Môtiers was separated from Yverdon by mountains; to reach it by road in a carriage entailed a long, roundabout journey. Rousseau, ever the eager walker, decided to go there on foot. He had very little luggage, for the trunk that M. de Luxembourg had sent from Montmorency had not yet arrived. Colonel Roguin 'insisted', as Rousseau put it in the *Confessions*, on accompanying him on the journey. They set out on 9 July, and after spending the night at an inn they arrived at the village of Môtiers in the Val de Travers on the morning of the following day. The scenic beauty, of the kind Rousseau most appreciated, consoled him as he and the colonel walked in the summer sunshine along mule tracks and footpaths across the Jura mountains; it did not, however, wholly banish from his mind the unpleasant thought that within a period of less than a month he had been exiled by two states and named as a criminal by a third, his own.

---

*Julie von Bondeli said: 'He departed as a sage, but not as a stoic, for he shed tears.'[61]
†'La gloire, l'intérêt, voilà son Dieu, sa loi; il pense en philosophe, et se conduit en Roi.'

2

MÔTIERS

Mme Boy's house in the village of Môtiers proved to be what she had warned Rousseau to expect—old, ill furnished, and in need of repair—but it had a certain rustic charm. Rousseau was especially pleased with the gallery, or covered terrace, which ran the length of the house outside the first floor on the south side, commanding a view of the waterfall of Môtiers and the distant Jura mountains, the very Swiss kind of landscape that he most loved and that, through his writings, was already beginning to stimulate a taste in others—a 'romantic' taste. The house is still there, remodelled and transformed into a small Rousseau museum, but not radically different in appearance from what is shown in eighteenth-century prints and drawings.[1]

Then, as now, the building was attached to a larger house and shared with it a courtyard and a barn into which, in the fulness of time, Rousseau found it convenient to escape when visitors importuned. His arrival in July 1762 deprived the occupant of the larger house of his monopoly of the premises, but that occupant was Mme Boy's brother-in-law, Major Girardier, second in command of the militia of the Val de Travers, and he received the new-comer cordially enough when Colonel Roguin introduced him. Indeed, until Thérèse arrived, Rousseau was invited by the Girardiers to take all his meals with them, as a paying guest at six *écus blancs* a month.*

Môtiers has retained much of the character it possessed when Rousseau knew it: one of a series of villages in the Val de Travers, a high mountain val-ley stretching from Pontarlier in France to the hills above the city of Neuchâtel. Môtiers then had only four hundred inhabitants; the houses were well spaced, and Mme Boy's was situated at the farthest extremity from the church, at the corner of the main street and the road that led to Fleurier. The village was surrounded by pastures and meadows, although the valley was noted less for agriculture than for mining, especially of asphalt, and for cot-

*On the same day he agreed to pay the local perruquier two *écus neufs* per annum for services.

tage industries such as lace making, clock making, and distilling. In his *Letter to M. d'Alembert* of 1758 Rousseau had painted an idyllic picture of happy cottagers of Neuchâtel 'making countless artifacts with their hands' and 'putting to use the inventive genius which nature gives them';[2] but what he found in the Val de Travers in the 1760s inspired rather less enthusiasm. He expressed particular disapproval of the extent to which the people had quit the land to work, for higher pay, in manufacturing.

As soon as Rousseau was settled, he wrote[3] a gracious letter of thanks to Mme Boy for letting him have her house: 'I think of you when I wake up and when I go to bed and all day long; and everything I see around me bears witness to your kindness.' He told her that Major Girardier, the major's wife, Anne-Marguerite, and their daughter, Adrienne, were 'showering friendship and attention' upon him, although he admitted that he missed the lively and affectionate society of the young girls in Mme Boy's family at Yverdon.

Mme Boy urged[4] him to treat the apartment as his own and to improve it at her expense in any way he pleased. She explained that she had instructed her agent to have any repairs that Rousseau wanted done. She said she hated the idea of taking rent from him for it: 'Thirty French livres is too much,' she protested, adding that she had often lent the place to friends but never used it commercially and that she was only too glad to have it occupied. This last sentiment was not shared by Major Girardier, who soon ceased to dissimulate his irritation at having to share the premises with Rousseau and Thérèse.

Another letter of thanks[5] Rousseau wrote—in careful calligraphy, with publication obviously in mind—was to M. de Moiry, expressing gratitude for the prefect's support at a time when he was being calumnied and unjustly pursued. He said he would have been overcome with despair but for the support and friendship that the prefect had lavished upon him.

The most important letter Rousseau wrote on the day[6] of his arrival in the Val de Travers was addressed to the governor of the principality, Lord Keith. Rousseau introduced himself as a poor author who had been proscribed in three states for saying what he believed to be true and useful. He explained that he was not asking the governor or King Frederick for grace, but simply suggesting that it would be a worthy act for them 'to grant me *le feu et l'eau* that the whole world has denied me . . . Determine my fate; I submit to your orders, although if you order me to leave, I shall not know where to go.'

It was an odd sort of petition, but the governor liked it, for he was an odd sort of man. George Keith was the last Earl Marischal of Scotland and himself an exile.[7] He had taken part as a young man in the Jacobite rebellion of 1715 and in consequence had been stripped of his estates in Scotland. He had served for many years as an officer in the Spanish army, and was then appointed by Frederick II as Prussian ambassador to the French court from

1751 until 1754. The governorship of Neuchâtel was a retirement job that Keith did not much like. His enthusiasm for the Jacobite cause diminished with time, and on the accession of George III in 1760 Keith was pardoned and restored to his rights and possessions in Scotland. Thereafter he often thought—or at any rate talked—of returning to his ancestral home of Keith Hall near Aberdeen; but he continued in the services of Frederick II at Neuchâtel on the off-chance of promotion to more congenial duties, although by 1762, at the age of seventy-six, there was not much that he could reasonably expect.

Despite his early allegiance to a Catholic prince, Keith had come to share the sceptical and anticlerical opinions of his royal employer and of his friend David Hume, so Rousseau's disgrace with the pious believers was a badge of merit in Keith's eyes. Keith was delighted to have Rousseau in his jurisdiction. He replied immediately[8] to Rousseau's petition, explaining that he was writing to the King for instructions but assuring Rousseau in the meantime of a welcome to the principality. Keith invited him to come as soon as possible to the gubernatorial château at Colombier and to stay as long as he wished. Keith offered to send a carriage to fetch Rousseau: 'You will find me an old man who is a bit of a savage, if perhaps somewhat ruined by the society of civilized barbarians.'

Rousseau had already drafted a letter[9] to the King himself in which he wrote: 'I have often spoken ill of you. I shall perhaps do so again, but having been driven from France, Geneva and Berne, I have just sought refuge in your lands . . . Sire, I desire no grace from you, and ask none. I am in your power and you may dispose of me as Your Majesty pleases.'

Fortunately, Rousseau did not send the letter, and Keith's intervention was successful. Frederick wrote promptly from the battlefield of Ditmansdorf,[10] instructing the governor to offer asylum to the 'unfortunate Rousseau'; he wrote again a few weeks later,[11] offering as a benefaction to Rousseau the miserly sum of one hundred *écus*—about fifteen pounds sterling—to be given him not as money, which he knew would be refused, but in the form of provisions. The King went on to say that 'if we had not been ruined by the war, I would have built him a hermitage with a garden, where he could live as he thinks our ancestors lived . . . I believe that the morals of your savage are as pure as his mind is wild.'

In transmitting this message to Rousseau, Keith made it sound more generous by telling him that Frederick was actually offering to build him a hermitage so that Rousseau had the satisfaction of refusing something worth having. Rousseau assumed it was Keith's idea to offer him the provisions—wood and coal—rather than money, but he really believed the King was offering him the house. 'Such generosity,' he wrote in the *Confessions*,[12] 'greatly affected me and made me forget the meanness of the hundred écus

without accepting either gift. Henceforth I looked on Frederick as my benefactor and protector, and became sincerely attached to him from that moment.'

Lord Keith lost no time in making the personal acquaintance of his new
protégé. Two days after Rousseau's arrival in Môtiers[13] he wrote to the intendant (or *châtelain*), Jacques-Frédéric Martinet, asking him to look after the
newcomer and to lend Rousseau a horse and carriage so that he could visit
Keith at his château at Colombier near Neuchâtel. The intendant decided to
take Rousseau there in person. In the *Confessions*[14] Rousseau describes the
visit:

My first feeling on seeing that venerable old man was of compassion for the
thinness of a body already worn out with years. But when I lifted my eyes to his
animated, frank and noble countenance, I was seized by a feeling of respect and
confidence which overcame every other emotion. He answered the short compliment I made as I approached him by changing the subject, and speaking as if
I had been there a week. He did not even ask me to sit down. The buttoned-up
Intendant remained standing. But I saw such a fond look in the fine and pierc-
ing eye of the Governor, that I felt at ease at once, and promptly sat myself down
without any ceremony on the sofa beside him. From the familiar tone he immediately adopted I knew he was not displeased with the liberty I had taken and
that he said to himself 'This is not one of the Neuchâtel people.'

Rousseau goes on to speak of 'the great similarity of character' that bound
him to Lord Keith, and of the warmth with which his own heart, 'at a time
of life when natural warmth diminishes', responded to Keith's friendliness.
Rousseau recalls how, shortly after their first meeting, the governor came
to Môtiers on the pretext of shooting quail, only to spend two days in
Rousseau's company without once touching his gun. Rousseau soon realised
that he had found in the Earl Marischal of Scotland a perfect successor to
the Maréchal-Duc de Luxembourg, a loving father figure; indeed he was
soon calling him 'mon père' and being called 'mon fils'. Rousseau went reg-
ularly once a fortnight to visit Keith at Colombier, but, scorning the intendant's carriage, he chose to go on foot, staying overnight at an inn at Brot on
the way. 'I often shed tears of tenderness on the road,' he recalls,[15] 'as I
thought of the paternal affection, the lovable virtues and the gentle philosophy of that worthy old man.' A room at the château, in the tower next to
the chapel, was always kept in readiness for Rousseau.[16]

Lord Keith was unmarried, but he maintained a large and unusual household, including an adopted daughter, Emetulla, a Moslem from Armenia;
Ibraham the Tartar, said by Keith to be related to the Grand Lama; Stéphan
the Kalmouk; and Motcho the Negro.[17] In the case of Emetulla, Lord Keith

had decided that she ought to convert to Christianity, if only for the purpose of marriage to a Christian bridegroom, and he enrolled Rousseau's help in teaching her; between them these unlikely instructors successfully prepared her for baptism into the Calvinist church of Neuchâtel with the new name of Marie.[18]*

In the meantime Rousseau had been establishing his own credentials as a member of that church. Paradoxically, for the subjects of a free-thinking king, the people of Neuchâtel were often religious bigots and their clergy were among the most narrow and intolerant of Calvinists. For several years public attention had been riveted on what was known as the Petitpierre affair.[19] Ferdinand-Olivier Petitpierre, pastor of the village of Ponts, had been accused in 1758 of having preached a sermon denying that the punishment of sinners in hell would be everlasting. The Vénérable Classe, or college in which the clergy of the principality were organised and disciplined, reprimanded him for disputing a received Calvinist doctrine, and instructed him to keep such heretical opinions to himself in the future. Petitpierre, however, maintained that his conscience impelled him to proclaim what he believed to be true, and in a sermon at La Chaux-de-Fonds in 1760 he again denied the eternity of punishments. He was told to retract or resign. On this occasion his parishioners supported him; an appeal was addressed to the secular authorities in the principality to nullify the action of the Vénérable Classe. The authorities were divided. Frederick II, called upon to intervene, could not dissimulate his impatience: 'If those buggers want to burn in hell for all eternity,' he said, 'it is not for me to stop them.'[20] However, he instructed the governor, who had been on prolonged leave, to return to Neuchâtel and restore order among his subjects. Keith reached Colombier in February 1762, which is why Rousseau found him in residence when he arrived in the principality six months later.

In his letter[21] to the intendant at Môtiers asking him to help Rousseau, Keith had suggested that Rousseau be put on good terms with the local pastor, since 'a voice in his favour in the Vénérable Classe would make his situation more tranquil.' The local pastor, Frédéric-Guillaume de Montmollin, was not one who would readily be expected to speak in Rousseau's favour, for Montmollin had been one of the most active of the Neuchâtel clergy in prosecuting Petitpierre for expounding views considerably less heterodox than those found in *Émile*. Why should Keith imagine that he might help Rousseau?

The truth that Keith knew well was that while Montmollin was a bigot, he was also an intellectual snob and a man of inordinate vanity;[22] he would predictably be thrilled at the opportunity to boast of having a celebrated au-

*She was duly married to a Christian bridegroom, but the liberality of Lord Keith's dowry atracted a fortune hunter and the marriage was unhappy.

thor as a parishioner and friend. He styled himself, and always signed his letters as, 'Le Professeur de Montmollin', for although his academic experience
was limited to that of headmaster of the small, private boarding school at
Môtiers, he had been awarded the title of Professor of Belles Lettres in an-
ticipation of the future founding—when King Frederick could afford it—of
a University of Neuchâtel. When Rousseau was introduced to him, the professor not only welcomed him to attend church services at Môtiers as a
parishioner but suggested he might care to partake, as a communicant, in the
Lord's Supper according to the Calvinist rite. Rousseau was readily persuaded, for in addition to any spiritual grace and comfort he may have derived from Montmollin's pastoral solicitude, such an association put a strong
card in his hand for his dealings with the authorities of Geneva, who could
not decently excommunicate a member of the sister church of Neuchâtel.

Rousseau had already incurred the hatred of certain Genevese clergy, but
he was more sensible of the hostility of those he saw as his two great enemies among the laity of the city. Writing to Moultou the day after his arrival[23] in Môtiers, he said he was holding his breath in his latest place of
refuge 'until such time as it shall please Messieurs de Voltaire and Théodore
Tronchin to pursue me and have me thrown out'. Once again he warned
Moultou that his friendship might prove dangerous and that correspondence
should not be too frequent since it was likely his letters were being intercepted and read. Rousseau added, however, that he felt forced in the circumstances to allow Moultou to publish a pamphlet in his defence; as an
experienced pamphleteer himself, Rousseau ventured to advise Moultou on
how to write it: 'avoid both satire and excessive praise, and cultivate sweetness and dignity in style.'

Rousseau was not alone in thinking that Moultou would be made to
suffer for his association with the author of *Émile*. Théodore Tronchin, with
whom Moultou was on rather more friendly terms than Rousseau realised,
gave Moultou the same warning. 'If you are not on your guard,' the doctor
wrote to him,[24] 'your religion will be suspect . . . Oh my dear friend, be prudent; you owe more to yourself; you owe more to your church than you owe
to friendship with a man who saps its foundation.' As for Moultou's plan to
publish a pamphlet in defence of Rousseau, Tronchin added: *'au nom de
Dieu'*—the Voltairians having an odd habit of speaking in the name of
God—'keep silent'.

Rousseau himself had second thoughts about encouraging Moultou to
write the pamphlet. In a letter dated 15 July[25] he explained that when he
had expressed the wish that someone should write a defence of *Émile*, he was
not asking Moultou to write one, and now Rousseau was alarmed at the
risks Moultou would run if he did so. If, however, Moultou was determined
to go ahead with the project, Rousseau said he could think of no one bet-

ter qualified. He insisted only that he not be consulted about the writing of it or be asked to read it in manuscript; he would wait to see it in print. As for the correspondence between them, if Moultou saw no danger in it, Rousseau said he would be happy to continue it.

In his reply[26] Moultou told Rousseau he was very unsure that he had the talent for writing the defence, but promised to do his best, and to burn the manuscript if it disappointed Rousseau. He thought of having it published in Zürich because, as he informed Rousseau's Zürichois friend Leonhard Usteri,[27] 'there is no longer any freedom in Geneva except for Voltaire.' In the end, however, Moultou abandoned the pamphlet unfinished.

Doubtless he had more than one motive for doing so. If he could not concentrate, it was partly because he had fallen in love with Anne-Germaine Vermenoux, a ravishing widow aged twenty-two who had come to live in Geneva, first with Moultou's wife's family, the Caylas, then with Professor Turrettini at Bossey. Moultou declared his love to Germaine, and compared it to that of St-Preux for Julie in *La Nouvelle Héloïse*. He sent her bouquets, and even wrote verses that recall, in their bold sensuality, Rousseau's courtship of Sophie d'Houdetot at the Hermitage:

> Dieu! Quel plaisir quand ses mains caressantes
> M'approcheraient de ses lèvres charmantes,
> Et que placé tout auprès de son coeur,
> Et consumé par sa brûlante haleine,
> J'expirerais dans le sein du bonheur
> En m'effeuillant dans le sein de Germaine![28]

It was an unfortunate passion since Moultou was a married man, a father, and a minister of religion; although it lasted three years, it seems to have remained unconsummated. Rousseau may have had some inkling of it since Moultou referred several times in his letters to a beautiful young woman who admired his (Rousseau's) books. What Moultou did not mention was that she was a close friend also of Rousseau's great enemy, 'the Juggler', Théodore Tronchin. The portraitist Liotard painted two pastels of Germaine's beautiful face, one for Moultou and one for Dr Tronchin.

While Moultou's efforts to write a defence of *Émile* faltered, Rousseau's other young friend among the Genevese clergy, Antoine-Jacques Roustan, finished what he set out to write, which was less a defence of *Émile* than a friendly critique of that book and of *The Social Contract*. Roustan's main criticism was directed at the chapter entitled 'The Civil Religion', in which Rousseau argued that Christianity was incompatible with republican government. Rousseau took no offence at this criticism, and even helped to get it published by Rey in a collection entitled *Offrande aux autels et à la patrie*.

Rousseau felt he could allow a friend to disagree with him, provided he was assured of that friend's sincerity and integrity. It was another matter altogether where Jacob Vernes was concerned. This ambitious young pastor took it upon himself to write from Séligny,[29] accusing Rousseau to his face of depriving Christianity of its most solid foundations. He protested that Rousseau's writings had troubled souls that had been strong in faith, robbed weaker brethren of the faith they had, and given victory to the libertines. Since Rousseau knew that Vernes was cultivating the favour of the prince of libertines, Voltaire, he could not bring himself to answer the letter. In fact, as will be seen, he went on to suspect Vernes unjustly of greater mischief; he failed to give Vernes the credit for being at least frank.

On 20 July, a Tuesday, Thérèse arrived at last at Môtiers. Her journey from Montmorency had lasted nine days and had not been altogether pleasant. Prone to misadventures when travelling,★ she was harassed by sexual advances from two young men on the public coach between Paris and Fontainebleau, and reduced to tears. She was rescued by a fellow traveller, one Abbé Grumet, who persuaded an official to reprimand the youths and force them to let her alone. At Dijon, where his journey ended—for the abbé was curé of Ambérieu-en-Bugey—he advised her to quit the public coach and hire a carriage for the rest of her journey. In her gratitude she revealed to him that she was Rousseau's housekeeper, and satisfied his curiosity by telling him what he afterward recalled[30] as 'many details of the life of that singular man'. Hearing Thérèse's account of the episode, Rousseau wrote[31] to the abbé, as soon as he found his address, to thank him for his chivalry toward her. Rousseau reported[32] at once her safe arrival to Mme de Luxembourg, again expressing his gratitude for the Maréchale's continued friendship to Thérèse and himself.

In the *Confessions*[33] Rousseau recalls the moment of Thérèse's arrival at Môtiers: 'What excitement we felt as we embraced! Oh how sweet are the tears of tenderness and joy! How my heart feasts on them! Why have I been made to shed so few of them?'

Thérèse was kindly received by everyone she met, and her presence in Rousseau's household seems to have occasioned none of the suspicions that had been raised in Geneva eight years earlier, even though the people of Neuchâtel had the same Puritan attitude to concubinage. Evidently, at the age of forty-one she looked like a housekeeper, plain and plainly dressed. Besides, she acted more than ever the part of the servant; sometimes when Rousseau had guests for meals, she was not allowed to sit at the table with them.[34] She also continued to be nurse to Rousseau in his all-too-frequent bouts of illness and constant need for catheters. When unwelcome visitors

★In 1754 she was molested in the coach by Gauffecourt on their way to Geneva and in 1766 she was seduced by James Boswell on their way to London.

began to importune, she became his guard and protector. Visitors were charmed by her simplicity of manners as well as her skill as a French country cook. Even Professor de Montmollin, for all his reputation as a Protestant bigot, offered her the use of his carriage so that she could attend Catholic mass in another village.

Thérèse's presence at Môtiers did not diminish Rousseau's indignation at the world's mounting hostility toward him. He wrote[35] to Mme de Luxembourg in bitter terms about his persecutions in Switzerland and elsewhere— even the Dutch having followed the French example in proscribing *Émile*—and he described how 'Punch' (Voltaire) and 'his *compère*' (Dr Tronchin) were 'manipulating all the marionnettes of Geneva and Berne' against him. On the other hand, Rousseau was able to tell the Maréchale about the warm welcome he had received from Lord Keith in Neuchâtel, and he sent her a copy of Colonel Pictet's letter as proof that he was not without friends even in Geneva. He explained that the Genevese had decided to put the colonel on trial: 'I think they are going mad. But I shall say nothing, write nothing and remain calm.' He ended on a more cheerful note, declaring that when he thought of the goodness shown by the Maréchale, the Maréchal, Prince de Conti, and Mme de Boufflers ('whom one must adore'), he wondered why he should complain about anything. He even withdrew his opposition to her idea of having his portrait by La Tour engraved for publication.

It was fortunate that Rousseau was in a mood to adore Mme de Boufflers, as she was increasingly assuming the role of the authoritarian nanny. In particular, she persisted with her argument that he ought to go to England. In July she wrote[36] at length warning him that however tranquil he might be at the moment, he would never find in Switzerland either resources to live on or freedom of the press. 'England alone would suit you,' she insisted. 'If you want to bring out a complete edition of your old works or perhaps new ones, you would have nothing to fear there. Contacts with your friends in France would be easier; every facility you need would be available to you, and I could hope to have the pleasure of seeing you again.' She enclosed a French translation of David Hume's letter to her as proof of his regard for Rousseau. But of course that was all it did prove. Rousseau could not fail to notice Hume's point that, being in Scotland, he was in no position to invite Rousseau to England.

As soon as Thérèse reached Môtiers their little *ménage* at Mme Boy's house began to take shape. Daniel Roguin had arranged for Rousseau's luggage from France to be conveyed in Thérèse's carriage to Môtiers. Rousseau no longer had to go to the Girardiers for his meals. Mme de Luze*—another

---

*Marianne-Françoise de Luze, *née* Warney (1728–1796), was the niece of Daniel Roguin and the wife of a prosperous textile manufacturer at Colombier, possessing an elegant country house near the governor's château.

member of the Roguinerie—wrote[37] from Neuchâtel to inform Rousseau
that two armchairs and twelve other chairs were on their way to Môtiers on
the instructions of Mme Boy.* The furnishings of the apartment continued
to be modest despite these additions to it, and there were really only four
rooms since the ground floor was not habitable. Rousseau's combined bedroom and study, which he called his 'laboratory', was the largest and the
quietest room, overlooking the courtyard at the back of the house.[39] It contained, besides the chairs, a curtained bed, a wardrobe, and some bookshelves
he put up himself. Thérèse's room was smaller, but brighter; it was furnished
with a cane chair, six other chairs covered in yellow material, two mirrors, a
chest with gilt fittings, and brightly coloured curtains. There was also a
fourth room, or 'petite chambre', which Rousseau described[40] to Mme de
Verdelin as containing a bed— 'a bad one, but with no bugs in it'—and an
armchair with a spinet across the arms. There was also a fair-sized kitchen[41]
with farm-house furniture, a 'noble' fireplace with a roasting pit, an oven,
and a stove.

Visitors appreciated Thérèse's cooking. One of them, François d'Escherny, recalled meals of succulent vegetables, gigot of mutton from the Val de
Travers prepared with wild thyme and perfect sauces, fresh trout from the
river Areuse, and, in season, quail and woodcock 'such as I have never eaten
in Paris'.[42] The wines were usually the flinty whites of Cortaillod, although
there were sometimes robust red Spanish wines presented to Rousseau by
Lord Keith. Escherny's only complaint was that while coffee was always
plentiful,† there were never any liqueurs. Given Thérèse's skill in the kitchen
and the poor reputation of the fare at the local inn, it is hardly surprising that
Rousseau always ate at home.

Visitors to Môtiers became increasingly frequent as soon as Rousseau's
whereabouts became known. A fair proportion of them came from German-speaking Switzerland, notably Berne and Zürich. Samuel Engel, president in 1762 of the Société Economique de Berne, complained that many
Bernese scientists and intellectuals were 'in love with Rousseau, admire him,
and protest against what they call the injustice that has been done to him'.[43]
These admirers included several other fellows of the same society, which indeed Rousseau himself had been invited to join; and he received testimonies
of friendship from Jean-Rodolphe Tshiffeli, Nicolas-Antoine Kirchberger,
Daniel Fellenberg, and Carolus Sturler, as well as the stalwart Vincent-
Bernard Tscharner. His most tireless Bernese champion was Julie von

*Rousseau, however, was determined to pay for the furniture and wrote to Mme de Luze, asking
her to send him the bill.[38]

†Roguin informed Rousseau on 23 July that he was sending him a supply of coffee and sugar, but
advised against hoarding since the coming of peace meant that shortages would be fewer in the future.[43] The Seven Years War did not actually end until the signing of the Peace of Paris on 10 February 1762.

Bondeli, at whose salon at Koeniz the intellectual cream of Bernese society assembled.[45] She was a formidable blue-stocking, so intensely serious that the poet Wieland, who loved her, complained that she drove him mad with her philosophical talk. Her adoration of Rousseau was almost fanatical. She was in effect the chief priestess in Allemanic Switzerland of the cult of Rousseau, 'das Haupt der Sekte von Rousseaus Bewunderen',[46] as she herself expressed it. She rejoiced in the knowledge that her Christian name was that of the heroine of La Nouvelle Héloïse. She gathered information about Rousseau from any source she could and passed it on to her numerous correspondents; there is hardly a letter of hers in which his name is not mentioned.

This Julie was, however, too shy to make Rousseau's acquaintance in person until many months after she had started to correspond with him. She declined to accompany Tscharner and Fellenberg when they went to visit Rousseau at Môtiers in the summer of 1762. One of their motives for the visit was to express the regret of the Patriotische Gesellschaft of Berne for the action of their government against Émile. When they apologised, Rousseau declared[47] to Tscharner that he had ceased to care about such things: 'I have fulfilled my mission, Monsieur. I have said what I have now to say. I regard my career as ended . . . Misfortune and adversity have robbed me of the little vigour of mind I have left, and now I am only a vegetating being, a walking mechanism. All that remains is a little warmth in my heart for my friends.'

After the visit, Tscharner sent a description[48] of Rousseau to Julie von Bondeli: 'For most of the time he had his back bent and his head bowed over his chest in a posture of meditation and dejection, but as soon as he spoke he lifted his head and revealed a pair of indescribable eyes . . . Although his health is wretched, he cannot stay still for long. He never sleeps, but calls sleeping what others call dozing after dinner.'

Julie von Bondeli was also told that Rousseau would get out of bed at two o'clock in the morning to make himself a pot of coffee, 'taking care not to wake up his housekeeper'.[49]

The Bernese visitor Rousseau seems to have preferred to the others was Nicolas-Antoine Kirchberger,[50] Baron von Liebestorf, whom he recalls in his Confessions,[51] saying 'his talents and his principles attracted me.' Kirchberger was an author and sometime president of the Société Economique de Berne, as well as a member of one of the leading Bernese patrician families. According to the account[52] of the visit he gave to Julie von Bondeli, 'M. Rousseau received me cordially, and when after half an hour's conversation, I wished to leave, he pressed me to stay. We spoke of The Social Contract. He left the room and soon returned with a copy of the book which he presented to me in the friendliest possible way. He took me to what he called his laboratory, and read me the sequel[53] to Émile.' Kirchberger told Julie von Bondeli he did not leave Rousseau until seven o'clock, and was then invited back the next day for dinner, when, he added, they drank her health with excellent Spanish wine. Rousseau had said to him as he left: 'I hate new faces, but when they are like yours, I am soon reconciled to them.'

Money, in those first months at Môtiers, was not a great source of worry to Rousseau, as he still felt flush with the 6,000 francs he had been paid by Duchesne and Guy for *Émile*. He realised, however, that his resources would not last for ever, even if he kept his expenditure down to what he considered the minimum, 1,440 francs a year. There was no opportunity in Switzerland, as there was in France, of his earning money as a music copyist. There remained the possibility of literary earnings, but the copyright laws of the eighteenth century were not favourable to authors; once a publisher had bought a manuscript, he was entitled to keep all the profits unless he chose to share them.

Rousseau's main publisher in Amsterdam, Marc-Michel Rey, wrote to him on 22 July,[54] begging him for news of his welfare. Rey reported that he had been unlucky with *The Social Contract*. The two thousand copies that he had sent to France had been refused admission by the censors; the bales of books had been left to rot for several weeks in a damp warehouse in Rouen, and then further damaged by sea water on the way back to Holland. Even in Amsterdam *The Social Contract* was proscribed. Rey said he was as yet far from recovering his investment in the book, so that even though he was bringing out a new edition of *Julie, ou la Nouvelle Héloïse*, there was no suggestion of that edition yielding any financial reward for the author. Rousseau's other Dutch publisher, Jean Néaulme, who had shared in the publication of *Émile*, had nothing to offer him but lamentations. Writing on 28 July,[55] he declared that as a result of the action against *Émile* by the states of Holland and West Friesland he had been made a criminal, and he also claimed to have been cheated by the French publishers, Duchesne and Guy, who had used his name to disguise their printing of the book in France.

Pierre Guy himself wrote[56] to Rousseau, expressing regret if their publishing house had contributed in any way to his misfortunes and adding that he had seen Mlle Levasseur before she left France on two occasions in the hope of being of service. Unlike Rey and Néaulme, Pierre Guy did not have much reason for complaint. Tipped off by Malesherbes, he had hidden his stocks of *Émile* in several warehouses around Paris before the police arrived at his offices; and it was not long before he was able to rescue the copies and sell them more or less openly. Despite the much-publicized interdiction of *Émile* by the Paris *parlement*, the French government turned its attention to suppressing *The Social Contract*,[57] a book subversive of the monarchy being of more concern to it than a book subversive of the church. Naturally, Guy said nothing of this in writing to Rousseau; he simply protested that pirate publishers were the only ones making money out of *Émile*.

Rousseau replied[58] dryly: 'Although pirating is inevitable when a book has a certain celebrity, I know too much about all that to believe you have as much to complain about as you say, and I hardly believe in the present situation that it is for me to console you.'

Evidently Rousseau's relations with all his publishers were at a low ebb, but he realised that his only hope of making money was to sell them something new, or something that could be made to look new, and once again he reverted to the idea of bringing out his *Complete Works*.

On 29 July 1762 Rousseau's first love, Mme de Warens, died at Chambéry. The Abbé Gaime, one of the curates on whom the Vicaire Savoyard was based, officiated at her funeral. It took some time for the news to reach Môtiers. M. de Conzié, who always claimed to be her devoted friend, wrote a long letter to Rousseau in September[59] in praise of *Émile* without as much as mentioning Mme de Warens's death. It was only when Rousseau asked him about her welfare that Conzié thought of informing him, saying[60] she had 'lived overwhelmed with illness and misery, forsaken by human injustice, but rewarded for her virtues and sufferings by a beautiful soul'. It is a fact that Mme de Warens died in penury, the few sticks of furniture she possessed being worth too little even to pay the wages she owed her servant.[61] It is also a fact that her rich friend and neighbour, M. de Conzié, gave not a sou to relieve the misery of the 'beautiful soul' of which he wrote so tenderly. In the *Confessions*[62] Rousseau speaks of her death as that of 'the best of women and mothers' and adds: 'if I did not believe I should meet her again in the life to come, my poor imagination would refuse to believe in the bliss that I hope awaits me there.'

In August Mme Boy planned to visit Rousseau at Môtiers on her way to inspect a farm she owned at Pierrenod to the south of the village in the nearby mountains. Roguin explained[63] to Rousseau that she would bring with her the money he had been looking after for him together with a credit note on M. de Rougemont, the Neuchâtel banker, 'who will render you all possible services'.

Her visit was delayed by what she called a 'fluxion of the eye', but she was well enough★ to set off on 20 August in a light carriage with her daughter, '*la petite blonde*' Madeleine-Catherine, and her cousin, Colonel Roguin, whose presence was due less to friendship for Rousseau than attachment to *la petite blonde*. According to the accounts[64] of Daniel Roguin, the money and credit notes Mme Boy took with her amounted to 4,331 French francs. Of this Rousseau felt able to invest 3,000 francs, and Mme Boy agreed to place it with her finance house in Lyons at 5 per cent annual interest. Some days later[65] M. de Luxembourg was able to inform Rousseau that the 1,000

★During her visit to Môtiers, however, she fell down and bruised herself.

francs he had invested on his behalf the previous year had yielded 75 francs interest, and he asked for instructions about its future use.

These figures give us an indication of Rousseau's fortune at that time. The 6,000 francs that Mme de Luxembourg had extracted from Duchesne and Guy for *Émile* was virtually the whole of his capital—now reduced to 4,000 francs as the remainder was needed for the expenses of living. Mme Boy was eager to help him. Forced to accept the 30 francs' rent for the house, she attempted to pay for repairs that were needed to make it comfortable. She also tried to persuade Rousseau to accept a flat she was having constructed in her farmhouse at Pierrenod as a summer retreat. He resisted the offer as he always resisted such benefactions, but at least he enjoyed his excursion to the mountains in the company of her party. Her farm was at an altitude of thirty-five hundred feet, and in the meadows around it Rousseau was delighted to find the wild Alpine flowers he had first learned to identify as a youth with Claude Anet in the hills around Chambéry. The views from Pierrenod were panoramic and the opportunities for mountain walks renewed his passion for that open-air exercise. He also took pleasure in the company of the Roguinerie, although he observed with disapproval Colonel Roguin's efforts to pay court to Madeleine-Catherine, Rousseau's favourite among Mme Boy's daughters. He was shocked at the idea—which Daniel Roguin encouraged—of the colonel's marriage to the girl. As he explained in the *Confessions*,[66] Rousseau considered the colonel too old* to marry a girl of fifteen, and, somewhat to the annoyance of Daniel Roguin, he conspired with the girl and her mother, who had a distinct repugnance to the thought of the marriage, to ensure that it did not happen.†

Nevertheless Rousseau himself seems to have been well aware of what it felt like for a man of fifty to be in love with a young girl. Among the manuscripts[67] in the Neuchâtel Public Library is a series of letters, drafted in the summer of 1762, 'to Sara', expressing the erotic desires of a 'grey beard' for a maiden. 'Sara' may have been inspired by a real person, for that Old Testament name was popular in the Calvinist principality, but it is more probable that like Julie in *La Nouvelle Héloïse*, she was a purely imaginary creature and that Rousseau wrote the letters either as a literary exercise or simply for the excitement he derived from a love affair experienced in fantasy.[68] The letters are passionate, inflamed alternately by ardour and bitterness. The writer knows he is too old to be in love, but he declares 'I burn for you, Sara, with the most cruel of passions. Do you dare chain to your chariot an ageing suitor . . . who, in his wild delusions, imagines he has claims to creature so young? Love and be loved, O Sara.' The second letter protests at Sara's in-

---

*Georges-Augustin Roguin was forty-four years old at the time.

†Eventually Colonel Roguin married Jeanne-Marie d'Illens, to whom Rousseau dedicated a quatrain.

difference: 'You despise my folly so much that you do not even mock me. Would that I had the happiness of believing that you were interested in me if only to tyrannize me.' The third letter speaks of two hours passed in her company; of her asking him for the tenderness of a father and of her weeping in his presence: 'I felt one of your tears fall on my face . . . I know that pity closes the heart to love, but it still has charms for me.' In the fourth letter he admits that he blushes for the love he has for her, and thanks her for her sweet, kind, and dignified reproaches. 'It is my destiny to burn until my last breath with a fire that nothing can extinguish. Without being able to escape from you, I say farewell for ever.' There is an unfinished draft of a fifth letter in which the writer confesses that what torments him more than the fear of losing Sara is jealous dread of losing her to a rival: 'No, my despair is not because I will not be loved, but because another will be loved.'

If he was thus let down in imagination by the maiden 'Sara', Rousseau continued in the real world to command the fidelity of more matronly females. 'I am in despair,' Mme Alissan—she who had once claimed to be his 'Julie'—wrote[69] from Paris. 'Your silence, always a torture for me, has become even more cruel.' It emerges from this letter that Mme Alissan had overcome her reluctance to make the acquaintance of Mme de Luxembourg and attempted to reach Rousseau by sending a letter through her as well as another through Daniel Roguin. But Mme de Luxembourg's letters were equally slow in reaching Môtiers. In mid-August[70] Rousseau was protesting to her that he had written three times since his arrival in Môtiers without receiving an answer. To Mme Alissan he counselled[71] patience, since his situation should excuse his delays in writing to her. He added, however, that even if her letters did nothing but scold him, he was always pleased to receive them, her friendship being one of those he cherished most.

A letter from Mme de Luxembourg dated 18 August[72] reached him before the end of the month and brought assurances of the abiding affection of herself and her husband to 'the dearest of friends, the most worthy to be loved and the most adorable of all men'. The Maréchale said she was certain that the King of Prussia must be charmed to have him in his territories, although she reminded Rousseau that he could also find refuge with Mr Hume or, much better still, with Mme de La Marck at Schleiden. She added some kind words about Thérèse: 'She has the most honest and upright heart that I know, and an infinite attachment to you.'

Mme de Luxembourg was right about the King of Prussia. Lord Keith was able to inform Rousseau on 16 August[73] that Frederick was happy to offer asylum to 'persecuted virtue'. There was, however, a further message to which Rousseau might have given careful thought: 'The King hopes (he says) that you will not write on controversial subjects which might excite too lively sensations in Neuchâtelois heads and occasion disturbances among a clergy already inclined to dispute and full of fanaticism.' Keith added that he had assured the King 'that you no longer read or write or speak'.

This last assertion was not entirely true, and Rousseau did not feel bound by the assurances Keith had given to Frederick. But at least he refused the request of his Genevese friends to write something they could use in his defence. In a letter to Marcet de Mézières[74] he explained: 'I am ill, dear friend; I need rest, which I shall never find in Geneva or among the Genevese. I have made up my mind to renounce my citizenship, and to do so publicly, but as I intend to consider only my own convenience and my honour, without allowing passion to intervene, I shall await the right moment to do this; and until then I shall allow my enemies to enjoy their triumph.'

This news distressed Marcet because, like several of Rousseau's other champions in Geneva, he wanted to exploit the despotic behaviour of the government toward Rousseau to the advantage of the political opposition. He implored[75] Rousseau to reconsider his decision. He insisted that the Petit Conseil had acted illegally in proscribing Rousseau and said he believed he could find, in collaboration with Paul Moultou, a means of having the ruling annulled: 'You will be free, my dear Jean-Jacques, no less than I am.' Marcet sent Rousseau a draft power of attorney,[76] which would empower him—Marcet—to petition the Petit Conseil for a copy of the indictment and then to appeal to the Consistory to assert its legal right to judge the case against the usurpation of the Petit Conseil.

Rousseau gave Marcet the power of attorney but expected no good to come of it: 'I think we should allow heads to cool down,' he suggested,[77] 'and not act precipitately when there is nothing to be lost by delay . . . So let us wait. The King of Prussia has just authorised my presence in his territories, so I have peace of mind and am in no hurry.'

Writing to Moultou at the beginning of August,[78] Rousseau expressed the fear that his letters to Geneva were still being intercepted since they took six days to reach their destination; he added that for this reason he would not write to 'our friend'—meaning Roustan—for fear of compromising him. 'In your case it is already too late. You are seen to be my friend, and in Geneva that is an unforgivable crime.'

Moultou tried to reassure Rousseau that his correspondence was not being tampered with. His latest letter, he pointed out,[79] had arrived without delay and with the seals intact. 'Why,' he asked, 'should the Swiss wish to know what you and I write to each other?' He agreed that it was thought a crime in Geneva to be a friend of Jean-Jacques Rousseau, 'but I hope to take that crime with me to the other world.'

Moultou exaggerated. In the salon of the Duchesse d'Anville and other places where he gazed in rapture at Germaine de Vermenoux, his devotion to Jean-Jacques was observed with urbane indifference. Without Rousseau having any knowledge, or even suspicion, of it, Moultou was increasingly in the company of Voltaire, although he continued in writing to Rousseau to refer to Voltaire, and to Tronchin, as enemies.★ This is not to say that Moultou was becoming disloyal to Rousseau; but as he led an increasingly *mondain* life he was acquiring those habits of insincerity and dissimulation that Rousseau always said were the inevitable product of polite society.

Writing to Rousseau on 21 August,[81] Moultou spoke with the utmost disapproval of Voltaire's latest anti-clerical publication, *Le Serment des cinquante*, as 'a horrible thing: never has Christianity been attacked in such a disgusting manner.' Rousseau had already read it and expressed to Keith[82] his indignation at the Genevese acceptance of that publication while they repudiated *Émile*: 'they keep their tolerance for atheists and burn anyone who dares to believe in God.' At the same time, Rousseau thanked Keith for having secured the promise of asylum from Frederick, and assured him of his wholehearted respect for the law and the prince. He also thanked Keith for the offer of shelter under his own roof at the château, but explained that he would rather stay at Môtiers and pay regular visits to Colombier: 'Here,' he wrote, 'I make ribbons with the women; at Colombier I shall be able to exercise my mind with you.'

Rousseau was referring here to the new hobby[83] he had taken up at Môtiers: weaving silk ribbons as he sat relaxing in an easy chair on the gallery and sometimes down at street-level, outside the front door, chatting to passers-by like a peasant's wife who had nothing better to do. It was part of a determined effort to make himself agreeable to the local villagers.

On 29 August Rousseau participated for the first time in holy communion at the parish church. Before he did so, he made a written application[84] to Montmollin for permission to take part, largely to afford some protection to the professor against any accusations from the Vénérable Classe of admitting an unbeliever to the sacrament. In this statement Rousseau declared that since his reunion in 1754 with the Church of Geneva into which he had been born, he had made a public profession of his adherence to Protestant Christianity:

I am attached in good faith to that true and holy Religion, and I shall be until my last breath. I wish always to be united to that church in public as I am in the depths of my heart, and however consoling it will be for me personally to participate in the communion of believers, I desire it, I assure you, more for the edification of those believers and for the honour of the Church than for my own advantage, for it would not be right for people to think that a man of good faith who reasons cannot be a member of Jesus Christ.

★'I abhor Voltaire.'[80]

In his published account[85] of the episode, Montmollin said that this declaration had given him great satisfaction, not only for the sake of M.
Rousseau and the church but because, as he freely admitted, it flattered his
amour propre to have such a great man as a parishioner: 'I saw it as one of the
most glorious events of my life.'

The declaration also pleased Rousseau's friends in Geneva, who had no
less than two hundred copies made for circulation in the city as evidence that
the author of *Émile* was a true Christian. 'You would not believe,' Moultou
wrote[86] to him, 'how much dismay your declaration has caused here to those
who do not like you, and what joy it has given those who do. Everybody
feels that after what you have done, there is no obstacle to your return to
Geneva and that our Consistory can do nothing against you, after the decision of Neuchâtel. Our pastors are too prudent. They will not set altar
against altar.'

Rousseau's declaration gave less pleasure to those in Paris. D'Alembert,
who had been pleading with Voltaire to stop tormenting Rousseau, lost all
sympathy with him on hearing that he had rallied to the church. 'I am no
more edified than you are by that mummery,' d'Alembert wrote[87] to Voltaire;
'I do not think it was necessary in order for him to dine and sup peacefully
and sleep in the lands of your former disciple, Frederick.' Mme de Boufflers,
who shared the anti-clerical sentiments of the *philosophes*, was no less disgusted by Rousseau's action. 'I have read that letter to the minister,' she
wrote,[88] 'and I confess that I do not approve at all . . . In the name of your
reputation, wait before you write anything more until your situation is better and your soul more tranquil.'

But Rousseau was in no mood to wait. He was itching to start writing
again and only inhibited by Frederick's desire that he should not publish anything controversial. Keith tried to put his mind at rest on this point: 'As for
the undertaking not to read, write, etc., I understand that, as you do, to
be a way of speaking that we do not need to take literally.' Rousseau did
not feel morally obliged to remain silent. 'I have promised myself not to
write any more, but, once again, I have promised only myself.' In other
words, Rousseau wanted once more to write for publication and intended
to do so.

At the end of August, two heavy trunks of his belongings arrived from
Yverdon. They included the Armenian costumes he had had made in Montmorency, and he decided to wear them as soon as the weather cooled. He
wrote[89] to Mme Boy, asking her to order some fur to attach to the edges of
the robe and to have a hat made of the same fur. These were not only prepa-
rations for what promised to be a cold winter in the Val de Travers, but part
of Rousseau's design to make the caftan more elegant. Visualising himself sitting in his caftan on his gallery weaving ribbons, he exclaimed: 'I have

thought as a man; I have written as a man and I have been called bad. Well, now I shall be a woman.'[90]

In a letter[91] to Mme de Verdelin he wrote: 'I wear a long robe; I weave ribbons. *Me voilà*, more than half a woman. If only I had always been one!' He told her how people were conspiring against him; how he was being persecuted by the 'nobleman Voltaire' and the 'juggler Tronchin' together with their numerous clique in Geneva and Paris. He also reminded her of his belief that his two 'Jansenist' neighbours[92] at Montlouis had, by spying on him, prepared the way for the *parlement* of Paris to prosecute him. He expressed the hope that Mme de Verdelin would one day visit him at Môtiers, and he thanked her for looking after his cat.

Mme de Verdelin was amused to learn that Rousseau had taken to weaving ribbons. She told him[93] she would like him to teach her the use of the spindle and promised in return to teach him the art of cookery—'I have been cooking my dinner and supper for the past fortnight.' In the same letter she said she did not attach much importance to the hostility of Voltaire: 'I am much more worried about the cold you will endure this winter in your mountains than about the trouble that Voltaire's intrigues will cause you.'

Rousseau was hardly qualified to teach the art of the spindle to Mme de Verdelin. He had to admit that he had been reproached for his weaving so rudely by Mme Sandoz, that he did not 'dare touch the spindle in the presence of those ladies'. Mme Sandoz was one of the few residents of Neuchâtel who maintained a literary salon in the city, and was living proof against Keith's claim that the society of Neuchâtel was composed of provincial bores.[94] She was, however, French by birth, a daughter of the Comte de Chaumont.

Rousseau's Swiss friends were less critical of his ribbons. One of the very first he made he presented[95] as a wedding gift to Anne-Marie d'Ivernois* on her marriage to Louis de Montmollin, a cousin of the professor. The ribbon was made of white and gold silk and was so cherished by the recipient that it can still be seen in a showcase at the Musée Rousseau at Môtiers. In the *Confessions*[96] Rousseau says he made presents of his ribbons to several young brides 'on condition that they promised to breast-feed their children'.

One day in early autumn Rousseau went to dine with Lord Keith at Colombier wearing his Armenian caftan. The governor expressed approval of the costume, greeting his guest in oriental fashion, 'Salamleki'. His adopted daughter, Emetulla, was thoroughly amused. She told another guest invited to the château—Mme Sturler—'A man from my country has arrived; at least one dressed as an Armenian. You will dine with him. Guess

---

*She was the daughter of Guillaume-Pierre d'Ivernois (1701–1775), the procurator-general of Neuchâtel. Not to be confused with her sister Isabella.

who he is.'[97] Before Mme Sturler could hazard a guess, Rousseau appeared.* Fortunately his Armenian costume met with her approval, and she sent the following account to Julie von Bondeli:[99]

The robe lent grace to his figure and the turban to his countenance, and his eyes doubled the effect. It was St.-Preux . . . At the table he spoke about the cotton factories in the country and the watchmaking workshops in the mountains which took labour off the land. He was told that industry brought money to the principality; but the devil took hold of him at the sound of the word *money*: 'You will have gold: you will roll in gold; but you will all die of hunger.' And then he growled, cried and gesticulated in a strange fashion. The uselessness of money and the simplicity of morals were his theses. In his anger he said such disagreeable things about the morals of the times, and especially about those of women, that everyone laughed like mad, while admitting that he was right.

From Amsterdam Rey sent Rousseau an affectionate letter in early September,[100] saying he had drunk a bottle of wine in his honour on hearing that he was safe and well in Switzerland. He gave a hesitant welcome to the idea of publishing Rousseau's *Complete Works*: he said that despite all the trouble he had had with *The Social Contract*, 'I am not against a collected edition, but we shall have to use precautions and I hope that with a little patience, all will go well.'

What Rey did not tell Rousseau was that he was planning to recoup his losses on *The Social Contract* by publishing an expurgated edition from which the offending chapter 'The Civil Religion' would be removed.

Rousseau's other Dutch publisher, Jean Néaulme, had embarked on an even more offensive enterprise. After the suppression of *Émile* in Holland, he set about publishing a radically changed and sanitized version of the book to be entitled *L'Émile chrétien* put together by Samuel Formey, a French literary journalist who had crossed Rousseau's path once before as the unauthorised publisher of his *Letter on Providence*. Néaulme complained in one of his letters[101] that as a result of publishing *Émile* 'I find myself dishonoured in the society in which I live,' and he made it fairly clear that he held Rousseau responsible for his distress.

In any event, Rousseau had no desire to have future work published by Néaulme, and if Rey remained unenthusiastic about publishing the *Complete Works*, the alternative Rousseau had in mind was Duchesne and Guy, who had at least paid him for *Émile*. Besides the *Complete Works*, Rousseau had a few other ideas for publication. One was the *Dictionary of Music*, for which

---

*From a letter Rousseau wrote to Mme de Luze it appears that she had sent him some lilac-coloured material for his caftan instead of the brown he had ordered. 'I shall have the air of a little charmer from Tiflis or Erivan,' he declared.[98]

he had been collecting material since he first started writing entries on musical subjects for Diderot's *Encyclopédie* in the 1750s. Another scheme was to collect into a single volume the critical comments that had been prompted by his novel *Julie*. Among them Rousseau was particularly impressed by those of Julie von Bondeli, saying to Caspar Hess[102] that her style 'combined solidity with colour, precision with charm, the reason of a man with the wit of a woman, the pen of Voltaire with the brains of Leibniz'. Despite this high praise, Julie von Bondeli was horrified at the prospect of her comments on Rousseau's novel being published. She prevailed on Leonhard Usteri to intervene in the matter, whereupon Rousseau explained[103] to her that he had not definitely decided to publish the book and that he would certainly not use her comments without her permission. In the end, he dropped the idea.

One project that Rousseau did not abandon was that of writing his autobiography, which Rey had suggested should form an introduction to his *Complete Works*. Remembering the four letters[104] of reminiscences that he had written to Malesherbes the previous January, Rousseau asked[105] the magistrate to return them to him. Malesherbes complied to the extent of having copies made to send to Rousseau; characteristically, he kept the originals. 'I have always loved and respected in you that true, strong, courageous and passionately virtuous soul that shines through all your writings,' Malesherbes wrote[106] in his covering letter; Rousseau, who did not know how much Malesherbes had been involved in the proscription of *Émile*, basked in his praise.

At Môtiers Rousseau continued to receive a stream of visitors, most of them new friends, although an old friend from Paris would occasionally appear. One such was Claude-Henri Watelet,[107] the tax farmer turned artist, who stopped off on a journey through Switzerland in the company of Marguerite Le Comte, an art student who had left her husband to live with him, and a travelling companion who bestowed a clerical blessing on their union, the Abbé Capette. According to one report[108] Rousseau went to dine with the party at the local inn, bringing with him 'a bottle of excellent wine from Beaune'. This report does not command ready credence since Rousseau is said elsewhere always to have refused invitations to dine at the local inn, and the only wines he is known to have possessed were local ones and Spanish wines presented by Lord Keith. The visit of Watelet, however, is authenticated by Rousseau himself, who mentioned it some years later in a letter[109] to Coindet: 'I owe M. Watelet, a very old friend . . . particular gratitude for coming to see me at Môtiers.'

Visitors from Zürich were more numerous than those from Paris. They included Leonhard Usteri, Johann Kaspar Lavater, Johann-Gaspard Schulthess, and Johann-Heinrich Füssli—this last being the historian, not the painter who bore the same name until he changed it to Fuseli on his emigration to England. The painter, who also became a friend of Rousseau, did not meet the author until a later date.[110]

One of the first Zürichois to visit Rousseau was Caspar Hess, a young professor of Hebrew who chose to spend his honeymoon in Môtiers in order to converse with the philosopher. An odd sort of honeymoon, perhaps, but one must remember that *La Nouvelle Héloïse* had established Rousseau as a romantic icon; to visit him was to reach what Byron called 'the birthplace of love'. Hess was the first, but not the last, of several *jeunes mariés* who took their brides to Rousseau in search of a nuptial benediction. Rousseau warned them all that romantic love did not last and that friendship was the only sound basis for matrimony.

After the visit Hess assured[111] Rousseau that the time he and his bride had spent with him had been the happiest of their lives. Rousseau in his reply[112] expressed no less pleasure at having made the acquaintance of the young couple. Their correspondence renewed the suggestion that had doubtless been made in conversation: that Rousseau should settle in Zürich.

There was much to recommend Zürich as a place of refuge. Its Reformation was the work of Zwingli, a less fanatical Protestant than Calvin; its commercial oligarchy was less oppressive than the hereditary aristocracy of Berne; and a spirit of a toleration prevailed in the canton long before it became one of the centres of the German-speaking Enlightenment. *Émile* had not been proscribed there, and Hess assured[113] Rousseau that the leading personalities of the city—among them Gessner, Bodmer, Hirzel, Breitinguer, and Usteri—were on his side. Even so, there were potential enemies. Usteri himself, writing[114] to urge Rousseau to come to Zürich, added, 'I would press you even more if I had not some grounds to fear our fanatics.' In any case, none of these suggestions that Rousseau settle in Zürich was accompanied by a concrete invitation.

Petitpierre, the Neuchâtel pastor who had been disgraced for denying the eternity of punishments, urged Rousseau to seek refuge in England, as he himself had done. His message was transmitted[115] by Rousseau's cousin Jean, who took the opportunity of expressing his dissent from the proposal. On the strength of his own experience of living in London, he predicted that the English would welcome Rousseau at first but abandon him as soon as they found out that his ideas were not theirs. Jean Rousseau also pointed out that the cost of living was high in England: 'You would need at least £200 a year.' He said the English despised all foreigners, although he had to admit that the English press was full of news about Rousseau and that English translations of *Émile* were selling well in London.*

Lord Keith had yet another idea. He himself was impatient to quit

---

*There were two translations on the London market: William Kenrick's *Emilius and Sophie* and M. Nugent's *Emilius*.

Neuchâtel, and he suggested[116] that Rousseau accompany him to his castle in Scotland, where David Hume resided in a small community of philosophers. He proposed that each should pay for his own keep, but for the rest 'there will be no regulations or laws in our republic, but each will rule himself in matters both temporal and spiritual.' Keith also offered money to Rousseau, dressing up the gift as an advance on the proceeds of the publication of his *Complete Works* in London.

On the same day[117] Keith wrote (in English) to David Hume, telling him that he had offered Rousseau 'lodging in Keith Hall', without inviting Hume to join him there. Keith described his new friend as 'gay in company, polite and what the French call *aimable*'. He added that while Rousseau 'gained ground daily in the opinion of even the clergy here' he was still being persecuted. 'This is not a country for him,' Keith wrote, 'Tho' it be to me a very great pleasure to converse with the honest savage, yet I advise him to go to England where he will enjoy *placidam sub libertate quietem*.'

Rousseau himself was feeling unsettled as autumn descended on the Val de Travers. Writing[118] to thank Mme Boy for some materials she had sent him for winter clothing and a renewed offer of a summer retreat at Pierrenod, he told her: 'I do not know how I shall endure the winter, and if I survive I do not know what will happen to me from one year to the next.'

Lord Keith continued to think of ways of helping Rousseau financially. He wanted to give him an annuity, but, feeling that Rousseau would refuse to accept one from him, he pretended that he had been authorised by Frederick to suggest one to him. He chose the wrong moment to do so, for Rousseau had just been hearing about Frederick's conquest of Silesia in the as yet unfinished European war.

'I have enough to live on for the next two or three years,' Rousseau wrote[119] to Keith in response to the offer of a pension. 'And I have never pushed foresight that far ahead. But even if I were starving to death, in the present situation of that good prince, and my worthlessness to him, I would rather eat grass and dig up roots than accept a morsel of bread from him . . . Let him make a glorious peace and restore his finances and rebuild his extended dominions, then if I am still alive and he has still the same benevolence for me, you will see if I shrink from his charity.'

This letter was accompanied by a present to Lord Keith of fruits from Rousseau's little garden— 'watered only with my tears'—and by another letter,[120] which Rousseau asked him to forward to Frederick:

Sire,
You are my protector and my benefactor, and I have a heart made to be grateful: I wish to discharge my debts to you, if I can.

You wish to give me bread. Is there no one of your subjects who lacks it?

Hide from my eyes that sword which dazzles and wounds me. It has done all too well in your services and the sceptre has been abandoned. The career of Kings of your ilk is great, and yours is far from its term. However, time presses and you have not a moment to lose to complete it. Consult your heart carefully, O Frederick! Can you decide to die without having been the greatest of men?

May I see Frederick the just and the feared fill his states with a happy people of whom he is the father and Jean-Jacques, the enemy of Kings, come to die of joy at the foot of his throne.

May Your Majesty deign to accept my zeal and my most profound respect.

Whatever Keith thought of this letter, he agreed[121] to forward it to Berlin, doing so in a manner that he hoped would ensure its being seen by the King's eyes only. At the same time he urged Rousseau to come to spend the winter at Colombier, where he was sure he would be warmer than at Môtiers. A week later,[122] however, Keith had to report that he himself had caught a bad cold, which he attributed to the fact that his bedroom at the château was too hot—his lazy servants put too many logs on the fire at once to save replenishing the fuel at frequent intervals—while elsewhere the place was too cold. Despite the fact that he hailed from the north of Scotland, Lord Keith detested the winter climate of Neuchâtel: 'I spent much of my youth at Valencia in Spain,' he explained, 'so I feel the cold more than the people of this country.' Besides, he assured Rousseau graciously, 'you make me yearn all the more for the return of good weather since you promise me that you will come then to Colombier again.' The one form of gift that Keith could persuade Rousseau to accept was wine, and as winter approached he ventured to offer[123] him vegetables as well: 'I have stored for the winter in the cellar more than I can possibly eat, and you would give me great pleasure if you would tell me what you would like.'

The winters in the Jura mountains were proverbially severe, and by the second week of October it was already snowing at Môtiers. Mme Boy's house, exposed to the winds and badly insulated, was draughty and cold. Daniel Roguin advised[124] Rousseau to accustom himself to the use of the local stoves, and also urged[125] him to have an open fire as well as the stove as a means of warming his feet. Roguin was afraid that Thérèse might have difficulty with the oven, but Rousseau himself had mastered that since he had started to bake his own bread—a privilege for which he had to pay the village baker a fee of one *écu blanc*.[126]

Rousseau was also able to dress warmly, as new supplies of clothes arrived from Mme Boy in Lyons. He had sent her very detailed instructions about the fur-lined robe he wanted to wear over his caftan, together with a fur hat, which he told her must not have 'the appearance of a night-cap'.[127] Encouraged by Roguin to wear the caftan even when attending church,[128] he was anxious that it not 'look like a dressing gown'. With this in mind he asked[129] Mme Boy to send him a striped silk belt to wear with the caftan; he had seen a real Armenian wearing such an outfit at Lord Keith's château and thought it looked very smart.

As winter drew nearer, Rousseau was no longer able to sit at his door weaving ribbons or chatting with villagers at the fountain, but he continued to cultivate their goodwill when he met them on his regular walks; he even taught some of their children to play the spinet. He took very seriously his new role as a communicant of the village church. In keeping with his philosophy of the simple life, he tried to find happiness in the society of simple people. But he failed to do so. They were too dull; the cold weather depressed him; and he felt ill.

'Je suis froid,' he wrote in a letter to Rey,[130] 'je suis triste, je pisse mal.'

3

A GOSPEL CHRISTIAN

Rousseau's letter to Montmollin, declaring his adherence to the Christian religion, gave joy to his friends in Geneva. Moultou assured[1] Rousseau that it had cleared the way for his return to the city, and Colonel Pictet urged[2] him to come back to a cordial welcome from 'the sound part of your co-citizens who will greet you with all the more pleasure because you are a living example of the most singular virtues.'

Rousseau was not persuaded by these assurances. 'My coming to Geneva,' he wrote[3] to Pictet, 'would be very dangerous to me and of no use to any-one else.' His enemies in Geneva were as scandalised by the news of his par-ticipation in communion as his friends were pleased. One Genevese elder of the church, Pastor Jean Sarasin,* promptly wrote[4] to de Montmollin to de-mand an explanation for what he called an 'astonishing' decision to admit Rousseau to the sacrament. A distant relation of Pastor Sarasin,[5] who had been among Rousseau's friends, this cleric proved himself one of Rousseau's most remorseless enemies. He addressed Montmollin with brutal frankness. 'A man who has written the books that Rousseau has written,' he declared, 'could not in good faith call himself a Christian or partake as such of the Lord's Supper.' As for the declaration in which Rousseau had assured Mont-mollin of his belief in the Christian religion, Sarasin said it appeared to him to be 'very equivocal and unsatisfactory' since it did not repudiate those pub-lished writings in which Rousseau had 'cast utter ridicule upon the religion of the Gospel while purporting to undermine the religion of Rome'.

Sarasin went on to say that he was sure that Montmollin must have inter-rogated Rousseau at length before admitting him to communion, and he asked for a full explanation of what had been said. This demand, like the rest of the letter, was couched in peremptory language. Sarasin did not even ad-dress the pastor by his cherished title of 'Monsieur le Professeur'.

*1703–1778.

Montmollin was rattled by the letter. He showed it at once to Rousseau and sought his help in drafting an answer. In his reply[6] Montmollin claimed that his decision had been amply justified. He said he had received from Rousseau the assurance of sincere belief in the Christian religion; he had questioned Rousseau about *Émile* and was satisfied with the explanation that that book was designed as a defence of Christianity against the materialism of the philosopher Helvétius and that its criticisms of religion were aimed at Catholic doctrines. He added that the Consistory of Neuchâtel had unanimously agreed that Rousseau could receive communion since that act was a public declaration of faith in Christ. Having received that formal approval, Rousseau 'had taken the sacrament with a humility and a devotion which had edified the whole congregation' of the parish at Môtiers.

Montmollin also paid tribute to Rousseau's character, saying that 'he has made himself loved and respected in these cantons by his sweetness, his affability, his moderation, his silence and by benefactions made without ostentation.'

Some years later, Rousseau recalled[7] being consulted by Montmollin about this letter. He said the professor had originally produced a draft in which he reported 'interviews' with Rousseau about his beliefs—interviews that had never taken place. Rousseau said he had protested but finally agreed to the letter being sent to Sarasin subject to certain changes that he made with his own hand. At the time, Rousseau described[8] Sarasin's letter to Montmollin as being 'full of bad faith, bad temper and ill will, to say no worse', but he made no criticisms, even to Moultou, of Montmollin's reply to Sarasin.

Moultou was soon able to report[9] to Rousseau that two hundred copies of his letter to Montmollin had been circulated in Geneva and that 'the whole citizenry is enchanted that you have come back to its way of thinking.' If this judgement was hardly true of the whole, it was true of one citizen who had been silent for several months: Jacques-François Deluc, Rousseau's old friend and the great champion of his plea in 1754 for readmission to his rights. A devout Calvinist, Deluc had been one of those most shocked by Rousseau's rejection in *Émile* of revelation and miracles, so shocked indeed that he had not written to the author or attempted to visit him at Yverdon or Môtiers. All Deluc had done was to send to Rousseau, through a friend they had in common, a copy of his own attempt at a defence of the Protestant religion against sceptical philosophy, a book entitled *Observations sur les savants incrédules*, in the hope that it might open Rousseau's eyes to the errors of his ways. Rousseau already knew the book, and knew it to be unreadable.

Deluc himself, however, had a high opinion of his own work and ventured to suggest[10] to Moultou that '*Émile* would not have been written if

M. Rousseau had read my *Observations* first.' Knowing that Rousseau felt wounded by Deluc's silence, Moultou tried to explain[11] that Deluc was still a friend: 'He condemns what you have written about religion, but he admires you and loves you.'

Deluc hoped to reinforce the impact of his own *Observations* by sending Rousseau a book by the English Protestant Humphrey Ditton, upholding the doctrine of the physical resurrection of Christ,[12] but Moultou dissuaded him. 'The man will make you die of boredom as the English Presbyterians did their poor King,' he warned[13] Rousseau; whereupon Rousseau assured Moultou that he was well able to protect himself: 'Sermons in print only bore those who choose to read them,' he observed.[14] 'Let M. Deluc come and preach to me in person; he will go away dissatisfied.' Even so, Rousseau admitted that he missed his old friend: 'They certainly take time to come to visit me,' he lamented, referring to Deluc and his two sons.

It was only when Deluc read a copy of Rousseau's letter to Montmollin at the end of September that he decided to cease ostracising the author of *Émile*. Indeed that letter seems to have had an electrifying effect on Deluc.[15] He took a copy of it to Moultou, saying, 'I bring you a draught of fresh water,' and he promptly wrote[16] to Rousseau at Môtiers to express his joy. He took a good many words to explain that while he approved of Rousseau's politics, he could never approve of the religious opinions set forth in *Émile*. Deluc suggested to Rousseau an explanation for his unfortunate departure from Calvinist orthodoxy, namely, that 'you have lived too long among the unbelievers and the superstitious to know the basis of true Christianity.' He expressed regret that Rousseau had not employed his talents to refute the scepticism of Voltaire, and went on to boast of his own success in that mission, recalling that he had once visited Voltaire to read aloud from the text of his *Observations sur les savants incrédules*: 'M. de Voltaire interrupted me as soon as I began and implored me to leave my manuscript with him for twenty-four hours so that he might read it with the closest attention.'

Rousseau was pleased to receive this letter, but in his reply[17] he did not conceal his feelings about past neglect: 'When other friends hastened to console me in my disgrace, I was surprised to receive no sign of life from the one among them on whom I had most counted.' Nor did Rousseau fail to point out that Deluc had been taken in by Voltaire: 'Your rectitude blinded you to the irony of his remark.' Nevertheless the tone of his reply was generally affectionate: 'I would be happy to see you, provided you do not preach sermons to me, for then we shall not understand each other.' He ended the letter by saying, 'I love you with all my heart . . . I need my friends . . . I embrace your dear sons and their good papa.'

While Rousseau encouraged Deluc to come to Môtiers, he advised Moultou[18] against such a visit: 'I do not think it at all prudent for you or Roustan to come to see me this year, for your journey would certainly not be kept secret.' Rousseau feared that Moultou would be punished by his fellow clergy for a known association with a notorious heretic. Moultou may not have shared these fears, but he had no enthusiasm to leave Geneva, even for a few days. A reason for this may be discerned in a remark in another letter[19] to Rousseau: Moultou asked if the ribbons Rousseau was weaving were really only to be given to brides, because he would like to have one for a 'beautiful, honest young woman who defends you at every opportunity and *vous aime à la folie*'. The young woman in question was obviously Germaine de Vermenoux; nothing would drag Moultou from her company.

Antoine Roustan was not persuaded by Rousseau's counsels of prudence. Although he was only a junior minister of the gospel and a schoolmaster at the Collège de Genève, with none of Moultou's wealth or social standing, he was willing to risk the sanctions of the church in order to visit Môtiers. He suggested[20] to Rousseau that without telling any lies he could conceal the motive for his journey: 'It would need many interdictions and fires and stakes to extinguish my friendship for you.'

At the end of September Roustan set out for Môtiers with two companions: another young minister and fellow schoolmaster at the Collège de Genève, Pierre Mouchon (who was a kinsman of Rousseau's), and a watchmaker named Christophe Beauchâteau. They journeyed on foot through the Pays de Vaud and over the Jura mountains, following the paths that Rousseau himself had taken through Fies and Mauborget to the Val de Travers. They arrived at Môtiers on 1 October and stayed for eight days, putting up at the local inn.[21]

Pierre Mouchon sent his wife an account[22] of the visit. He told her 'he fell from the clouds' on seeing his illustrious kinsman for the first time:

You have no idea how charming his company is, what civility of manners, what depths of serenity and of gaiety there is in his conversation! You may have expected a different portrait. Did you imagine a bizarre sort of man, always solemn, often brusque and rude? Nothing could be farther from his true character. To a sweetness of countenance is added an expression full of fire, his eyes sparkling with incomparable vivacity. And when a subject interests him, his eyes, his mouth, his muscles, his hands all speak with him. It would be very wrong to imagine him a malcontent, a perpetual censor—not at all, he laughs with those who laugh, he teases, he chats with children and jokes with his housekeeper, Mlle Levasseur.

Rousseau, who had given up an invitation to stay with Lord Keith in order to receive his Genevese visitors, spent hours in their company, and only refused to join them when they went to dine at the parsonage with Professor de Montmollin. 'He never eats away from home,' Mouchon explained to his wife. Both Roustan and Mouchon were persuaded to preach[23] at the parish church while they were at Môtiers, and Montmollin doubtless was encouraged by the support of two Genevese ministers at a time when he was being tormented by Pastor Sarasin, even though their rank was very junior to his.

Apart from their dinner at the parsonage, the Genevese visitors took most of their meals with Rousseau; between meals he led them on long walks, sometimes in the woods, sometimes toward the mountains where the snow was already falling. One evening, according to an anecdote told by Mouchon,[24] Rousseau suggested to his guests as they sat around the fire in his kitchen that they renew an old folk custom of taking turns rotating the roast meat on the spit while telling a story or fable. The story Rousseau told when his turn came was *La Reine fantasque*,[25] a fairy tale he had written in 1756 about a queen who baptises her son Caprice and her daughter Reason only to discover that their characters contradict their names. His listeners, it is recalled, were 'delighted by the pleasure and varied tone of his voice, his vivacity of gesture and the animation of his countenance as he recited the tale'. Rousseau sent the manuscript of *La Reine fantasque* to Rey but discouraged him from publishing it—it was, he said,[26] a mere scribble, a 'barbouillage'.

It seems that Montmollin told Roustan and Mouchon about the letter he had written to Sarasin that explained his reasons for admitting Rousseau to communion. They wanted copies of it, thinking it could be circulated in Geneva to reinforce the effect that Rousseau's letter to Montmollin had already had in winning public opinion to his side. Sarasin, clearly seeing that the circulation of the letter would have just that effect, resisted the proposal.

Writing to Montmollin on 12 October,[27] Sarasin adopted a more unctuous approach than that of his earlier letter. He said he prayed for God's blessing on the pastor's efforts to save a penitent's soul. But he also renewed his attacks on Rousseau's published writings and argued that even if the Vénérable Classe of Neuchâtel had authorised Rousseau's admission to communion, it had by asking the government to suppress *Émile* and *The Social Contract* confirmed his own judgement of those books. In these circumstances, Sarasin felt that Rousseau should be required to repudiate publicly the heretical opinions he had expressed in order to destroy the poison that— 'against his intention'—his books had injected into people's minds. Sarasin ended his letter by congratulating de Montmollin fulsomely on his recent appointment by Frederick II as Chapelain du Roi and Ministre de la Cour— although we cannot doubt that, given the notoriously atheist character of the King and Court in question, Sarasin must have considered those appointments as ridiculous as the professorial title he studiously omitted to ascribe to his correspondent.

Roustan, who had the measure of Montmollin, tried by the simple method of flattery to persuade him to allow his letter to Sarasin to be circulated. 'We met at Môtiers not one but two philosophers,' Roustan wrote[28] to Montmollin after the former's departure. 'How fortunate is Monsieur Rousseau to have found a wise pastor; how fortunate is the religion that has such heralds.' Roustan begged the professor (for as such Roustan addressed him) to allow his letter to be published in the interests of Christianity notwithstanding Pastor Sarasin's objections.

All three of Rousseau's Genevese visitors wrote him letters of thanks for his hospitality. Roustan said[29] that meeting Rousseau had been an inspiration: 'In whatever situation I find myself in future, I shall think of the Sage of Môtiers, who can hardly ever sleep, is afflicted by infirmities, tormented by a crowd of powerful enemies, but is always patient, laughs with his friends, and draws serenity, calm and peace from the purity of his heart.'

Mouchon was hardly less eloquent. He assured[30] Rousseau that his eight days at Môtiers had been 'the epoch of my life' and that in the routine of a schoolmaster's tiresome job the memory of the visit 'restores my serenity'. The watchmaker Beauchâteau reported[31] that the journey home from Môtiers to Geneva had been easier than expected: it had taken them three days, spending their first night at Vitteboeuf and the next at Morges. Beauchâteau also informed Rousseau that while the author's enemies were still active in Geneva, 'the virtuous elements regard you as their leader' and that 'your friends have the delicious pleasure of finding more and more people who agree with them.'

Indeed, there is every evidence that public opinion in Geneva was being mobilised on behalf of Rousseau. Once Deluc entered the struggle, he brought all his political experience and authority to bear in the organisation of what became a campaign. Rousseau's supporters decided to test public opinion by challenging the re-election of procurator-general Robert Tronchin, who was held responsible for the indictment of *The Social Contract* and *Émile*. The election, in which every citizen had a vote, was scheduled for 12 November.

Five weeks before that event, Deluc went to Môtiers to discuss with Rousseau the strategy to be employed against Robert Tronchin. He had a second purpose, rather less alluring, of completing Rousseau's conversion to Calvinist orthodoxy. Moultou warned[32] Rousseau of this, saying that Deluc 'is wild to have you think as he thinks'. Rousseau had a ready response: 'M. Deluc is an excellent friend,' he replied,[33] 'full of sense and probity and virtue. He is the most honest and the most boring man there is.'

Deluc travelled to Môtiers on horseback, but the weather turned extremely cold as he rode across the Jura mountains. He was taken ill with what he called a colic and arrived on Rousseau's doorstep a sick man. He was put

straight to bed with a hot broth. Rousseau wrote[34] to Deluc's two sons, reproaching them for letting him travel in such inclement weather; he assured
them, however, that their father was under the care of a very good doctor at
Môtiers. Thérèse nursed the invalid, and Rousseau was spared from having
to hear any of his sermons. After two days he was able to inform[35] Deluc's
sons that their father was well again and would be coming home, not on
horseback, but by carriage on the easier route along the Val de Travers,
through the city of Neuchâtel and across the lake 'in the company of
M. d'Ivernois'.

The M. d'Ivernois in question was François-Henri d'Ivernois, a merchant
of Geneva and a cousin of the d'Ivernois of Neuchâtel, with whom
Rousseau had made friends at Môtiers. Like Deluc, François d'Ivernois was
active in Geneva on the side of the citizens' opposition to the government,
and his presence at Môtiers suggests that his conversation with Rousseau
would have had more to do with politics than with theology. Rousseau attached great importance to the campaign against the re-election of Robert
Tronchin, but he was reluctant to facilitate his supporters' efforts by supplying further evidence of his attachment to the Reformed religion and dis-
tancing himself from the Vicaire Savoyard.

'Is it not amusing that it should be I who has to make reparations for the
affronts I have received?' Rousseau remarked[36] to Moultou. Deluc suggested
that Rousseau supply 'clarifications' of his published opinions to help persuade the Genevese voters that he was a genuine Christian who had been
unjustly treated by Robert Tronchin and the Petit Conseil.

After Deluc had left for home, Rousseau explained[37] to Moultou: 'It is not
I who want to offer "clarifications". It is the good fellow Deluc who wants
me to provide them, and I am sorry I cannot satisfy him because he really
won my heart on this visit, and I was more pleased with him than I expected
to be.'

Another piece of evidence that Deluc wanted for his campaign was a copy
of Montmollin's letter to Sarasin that set out his reasons for readmitting
Rousseau to communion. Moultou joined Deluc in explaining[38] the importance of this to Rousseau, but Rousseau refused[39] to say a word to Montmollin on the subject, fearing that Montmollin might be compromised.
Rousseau told Moultou that if he wanted to see the letter, he should speak
directly to Sarasin about it. This advice was fruitless, for Sarasin was in no
mind to serve the interests of Rousseau's friends as the day of the election
approached. Indeed Sarasin had already warned[40] Montmollin—now addressed as Monsieur le Professeur—of plans to publish the two letters they
had exchanged in September, and urged him to take whatever steps he could
to prevent publication. Sarasin reverted to the subject in a later letter,[41] saying he was very annoyed at the indiscretion of those who were pestering

Montmollin for copies of the letter. To Sarasin's satisfaction, Montmollin refused to release the letter.

Unable to secure this letter for their purposes, Rousseau's champions pressed him again for written 'clarifications' of the religious opinions contained in *Émile*. Not only Deluc, but Pictet[42] and Moultou thought this was necessary. Even Montmollin, for reasons of his own, urged[43] Rousseau to write a 'second letter' explaining his religious beliefs. Rousseau yielded reluctantly. He informed Deluc on 18 November[44] that he had agreed to write a 'second letter' to Professor de Montmollin, but added: 'I have decided to adopt a firmer tone than one likely to please the people who would like me to crawl.' Nevertheless Rousseau agreed to sign a letter[45] drafted in collaboration with Deluc, Moultou, and de Montmollin in which he asserted, among other things, that 'If I had always lived in Protestant countries the Profession of Faith of the Savoyard Priest would not have been written.'

By this time it was too late for the letter to influence the election in Geneva, and the draft was never published. On 21 November Robert Tronchin was re-elected by 800 votes to 400. Rousseau, plainly disappointed, lost patience with Geneva. On the other hand, he had not yet tired of religious controversy. Despite the King's desire that he abstain from such activity while living in the principality, Rousseau spent hours in his 'laboratory' writing a defence of *Émile* that he intended to publish. This essay had nothing to do with Geneva; rather it was prompted by the publication in France of a *mandement* against *Émile* that was signed by Christophe de Beaumont, Archbishop of Paris. Rousseau set about answering this document with a pamphlet of some forty thousand words. When others attacked *Émile* in print he was content either to roll with the punches or, as he once said, to spit on his critics, but Christophe de Beaumont was different. Rousseau respected Beaumont more than he did most bishops because he, too, had once endured exile rather than submit to the dictates of the French government in church policy. Rousseau saw the archbishop as a man of conscience like himself, a worthy adversary. Again Rousseau proved himself a superb polemist; his pamphlet[46] is a masterly fusion of reasoning and rhetoric. He wrote it in the form of a letter from a humble citizen of Geneva to a prince of the church, addressing Beaumont with his grandest titles: 'Archevèque de Paris, Duc de Saint-Cloud, Pair de France, Commandeur de l'ordre du St. Esprit, Proviseur de la Sorbonne etc.' He began by asking: 'Why, Monseigneur, should I be speaking to you? What language have we in common? How could we understand each other? What could there be between us? And yet I must reply to you. You yourself force me to. If you had simply attacked my book, I could have let it pass. But you attack my person, and the greater your authority among men, the less free am I to remain silent when you seek to dishonour me.'[47]

Rousseau goes on to comment on the action of the *parlement* of Paris against *Émile*, 'a book published in a Protestant country by a Protestant author over whom the Parlement had no jurisdiction'.[48] The action cannot, he argues, have had a religious motive; atheists such as Spinoza have been welcomed in France, their books freely printed and sold, while 'the defender of the cause of God is stigmatized, tormented, pursued from state to state . . . without consideration or pity.'[49] That is bad enough, but what is more astonishing is that 'a virtuous man, as noble in his soul as in his birth, an illustrious prelate who ought to reprimand such shameful procedures, should authorise them.'[50]

Rousseau invites the archbishop to explain why he did not issue *mandemants* against the *Discourse on Inequality*, the *Letter to M. d'Alembert* or *Julie*, 'which you must have read since you judge them',[51] when they set forth the same principles and the same ideas as *Émile*. Rousseau admits that he ought not to have been wholly surprised at the Paris *parlement's* persecution of him since it was dominated by Jansenists, who, as he had predicted in *Émile*, would collectively prove as intolerant a master as their Jesuit enemies; but, he adds, he could not have expected that 'the fearless Monseigneur de Beaumont, who has never yielded to any power or made peace with the Jansenists should become their satellite and the instrument of their animosity against me, and rather than be accused of lack of zeal, prefer to undertake an act of cruelty'.[52]

Rousseau asserts once again that he is a Christian 'as a disciple not of priests, but of Jesus Christ'.[53] He observes that the archbishop has denied him the title of a Christian because he refuses to accept the doctrine of original sin, and he argues in his defence that this doctrine comes from St. Augustine and the theologians rather than from the Gospel. Moreover, he denies that this doctrine can be reconciled with the church's own teaching that the Christian emerges from the sacrament of baptism as clean as Adam came from the hands of God. As for the assertion that we are all guilty because of the sins of our forefathers, Rousseau asks how any Christian can believe God to be so unjust as to punish us for sins we have not committed.[54]

Rejecting the doctrine of original sin, Rousseau restates the central theme of all his writings—that man is good by nature and corrupted only by society. He summarises the argument of the *Discourse on Inequality*, according to which man's original *amour de soi*, which is innocent, develops as individuals come into contact with others into *amour propre*, the source of wickedness and conflict. Sin, Rousseau agrees, is everywhere, but he says it emerged only after men left the state of nature to live in communities.

'Monseigneur,' Rousseau declares, 'I am a Christian, a sincere Christian according to the teaching of the Gospel.'[55] He goes on to say that the Gospel shows Jesus— 'my Master'—speaking little about dogmas and much about duties. 'When Jesus invokes the Law of the Prophets he dwells on virtuous actions rather than on sets of beliefs and tells us that he who loves his brother has fulfilled the law.'[56]

Rousseau rejects the archbishop's claim that a Christian is required to believe in miracles. He admits that there is an abundance of testimony in support of miracles, 'none more complete than testimony to the existence of vampires.'[57] But does that mean one is to be damned for not holding such a belief? Rousseau says he is very willing to be shown a miracle—but would prefer 'to ascribe it to magic than to recognize the voice of God in any demonstration against reason'.[58]

He turns next to the accusation that *Émile* is a danger to public order. Rousseau reminds the archbishop that he insisted in that book on the duty to obey the laws of one's own country in matters of religious forms and observation. While pleading for toleration, he had expressly acknowledged the right of the sovereign to forbid the introduction of new sects and strange religions, and had simply argued that once different religions are established and tolerated in a country 'it is unjust and barbarous to destroy them by violence.'[59]

He reminds Beaumont that the Profession of Faith of the Savoyard Priest—the feature of *Émile* on which the archbishop's criticism is centred—is divided into two parts. The first and most important, Rousseau points out, 'is designed to combat modern materialism, to establish the existence of God and natural religion with all the force the author can command'.[60] The second part, 'shorter and less systematic, sets out certain doubts and difficulties concerning revelation, while affirming certitude in the purity and holiness of Christian teaching'. Rousseau observes with sorrow that only the second part has attracted the attention of Monseigneur de Beaumont even as it did that of the magistrates of the Paris *parlement*. '*Émile* was written by a Christian in defence of religion,' he concludes, 'and all you have to answer my reasoning is abuse and burning at the stake.'[61]

The first publisher Rousseau thought of for the *Letter to Archbishop Beaumont* was Rey. In a letter dated 16 November[62] Rousseau explained that he had been forced against his will to take up his pen again, and, if his lamentable state of health allowed him to finish what he was writing, he would send the result to Amsterdam: 'See if you would like to print it: but in any case, secrecy and diligence are essential.' A fortnight later,[63] Rousseau informed Rey that the manuscript on which he had been working for the past two months would be ready within six weeks. He wanted to have it published in secret, although he assured Rey it was something that could safely be printed in Holland since it criticised only a Catholic priest. Rousseau added that if Rey decided to accept the pamphlet, he should not lose a moment in having it printed, if only to keep it out of the hands of pirate publishers.

Despite this last remark, Rousseau's impatience to see the *Letter to Archbishop Beaumont* in print was so great that, having received no word from Rey by 17 December, he wrote[64] on that date to one of the most notorious pirate publishers in France, Jean-Marie Bruysset, offering him 'a defence of *Émile*' that must have been the same manuscript sent to Rey. Bruysset declined[65] the opportunity, saying 'a father of a family dare not risk the storms that a defence of *Émile* will inevitably provoke.' Such prudence was uncharacteristic of Bruysset. One may assume he saw no profit in publishing the work.

By the time Bruysset's refusal reached Rousseau, he had received from Rey an assurance[66] of his willingness 'to publish anything you would like to send me' and a renewed plea for Rousseau's autobiography. Rey made no mention of any payment for copyright, but he did at least inform Rousseau that the three hundred francs of Thérèse's annuity for the year 1763 would be paid in advance by his agent in Neuchâtel.

During this period, Rousseau kept in touch with his Paris publishers, Duchesne and Guy, partly in order to have books sent him from their bookshop and also to keep alive the possibility of their publishing his *Complete Works* and the *Dictionary of Music*, both potential sources of revenue to the author. Guy had in fact already made plans for a provisional collected edition[67] and even engaged a writer, the Abbé Joseph de La Porte, to edit the volumes. Rousseau seems to have learned of the project from his old friend in Paris, Toussaint-Pierre Lenieps, before he heard from Guy himself. Lenieps reported to Rousseau in mid-November[68] that La Porte was gathering material for a collected edition and had visited him in search of anything that might be included; again in December[69] Lenieps informed Rousseau that the abbé wanted to include the long letter[70] Rousseau had written to him in 1759, detailing his grievances against the Paris Opera over *Le Devin du village*. Guy said nothing about this in his correspondence with Rousseau throughout 1762. Not until January 1763[71] did Guy give some intimation of his plans, and even then he said only that his publishing house would like to bring out a provisional edition of Rousseau's *Collected Works*, that the Abbé de La Porte would like to edit them, that Mme de Luxembourg was strongly in favour of the project, and that he, Pierre Guy, was approaching Malesherbes for police authority to publish them; only Rousseau's consent was needed. Guy made it clear that what he had in mind was an interim collection, and that would not compete with the *Complete Works* that Rousseau intended one day to produce and that Guy, in turn, hoped to publish. Again, no mention was made of any fee for the author.

Rousseau's women friends in Paris continued to fret about his poverty in Switzerland, his isolation, his health, the cold weather, and also his resistance to their efforts to help him.

'Why are you so cross with me?' Mme de Boufflers asked in a letter dated

10 November.[72] Rousseau answered[73] her squarely: 'I have always approved of my friends giving me counsel, but not orders. I want them to advise me but not to govern me. You have deigned, Madame, to honour me with the solicitude of a friend; I thank you for it. Confine yourself to that, and I shall thank you even more.'

Mme Alissan irritated him almost as intensely with her complaints that he was neglecting her. He tried[74] to make her understand that he was 'overwhelmed with letters, memoranda, verses, praises, critiques and dissertations' from correspondents who expected to be answered. 'I would need ten hands and ten secretaries to deal with them all.' He begged her to terminate their correspondence, but, far from agreeing to this, Mme Alissan replied[75] with another long letter urging him to be patient with her because this time she had news for him. In Paris she had recently attended a performance of *Le Philosophe prétendu*, a play by Desfontaines (from a story by Marmontel), in which Rousseau was mocked. Mme Alissan reported, however, that during the play a man seated near her had put up a magnificent defence of the victim. From her description of his champion as 'a man with a large wart' Rousseau guessed it must have been the Marquis de Croismare, with whom he had made friends at the Hermitage. This letter evidently pleased Rousseau; instead of renewing his plea to Mme Alissan to end their correspondence, he urged[76] her to write again telling him more about herself. As he had never met her, he had to imagine how she looked: 'I believe your face torments me more than it would if I had seen it,' he declared. 'If you will not tell me how you are made, you must at least tell me how you are dressed, so that my imagination may fix on something that I know to be yours.'

Mme Alissan was quick to respond. She described[77] herself as having dark-brown hair, well arranged; a perfectly oval face with a high forehead, black, well-arched eyebrows, deep-blue eyes, an aquiline nose, a small mouth, white and healthy teeth, and a good chin; and a countenance that bespoke contentment rather than gaiety, goodness more than sweetness, soul more than wit. 'From that portrait,' she asked, 'will you think me as beautiful as an angel? Not at all. I do not have one of those faces that people look at twice.' Her gown, made of grey satin and decorated with pink *mouches*, suited her modesty, she explained. She did not follow the rule of the portraitist in *Émile*,[78] who, 'failing to make you look beautiful, makes you look rich.'

Mme de Chenonceaux was another of Rousseau's women friends who kept up an affectionate correspondence from Paris. Having secured one of the copies of *The Social Contract* circulating on the black market in France despite the government's efforts to suppress them, she wrote to say she was glad the author was safe in Neuchâtel because, as she put it, 'if you had been here, you would have been stoned.' She spoke of visiting Rousseau in his refuge since she had plans to go to Lyons and had heard that a detour to Môtiers would add only twenty-five or thirty leagues to the journey. The purpose of this trip was an unhappy one—to visit her wastrel husband, M. Dupin's son, in the debtor's prison at Pierre Encise. The fairly cheerful tone of her letter, however, suggests that she had recovered at least from the worst part of her nervous breakdown.

Mme de Chenonceaux never made the journey to Môtiers; but a friend who eventually did so was Mme de Verdelin, who wrote to Rousseau at the end of December,[79] saying that she had found a beau for his old cat but still lamented the loss of her own lover, Adrien de Margency. 'The greatest sorrow for a woman is not to have been disappointed in her choice; it is to have known love. One must mistrust oneself for the rest of one's life.' She told Rousseau that she found consolation in his books: 'I read *Émile*; I read *Julie*, that sublime *Julie*, and I became more patient.'

Mme de Verdelin added that she was still worried about Rousseau's health in the cold climate of the Jura mountains. And indeed Rousseau did fall seriously ill again in December. In a letter to Moultou he reported[80] that a bad cold had developed into a fever, and 'it seems my old bladder wants to block itself up completely.' Swiss winters did not suit him. But the causes of his illness were perhaps not entirely external and physical. They always seemed to coincide with some form of moral tension.

The failure of his friends' efforts to recruit more than a minority of the voters on his side against Robert Tronchin had plunged Rousseau into renewed despair about his native country. Deluc and other political activists in Geneva did not share his depression; they were far from regarding the re-election of Robert Tronchin by a much-reduced majority as a total defeat. They wanted Rousseau's help to press on with the efforts of their party in its struggle against the government. Rousseau was disinclined to co-operate. 'I detach myself further and further from Geneva every day,' he confided to Moultou. In the same letter[81] he encouraged Moultou to act on his intention to resign from the ministry: 'It is necessary to leave and not have oneself dismissed.'

By this time Rousseau felt so ill that he believed he was going to die. He began to fret about the situation of Thérèse if that should happen, and wrote to Keith to ask whether the law of Neuchâtel would allow him to bequeath all he possessed to her.

News of his illness reached Daniel Roguin, who wrote anxiously on 21 December[82] to Thérèse, begging her to send him bulletins three times a week on the state of health of 'our dear friend'. Letter writing, of course, did not come easily to Thérèse; fortunately, the crisis of Rousseau's illness had passed by the time Roguin's request reached her.

Lord Keith had already done something to ease Rousseau's anxieties about Thérèse's future. He drafted[83] for Rousseau a testamentary deposition that he believed would serve the purposes of a will, avoid death duties, and ensure that Thérèse received everything. He also promised to do what he could

for Thérèse should the need arise: 'If my estate were not entailed, I would
do something immediately to put your mind at rest; but I have first to provide for my own children, Emetulla, Ibrahim and Stepan, but once their
affairs are settled I will look after yours.' He also promised to come to visit
Rousseau at Môtiers.

At the same time[84] Keith instructed Martinet, the intendant at Môtiers,
to 'look after M. Rousseau's housekeeper' in the event of the philosopher's
death, and expressed his hope that it would be possible for Rousseau to leave
all his possessions to her without the formalities of a sealed will. By the end
of December, however, Rousseau was well enough that Keith was able to
think of more cheerful ways of helping him; he wrote[85] to Martinet, saying,
'Since you like my wine, I am sending you a little extra so that you can offer
some with New Year greetings to your honest savage in the cold climate of
your mountains.'

It seems that Martinet must have given Rousseau further information
about the law of inheritance in Neuchâtel, for Rousseau decided to draw up
a more elaborate will[86] than the brief deposition suggested by Keith. In it he
named as his sole heir Thérèse Levasseur, 'my housekeeper', leaving to her
'everything that belongs to me and that can be transmitted . . . including my
books and papers, and the proceeds of my publications, only regretting that
I cannot better repay the twenty years of care and devotion that she has given
me and during which she has received no wages'. He went on to exclude
from his succession all his relations, although he bequeathed to the closest,
his aunt Suzanne Goncerut and his cousin Gabriel Rousseau, a nominal five
sols 'not from contempt or derision, but to satisfy the law of the country
where I live'. He expressed one other wish—not as a formal stipulation but
as something in the public interest—that his body be subject to an autopsy
to ascertain the exact nature of 'the strange affliction which has tormented
me for so many years'.

To this end, Rousseau added a 'note sur la maladie'[87] in which he recorded
the following details:

[I] That he had been tormented for twenty years by the retention of urine,
which had been diagnosed as due to a stone, until Frère Côme had established that there was no stone.

[II] That at no time could he pass urine freely, but felt a constant pressure
which he could never relieve; he feared the ever-diminishing stream would
sooner or later cease altogether.

[III] That there was a blockage in the urethra against which the *bougies*★
of M. Daran had ceased to be effective.

★These probes were much in fashion for the treatment of venereal disease; since Rousseau made
no secret of the fact that he used them, it was readily assumed that he suffered from the same affliction as those other users.

[IV] That this obstruction receded further into the bladder as the years passed.

[V] That baths and diuretics only increased his pain; blood–letting produced no relief; and physicians and surgeons had failed either to explain or to cure his affliction.

[VI] That Frère Come had diagnosed a swollen and scirrhous prostate gland,[88] so the seat of the problem must be in the prostate or the neck of the bladder or in the urethra, 'and probably in all three.'

[VII] That the problem was *not* the result of venereal disease, 'for I declare I have never had a disease of that kind.'

Rousseau signed the will on 29 January 1763; but he seems not to have deposited it with Martinet[89] until several months later, when he began, once again, to fear that he was dying. By February he had started to feel better.

In January, during the worst of Rousseau's illness, Moultou had suggested[90] that he come to Geneva, where he would be better placed for medical treatment; if he feared recognition, he could come incognito and stay outside the city confines. Moultou assured Rousseau that he was dedicated to preparing his defence: 'I work for you; I revise, I correct.'

But was he? Other evidence shows that Moultou was rather busier helping Voltaire preparing his treatises on toleration. Although he said nothing about it in his letters to Rousseau, Moultou was becoming ever more intimate with Rousseau's greatest enemy. The first of many letters exchanged between Moultou and Voltaire in the archives at Geneva seems to have been written in November 1762.[91] In it Voltaire says, 'I am extremely pleased by your equitable and tolerant way of thinking and very grateful for your goodness to me.' In December Moultou must have visited Voltaire at Ferney because, in a letter written on Christmas Day,[92] Voltaire tells him 'everyone at Ferney was charmed by you.' He adds, 'You write with clarity and eloquence; you embellish everything you touch.' On 2 January[93] Voltaire sent Moultou the draft of his treatise on tolerance for him to revise: 'add anything you like to it'; a week later[94] we find Voltaire urging Moultou to come again to sleep at Ferney 'with or without our Arian'.

The Arian* was Jacob Vernes, the ex-friend whom Rousseau suspected of the deepest perfidy; but he was, in fact, more innocent than Rousseau suspected and certainly more open than the devious Moultou, who was falling more and more under Voltaire's spell.

Je prends la liberté de vous embrasser de tout mon coeur,' Voltaire wrote[95] in another letter to Moultou; and in writing to the Marquis de Souvernet,[96] Voltaire referred to Moultou as 'the man I esteem the most in the world and in whom I have the greatest confidence'.

*So called because Voltaire ascribed to Vernes the Arian belief that God alone is divine, and Christ a created being.

Unaware of all this, Rousseau might have said the same of Moultou, and indeed while Voltaire was pressing Moultou to come to Ferney, Rousseau was also soliciting his company. He wrote to Moultou on 20 January 1763:[97] 'Tell me, dear Moultou, if I regain enough strength to stand up this summer, could you spare two or three months to pass more or less tête-à-tête? I would not choose Môtiers, or Zürich or Geneva for the purpose, but a place where we should not be sought out by intruders . . . Think about it, and let me know how you feel. It would not mean a long journey. The more I think about it, the more I find it charming. It is my last castle in Spain.'

4

THE TOCSIN OF SEDITION

The winter of 1762–63 was one of the coldest of the century. The Thames and the Seine were frozen over, and snow on the plains of Switzerland was almost as thick as on the mountains. Daniel Roguin wrote[1] anxiously to Rousseau from Yverdon, urging him to keep warm as he did, by sitting on top of his stove; but Rousseau felt too ill even to leave his bed. Yet he kept working. Having sent the manuscript of the *Letter to Archbishop Beaumont* to Rey at the beginning of January, he continued to pester the publisher with emendations and improvements. He also vented to Rey[2] his anger at Néaulme for publishing Formey's distorted version of *Émile* and at Duchesne and Guy for undertaking a collected edition of his writings that he believed would prejudice the *Complete Works* on which he was counting for a future livelihood: 'without that resource I shall not know where to turn, and I would rather starve than beg.'

These words prompted Rey to place in the francophone gazettes that were printed in Holland an advertisement denouncing both Néaulme and the Paris publishers. Far from appreciating this gesture, Rousseau was furious. He reproached[3] Rey especially for the attack on Duchesne and Guy, saying it exceeded the bounds of decency and 'will compromise me also with M. de Malesherbes'. He went so far as to say, 'you have done me a greater injury than the Paris *parlement* did me.' By this time Rousseau had second thoughts about the wisdom of publishing his *Letter to Archbishop Beaumont*, but the letter[4] he sent Rey expressing these doubts reached Amsterdam too late to abort the project, which Rey had had set up in type with unusual speed despite his belief that the book would 'make the author more enemies than ever'.

Rousseau seems to have overcome his anxiety about the *Letter* fairly briskly and resigned himself to whatever consequences it might have. He concentrated on moderating the harm Rey's advertisement had done to his standing with Duchesne and Guy, with whom he was still hoping to do profitable business. Guy himself wrote[5] to Rousseau, trying to persuade him that the collected edition being edited by the Abbé de La Porte would not prejudice the *Complete Works* that Rousseau himself planned to compile in the future. Indeed, Guy argued, so many bad private editions of Rousseau's books were on the market that it was in the author's interest to have a good one printed in France. Guy also informed[6] Rousseau that Mme de Luxembourg approved of the project and that he was meeting her to settle how much to pay Rousseau. This last prospect may have encouraged certain hopes in Rousseau since Mme de Luxembourg had made the publishers give him six thousand francs for *Émile*; in the event, they paid him only fifty louis, or twelve hundred francs, for La Porte's collection. Rousseau remarked[7] mournfully to Lenieps: 'Messieurs La Porte and Duchesne appropriate my property with as much nonchalance as if it were their own . . . In Paris they first burn my books and then they print them and I cannot prevent it.'

What Rousseau did succeed in stopping was La Porte's design to use as a frontispiece an engraving of La Tour's portrait of the author, then in Mme de Luxembourg's possession. Rousseau raised no objection, however, to the engraving's being published separately, without his name, and bearing only his motto, 'vitam impendere vero'. La Tour made a copy of the portrait from the engravers to work from, and even offered to give that copy to Rousseau as a present—an offer that Rousseau characteristically, but for once fairly graciously, declined, then later changed his mind and accepted.

As the arctic weather eased in February, Rousseau's health improved, and he even managed to go to church. Montmollin attributed[8] the author's recovery to 'little homely remedies' Montmollin himself had recommended, together with 'the consolation of holy communion' he had administered. But Rousseau was not the only invalid in Môtiers at that time. Montmollin's daughter, Lisette, aged twenty, was so gravely ill that Rousseau told[9] Mme Boy he expected the 'good and lovable girl' to die, even as he expected to die himself. The only person who actually died in the village, however, was Rousseau's neighbour, Major Girardier, and his death caused no great grief. Since Thérèse's arrival, Rousseau's relations with Girardier had been strained to such a point that, he admitted to Mme Boy in January 1763, 'I have no longer any communication whatever with him.' On 6 February[10] he had to inform her that the major had died the previous evening, adding that since he himself had been too sick to act, he had sent Thérèse next door to render *les derniers devoirs*. When Daniel Roguin heard of Girardier's death, he made no pretence that it was bad news for anybody, not even for the widow and daughter; 'if usage permitted,' he declared,[11] 'it would be a case for congratulation rather than condolence.'

While he was housebound by the winter snows, Rousseau found time to answer M. de Luxembourg's request for a description of his 'new abode'. In his careful calligraphy, he wrote two long letters[12] about the Val de Travers and its inhabitants, an account more flattering to the place than the people. In contrast to his encomium of the uncorrupted mountain folk of Neuchâtel in the *Letter to M. d'Alembert*, published five years earlier, Rousseau is wholly critical of his neighbours, although he admits that the differences lay as much in the observer as in the observed. The people of Môtiers, he writes, are very Swiss and as such offer a bizarre mixture of the primitive and the *recherché*; 'they dress up under their pine trees as if they were in Paris,' combining the refined and the rustic, the luxurious and the crude. Their misfortune, he suggests, is that their taste for money originally led them to become mercenaries in foreign armies, and returning mercenaries brought corruption with them. The Swiss themselves never produced much other than cheeses, horses, and men, but immigrants from other countries, especially Protestant refugees from France, introduced industries, with the result that the inhabitants of the Val de Travers quit the land to earn better wages in factories and workshops set up in the most remote and unlikely places.

Rousseau admits that his neighbours are good citizens—just, charitable, loyal, and brave; but, he adds, they are also cunning, stubborn, jealous, inquisitive, and avaricious. The inhabitants of Neuchâtel under their royal sovereign enjoy about as much liberty as the Swiss of the republican cantons, but the distinction of living under princes has, he suggests, gone somewhat to their heads; they put on grand manners and fanciful airs without, alas, much taste. They are also vain. He notes that they are deeply impressed by a marquis or a count; having no nobility of their own, they give themselves an abundance of titles, and one has to take care to address the holders of such ranks as 'Monsieur le Justicier, Monsieur le Professeur, Monsieur le Docteur', and so forth: 'If I had kept my old trade,' Rousseau adds, 'I should doubtless be Monsieur le Copiste.'

A more serious criticism of the people is that 'while they are not without morals, they are without principles: their Christianity consists simply of going to Church every Sunday, for they have no Christian love of their fellow men.' And while Rousseau acknowledges that he has been received by the local pastor with unexpected kindness, he adds that the clergy of Neuchâtel generally are bigoted and quarrelsome: 'They welcomed me by suppressing my books.' It is thanks to the protection of Lord Keith alone, he explains, that he himself has been left in peace.

In his second letter, Rousseau describes the valley in which he has sought refuge. He has found it more beautiful as he has learned to know it better. The level ground around the river makes for easy walking, while climbing the mountain slopes is rewarded with a surprising variety of scenic views;

forests, gorges, waterfalls, rocks, streams, and grottoes invite exploration, and everywhere 'botany yields up its treasures to those who understand that science,' his own understanding, he admits, being all too limited.

As he writes, everything is covered with snow, but he recalls the previous summer, when all was green and sunlit and he swam in the Areuse, 'a very pretty river, as clear and sparkling as silver and filled with trout'. He says he would like to have lived in a really isolated chalet he had seen on the north slope above the valley. Even the house he has in the village, however, commands an impressive view of the Jura mountains and faces a superb waterfall, while 'I have under my window a very beautiful fountain the sound of which is one of my joys.'

The Maréchal de Luxembourg was not the only correspondent to whom Rousseau found time to write at length that winter. The friendly letter from David Hume, written the previous July, did not reach Rousseau until February, and in thanking Hume for it, Rousseau explained[13] his present situation. He said that many things made him wish to come to England, especially as he had received nothing but affronts and outrages from the country where he had hoped to find consolation; but, thanks to the goodness of Hume's compatriot, Lord Keith, he had found not only a refuge but 'Scotland in Switzerland'. He hoped only that his health would one day enable him to join the two of them in Scotland itself, where 'your common homeland will become mine.'

Another correspondent on whom Rousseau lavished more than usual attention was Mme Alissan, whose description of her appearance in one of her long letters seems to have caught his fancy; we find him replying[14] to her, not only at equal length, but in distinctly flirtatious language. He quotes Italian poetry to her, and says of himself, coyly, that while it is unbecoming for a man of fifty to take such a curious interest in the details of a woman's appearance, he cannot restrain himself. Misreading a remark in her letter about the whiteness of her face compared to the rest of her skin,* he declares: 'I would not wish for all the world to have to gaze upon that perfectly oval face which is the whitest part of your person . . . lest in order to appreciate the complexion of the face, my indiscreet imagination should—no matter how sensitive to the cold you are—strip a thousand veils to find other parts of the body to compare it with.' Then he asks, 'Tell me how old you are.'

Rousseau was playing with fire. He must have realised that Mme Alissan was in love with him, and that what was just a game for him would stir deep emotions in her. Indeed in her next letter,[15] in which she informed him that she was thirty-two, she actually suggested that she might move to Switzerland in order to be nearer to him. She asked if he knew of any property for

---

*In her letter of 13 January 1763 Mme Alissan had said that her face was the least white part of her person as a consequence of smallpox.

sale there, although she feared that as a Catholic she might not be allowed to buy land in a Protestant canton. At the same time she asked if she might in future address him as 'mon ami' rather than 'Monsieur'.

Rousseau put up some playful resistance to her dropping the 'Monsieur', but mentioned in his reply[16] a property near Yverdon that he believed to be for sale. As for her age, he recalled that 'my last passion, which was certainly the most violent, was for a woman over thirty years old.* She had the same taste in *coiffure* that you have, and yours could not be more attractive; she was always charming, and in the way she wore her hair, she was adorable . . . But she loved another, and she had nothing more than friendship for me.'

In her reply[17] Mme Alissan expressed interest in the property near Yverdon, but explained that she had not yet access to the funds that would be needed to buy it. She said that while she had many things to tell Rousseau, she would wait for the 'subject of *Monsieur* to be settled first', for what she had to say was to be said to an *ami*. After this, Mme Alissan fell silent for several weeks, and Rousseau became concerned enough in early April to write[18] begging for news from her. She answered[19] at length, explaining that her silence was due to unhappiness at home, where she was ill used by an uncongenial husband, and by others to whom she had always shown kindness. She also reproached Rousseau for his failure to satisfy her curiosity about himself. 'They say you have published a new book.† It is terrible that the public knows what you are doing before I do.' In the same letter she mentioned that a woman artist was painting a portrait of her, and asked Rousseau if he would like to see it.

He assured[20] her that he would not only like to see the portrait, but to possess it, and he urged her to have a copy made at his expense. Moreover, to end the bantering about 'Monsieur', he suggested using Christian names, only he had to confess he had forgotten hers.

By return of post, Mme Alissan informed[21] him that her Christian name was Marianne and confessed that the warmth of his letter had carried her away. She said she was willing to send him her portrait, but not to have a copy made for him, because that would lead to talk—and she did not want her friendship with him to become known. Rousseau took a long time to answer[22] this letter, although when he did so he expressed delight at learning her Christian name: 'O charming Marianne . . . Sweet Marianne . . . Of all the things I know of you a thousand delight, and none displeases.' He went on to scold her gently for not letting him have a copy of her portrait, claiming that if he was to be accused of meaning something to her he ought to have the corresponding rights.

By this time, however, it is clear that Rousseau had too many other things

---

*In fact, Sophie d'Houdetot was only twenty-six in 1756.
†The *Letter to Archbishop Beaumont*.

on his mind to continue the attention he had given earlier to flirtatious correspondence with Mme Alissan. What had diverted him when he was in poor health, idle, and housebound in winter could no longer command his interest when the snows melted and his health recovered; then the 'marmot', as he called himself, emerged from hibernation to become a 'bear', running around the countryside, receiving dozens of visitors, inundated with correspondence, and drawn even deeper into the political strife of Geneva.

In February, Lord Keith had paid a short visit to Geneva, where he was reported to have intervened—unsuccessfully—with the authorities on behalf of his protégé. Keith also made the acquaintance of Moultou,* and he took back to Neuchâtel a letter Moultou had written to Rousseau that was intended for Rousseau's eyes only and was to be destroyed as soon as it was read. Since Rousseau obeyed these instructions, we do not know precisely what Moultou wrote, but Rousseau's reply[24] reveals the general message of the letter and his reaction to it. Moultou urged him to make a submission to the Consistory of Geneva to secure a certificate of Christian orthodoxy, which could be used to effect a reversal of the Petit Conseil's edict against him.

Rousseau was outraged at the suggestion, which he recognised as similar to that put to him six months before by Voltaire; indeed, as he wrote to Moultou, this was worse, for Voltaire had advised only a 'quarter of the grovelings you advise now'. It was, Rousseau declared, unthinkable 'that I at my age should solicit like a schoolboy certificates from the Consistory' and only strange that Moultou should imagine such a thing possible. 'I do not know what has happened to you, but you have certainly changed your tune,' he wrote, before ending the letter with a cold 'Adieu'.

What had happened, among other things, is that Moultou had been seeing more of Voltaire. He had developed a habit of visiting Ferney every Saturday, often together with Suzanne Curchod, Gibbon's jilted fiancée, who had been a governess to Moultou's children and now often acted as a *dame de compagnie* to Moultou's beloved Mme de Vermoneux. Rousseau did not know the extent of the growing intimacy between Moultou and Voltaire, but he smelt a rat, and his attitude to the man he had thought of as his best friend in Geneva began to change.

Moultou tried to persuade Rousseau that he had misunderstood his proposal. 'I am not asking you to make any kind of retraction,' he wrote.[25] He was simply reminding him that 'one must obtain by gentleness what one cannot get by violence or an appeal to justice.' As for Rousseau's reference to Voltaire, Moultou wrote:[26] 'Do not be disturbed about him. I shall be seeing him again. I know him. He wants a reconciliation with your reputation.

*'I am very pleased with him . . . I believe you can count on his friendship and on that of many others,' Keith wrote to Rousseau.[23]

Hume's letter* has shaken him. But at the moment what is important is that you should be on good terms with him. We shall see. Count on me.'

Moultou also told[27] Rousseau that he was being punished in Geneva for his friendship with Rousseau. He had expected to be appointed by the elders of the church to a benefice, that of Chêne, but had been passed over in favour of another minister, five years his junior, and he did not doubt that it was because he was a known champion of *Émile* and its author. 'I confess,' he wrote, 'that I have never felt a more bitter sorrow.'

While Moultou admitted to Rousseau that he continued to visit Ferney, he did not reveal how frequently, and he even made out[28] that he did so only at the request of the Duchesse de Grammont, who took an interest in the Calas case and wished him to discuss it with Voltaire. Once again, Moultou told Rousseau that Voltaire wanted a reconciliation. Rousseau reported[29] this to Lord Keith with a measure of scepticism: 'Do you know, Milord, that Voltaire is trying to make it up with me? Nothing is foreign to the talents of that great actor . . . I am quite willing if he wants to forget everything. I swear to you that of all the Christian virtues none costs me less than forgiving an injury.' To Moultou himself Rousseau wrote:[30] 'M. de Voltaire makes you think he likes me because he knows you like me. With people of his own ilk he speaks another language.'

Rousseau was not far wrong in this last conjecture, to judge from a remark in a letter[31] from Voltaire to d'Alembert: 'Jean-Jacques weaves ribbons with the mountain folk of his village: one must hope he does not use his ribbons to hang himself.'

When Moultou saw the text of Voltaire's *Treatise on Toleration*, he described it[32] to Rousseau as an 'abominable book'. This is a puzzling remark, for nothing in that book—which Voltaire had deliberately written to influence Christian readers—could be construed as objectionable to Moultou, who espoused toleration and a minimal creed. It is hard to believe that Moultou wrote those words simply to give Rousseau the impression that he was no friend of Voltaire's, although he may have done so. Another possible explanation is that the text Moultou saw contained some anti-Christian utterances that were removed from the final version published six months later; it is indeed reported[33] that Moultou and Vernes went to Ferney in February 'to try to make Voltaire change and revise certain provocative passages'. It is unlikely, however, that Moultou described the *Treatise* as an 'abominable book' to Voltaire himself when he received an advance copy of what Voltaire called his *petit ouvrage* in April. None of Moultou's letters to Voltaire has been traced, but Voltaire's letters to Moultou dating from the time bear witness to an unclouded friendship: 'When are you coming to see a poor

---

*David Hume's letter to Mme de Boufflers in praise of Rousseau had been widely circulated.

old blind man?[34] ... [C]ome and lay the foundations of Reason. Be its apostle.'[35] Voltaire would not have written thus to someone who had criticised his book to his face.

Moultou was not alone in his belief that Rousseau should make some statement to the authorities of Geneva to facilitate the annulment of the edict against him. By the early months of 1763, Deluc came to share that point of view. At the time of Keith's visit to Geneva, Deluc urged[36] Rousseau to write a statement of his religious beliefs, which could be used in the campaign to rescind the edict of the Petit Conseil. Deluc even had the temerity to draft a few sentences that he urged Rousseau to incorporate in the statement, including an expression of regret for having provoked misunderstandings, an acknowledgement of a 'truly divine Revelation', and an admission that he failed to acknowledge 'how much the religion of the citizens of Geneva was part of their patriotism'.

Rousseau refused to do what Deluc asked of him, saying[37] he had no declaration to make to the Genevese. If explanations of his religious beliefs were wanted, they could be found in his published writings; 'I have nothing else to say.'

In fact, Rousseau was hoping that his *Letter to Archbishop Beaumont* would settle all doubts and prompt the Genevese authorities to relent. It did not do so. When the *Letter* was published in April, the French resident in Geneva, Monpéroux, wrote[38] to the First Syndic, asking him to take steps against an 'insolent attack on the Archbishop of Paris'.* Within forty-eight hours the Petit Conseil had complied with his wishes, and forbade the printing or reprinting of Rousseau's pamphlet. At this point Rousseau lost his patience, and he did what he had been contemplating for several months: he renounced his Genevese citizenship.

He felt reasonably secure in doing this because Lord Keith had secured for him a certificate of nationality in the principality of Neuchâtel. It was an act of kindness Keith undertook just before leaving Neuchâtel and retiring from his governorship at the end of April 1763. Before leaving, Keith renewed[39] the invitation to Rousseau to join him in Scotland and promised to arrange an annuity for him. In the *Confessions* Rousseau writes[40] of Keith as 'the one man on earth still worthy of my friendship' and recalls how 'of his own accord he sent me a certificate of naturalisation which seemed a certain means of preventing me from being driven from the country. The village of Couvet in the Val de Travers followed his example and enrolled me as a burgess.' One notes that it was a neighbouring village that conferred this honour on Rousseau, not the one where he lived. He was not altogether popular in Môtiers, and he knew it. In a letter to Mme Boy,[41] he declared that while

---

*Ironically, Archbishop Beaumont was soon indicted by the French authorities for his open defence of the Jesuits; to avoid a worse incarceration he sought refuge in the monastery of La Trappe.

he was grateful to occupy her house 'I would if I were in better health seek to live among people who viewed my presence with greater pleasure.' He told her he looked forward to moving in the summer to the apartment she was having remodelled for him on her farm on the mountainside at Pierrenod.

Rousseau's friends in Geneva were dismayed by his renunciation of citizenship; several wrote begging him not to lose interest in their affairs and urging various courses of action. Deluc and Moultou no longer agreed. Deluc wanted to keep the Rousseau case at the centre of a campaign to defend the citizens' rights against the Petit Conseil; Moultou urged him to do nothing that would disturb the peace of the city. To a certain extent there had always been a difference between these two men. Moultou was unorthodox in matters of religion but conservative in politics, while Deluc was orthodox in religion and liberal in politics. In the past Rousseau's attitude had been closer to Moultou's; indeed in the *Confessions* he claims[42] that he had always sought to preserve the tranquillity of Geneva and refused to participate in rebellious movements. But once he had himself become a victim of Genevese intolerance, Rousseau was more sympathetic to Deluc's politics than he was to Moultou's. He tried[43] to assure Colonel Pictet that renouncing his citizenship did not mean renouncing his friendships and that 'while I shall never live there, I shall always love Geneva.' What he loved, however, was a certain idea of Geneva; the actual city and its people provoked increasing contempt.

In the spring of 1763 he found relief from 'the imbecile citizens of Geneva and their politics'[44] in the company of a young Hungarian, known as the Baron de Sauttern, who arrived in Môtiers with the declared intention of settling there as Rousseau's pupil. Rousseau took an instant liking to him, and the two became constant companions for the next four months. Jean-Ignace Sautternmeister von Sauttersheim—for such was his actual name—was a good-looking man of twenty-five; he introduced himself as a former officer of the Imperial Army who had served as an aide-de-camp to General Nadasty, been wounded in the siege of Bude, then lost his commission as a result of converting to the Protestant religion. He spoke hardly any French, and, as Rousseau knew no Hungarian or German, his visitor had to communicate in Latin. Nevertheless conversation flowed freely, and, to the great satisfaction of Rousseau, Sauttern proved to be an enthusiastic walker, joining him cheerfully on his daily outings and scrambles in the mountains.

In the *Confessions* Rousseau recalls[45] that of all the acquaintances he made at Môtiers,

there was only one who won my affection . . . His looks, his deportment and his manner matched his conversation . . . My heart does not know how to give itself by halves. Soon he had all my friendship and we became inseparable . . . I took him to meet Lord Keith, who received him with great cordiality . . . He spoke of his family, his affairs, his adventures and the Court of Vienna, about which he seemed to have a detailed knowledge. In short, I found in him a sweetness of nature in every situation, manners not only polite but elegant, great neatness of appearance and an extreme delicacy of speech—in short, all the marks of a man well-born and bred.

Soon after this polished figure introduced himself, Rousseau received the first of several warnings against him. François d'Ivernois reported[46] from Geneva that a Hungarian in the service of France had been sent to Môtiers to entrap him. Rousseau refused to believe this but decided to take the risk of putting Sauttern to the test. As he explains[47] in the *Confessions*, he invited his young friend to accompany him on an excursion to Pontarlier on French soil, where, if it was true that Sauttern was a French agent, Rousseau would be at his mercy.

'As soon as we arrived there, I put the letter from M. d'Ivernois into his hands, and after giving him an ardent embrace, I said "Sauttern has no need of proof of my confidence in him, but it is necessary to prove that confidence to others." No harm came.'

After this episode Rousseau wrote[48] to Usteri: 'I am convinced that the suspicions about M. de Sauttern which have been communicated to me have not the least foundation. I continue to see him with great pleasure and hope to be able to count him among my friends.'

Sauttern was not a spy, but neither was he what he pretended to be. Rousseau learned in time that he was not a Protestant victim of religious persecution, but a refugee from his creditors; not a former officer in the Imperial army, but a former clerk in the Imperial archives. He had never been wounded in battle. Perhaps he was not even entitled to be called a baron, although the records show that he was the son of Joseph-Emmanuel Sauttern-meister von Sauttersheim, Burgermeister of Bude, who had inherited an imperial title of nobility that could arguably be translated as 'baron'. In any case, while Rousseau could not deny that Sauttern told many lies about himself, Rousseau insists[49] in the *Confessions* that 'I shall never doubt that he was a true nobleman,' and he adds[50] that Lord Keith, 'who knew the world', shared this opinion.★

Egalitarian as Rousseau claimed to be, there can be no doubt that the thought of Sauttern's rank endeared him to Rousseau, just as the absence of rank in such a young man as François Coindet, for example, disqualified him

★In fact, Keith suggested to Rousseau on 11 June 1763 that Sauttern must be an impostor.[51]

from the full intimacy of friendship.* Even when Sauttern added disgraceful conduct to his mythomania, Rousseau forgave him. Conceivably he remembered his own youthful impostures as Vaussore de Villeneuve and Mr Dudding, and refused to condemn in another things he had done himself. In any case, he adored the boy.

In the *Confessions* Rousseau speaks[53] of Sauttern's spending two years at Môtiers. In fact it was less than five months, but Sauttern was still there when Moultou paid his long-delayed visit. Moultou stayed twelve days, but showed none of Sauttern's willingness to go for long walks with his host. Nevertheless he seems to have kept silent about his desire to effect a reconciliation with Voltaire, and expressed no dissent from Deluc's proposal to mobilise the citizenry of Geneva against the Petit Conseil on behalf of Rousseau. Indeed Moultou was at Môtiers when Rousseau wrote the letter that was to become notorious as the 'tocsin of sedition', and he carried it back to Geneva with him.

Marc Chappuis, a longtime acquaintance, if also one whom Rousseau mistrusted after he had ousted Gauffecourt from the salt monopoly at Geneva, ostensibly supported Deluc's campaign on behalf of Rousseau but secretly acted in league with the government. On 18 May Chappuis wrote[54] to Rousseau, urging him to withdraw the renunciation of his citizenship and pay a *visite de civilité* to the syndics of Geneva, who, Chappuis suggested, would then be willing to moderate the severity of their edicts.

Rousseau rejected this proposal, asserting in his reply[55] to Chappuis that to remain a member of a state that had publicly stigmatised him as a criminal would be to accept dishonour. He went on to point out that the constitution of Geneva allowed its citizens, even five or six of them, to make *représentations* in cases in which they disapproved of the proceedings of the government. As it was, the world could see that the citizens of Geneva had done nothing to defend him. The procedure of a *représentation* was simple, yet no one had used it: 'I confided my honour to you, O citizens of Geneva, and I was at peace, but you have taken so little care of that trust that you have forced me to withdraw it.'

The message of the letter was clear. Rousseau expected the citizens to make a *représentation* on his behalf. This was what Deluc wanted to happen, and Rousseau took the precaution of asking Moultou to show the letter to Deluc before it was delivered to Chappuis. He hoped to see the letter circulated in Geneva, and he suspected that Chappuis might not agree to do this or, worse, might circulate a distorted version of it.

In the event, Deluc himself had copies made and circulated, with the re-

---

*'The very plebeian origins of Coindet explain the nature of the relationship that was established between him and his illustrious compatriot.'[52]

sult that a group of citizens finally made a formal *représentation* on Rousseau's case. Because the letter to Chappuis was seen to have inspired this move, it came to be called, by Rousseau's enemies, the 'tocsin of sedition'.

Moultou, on his return to Geneva, wrote a very affectionate letter[56] to Rousseau, saying he had learned to love him, 'not only in your books, but in your house, your study and your dressing gown—I shall always love you.' At the same time Moultou voiced his fears that he was not loved in the same way in return: 'if only you had judged my heart as I have judged yours.' Moultou did not forget to thank Thérèse for her kindness to him or to send greetings to 'the Baron, who completely won my heart'. He expressed no doubts about Rousseau's letter to Chappuis, but as the public unrest provoked by that letter developed, Moultou became nervous. He soon complained[57] to Rousseau that Deluc was engaged in injudicious political activity, and he urged Rousseau not to come to Geneva 'or even write to anyone here until I advise you'.

Rousseau had evidently spoken of passing through the city on his way to visit Les Charmettes at the invitation of Conzié, to whom he had said[58] he was eager 'to occupy for several days the modest cell you have prepared for me in your house' and 'to cover with flowers and tears the grave of that incomparable woman whose eyes you closed'—Mme de Warens.

In the event, Rousseau was able to assure[59] Moultou that he had no plans to come to Geneva since he had put off the visit to Les Charmettes and decided instead to go to Zürich. In June he set out with Sauttern, planning to visit Usteri and Hess and other friends in Zürich, to pass Berne on the way to visit Julie de Bondeli, but to hurry through Yverdon without visiting the Roguins, 'for fear', as Rousseau afterwards explained,[60] 'of being overwhelmed by the caresses of so many friends'. They travelled much of the way on foot, but they did not get beyond Estavayer on the southern shore of Lake Neuchâtel, for at that point the midsummer weather became so wet and stormy that they abandoned the trip and went home.

Back at Môtiers, Rousseau found a letter[61] from Deluc, informing him that forty citizens had agreed to support a *représentation* to the government on his behalf. Rousseau congratulated[62] Deluc and his fellow *représentants* on a proceeding that 'does you honour'. The central argument Deluc advanced was that the action taken against Jean-Jacques Rousseau was illegal on the grounds that the Petit Conseil had no right to regulate religious affairs, which Article 88 of the constitution assigned to the Consistory.

Moultou informed Rousseau on 25 June[63] that the majority of citizens supported the *représentation* but that he himself had had to cut off relations with Deluc in order to placate his father and his father-in-law (Guillaume Fuzier Cayla, a prominent patrician), who were alarmed at the disturbance Deluc was provoking. A few days later[64] Moultou admitted to Rousseau that he shared the same fears. He asserted that Deluc was becoming violent in his fanaticism; passions were becoming inflamed, and he begged Rousseau to put pressure on Deluc to end the agitation—even to make to the First Syndic a public declaration deploring any disturbance to the peace being instigated in his name.

At first Rousseau seemed to accept Moultou's account of the situation, and he even urged[65] Deluc to take no further action beyond the original *représentation*. The Petit Conseil's brisk rejection of that *représentation*, however, prompted Rousseau to change his mind, to reject Moultou's advice once and for all, and give his full support to Deluc.

The bad weather in the summer of 1763 undermined Rousseau's health, although he still hoped to be well enough before long to join Lord Keith in Scotland. In an affectionate letter[66] to Charles Duclos, he explained that while France was the country he loved best, he would rather have a British than a French friend, for 'I once had many friends in France, but since my disgrace I have kept only two.' At the same time he spoke bitterly about the Genevese: 'they punish me for the harm they have done me.'

The one* male friend Rousseau had in mind besides Duclos was presumably M. de Luxembourg, from whom he continued to receive regular letters despite the Maréchal's failing health and heavy duties at court. More than once in the summer of 1763, the Maréchal begged[68] Rousseau to keep him informed of his welfare and his plans, sending Rousseau his news, and expressing the hope that Rousseau would visit him on his way to Scotland. Mme de Luxembourg seems not to have found time, as her husband did, to write often to Rousseau, and he soon numbered her, not altogether justly, among the friends who had forsaken him.

He had no reason to complain of two other French women friends, Mme de Verdelin and Mme de Chenonceaux, who remained assiduous correspondents, except for the short interval during which Mme de Chenonceaux suffered a nervous breakdown. Mme de Verdelin reported[69] this last of Mme de Chenonceaux's many misfortunes to Rousseau, suggesting that her friend had 'gone out of her mind' as a result of the misconduct of her husband, Dupin de Chenonceaux, who had ended up in the debtors' prison at Pierre Encise. At the same time Mme de Verdelin forwarded a present of cuffs embroidered by her daughter Léontine, and sent him news of the cat he had left in her care: 'she is well, but I cannot pretend that she loves me.'

*To say that he had only two French friends left was to forget, among others, Claude-Henri Watelet, who had made the difficult journey to Môtiers to visit Rousseau, and Alexander Deleyre, who kept in touch by letter, and only failed to visit Rousseau because he had a job in Parma, where he was poorly paid and given no leave by his employer the Duke. Deleyre also had family problems, as he explained to Rousseau in one of his letters. His young son had a deformed foot 'which is doubly unfortunate in Italy where defects of nature are despised', but he was still trying to educate the boy according to the teaching of *Émile*.[67]

Rousseau expressed[70] a decent concern about Mme de Chenonceaux's illness, recalling that he had always disapproved of a marriage that had been arranged for her against her inclination. As usual the thought of another's suffering prompted him to speak of his own: 'Mme de Chenonceaux is not alone; I too groan under many misfortunes.' Only the goodness of Lord Keith, he said, had saved him from disaster.

In thanking Léontine for the present of the cuffs, he said he would not wear them on his sleeves, where the caftan would hide them, but around his neck 'like an order of chivalry'. On the subject of his cat he added, 'I forgot to tell you that she likes to eat during the night.'

Writing again in June, Mme de Verdelin told[71] Rousseau that she had visited his old cottage at Montlouis and found the garden in good shape, the lime trees as he had left them, and the flowers climbing freely on the trellis to provide a shady bower. She had thought of taking Rousseau's cat back there to amuse her: 'she sleeps under my bed again, but she loves me no better'. Mme de Verdelin said she had visited Thérèse's old mother at Deuil: 'She is in good health and by no means as penurious as she may have said she is.' The letter shows that Rousseau was still contributing to the upkeep of Thérèse's mother, notwithstanding well-publicised allegations to the contrary.

Mme de Chenonceaux was sufficiently recovered from her nervous breakdown to write to Rousseau in July,[72] saying that she had rented a little house with a garden in Paris away from her parents-in-law, the Dupins, with whom her relations had long been strained. As her husband was still in the debtors' jail at Pierre Encise, she lived alone on an annual income of twelve thousand francs, 'which is not much for Paris',* but she was content with her lot. She sent Rousseau a cordial message from an old friend, the Abbé de Condillac, and tried tactfully to suggest a reconciliation with a young friend, François Coindet, who had charmed her as he had others of Rousseau's aristocratic admirers.

Mme de Chenonceaux's plea for François Coindet may have been well timed, for it reached Rousseau just when he was losing the company of another young friend, Sauttern, who had been suddenly summoned—or so he said—to return to Hungary on urgent family business. He had not even time to settle his affairs at the local inn where he had lodged, and simply asked Rousseau to take charge of the baggage he left there. Rousseau sent Thérèse to rescue Sauttern's clothes—and his pistols—which he sent on to him, and he kept his heavier belongings in his house, pending the traveller's return. Soon another reason was suggested for Sauttern's abrupt departure: a maid

*Rousseau had lived in Paris on less than fifteen hundred francs a year.

at the inn declared that she was pregnant by him. Rousseau refused to believe her.

In a letter[73] to Daniel Roguin, he spoke of an infamous slander put out against Sauttern by an 'abominable sow' at the inn. He said he would never believe that 'someone as sensitive and cultured as the Baron' could have slept with 'the most diseased and stinking slut, the most hideous monster Switzerland has ever produced'.

However, when Rousseau reported the accusation to Sauttern, his equivocal reaction—Sauttern asked if the girl could prove the child was his[74]—convinced Rousseau that he was guilty. In the *Confessions*[75] he says he was not alone in being dismayed by Sauttern's conduct: 'the most *aimable* ladies of the neighbourhood, who had lavished their charms upon him to no purpose, were furious.'

Sauttern did not go to Hungary, but to Strasbourg, where, according to Rousseau, 'he caused some disorder in a family in that city by seducing a married woman.' The philosopher heard about this because the husband, knowing Sauttern to be Rousseau's friend, took the unusual step of writing to Rousseau to expound his grievances. Far from being embarrassed by this approach, Rousseau says in the *Confessions*[76] that 'I took every care to direct the young woman to virtue and Sauttern to his duty.'

The correspondence[77] shows that Rousseau treated Sauttern with unusual indulgence. His reproaches were gentle; he even sent Sauttern a gift of money.

At the beginning of August Rousseau became so ill that he contemplated suicide. He confessed as much in writing[78] to Charles Duclos: 'My unending and unrelieved pains have put me in the exceptional situation described by Lord Edouard to St.-Preux.'* Rousseau bade his old friend farewell, and in a postscript he asked him to undertake, after Rousseau's death, to persuade Duchesne to give Thérèse the fifty louis he had promised to give him. 'What a soul that good girl has! What fidelity! What affection! What patience! She has been my one consolation in my sufferings, and made me bless them . . . She has a heart like mine.'

The desire to end his life receded as the worst of his pains eased, but he was still in low spirits when he wrote[80] to Mme Boy a fortnight later to explain that he was not well enough to make use of the summer retreat she had had prepared for him at Pierrenod—something he sincerely regretted, if only because he had come to loathe the village where he was, as he told her with somewhat brutal frankness: 'Apart from a very few people, I regard Môtiers as the most evil and poisonous place one could inhabit.'

---

*'When violent suffering of the body is incurable, it is justifiable for a man to end his own life.'[79]

In the same letter Rousseau mentioned the hostility of the villagers of Môtiers toward Thérèse. He may have exaggerated this, but there is no doubt that she felt the dislike to be mutual, and Rousseau continued to fret over what her future would hold after his death. Daniel Roguin tried to relieve his anxiety by promising[81] to look after Thérèse at Yverdon as 'one of my own nieces'. But thinking she would never be happy anywhere in Switzerland, Rousseau hit on the idea of writing[82] to the curé who had befriended Thérèse on the journey from Montmorency, the Abbé Grumet, asking if he would help her again by finding a retirement home for her in his parish at Ambérieu. The kindly priest agreed,[83] approving warmly of what he understood to be the pious desire of a true believer to retire from a Protestant country to a Catholic one. 'But must we endure the sorrow of losing you, Monsieur, in order to receive her? You are not so advanced in years, Monsieur, . . . You have within you the resources for recovery.'

Rey expressed no less confidence in Rousseau's capacity to overcome his afflictions. Writing[84] to him that same August Rey first expressed sympathy for Rousseau's sufferings, and then suggested brightly that he should make a journey to Holland on his way to join Lord Keith in Scotland, on foot as far as Basle and then by boat down the Rhine. This idea of walking some hundred miles across the Swiss mountains reminded Rousseau of Diderot's notorious suggestion that he walk behind Mme d'Epinay's carriage from Montmorency to Geneva, and he did not take kindly to it.

Fortunately, by the time he received Rey's letter Rousseau felt better. His physical condition was often governed by his moods, and after his spirits had been lowered by the departure of Lord Keith, disappointment over Sauttern, and dissatisfaction with Moultou, he was cheered by a visit of two French noblemen with whom he quickly made friends. These visitors arrived at Môtiers in such strange guise that they were taken at first to be smugglers. They came on foot, each leading a mule bearing his luggage, and, as Rousseau puts it in the *Confessions*,[85] 'this manner of travelling, so much to my own taste, and so little to that of the French nobility, won them my friendship and their conversation improved it.' They introduced themselves as the Chevalier d'Astier de Cromessière, a retired infantry captain, and Comte Charles de La Tour Du Pin-Montauban, chamberlain to the Duc d'Orléans. It was the beginning of an on-again, off-again relationship that lasted for years, one that became stronger with d'Astier, whose open manner especially recommended him to Rousseau. Among other things, Rousseau recalls[86] that d'Astier spoke 'at length, and perhaps on purpose, about the freedom of the press in Avignon, near his home'. Always on the lookout for somewhere to publish his work without fear of censorship, Rousseau made a note of this, and it was not long before he was taking advantage of d'Astier's connections with the book trade of the papal enclave.

To Rousseau's pleasure, d'Astier promised[87] after their departure to return the following spring.

Soon after these visitors left, Rousseau received a letter[88] from Deluc begging him to come to Geneva and participate in the campaign of opposition to the government: 'Your fellow citizens,' Deluc wrote—unwilling to accept the fact that Rousseau had ceased to be a citizen—'have more confidence in your lights for the defence of our laws.' Rousseau refused[89] to go, but he did agree to offer advice to the citizens on their strategy. After the first *représentation*, with four hundred supporters, had been answered by the Petit Conseil, a second *représentation*, with six hundred supporters, was dismissed without a reply. A third *représentation* was then submitted on 20 August, making an even bolder assertion than the previous two—namely, that the citizens' own Grand Conseil, or General Assembly, as opposed to the Petit Conseil, had the right, as the legislative body in the state, to determine the meaning of the laws. To this third *représentation*, the Petit Conseil replied at length, defending the *droit négatif*, as they called the right to accept or reject any *représentation* from the citizens.

At this stage, Rousseau drafted a further *représentation* for the citizens, but it was overcome by events and was never sent. A new element entered the dispute with the September publication of a closely reasoned pamphlet, *Letters from the Country*, defending the Petit Conseil's action; it was anonymous, but the author was generally known to be the procurator-general Robert Tronchin. Its publication had the effect of winning a considerable measure of support for the government among the citizens, who were henceforth divided into two hostile parties, opponents of the regime coming to be known as *Représentants* and supporters as *Négatifs*.

Moultou tried to distance himself from all this, not only from the *Représentants*, but also from Geneva. He found a country retreat at Bière in the canton of Vaud, where, as he informed[90] Suzanne Curchod, 'one reads Rousseau but does not talk about him, where there are no *représentations*, no cabals, not a word of politics . . . and where solitude calms the soul.'

In truth, Moultou's 'solitude' was less than complete. He was away from his family, but he was not alone, for Bière was also the country retreat of the *belle veuve* Mme de Vermenoux. While there Moultou volunteered[91] to visit Rousseau at Môtiers, but Rousseau did not press him to come. When Moultou returned to Geneva in the autumn, he told[92] Rousseau that he found the city intolerable and that he was looking for some property in the country to which he could move—no further than Morges—'so as to be closer to you'. Morges, in fact, was not at all close to Môtiers, but it was close to Bière.

Rousseau's reply[93] to this letter was short and sharp: 'You think of changing your abode, which is excellent; but it would be even better to begin by changing your profession, since the one you have can only dishonour you.'

Moultou was too wounded by these words to reply, and his correspondence with Rousseau lapsed for more than a year. Moultou attributed Rousseau's coldness to his own refusal to support the *Représentants*, although he told[94] Usteri that he had broken with Deluc and his friends only out of filial duty. Even so, it is clear that Moultou himself shared at that stage the political views of the *Nègatifs*:[95] the *Représentants*, he wrote,[96] 'want the people to have the right to take to their own council any matter they please to stir up; imagine the anarchy to which that would reduce us!'

It is equally clear that Rousseau was by this time wholeheartedly behind the *Représentants*; when Deluc urged him to write a reply to Robert Tronchin's *Letters from the Country* he did not hesitate to agree,[97] asking only that Deluc[98] provide material about the history and constitution of Geneva. Deluc set about collecting the data, and Rousseau received more useful material from Lenieps—whose opposition to the Geneva government dated back to the civil strife of 1737, and who had since lived in exile because he had never accepted (as had Deluc and the other moderate liberals) the French mediation of 1738. Lenieps was naturally delighted to see people in Geneva coming around to his way of thinking, and in encouraging Rousseau to refute Robert Tronchin he suggested[99] that 'the unique burning style' of Rousseau's pen was all that was needed to give expression to the citizens' cause. Rousseau decided that his reply to the *Letters from the Country* would be called *Letters from the Mountain*, but he said nothing about the project when he wrote[100] to Rey at the end of the year. His conversations with d'Astier had prompted the idea of having the letter published in Avignon. Indeed, already in November we find d'Astier writing[101] to Rousseau to recommend a publisher of his acquaintance, Jean-Louis Chambeau, and Chambeau himself expressed[102] the warmest enthusiasm at becoming Rousseau's publisher. Chambeau's letter did, however, contain a note, which Rousseau did not fully heed, warning that his freedom was not what he wished and that he could accept only a manuscript that was assured of a 'tacit permission' from the French authorities.

Work on the *Letters from the Mountain* took up much of Rousseau's energy in the ensuing months. In a letter to Mme de Verdelin[103] he said, 'I would like to write to you every day: I have thousands of things to tell you, but I am miserable, ill, obsessed, discouraged.' He said he could hardly wait for the winter snows to close access to his village and thereby put an end to the constant stream of visitors★ who were tormenting him. Replying to this letter on 23 November,[104] Mme de Verdelin was able to tell him that heavy snow

---

★Even as he wrote he had two Swiss visitors at the house: Jacob Wegelin (1721–1791), a professor of philosophy and pastor from St Gallen who had written an imaginary dialogue on Christianity between Rousseau and Jacob Vernes, and Johann Schultess (1741–1830), a young *littérateur* from Zürich.

had already fallen in Paris, where she was nursing a very sick husband. She consoled herself in her anxiety with the thought of visiting Môtiers in the spring, helping Thérèse in the kitchen, cleaning vegetables, and cooking her Saintonge stew for them. Strange as it may sound, the Marquise de Verdelin was in the fulness of time to do just this.

Writing to her again a month later,[105] Rousseau declared that she was the only person whose feelings of friendship had not cooled toward him because of his misfortunes. Even the Luxembourgs disappointed him: 'The whole household maintains the most deadly silence where I am concerned—although in the case of the Maréchal I know he is on duty and I must wait.'

At about this time, however, Rousseau received an unexpected, very affectionate letter[106] from Mme de Boufflers. It appears that she had heard from Lord Keith that Rousseau imagined her to be angry with him, as indeed he might well have been after all the scoldings contained in her letters from Paris and her silence after she had gone to England. She assured him that in fact she was as much his friend as ever and explained that during her stay in England she had looked everywhere for a place where he might find a congenial refuge.

In his reply[107] Rousseau expressed his joy at having kept a friendship he feared lost. He said his greatest hope was still to end his days with Lord Keith in Scotland, but his wretched health made that prospect seem remote. He expressed no interest in her suggestion that he go to England. He had already[108] made it clear to Mme de Verdelin that if he had the choice he would go to France, 'the country where I have spent the best years of my life'. He told[109] one of his Swiss visitors: 'I would rather die in a Catholic country than a Protestant one; the Catholic clergy preach intolerance, but the Protestants practise it.'

Rousseau's correspondence with Mme Alissan had lapsed during his severe illness in the summer, and in her anxiety she had taken the bold step of writing, under an assumed name, to Mme Boy to find out how he was faring. Mme Boy was able to report[110] from Pierrenod in mid-August that although Rousseau had been a very sick man, he was now recovering. Learning of her enquiry, Rousseau himself thanked[111] his *très bonne Marianne* for her solicitude and begged her to send him the portrait she was having painted: 'I suffer, dear Marianne, and my body silences my heart . . . but perhaps the sight of your portrait will revive a feeling that is subdued by pain.'

Mme Alissan went to great trouble to have the portrait neatly packed and taken to Switzerland by a private traveller: 'Now you can judge for yourself,' she told[112] Rousseau, 'the face of the woman whose soul, mind and behaviour you have judged so sternly.' Rousseau's acknowledgement[113] of the portrait was prompt but curt. Instead of making those comments on her appearance that she awaited so nervously, he simply said that he felt, as he looked at her portrait, 'like St-Preux contemplating the portrait of Julie in *La Nouvelle Héloïse*'.

In the novel, St-Preux is said to have experienced ecstasies, but it is obvious—and was all too obvious to Mme Alissan—that Rousseau had not done so in contemplating her portrait. When he packed it up to send back to her a week later, he scribbled[114] one coldly polite sentence saying that her portrait had 'compensated with pleasure the pain I feel in losing it'.

If Rousseau could hardly bring himself to express any interest in the portrait of Marianne, he made a great fuss about his own portrait. First he complained[115] to the publishers about the engraving Litret had made from La Tour's original because it showed him in French dress: 'It would be more graceful if it showed me in the Armenian costume, which I always wear nowadays and which suits me better.' The publisher Guy duly engaged Cathelin to make another engraving, this one depicting the philosopher in a fur-lined robe and a fur hat. But again Rousseau found fault[116] with it: the cap was too high, the fur too fluffy. Guy acted on his criticisms and was able to assure[117] Rousseau that La Tour had personally retouched the drawing, and even brought in an Armenian model to get the costume right. Rousseau was satisfied enough with the final outcome to order several copies for distribution among his friends.

These friends did not include Mme Alissan, who was reduced to bitter tears by the brevity and empty *politesse* of his comments on her portrait. She protested[118] that he could at least have said something, flattering or otherwise, about the face it depicted. This only prompted him to put her down more firmly than ever. 'Madame,' he wrote on Christmas Day[119]—for she was no longer 'Marianne'—'I reply to your reproaches with facts'—and he told her about his poor health, his demanding visitors, the exercise he had to take every day, the prolonged use of catheters, and 'a serious piece of writing' on which he was working: 'I declare to you that this is my last apology.'

The 'serious piece of writing' was the *Letters from the Mountain*, and the most demanding of his visitors was Deluc's son Jean-André, who had arrived at Môtiers with a case full of papers for Rousseau to consult in writing the work but who then promptly fell ill, much as his father had done when he visited Rousseau a few months earlier. Deluc *fils*, who had been suffering from fevers for some time, had made the journey only because of the importance Rousseau placed on the documentation he needed for his refutation of Robert Tronchin, although the true purpose of the visit was a closely guarded secret. Rousseau was successful at least in preventing Montmollin from finding out what he was doing, to judge from a letter[120] the pastor wrote to Sarasin, in which he said he had heard Rousseau tell young Deluc that 'he wanted to hear no more about *représentations*, was angry at being implicated in them, and, having a new nationality, wanted to forget all about the old.' Rousseau may afterwards have regretted deceiving Montmollin in this way, for Montmollin's discovery of the deceit marked the end of his goodwill toward him.

The *Letters from the Mountain* were intended to rebut Robert Tronchin's argument in his *Letters from the Country* by showing, first, that Rousseau's books were not subversive of government and religion and, second, that the ruling élite of Geneva was systematically violating the constitution of the republic. On the first charge, Rousseau claimed that Geneva had been in his mind all the time in writing *The Social Contract*; he had not tried to invent another utopia like Plato's *Republic* but to depict a real state as 'an exemplar for all Europe'.[121] He added: 'What a bitter irony it is that no other country in Europe has banned the book except the one to whose constitution it is such a tribute.'★

Wisely Rousseau did not elaborate on his claim that the republic described in *The Social Contract* corresponded to the state of Geneva, for the differences between the two were significant. The civil religion of Geneva was, of course, Protestant Christian, that of *The Social Contract* non-Christian; the citizens of Geneva were a privileged minority that made up less than a third of the population, whereas in the republic of *The Social Contract* every man is a citizen. Moreover, in his *Letters from the Mountain* Rousseau does not appeal to the same republican principles that he asserts in *The Social Contract*. He has indeed been criticised[†] for invoking a principle of government—the division of sovereignty and the balance of powers—that he specifically rejects in *The Social Contract*.

It must be remembered, however, that the *Letters from the Mountain* is an exercise in polemics, not in political philosophy; Rousseau's strategy was to accept Robert Tronchin's statement of the forms and principles of the constitution of Geneva, and then to show that they had not been respected by the Petit Conseil. He judges the rulers of Geneva not by the standards of *The Social Contract* but by the laws of the republic: its original constitution and the rules established by the Act of Mediation of 1738. These principles incorporate the idea of a balance of power: 'What better government is there,' Rousseau asks, 'than one of which all the parts are held in perfect equilibrium, where the individuals cannot transgress the law because they are subject to magistrates and the magistrates cannot transgress it because they are supervised by the people?'[123] A few pages later, he refers to Robert Tronchin's having 'rightly cited England as a model of the current balance of power'.[124]

Compared to the well-known remark in *The Social Contract*[‡] about the English being free only on election days, this praise of England might sug-

---

★In fact, *The Social Contract* was banned by the courts in Holland and by the censor in France.
†Among others by Jean-Daniel Candaux in his introduction to the Pléiade text of the *Letters*.[122]
‡'The English people think they are free. They are badly mistaken. They are free when they elect Members of Parliament; as soon as those are elected, the electorate is enslaved; it is nothing.'[125]

gest that Rousseau had abandoned his radical, democratized republicanism for the Whiggish politics of Locke or Montesquieu. Indeed it is sometimes suggested that he moved to the Right in his politics. It would be closer to the truth to say that he moved to the Left: whereas in 1755, when he wrote the Dedication to the *Discourse on Inequality*, he held the view that everything was in order in Geneva, the people united, harmonious, and free, he had now come to think, with Deluc and Lenieps, that the people of Geneva were being, and had long been, oppressed by their rulers, and he was willing to support resistance to that oppression.

He was not holding up the constitutional monarchy of England as an ideal, but suggesting[126] that the balance of powers, which preserved liberty in England, had been forsaken in Geneva when the executive body took all power into its hands and instituted a despotism worse than that of many monarchs.

The King of England, invested by the laws with great power to protect them, has no power to infringe them, for no one in such a case would obey him, each would fear for his head; the Ministers themselves are lost if they alienate Parliament, where their conduct is examined. Every Englishman, sheltered by the laws, can stand up to the Royal power, and the least of persons can obtain genuine redress if he is wronged . . .

In Geneva the power of the Petit Conseil is absolute in every respect. The Petit Conseil is Minister and Prince, petitioner and judge at the same time; it orders and it executes; it has power in its hands to do everything; nothing it does can be questioned; it renders account of its conduct to nobody; it has nothing to fear from the legislative body, which has no right to speak without its permission.

Having studied all the material provided by Deluc and Lenieps, Rousseau is able to appeal, in the best Whig style, to the authority of an ancient enactment—pointing out, for example, that in the fifteenth century the Conseil Général, or General Assembly of Citizens, the legislative organ of the state, met frequently whereas in more recent times it has met only at the pleasure of the executive, the Petit Conseil. The Petit Conseil has not taken sovereignty out of the hands of the General Assembly by any one single act or coup but by a series of more or less covert manoeuvres over a period of many years. One incident Rousseau cites is the construction of expensive fortifications in 1714 after a citizens' rebellion. This gave the magistrates the opportunity to impose heavy taxes on the citizens to pay for the buildings, to import a garrison of foreign soldiers to man them, and then to use those soldiers to subdue the citizens.

Rousseau recalls a number of other instances in which the Petit Conseil had contrived to diminish the power of the General Assembly while keeping up all appearances of respecting the constitution. Occasionally summoning the citizens and burgesses to vote, but only as they were instructed to vote, refusing to listen to any voice outside its own closed walls, and riding roughshod over the laws of the state in governing by fiat, the magistrates of Geneva have, he asserts, made themselves its masters:

'When one considers the rights of the citizens and burgesses of Geneva brought together the General Assembly, nothing seems more brilliant. But considered as they really are, what have these same citizens and burgesses become? Slaves of an arbitrary power, they are delivered up defenceless to the mercy of 25 despots. The Athenians at least had thirty.'[127]

What had started out as a pamphlet grew to the length of a book—the *Letters from the Mountain* is one and a half times the length of *The Social Contract*—but its robust eloquence preserves the character of a pamphlet, a party manifesto for the *Représentants* to match the manifesto that Robert Tronchin had provided for the *Négatifs*. It was something the *Représentants* needed, for such was the success of the *Letters from the Country* that a solid majority of the citizens at the General Assembly in the New Year 1764 voted sheepishly for the list of candidates for public office drawn up by the Petit Conseil. The *Représentants'* objection to Rousseau's case being judged by the Petit Conseil instead of the Consistory was effectively nullified when the Consistory announced that it would have judged the case in the same way. No more was said about the General Assembly's right to legislate and interpret legislation.

The protest movement had died down to a point that Deluc and his friends pinned all their hopes on Rousseau's intervention to revive it. They took great care to keep secret the fact that he was writing a reply to Robert Tronchin, and did not even communicate with him by letter while he was at work on it. Afterward, when the reply was in the press and they renewed their correspondence with him, they referred to the *Letters from the Mountain* by a code name: the *Airs de Mandoline*.[128]

'MARMOT' AND 'BEAR'

The early months of 1764 witnessed the publication of several works of interest to Rousseau. Antoine-Jacques Roustan's *Offrande aux autels et à la patrie*, containing a decent critical appraisal of *Émile*, was brought out by Rey and promptly burned by the Petit Conseil in Geneva at the behest of the French resident. Roustan himself escaped the melée on being appointed a chaplain at the Swiss Church in London. Duchesne and Guy published Rousseau's short essay, *Imitation théatrale*, which was intended to supplement the argument of his *Letter to M. d'Alembert* with an abridgement of Plato's teaching on the evils of the drama. Voltaire was impatient to read it: 'Send me Jean-Jacques' latest vomitings on the theatre,' he wrote[1] to his bookseller. Soon afterward Duchesne and Guy published La Porte's collection of Rousseau's writings, for which Rousseau had been offered, but not yet received, fifty louis. Rousseau graciously congratulated[2] La Porte on his editorial work, but he made it clear to the publishers that he did not and would not acknowledge the books as his. For this reason he refused at first to accept any complimentary author's copies, but afterward relented in order to have one set sent to a new library his friends were setting up in Yverdon and another sent to Mme Alissan. This latter was intended as a peace offering to his unhappy admirer, who had complained[3] that his callous reaction to the sight of her portrait had made her ill. The gift had the desired effect, and the two were soon addressing each other, in their resumed correspondence, as '*chère* Marianne' and '*mon cher* Jean-Jacques'.

The winter snows kept Rousseau shut up in what he called his prison for most of the time, and in a sick bed for much of it, although he did go out occasionally to chop wood as an exercise that, by making him sweat, he believed did himself good. He made his prison more tolerable by acquiring a dog ('Sultan') and a cat just as he had had at Montmorency. He also enjoyed human companionship in the person of Isabelle d'Ivernois, his young and cultured neighbour, who, as he recalls in the *Confessions*,[4] 'came to pass with

Thérèse and me long evenings which she made shorter with her intelligence and the mutual outpourings of our hearts. She called me "papa" and I called her my daughter.'

If the stream of uninvited visitors dried up in the cold weather, letters continued to reach him by the score, and even after spending hours writing material for publication, he still managed to answer most of them. One correspondent on whom he lavished much time and attention was Prince Louis of Würtemberg, who had moved to Lausanne disappointed with the rewards he had received from the Austrian Empress for service in her armies. He was an admirer of Rousseau and was trying to bring up his infant daughter on the principles of *Émile*, but having observed that the system of *Émile* was designed exclusively for boys, he approached[5] Rousseau for advice in adapting it to the upbringing of a girl. The girl being still very young, Rousseau was able to concentrate at first on purely physical methods: breastfeeding and a spartan regime of cold baths, light covering, and barefooted outings in all weathers. Since the child was destined to die at the age of twelve, Rousseau's method cannot be deemed a total success in her case; nor for that matter can her father be cited as a dutiful exponent of Rousseau's philosophy, for on ascending the throne of Würtemberg, he proved a most reactionary ruler. But in the years of the infancy of little Sophie—for such was the Rousseauesque name they gave her—all was sweetness and light and obedience to nature in the princely household. The happy father could report[6] to Rousseau that the child flourished in her nakedness; she never caught cold, never cried, smiled at everyone, and was not at all afraid of thunder or lightening.

Dr Tissot, he had to say, uttered dire warnings against leaving the child unclothed in winter, but the Prince promised to follow Rousseau's instructions to the letter, and indeed Rousseau insisted[7] that his system must be adopted in its entirety or not at all. He was touched by the Prince's fidelity, and praised that of the mother in agreeing to breast-feed her child: 'It is rare for a woman of her rank★ to undertake the duties of a mother and love them.'

Pleased with the progress of his daughter, Prince Louis proudly informed[9] Rousseau in March 1764 that his wife was expecting another child and proposed once again that she nurse it. At this stage, addressing Rousseau as *mon cher maître*, the Prince started to unburden himself of his own troubles, complaining especially about the ill treatment he was receiving from Maria Theresa, 'for whom I shed my blood in battle with the joy of a martyr.'

In assuming the role of moral counsellor, Rousseau urged[10] the Prince to rise above the opinions and behaviour of others and to see happiness within

---

★Princess Louis was of noble but not royal birth. Boswell, an even greater snob than Rousseau, exclaims in his journal '[Prince Louis] . . . married a *Comtesse*, which was an unpardonable degradation.'[8]

himself. Rousseau also advised him to look for love and friendship outside the relationships imposed on him by his rank and station: 'that is the lesson I have learned in the course of a life which has enabled me to observe and compare all conditions of men from the humblest to the greatest.'

The Prince assured[11] Rousseau that he was very willing to accept his guidance: 'What situation could be sweeter than mine? I have Sophie for a wife, Sophie for a daughter and Emile's tutor as my master and friend.'

Soon after the birth of his second child, the Prince reported[12] that the mother's milk had 'dried up in her pretty breast.' Rousseau's response to this problem was to suggest[13] that it was all the Prince's fault. Surmising on the strength of the reference to the 'pretty breast' that the Prince wished, in the manner of Louis XV, to preserve it for his own pleasure from the depredations of a sucking child, Rousseau wrote sternly: 'The *voluptés conjugales* are transitory and the pleasures of a lover do not make the happiness of a father and husband.'

Prince Louis denied[14] the accusation haughtily: 'You do not know me . . . I have given up everything for virtue—pleasure, glories, fortune.' As for his wife's milk, 'You are mistaken; there was none.'

The second child—also a daughter—proved less robust than her sister;* but she too was duly given the upbringing prescribed by Rousseau once she had been weaned from her wet nurse. She too went, as soon as she could toddle, barefoot in the snow, even though her elder sister developed chilblains.†

While Prince Louis prided himself on having won the friendship of Rousseau, Paul Moultou lamented the loss of it. Although it was he who broke off their correspondence, he believed that Rousseau's heart was hardened because Moultou had refused to support Deluc and the citizens' party against the Petit Conseil in Geneva; even if largely motivated by consideration for his patrician family, Moultou was no less sure that his attitude had been correct. As he explained[17] to his friend Élie Reverdil, he had supported Rousseau and *Émile* without joining the movement to displace Robert Tronchin and undermine the government of Geneva. He dreaded civil unrest and had tried to persuade Rousseau to make his supporters end their agitation. Rousseau had refused, with the result that he, Moultou, found himself hated on both sides, by the clergy and civil authorities because he defended *Émile* and by Deluc and the *Représentants* because he defended the *droit négatif* of the Petit Conseil.

*Boswell, who saw them both in December 1764, described the elder in his journal as a 'stout lass', adding, 'The other was more delicate; but they both seemed healthy and gay.'[15]
†'Chilblains have caused her terrible pains, but thanks to the care of Dr Tissot, she has been cured,' the Prince wrote in November.[16] He added, 'This Dr Tissot is another Rousseau.' Since Dr Tissot opposed Rousseau's spartan methods, the remark is puzzling.

Adding to Moultou's chagrin was the departure of Mme de Vermenoux to live in Paris. He unburdened[18] his sorrow to Jean-Louis Garcin, a friend from college days, who had become a private tutor in Leyden: 'I have been seeing her for three years, and now I no longer have her near me . . . I am alone, without friends . . . O God, am I not in love with her!'

Mme de Vermenoux was clearly not in love with Moultou. In Paris she set her cap at Jacques Necker, the glamorous banker and economist who was later to achieve fame as first minister to Louis XVI. She did not succeed. To everyone's amazement he preferred, and married within a few weeks, the beautiful widow's rather plain companion, Suzanne Curchod. Moultou, on the basis of a long platonic friendship with Suzanne, begged[19] her at one point to try to promote a reconciliation between himself and Rousseau, but soon afterward he declared[20] to her: 'Rousseau is nothing to me any more, and he will never be anything to me.'

The appearance of La Porte's collection and its reported success prompted Rousseau to think that the time was ripe for him to get his own definitive edition, the *Complete Works*, into print. He envisaged it as being a well-illus-trated and well-printed publication, and he approached his artist friend Claude Watelet in the hope of securing Watelet's collaboration. The artist, who received the message on a visit to Rome, agreed[21] readily. As a publisher for the works, Rey was Rousseau's first choice. He told[22] Rey that the pro-ject was 'of the greatest importance to me as the only source of a future livelihood, since I am in no condition to produce any more work.' Rey was too short of capital just then to commit himself, and Rousseau did not tell Rey that he was in the process of producing the *Letters from the Mountain*, as he was planning to have that book published in Avignon.

Captain d'Astier, who was acting as Rousseau's agent in Avignon, in-formed[23] Rousseau in April that his friend, the publisher Louis Chambeau, was eager to have the manuscript but would not be able to pay the author more than twenty-five or fifty louis for it. d'Astier volunteered to come to Môtiers to collect the manuscript, but Rousseau, unwilling to put his friend to so much trouble, proposed instead to send it to d'Astier by instalments, in packets too small to excite curiosity. D'Astier encouraged[24] Rousseau to believe that the book could be printed and published in two months, but soon after he had received the first two instalments of the text he had to in-form him that the Inquisitor at Avignon, to whom all material published in that papal enclave had first to be submitted, refused to licence it. Astier was as much surprised as dismayed by this decision, which he attributed[25] to new circumstances surrounding the expulsion of the Jesuits from France; surely, though, both he and Rousseau were most unworldly in having ever expected the Inquisitor to sanction a book in which St. Paul is described as a 'natural persecutor'[26] and Christian miracles are dismissed as illusions.

Despite the celerity of d'Astier and the Inquisitor in attending to their business, the publication of the *Letters from the Mountain* was delayed by these proceedings, and it was July 1764 before Rousseau could send the manuscript to Rey, the publisher whom prudence would have dictated in the first place. Although Rousseau warned[27] Rey that the book would make him enemies in Geneva, Rey not only agreed[28] to publish it before seeing the manuscript but also promised to have it in print by November.

Rousseau's anxiety about Thérèse's future was relieved somewhat by a message[29] he received from Lord Keith offering her a present of one hundred louis. Lord Keith had gone to Scotland, taken an instant dislike to the place, and decided to sell his property there and return to Germany. Having done well in the sales, he begged Rousseau to let him use some of the money to help Thérèse. For once Rousseau accepted[30] a benefaction gracefully, asking only that it be paid as an annuity rather than as a lump sum that he would not know how to invest.

By this time Rousseau had come to regret having asked the Abbé Grumet to help Thérèse, for he learned that his letter to the kindly curé had been not only circulated in Ambérieu but printed and published in Paris. Rousseau reported[31] this with understandable irritation to Mme de Verdelin, who had also volunteered to look after Thérèse if the need arose. Grumet, being reprimanded, denied[32] that he was responsible for the publication, claiming that a visitor to his house had copied the letter behind his back and circulated it without his knowledge or consent: 'I am not guilty, but I need your indulgence.'

Mme de Verdelin continued[33] to take an interest in Mme Levasseur on behalf of Rousseau and Thérèse, and even when she could not visit her herself, she made sure from the local curé at Deuil that the old woman lacked nothing. In the meantime, Mme de Verdelin had for some months been nursing a very sick husband, and in December he died. Rousseau urged[34] her to regard this as a blessing: 'he has gained more than you have lost.' But while Rousseau thus briskly disposed of the subject of her husband's death in two sentences, he wrote at some length about the effect of the changed situation on her attitude to her former lover, Margency, who had ended their adulterous relationship on developing religious scruples but was once again eager to see her. Rousseau pleaded with her to treat him kindly. He said in one letter[35] that he could well understand Margency's desire to return 'once he could act on his feelings without crime', and he urged Mme de Verdelin to listen to her own heart in responding to Margency's renewed approach to her. But when she told[36] him she had resolved to live henceforth for her children and not for an old passion, he assured[37] her of his confidence in the rightness of her decision as one of 'virtue and reason.'

In the spring of 1764 there appeared in print a pamphlet entitled *Lettre à l'Archevêque d'Auch de J.-J. Rousseau, Citoyen de Genève.* Virtually every reader recognized it as a badly written forgery,★ but one who took it to be genuine was Alexandre Deleyre, who blotted his copybook once again with Rousseau by writing[38] from Parma to congratulate him on it.

Although he never believed that any discriminating reader could possibly think the pamphlet was his,† Rousseau had already asked[40] Duchesne and Guy to publish a denial. This denial contained a reference to Voltaire that caused consternation at Ferney. It named Voltaire as 'the most ardent and most adroit of my persecutors'. Since Voltaire was still pretending to be Rousseau's friend and benefactor, he was outraged: 'What do you think of that lunatic Jean-Jacques?' he asked[41] Théodore Tronchin. 'He wants to make war, but I will not field my troops against him.' Such, however, is exactly what Voltaire proceeded to do, although he did not strike until Rousseau made himself more vulnerable by the publication of the *Letters from the Mountain*.

On 18 May Rousseau's 'daughter' Isabelle d'Ivernois was married to Frédéric Guyenet, lieutenant-civil, an administrative official to the intendant of the Val de Travers, Jacques Martinet. She was henceforth known as 'Madame la Lieutenante'.

Although the marriage did not turn out to be a particularly happy one, it started brilliantly, with much feasting and dancing in the village. During the festivities, Rousseau made a new friend, François-Louis d'Escherny. Aged thirty-one, the son of a prosperous Neuchâtel family, and a future count of the Holy Roman Empire, d'Escherny had rented a house in Môtiers several months earlier in the hope of making the acquaintance of Rousseau,[42] but despite having a letter of recommendation from his kinswoman Mme de Luze, he had not succeeded in meeting the philosopher. Rousseau may have dreaded another Baron Sauttern, for when d'Escherny wrote to introduce himself as a fellow lover of solitude, Rousseau replied[43] laconically that he was sure neither lover of solitude would wish to disturb the solitude of the other. Once brought together at Isabelle's wedding, they promptly became friends, if never as intimate as d'Escherny claims in his boastful and sometimes inaccurate memoirs.[44] What recommended him to Rousseau was a love of Italian music, a talent for it, and a certain knowledge of it acquired while living in Leghorn. They sang Italian airs together while Rousseau played the spinet and d'Escherny the harp. They also went hiking in the mountains, although d'Escherny certainly exaggerates when he says he 'walked a thousand leagues with Rousseau'. He has kind words for Thérèse in his memoirs, praising her cooking and the care she took of Rousseau, and

---

★This pamphlet, an attack on the Jesuits, is said to have been written by Pierre Firmin de La Croix, a Jansenist.

†Bachaumont wrote: 'One cannot ape an author as original as Rousseau.'[39]

reproaching Rousseau for not letting her sit at the table with them when he was invited to dine. D'Escherny also says she made Rousseau unnecessarily suspicious of the villagers of Môtiers by telling tales, true or false, about their hostility toward him.

D'Escherny recalls[45] singing duets with Rousseau in the moonlight beside the River Areuse before an audience of young village girls, although he is not flattering about Rousseau's voice: 'mediocre in French and rather bad in Italian'. He even asserts, falsely, that Rousseau could not speak Italian. Rousseau's occasional coldness toward him he attributes to Rousseau's jealousy of his superiority in singing, but he nevertheless maintains that Rousseau appointed him in Môtiers his 'grand master of ceremonies'.

If d'Escherny's memoirs are less than wholly reliable, much that he says is confirmed by another young man who made Rousseau's acquaintance at the same time. This was Jakob-Heinrich Meister, remembered in literary history as Grimm's collaborator and successor as editor of the *Correspondance littéraire*, but at that time a nineteen-year-old curate from Zürich. Fortunately he was as yet unknown to the man whose name could not be spoken in Rousseau's presence. In letters[46] to his father that bespeak a future journalist, Meister describes how with a French friend named Mègre he travelled fifty leagues on foot to visit Rousseau and had been very warmly received. He had expected to meet an invalid but instead found 'the most sprightly man you could imagine, one in most vigorous health'. Meister's visit took place in June, by which season the 'marmot' and sick man of the winter months had once again been transformed into the 'bear' of the summer, who astonished others besides Meister with his energy. Meister describes his host's appearance:

His complexion is swarthy, the eyes so black that the whites afford a dazzling contrast. Cathelin's portrait expresses the physiognomy rather well and Littret's captures the detail but not the whole; neither has caught the face at its most expressive moments. When M. Rousseau's soul is peaceful, his look is altogether sweet. Then when he is agitated, his whole passion flares up in his eyes and his look is as penetrating as lightning. He speaks with that same harmonious celerity, that eloquence and precision one admires in his writing. His whole manner is urbane, but he is not quite as polite as he might be without cost to his freedom.'

'We spoke about his books,' Meister continues; 'M. Rousseau said, "Books do more harm than good. They injure those who do not understand them, and they are useless to those who do."'

Meister's French companion, Mègre, asked Rousseau what was the secret of his literary style that everyone admired so much. 'The only secret,' he replied, 'is that I believe strongly in everything I write; whether it is true or not, I think it is true.' Mègre, who came from Nîmes, tried to interest Rousseau in the antiquities of that place, but Rousseau said the subject bored him: 'I like only living things.' He told them he was not interested in architecture and admitted he did not much care for paintings. He went on to explain his love of prints: 'They leave my imagination free to colour them as it pleases; then I think I see the objects as they are in nature.'

Rousseau told his visitors that he liked only Italian poetry and detested French; his favourite authors, besides those of the Scriptures, were Plutarch, Tacitus, and Homer among the ancients, Buffon, Montesquieu, and Gessner among the moderns. He told them about his publishing plans and spoke without bitterness of Voltaire and Diderot. 'Even his voice,' Meister writes, 'was enchanting. I have never heard one more harmonious. He accented every word with force, precision and ease. Whatever he described, one could believe one saw.'

Meister gives an account of a walk with Rousseau. Both he and Mègre found the going hard. Rousseau had promised to take them only on the easier paths. 'However,' Meister adds, 'those easier paths were up very steep mountains and across very rough stones.' He says the experience was thrilling, even though he could not hold Rousseau to a sustained conversation as they scrambled and climbed over the rocks. When they seemed to have lost their way, Mègre exclaimed bravely: 'How good to be lost with the illustrious Rousseau!' whereupon Rousseau protested, 'No compliments, please. Would you not rather be lost with a pretty girl?' When Rousseau noticed his visitors sweating and panting behind him, he said 'I am not tired, gentlemen . . . If you are, go back and leave me alone.' They carried on, and when they peered nervously from a summit, Rousseau told them he had no fear of falls: 'I always let myself go. If I slip in the mountains I just slide on my behind and I reach the bottom without the least harm. Such is the philosophy of children, and I have made it my own.'

Meister, who prided himself on his French, was invited by Montmollin to preach at the village church. On that occasion, however, Rousseau was not in the congregation, for he had just heard news which left him too stricken with grief to leave his room: the death of the Maréchal de Luxembourg. Seldom at his best in writing letters of condolence, Rousseau then wrote to Mme de Luxembourg one of his worst.[47] He said he would not have written to her at all if he had known anyone who was dearer to the friend he had lost:

But with whom can I better lament that loss than with the one person in the world who feels it most? Ah, how can those he loved remain divided? Will their hearts not unite at least to weep for him? And if your heart no longer speaks to mine, please take an interest in my misfortunes for the sake of one who did—as you well know. But there I flatter myself too much. No doubt he had ceased to take that interest, and following your example he forgot me. Alas, what have I done? What is my crime if it is not to have loved you both too much? . . . Death alone could take his affection from you. But I lost you both while he and you were still alive. How much more to be pitied am I than you?

This letter is the more shocking for having been written at a time when Rousseau was in good health and, according to the testimony of d'Escherny and Meister, good spirits; not a product of winter and sickness like most of his paranoid outbursts, but something which dates from the best and busiest summer of his life in exile. The widow's reply[48] to the letter was of a sweetness to put him to shame:

It is my tears that I wish to mix with yours. I might have believed that in my grief I would have had the greatest consolation from you. Instead, Monsieur, I find that I must justify myself, and what is even more terrible and more pressing, that I must justify M. de Luxembourg, who loved and respected you and counted on having no better friend in the whole world than you.

She went on to explain that in the last four months of his life, her husband had been too ill to write letters, but had always spoken most fondly of Rousseau and felt his absence most painfully. She begged Rousseau to repent a little the injustices he had done to a dear friend's memory: 'In the name of God do not add your indifference to my great grief and be sure that I shall always love you in my most tender heart.'

This letter produced at least a fairly decent response[49] from Rousseau. He did not express any regret for the injustice of his earlier assertions, but he did thank Mme de Luxembourg for having 'transformed my despair into precious, sweet tears with which I shall honour the Maréchal's memory every day of my life'. Mme de Luxembourg was evidently comforted by this change of tone, but their relationship was never restored to its former intimacy, and in the *Confessions*[50]* Rousseau puts the blame for this on her: 'In spite of several affected and increasingly rare demonstrations of friendship, Mme de Luxembourg hid less successfully from day to day her altered feelings towards me.'

Rousseau did not lack friends at this period of his life, making several new ones among the more enlightened patricians of Neuchâtel who came to summer retreats in the Val de Travers. Among these was Colonel Abraham

---

*In the *Confessions* Rousseau goes on to say that Pierre Guy informed him that he had been left a bequest in the Maréchal's will. After some reflection he says he decided to accept it, but then heard nothing further about the matter. There is no such bequest in M. de Luxembourg's will or codicils, nor any reference to one in the correspondence between Guy and Rousseau.

de Pury, who had a chalet in the mountains to the north of Môtiers, 'Mon-lési', where he entertained his highbrow friends in what he called his '*salon des philosophes*'. Two were of particular importance to Rousseau. The first was Jean-Antoine d'Ivernois,★ a physician by profession who was also an authority on the flora of the Jura. He became Rousseau's unpaid instructor in botany and, as Rousseau recalls,[51] 'inspired me with a taste which became a passion'. With Monlési as a base, Dr d'Ivernois took Rousseau on several botanising expeditions, thus giving a new focus to his *promenades pédestres*. The second friend Rousseau acquired at Monlési was even more important to him, indeed becoming almost at once his closest, and incontestably his most useful, friend: Pierre-Alexandre Du Peyrou.[52]

In the *Confessions*[53] Rousseau describes Du Peyrou as an 'American'. In fact he hailed from Dutch Guyana, where his Huguenot family had emigrated after the Revocation of the Edict of Nantes. He was a handsome man, with a dark complexion attributed to the sunburn of the tropics, but already afflicted at the age of forty-five, when Rousseau first met him, with deafness and gout. He was socially gauche, cold, reserved, and, as Rousseau puts it, 'Dutch',[54] despite having lived among the *philosophes* of Paris. His situation at Monlési was also rather odd;[55] he was a rejected suitor of Mme de Pury and was eventually to console himself for losing her to the colonel by marrying at the age of forty their daughter Henriette, aged eighteen, while still rather more in love with the mother. Du Peyrou was also rich, having inherited an enormous fortune based on the slave labour of the Dutch colonial plantations. Rousseau says[56] that he totally forgot in Du Peyrou's case 'the objection I had against the Baron d'Holbach, that he was too rich, and I believe I was wrong.' The chief merit that Du Peyrou had in Rousseau's eyes was his simplicity, 'which always reminded me of Lord Keith'.

Du Peyrou was still a bachelor at that time, and Rousseau urged him to join in the study of botany under Dr d'Ivernois: 'When one has botanised all day one is not sorry to go to bed alone at night . . . it is more pleasurable to analyse a pretty flower than a pretty girl.'[57]† In his *Reveries*[58] Rousseau mentions a botanising expedition with Du Peyrou and other friends from Monlési that took them to Mont Chasseron from the summit of which they could see seven Swiss lakes.‡ D'Escherny in his memoirs[59] gives a full account of the trip. He describes how the party set out with their provisions—blankets for the night, together with a picnic of patés, poultry, venison, and

---

★Not to be confused with his brother and Isabelle's father, Guillaume-Pierre d'Ivernois (1701–1775), former procurator-general or her brother Charles-Guillaume d'Ivernois (1732–1819), newly appointed treasurer-general, or with her cousin François-Henri d'Ivernois (1722–1778), the Geneva merchant.

†Du Peyrou married Henriette de Pury five years later.

‡On a clear day at sixteen hundred metres the lakes of Neuchâtel, Geneva, Bienne, Morat, Joux, Brenet and St-Point are visible.

a good supply of wine—loaded on the back of a mule. The organisation, according to d'Escherny, was almost military: Colonel de Pury, carrying a compass, acted as navigator; Du Peyrou had charge of the herbarium; d'Escherny himself, as quartermaster, made the camp fires and prepared the coffee; Rousseau, 'as the senior member of the little group, was the captain, in charge of discipline and order'. Like Meister, d'Escherny comments on Rousseau's agility. He notes how Rousseau climbed 'like a goat' toward the summit while Du Peyrou dragged his feet painfully in the rear. After a long day in search of plants the party ate their supper and enjoyed 'excellent coffee' (for d'Escherny has no inhibitions in praising his own accomplishments) before making their beds on straw in a peasants' barn: 'The next morning the usual question was put: "Did you sleep well?" Rousseau said: "As for me, I never sleep," whereupon Colonel de Pury in his brisk military way stopped him short, saying "Good God, Monsieur Rousseau, you amaze me. I heard you snoring all night—it is I who never slept.'"

On the way back to Môtiers, the fine weather gave way to a dramatic storm, during which, says d'Escherny, Rousseau uttered a fervent hymn to the elements. Rousseau's own account in a letter[60] he wrote to Mme de Luze is less ecstatic: 'I have just returned from Chasseron, covered with mud up to my waist and soaked to the skin.'

Rousseau moved around a great deal in the cantons of Neuchâtel and Vaud that summer, partly to avoid the stream of visitors who came to his house, partly in search of a new home, since he was fed up—and Thérèse even more fed up—with Môtiers. His companion on some of these journeys was François d'Ivernois, who was involved in the publication of the *Letters from the Mountain* and the distribution of it in Geneva, and who was also the chief intermediary between Rousseau and the other leaders of the *Représentants* in that city. He had been unable to attend the wedding of his cousin Isabelle in May because his wife was just then giving birth to their eighth child, but he went to Môtiers a few days later to discuss with Rousseau the promotion of *Letters from the Mountain* and its place in the strategy of the coming struggle against the Petit Conseil.

In June Rousseau met François d'Ivernois at Brot to begin a journey on foot lasting several days. They took what d'Ivernois called the *sentiers raboteux* from Brot to Yverdon, then walked to the village of Goumoüens, where they put up at the local inn and undertook several excursions in the neighbourhood. In the *Confessions*[61] Rousseau describes François d'Ivernois as a bore and a pest, and speaks of their three days at Goumoüens as an ordeal, but the letters Rousseau wrote at the time are full of friendly words to, and about, him. François d'Ivernois was the only *Représentant* leader to whom, having worked out a simple code, Rousseau wrote freely about Genevese politics at that period, regarding him as less extreme than Deluc and less indiscreet than Lenieps.

It has to be remembered that Rousseau wrote the later chapters of the *Confessions* at a time when he took the bleakest view of everything and everybody. In the summer of 1764, he was in a mood to think kindly of his fellow men, even though he had started to develop sciatica. François d'Ivernois did him numerous services, including the sale of the carriage he had used in his escape from France; d'Ivernois sent him presents that were gratefully received, and Rousseau responded in kind. Rousseau even used his influence with Lord Keith to secure for d'Ivernois letters of nobility from Frederick II.

Among others who benefited from Rousseau's geniality that summer was François Coindet, whose years of disgrace came to an end. First in a letter[62] to Duchesne, Rousseau asked for news of Coindet, having somehow learned that he had been demoted at the bank where he worked. Then Coindet himself wrote[63] to Rousseau, saying that Rousseau's enquiry had 'prompted the sweet hope that our friendship is not entirely extinguished'. Rousseau said in his reply,[64] 'You are wrong to think I ever lost my friendship for you. I am always the same, and if certain of your manners displeased me . . . I have never ceased to take an interest in you.' Rousseau went on to suggest that Coindet make himself useful by buying prints in Paris on his behalf—'pretty ones that do not cost much, especially portraits of celebrated men and women for which I have a predilection'. Coindet promptly seized the olive branch and, as Rousseau's agent in collecting prints, secured his continued goodwill.

Another friend who benefitted from Rousseau's genial mood was Sautternsheim. Rousseau sent him a present of ten louis, and, in a letter[65] to an Austrian acquaintance, he said of Sautternsheim—by no means truthfully—'I know only honest things about him: he is not at all an adventurer.'

Even Alexandre Deleyre came in from the cold. After Deleyre apologised[66] for mistakenly attributing the badly written *Letter to Archbishop d'Auch* to Rousseau—and reported that Condillac had been equally deceived—Rousseau apologised[67] in turn: 'I feel I got angry without reason in a situation where you should have been corrected not attacked.' He promised to keep in touch but explained that he was too overwhelmed with correspondence to write to his old friend as often as he would wish. He gave[68] the same explanation of his silence to Mme Alissan, hoping that she would 'accept friendship instead of letters'.

It was not only correspondence that claimed his time; he travelled as well. In August he set out on a journey to Aix-les-Bains, hoping to find some relief there for his sciatica, and then went on to see Conzié at Les Charmettes

and Gauffecourt in Lyons. At Thonon on the Savoyard shore of Lake Geneva
he had a political meeting with a group of *Représentants*.

During the voyage across the lake he saw in the distance the spires of
Geneva, and, as he afterward informed[69] Lord Keith, 'I sighed the kind of
bitter sigh I would once have sighed for a perfidious mistress.' The conference at Thonon was stormy.[70] There were six Genevese in the party: Jean-
François Deluc and his son Jean-André, Jacques Vieusseux, Pierre Vieusseux,
François d'Ivernois, and Jacob Voullaire. Rousseau had insisted[71] there be no
women present; he wanted no civilities to inhibit the exchange of views, nor
did they. Deluc *père* put the case for radical action—and we may assume he
did so at his usual tedious length. Voullaire, the youngest, who was also the
most conservative, objected vigorously to any policy that would be injurious
to the constitution. Tossed between Deluc on the left and Voullaire on the
right, the conference finally decided to concentrate all efforts on the next
elections for public offices in Geneva, when citizens would have the opportunity lawfully to approve or reject candidates nominated by the Petit Conseil. Rousseau's friends counted on having his *Letters from the Mountain* in
print in time for those elections; it was also agreed that the *Représentants*
should themselves publish a set of replies to Robert Tronchin, although even
those who thought as highly of their own literary gifts as did Deluc *père*
could not expect their arguments to have anything like the impact of
Rousseau's.

By the time the conference ended, the weather in Thonon changed for
the worse, and once again Rousseau, feeling unwell, had to abort a journey.
He went directly to Môtiers, hoping to see Mme de Verdelin. The marquise
was spending the summer at Bourbonne-les-Bains for the sake of her daughter, who was receiving treatment there for an affliction of the limbs, and she
had promised to make what seemed to be the reasonably short journey to
Môtiers to visit Rousseau before they returned to Paris. In the event the girl's
treatment was ended early, and Mme de Verdelin had to inform[72] Rousseau
that she would not be able to visit him until the following summer. Rousseau
was irritated by the change of plans. He even claimed[73] that he had given
up going to Aix-les-Bains expressly in order to keep his appointment with
her.* In the same letter he rebuked her on another score. He had found out
from Thérèse that Mme de Verdelin had asked her for the name of his
banker, with the obvious aim of making a discreet financial donation. He
wrote: 'You labour, Madame, to deprive me of domestic peace, the one good
that I have left and for the loss of which all your goods would never com-
pensate. I declare to you that I dislike devious benefactions, and you oblige
me now to renounce them once and for all. When I am in need I will tell

*Two days later he wrote to Keith: 'From Thonon I had to turn back, ill, and under a continual
rain.'[74]

you and you can do what you please for me. In the meantime, Madame, kindly cease disturbing my life. I have enough troubles without that.'

Having written these harsh words, Rousseau suggested he might go to Pontarlier or Besançon to meet Mme de Verdelin and her daughter on their way back to Paris, but he said no more to mitigate the severity of his reproaches. The rendezvous proved impracticable, but as soon as she reached home, Mme de Verdelin wrote[75] to justify her attempt to make a gift to him. She said that her husband had left her well off, with more than enough* to provide for herself and her daughters, especially as they were about to move to a small apartment in a convent and would employ only four servants. She wanted to share her wealth with Rousseau, and she added that he ought to know her heart well enough to understand that her motives were not those of the kind of people who tried to patronise him.

Rousseau was in fact rather more prosperous than usual at that time, as money owed him by Rey and his Paris publishers finally reached him. He was able to assure another friend who was anxious about his finances,[76] Mme de Boufflers, that 'necessity, even abundance', was not lacking. He also told Mme de Boufflers that he was looking for somewhere to live that was more suited to his tastes than Môtiers, and that he was enjoying his new hobby, botany: 'It is the true occupation for an active body and a lazy mind.' He mentioned his great sorrow at the death of a friend they had in common, M. de Luxembourg. Fortunately, perhaps, he did not learn in time of the death of Mme de Boufflers' husband to write her one of his maladroit letters of condolence, although her mourning was probably more formal than felt: her real chagrin came when her lover, the Prince de Conti, disappointed her hopes of marriage, on the grounds that it would force him to give up his position, palace, and handsome emoluments as Grand Prior of the Chevaliers de Malte, an order dedicated to chastity.

As the summer storms gave way to a fine autumn, Rousseau set off on the move once more, despite his sciatica. He visited Mme de Luze at Le Bied in the Vallée de la Sagne; he went on botanising expeditions to La Robellaz and Le Creux-du-Van; he installed himself for a week with Thérèse at a chalet at Champ-de-Moulin near Brot. It was while he was resting with Thérèse at his favourite inn at Brot—that of La Couronne, run by the Sandoz family— that he was spotted by yet another inquisitive admirer, Count Charles von Zinzendorf, imperial chamberlain from Vienna, who was on his way to seek out Rousseau at Môtiers. According to the Count's journal,[77] Rousseau accepted the intrusion very politely, and then rewarded—or punished—the Count's interest by taking him for a long and exhausting walk on rough paths

---

*She said he had an annual income of twenty thousand francs, rather more than Madame Chenonceaux's twelve thousand but still relatively modest. Voltaire allocated twenty thousand francs to his mistress, Mme Denis.

around the Gorges de l'Areuse, where, the Count noted 'We had to leap from rock to rock like goats.' After dinner at the inn, Rousseau took him on another alarming climb to the top of the precipice of La Clusette. Apparently Thérèse talked too much for Zinzendorf's pleasure, but his curiosity about Rousseau was amply satisfied afterward in the parsonage at Môtiers, where Montmollin entertained him with stories about his illustrious parishioner.

An invitation that gave unmixed pleasure reached Rousseau at about this time. A Corsican officer, Captain Buttafoco, asked[78] Rousseau to draft a constitution for his people, who had for some time enjoyed de facto independence from their nominal sovereigns in the Republic of Genoa but had yet to set up a state of their own. In *The Social Contract*[79] Rousseau had expressed the hope that 'some wise man will teach those brave people how to conserve their liberty,' and Buttafoco claimed the authority of Pasquale Paoli, the 'General of the Corsican Nation', in suggesting that Rousseau himself should be that wise man.*

Rousseau was thrilled. 'The very idea,' he assured[81] Buttafoco, 'lifts my soul and transports me.' He had doubts about his capacity to undertake the commission, but 'if it is beyond my powers,' he said, 'it is not beyond my zeal.' Buttafoco brushed aside all difficulties and promised[82] to send Rousseau whatever material concerning the history and laws of Corsica he would need in drawing up the constitution. Rousseau made no secret of the commission, and spoke proudly about it in letters and conversation, although he was annoyed when the *Gazette de Berne* announced that he had been asked to go to Corsica as its governor, for that, he felt, only made him look ridiculous.

His suggestion to Mme Alissan that she accept his friendship instead of his letters was not well received. 'My dear Jean-Jacques,' she protested,[83] 'No one will love you, my adorable friend, as I do . . . Of course I want letters, for the precious friendship you offer me can have no other expression.'

Seeing there was no way to cool her ardour, Rousseau decided to make good use of it by asking her to do him a favour in connection with his portrait, evidently unembarrassed by his bad behaviour in the matter of her portrait. Rousseau had decided to accept from La Tour the second copy† the artist had made of the celebrated 1753 portrait and promised[84] him, in thanking him for it, that 'It will never leave me, that admirable portrait which somehow makes the original worthy of respect.' He was impatient to have it

*In fact, Buttafoco had no such authority. He was already in the service of the French, who wished to end the sovereignty of Genoa over Corsica only to impose (as in the event they did) their own.[80]

†The original remained in the possession of Mme de Luxembourg. In a letter to Rey Rousseau declared that La Tour was the only artist who had painted a true likeness of him.

at Môtiers, and, knowing that Marianne's friend Henri Bréguet, a merchant in the Val de Travers, was returning from Paris to Switzerland, Rousseau asked[85] her to ask Bréguet to bring the portrait with him. Mme Alissan promptly agreed[86] to do this but was bitterly disappointed when the portrait passed through her hands so securely wrapped up and sealed that she had to hand it to Bréguet's coachman unseen.*

Silence on the part of Mme de Verdelin, who was too taken up with family problems in Paris to attend to her correspondence, caused Rousseau some anxiety, for he was genuinely fond of her, and in November he took the unusual step of writing[88] to one of her friends, Vicomtesse d'Aubeterre, for news of her. Mme de Verdelin herself replied,[89] explaining her difficulties as a widow in bringing up her daughters and the trouble she was having with the workers in preparing their new home. She added that she was planning to take the afflicted daughter once more to Bourbonne for the hydropathic treatment. Rousseau suggested[90] that nature would afford a more effective cure, but he urged her to take the girl to Bourbonne all the same since the trip would facilitate a visit to Môtiers: 'if the treatment is useless for her, it is extremely necessary for me.'

Things continued to go well for Rousseau in the later months of 1764. He was especially pleased to receive from a bookseller in Neuchâtel, Samuel Fauche, an offer to publish the *Complete Works* on which he set such store.[91] Fauche even offered to have the printing done in Môtiers so that Rousseau could supervise it. Since Rousseau attached great importance to accuracy in printing—and had indeed been tormenting Rey and others for several weeks with corrections and errata for the *Letters from the Mountain*—the prospect of having the *Complete Works* set up in Môtiers made the offer particularly attractive to him. The only doubt he had was whether Fauche commanded the financial resources to make the project a success.

Rousseau calculated that his *Complete Works*, brought out in an octavo edition of six volumes and a duodecimo edition of fifteen volumes, should yield a profit of one hundred thousand francs, of which the author's share would be one quarter. Such, at any rate, he reckoned if the books were published in Amsterdam or Paris. But could the same profit be made in Neuchâtel? He decided to consult Du Peyrou on the subject. Informing him of Fauche's offer, Rousseau explained[92] his desire to see his life's works published in a form that would be 'a masterpiece of typography' and also provide an income for the rest of his days.

Du Peyrou responded by offering personally to sponsor the project. He had already tried without success to help Rousseau materially. He had taken Rousseau on a botanising expedition in the autumn to Cressier between the

---

*'Wrapped up! But wrapped up—as by the hands of Jealousy! Ah my friend, this is terrible.'[87]

lakes of Neuchâtel and Bienne in the hope of persuading the philosopher to move to a little house he owned near his estate at Bellevue;[93] but this offer bore too much the appearance of patronage to be accepted. Du Peyrou's proposal to invest in the *Complete Works* did not meet the same resistance. The advice he gave[94] Rousseau was to demand of Fauche the authority to choose the paper, the typeface, the ornaments, and the illustrations, the opening of a subscription list before publication, and certain guarantees concerning the resources at Fauche's disposal. For his part, Du Peyrou offered to finance the author's fee in the form, if he so desired, of an annuity.

This offer Rousseau accepted[95] with alacrity and gratitude, at the same time asking Du Peyrou, as a man of business, to deal on his behalf with Fauche and his associates: 'The service you offer me is the greatest I could possibly receive in my present circumstances.' Rousseau had enough confidence in the successful outcome to invite[96] Alexandre Deleyre to write a preface for the *Complete Works*. 'I am in no state to write one myself,' he explained. He also renewed[97] his invitation to Watelet to take charge of the illustrations, and secured his consent.[98] He did not doubt that with Du Peyrou's enormous fortune behind it, the project would succeed. In his excitement he even allowed Du Peyrou to contemplate further acts of homage. When his friend suggested[99] adding a monument to the author of *Émile* to the Egyptian temple he was erecting as a feature of his splendid new house in the city of Neuchâtel, Rousseau declared[100] that the idea had moved him to tears: 'I have your friendship now; believe that I am not unworthy of it.'

Rousseau's heart seems to have warmed toward others. Hearing that Rey had dispatched a consignment of the *Letters from the Mountain* to Paris, Rousseau sent[101] Duchesne the names of those who should receive presentation copies. The list gives us an indication of the people in Paris he regarded then as friends. The women are the Maréchale de Luxembourg, the Comtesse de Boufflers, the Marquise de Verdelin, the Marquise de Créqui,* Mme Alissan, and Mme de Chenonceaux. The men are Watelet, Duclos, d'Alembert, Panckoucke,† Lenieps, the painter La Tour, Coindet, Lorenzi, and Rougemont.‡

The copy destined for d'Alembert may be seen as a peace offering. Rousseau had said à propos of him in writing[103] to Watelet: 'M. d'Alembert has sent me greetings several times, and I am sensible of that kindness on his part. I have wronged him, and I reproach myself. I fear I have been unfair to him, but I have to say that my unparalleled and innumerable woes and the

---

*Mme de Créqui went in person to the publisher's office to thank them for the book, but her correspondence with Rousseau seems to have lapsed.

†Charles-Joseph Panckoucke, who never gave up hope of becoming Rousseau's publisher,[102] sent him books and literary gossip from time to time.

‡M. de Rougemont, a banker from Neuchâtel established in Paris, provided a channel for transferring money to Rousseau in Môtiers, on the rare occasion when the service was needed.

atrocities I have endured have made me suspicious and ready to believe the worst of people. But I am not afraid to confess my errors and to correct my faults.' To the stalwart Duclos, he exclaimed:[104] 'How can you be such a decent man and not get yourself hanged?'

One visitor who disarmed all suspicion, who conquered Rousseau completely with a mixture of impudence and charm, was James Boswell, yet another young man—for Boswell was then only twenty-four—who arrived at Môtiers in search of an interview. He travelled on horseback, took a room at the inn, cast an experienced eye over the female staff, but, wiser than Sauttersheim, concentrated on the serious business of getting to know the philosopher. He made several drafts of a letter to introduce himself. He had already sketched out one[105] beginning 'I am a Scot of ancient lineage,'[106] then scrapped it in favour of one beginning 'I am a Scottish laird of ancient lineage.' Never one to sell himself short,* Boswell opted for blatant self-advertisement: 'I introduce myself, Monsieur, as a man of singular merit . . . Believe me, you will be pleased to have met me . . . although I am only a young man, I have had an experience of life that will amaze you . . . I find myself in a serious and delicate situation, in which I need your advice . . . So open your door to one who dares to tell you that he deserves to enter it.'

The stratagem worked. A note[108] came back the same day: 'I am ill, suffering, in no state to receive visits. However I cannot refuse that of Monsieur Boswell, provided that out of consideration for my condition, he makes the visit short.'

In his journal[109] Boswell describes how he put on his finest clothes—coat and waistcoat in scarlet with gold lace, buckskin breeches and boots, under a greatcoat of green camlet lined with fox fur—and went nervously to Rousseau's door, where he found Thérèse waiting for him: 'She was a little, lively, neat French girl and did not increase my fear.' She took him up to the kitchen, where the 'wild philosopher' eventually appeared, 'a genteel black man in the dress of an Armenian'. They talked together standing or walking around in Rousseau's bedroom. Afterward Boswell recorded, in imperfect but adequate French, their conversations. He noted telling Rousseau he had a card of recommendation from Lord Keith, and having to admit, when Rousseau asked to see it, that he had lost it. On this first visit they talked only of general topics. Rousseau spoke warmly of Lord Keith and King Frederick, criticized the clergy, attacked the French, praised the Scots, and told Boswell about the invitations to prepare a constitution for Corsica.† Despite

---

*Fortunately, he did not style himself on this occasion, as he did elsewhere, 'Baron Boswell d'Auchinleck'.[107]

†Boswell offered to be Rousseau's ambassador to Corsica, but although Rousseau brushed the idea aside as a joke, it was the beginning of Boswell's intense interest in the subject and led to his eventful visit to the island in 1765.[110]

the fact that, according to his own account, Boswell kept grasping his host's hand and thumping him on the shoulder, he was asked to come again.

Boswell had obviously made a good impression on Rousseau, and he turned his attention next to Thérèse, partly to facilitate his access to Rousseau, partly because he did not find her unattractive, notwithstanding the fact that she was rather plain and at forty-two old enough to be his mother. Meeting her in the street, he made her promise to let him know when Rousseau could receive him again. He did not have to wait long. On the second occasion, he found Rousseau in a more cheerful mood. They talked much about the Abbé de St-Pierre, whose writings on peace Rousseau had edited for publication. Rousseau described the abbé as a man of high political ideals who was altogether open about his several mistresses and natural children. He then said to Boswell, 'If you become a Member of Parliament, you must try to be like the Abbé de St-Pierre.'

The talk about the abbé's sex life emboldened Boswell to bring up the subject of his own, to unburden himself of the feelings of guilt that ruined, in a Calvinist born and bred, the pleasures of the alcove, without hindering the search for more. When Boswell told Rousseau he had converted to Catholicism and was planning to enter a monastery in France, Rousseau exclaimed: 'What folly!' And when Boswell asked Rousseau if he was a Christian, Rousseau said: 'I pride myself on being one,' and then named, without further comment, the three persons of the Trinity. Boswell told Rousseau he had a melancholy nature and asked Rousseau if his nature was the same. Rousseau declared that his nature was serene, and that melancholy feelings had come only with persecution. When Boswell told him, 'I cannot be happy. I have done too many wrongs,' Rousseau urged him to begin his life anew: 'God is good, because he is just. Do good. You will wipe away all the wrongs.' When Boswell asked Rousseau if he would take charge of him as his director of conscience, Rousseau protested: 'I cannot . . . I am in pain . . . I need a chamber pot every minute,' but he promised to see Boswell again.

Boswell then went away to write a memorandum about himself which he gave to Thérèse to give Rousseau. He explained the problem he had mentioned in his first letter, the 'serious and delicate situation.' This concerned an affair he had been having with a married woman* in Scotland, the wife of one good friend and the daughter of another. What should he do about it? Rousseau advised him to end the affair: 'You should say to your mistress, "Madam, all this is against my conscience, and it cannot go on." She will applaud you; if not, she is contemptible.' Boswell then asked: 'Suppose she threatens to tell her husband if I break it off?' Rousseau replied: 'First, she will not. Secondly, you must not do wrong for the sake of good.'

*She was Jane, daughter of Lord Kames, and wife of Patrick Heron, who eventually divorced her, citing a co-respondent other than Boswell.

Boswell confessed that he would like to have thirty wives; 'and why not, as they do in the Orient?' Rousseau replied that wives in the Orient were slaves. When Boswell pointed out that the Old Testament permitted polygamy, Rousseau reminded him that he was a citizen, and should obey the laws of his own state. Boswell then asked if he could allow himself to seduce a married woman in France or Italy, where adultery was tolerated in polite society. Rousseau exclaimed: 'They are corpses. Do you want to be a corpse?'

In his journal Boswell notes that Thérèse left the room when he brought up the subject of women, and that Rousseau reproached him, saying, 'Look, you have driven Mademoiselle away.' But evidently Rousseau spoke good-humouredly because Thérèse returned, and Rousseau invited Boswell to come back the next day for dinner, 'provided you are not greedy'.

Boswell arrived early, and, as he puts it, 'pretended to help Mlle Levasseur make the soup', which probably means he had started to flirt with her.★ He continues (in English):

We dined in the kitchen, which was neat and cheerful. There was something singularly agreeable in the scene. Here was Rousseau in all his simplicity in his Armenian dress . . . His long coat and nightcap made him look easy and well. Our dinner was as follows: (1) A dish of excellent soup. (2) A bouilli of beef and veal. (3) Cabbage, turnip and carrot. (4) Cold pork. (5) Pickled trout which he jokingly called tongue. (6) Some little dish which I forget. The dessert consisted of stoned pears and chestnuts. We had red and white wine. It was a simple good repast. We were quite at our ease.

This meal is similar to that recorded by d'Escherny, except that whereas d'Escherny says that Thérèse was never allowed to sit at the table with guests, Boswell notes that she ate with them. He would probably have made a great fuss if she had not. He did not hesitate to stand up to Rousseau, nor did he moderate his attentions to Thérèse in Rousseau's presence. Before he left, he promised to write to her from Geneva and he asked what he might send her as a present. She said she would like a garnet necklace.

Rousseau and Boswell parted with moist eyes. Boswell said, 'You have shown me great kindness, but I deserve it.' Rousseau replied, 'Yes. You are a rogue, but a nice rogue. A rogue I like.' As Boswell was on his way to Italy,† Rousseau gave him a letter of introduction[111] to Alexandre Deleyre in Parma. In it he described Boswell as 'a young man with a troubled soul and black thoughts,' and he urged Deleyre to discuss moral subjects with him 'only in the most consoling and tender aspects' since his young friend was 'a

★He also made a point of going with Thérèse to distribute alms to poor people of the village.
†Rousseau advised him to spend his time there in studying the fine arts.

convalescent who will surely be killed by the least relapse.' These words suggest that Boswell may have unburdened his soul to Rousseau in more dramatic fashion that his journal discloses; but whatever he had done, he had won Rousseau's sympathy.

He had no less success with Thérèse. He bought the promised garnet necklace, and sent[112] it from Geneva as 'a modest token from a worthy Scot', adding 'I shall never forget your accomplishments. You weave. You cook. You sit at the table. You make jokes. You get up; you clear the table; the dishes are washed; all is tidy and Mlle Levasseur is with us again. Only a conjurer could perform such feats.' He begged her to write to him from time to time, as she had promised.

Writing on the same day[113] to Rousseau himself, Boswell expressed the hope that he would not mind 'if I write sometimes to Mlle Levasseur. I swear I have not formed a design to abduct your housekeeper.' Abduct? Rousseau could feel safe on that account. Boswell did not abduct, he seduced, and Thérèse was already a target.

Rousseau's friends in Geneva waited impatiently for the arrival of his *Letters from the Mountain*. Elaborate schemes were devised for smuggling the books into the city. They were wrapped in bundles of cloth, labelled as textiles, and addressed to the warehouse of Jacques Vieusseux's general import business. Rey, who was notoriously thick-headed in certain matters, almost ruined the enterprise by addressing the bundles to 'Messrs. Vieusseux, Booksellers.'

The first elections of the season in Geneva found the *Représentants* ready for action, and Deluc *père* was able to report to Rousseau on 20 November[114] that a success had been scored in the voting for state auditors. The Conseil Général★ had declined to confirm the list of candidates nominated by the Petit Conseil, accepting only one, Isaac-Robert Rilliet, who was believed to be less hostile than others toward reform. A new election was demanded for the place of second auditor, and on that vote the citizens returned Ami de Rougement, who had originally been rejected by the Petit Conseil. The post of auditor was not of great political significance, but the mere assertion of the Conseil Général's will against the magistrates' demands created an atmosphere of tension.

It was amid these ominous stirrings that the *Letters from the Mountain* arrived in Geneva like 'a firebrand in a powder magazine', a phrase used in a letter[115] from François d'Ivernois to Rousseau and often repeated. One or two magistrates proposed burning the book immediately, and Voltaire wrote impassioned letters urging them to do so. Posing as a champion of Chris-

---

★Voltaire called it 'the council of 1,600', for such was the number of its members, a minority in a population of nearly 5,000 adult males. The 'democratic' element in Geneva was only relatively democratic.

tianity, he pressed[116] his best friend on the Petit Conseil, François Tronchin, to ensure that the government acted against a 'seditious blasphemer' and put a stop 'to the audacity of a criminal' not simply by burning the book but by punishing the author 'with all the severity of the law'.

The majority of magistrates hesitated, however, less perhaps from the indecision of which Voltaire accused them than from fear of making matters worse by precipitate action. The Petit Conseil voted to refer the *Letters from the Mountain* to Robert Tronchin, the procurator-general. He refused to give advice, on the grounds that as the author of the *Letters from the Country* he was a party in the case. The subject was adjourned while the magistrates prepared to confront the citizens on the broader issue of the legislative powers of the general assembly and the forthcoming elections of syndics.

The *Letters from the Mountain* made Rousseau many new enemies as well as inflaming the animosity of those he already had, but it also won him back one old friend. Paul Moultou was so delighted by the book that he ended his proud silence and begged[117] to be re-admitted to Rousseau's favour. Such enthusiasm for the *Letters from the Mountain* is surprising in view of Moultou's known political sympathies; as a conservative, he might have been expected to react to the book as that other conservative David Hume did in saying,[118] 'I disapprove particularly of the seditious purpose.' By this time, however, it seems that Moultou had lost all his illusions about Geneva. He had given up preaching and taken the first step toward renouncing his holy orders. His feelings of alienation extended from the church to the state. Indeed, after the departure of Germaine de Vermenoux, he seems to have felt he had nothing to keep him in Geneva. He spoke of emigrating to Berlin or Paris, and he applied through the Duchesse d'Anville for a passport to go to France. She secured[119] one for him with the proviso 'that you do not preach Calvin or Rousseau'.★

Moultou's praise for the *Letters from the Mountain* was unrestrained: 'A century from now,' he predicted[120] to the author, 'your virile writings will break all the chains of Europe, and religion, being better understood, will no longer produce victims nor sanctify persecutors. So try to bear the outrages of your contemporaries, for in persecuting you they put the seal of truth on your writings.'

Rousseau received Moultou's appeal with pleasure, but also with a certain element of mistrust. 'It was very cruel,' he replied,[122] 'that each of us, equally eager to keep the friendship of the other, should have believed that he had lost it . . . Your silence broke my heart. If you come back sincerely you will restore my life to me. Unfortunately I observe in your letter more words of praise than words of feeling. I can praise you, too; I would give my blood for

★Mme d'Anville did not share Moultou's opinion of the *Letters from the Mountain*: 'Rousseau wants to overthow his own country,' she protested.[120]

your friendship.' He ended by urging Moultou to leave Geneva as well as the ministry: 'You were not made to live in that place.'

Rousseau wrote less scornfully of Geneva in letters to his friends among the *Représentants*, and indeed he continued to offer them advice on organising their activities. These efforts were rewarded in the Near Year elections for syndics. While Deluc *père* could not claim a complete victory for his party, he was able to report[123] to Rousseau that the most liberal of the candidates, Jean Jallabert, had topped the list with 781 votes. This result was the more gratifying to Rousseau since Jallabert, a noted scientist, had long been well disposed to him personally.[124] The second successful candidate, Leonard Buisson, won 688 votes, and there were 605 votes supporting a proposal for a new election. Voltaire's friend François Tronchin received only 386 votes.

The Petit Conseil was put on the defensive, and the magistrates decided to defend themselves by devising some cosmetic reforms to placate the *Représentants* and also by making sure that if the situation got out of hand, they could rely on the intervention of the French, as a mediating power, to fortify their authority. They continued to take no action against the *Letters from the Mountain*; the *Représentants* had asked for other things besides redress for Jean-Jacques Rousseau, and the magistrates hoped that if carefully handled that particular subject might be allowed to drop from the agenda.

Voltaire was less patient. He wanted to see Rousseau receive 'the very severe punishment that such a scoundrel deserves'.[125] It is difficult to understand why Voltaire should have hated Rousseau so much; perhaps Voltaire did not understand it himself, since he always denied acting against Rousseau in communicating with anyone who was well disposed toward Rousseau. 'He maintains that I persecute him,' Voltaire wrote[126] to d'Alembert, 'at a time when I am helping him and I am being persecuted myself.' He told[127] the same story to Mme de Luxembourg: 'I have defended M. Rousseau here, Madame, and yet he says that Monsieur Tronchin and I are his persecutors.' Voltaire also tried to persuade Moultou, who continued to visit him, that Rousseau was mistaken in thinking of him as an enemy.

Behind this false facade, Voltaire prepared his most vicious attack. Failing to put Rousseau on the scaffold, he put him in the pillory. In the guise and the crabbed literary style of Calvinist pastor, he wrote a short pamphlet against the *Letters from the Mountain* with the title *Le Sentiment des citoyens*[128] and had it published in Geneva. In it, Rousseau is condemned as a blasphemer against Christ and a hypocrite:

Is this writer a scholar who debates with scholars? No. He is the author of an opera and two unsuccessful plays. Is it a decent man driven by mistaken zeal to address indiscreet reproaches to virtuous men? Alas, we have to declare with sorrow and shame that it is a man who still bears the deadly marks of his debauchery and who in the costume of a mountebank drags with him from village to village and from mountain to mountain the wretched woman whose mother he killed and whose children he exposed at the gates of an orphanage . . . abjuring all natural feelings even as he strips himself of honour and religion. It is he who dares to give advice to our fellow citizens . . . It is he who speaks of the duties of society.

Here was a blow below the belt, and Rousseau took it badly. Not for one moment did he surmise that Voltaire was the author. Deceived by the style, he guessed that Jacob Vernes had written the pamphlet, and his suspicions against Vernes became so obsessive that he would not listen to any denials. From the day on which he received and read this pamphlet, 31 December 1765, Rousseau's capacity for clear judgment faltered. It was a wretched end to a year that had, on the whole, been a fairly happy one.

The *Letters from the Mountain* brought the author a few words of admiration, chiefly from the Genevese friends for whose benefit he had written it: the Delucs, François d'Ivernois, Vieusseux, Lenieps. It also brought praise from friends in the Bernese republic—Daniel Roguin, Prince Louis, and Julie von Bondeli, who actually declared[129] it to be 'the best of his books'—while the friends in Paris to whom he had sent presentation copies easily found polite things to say about it; Geneva was not a subject to stir passions among them. Mme de Chenonceaux was duly flattered to find in the book a statement[130] that *Émile* had been written 'at the request of a young and lovable mother, who understands philosophy and the human heart. With her looks she is an ornament to her sex; by her genius she is an exception.' Mme de Chenonceaux knew that she was that mother, and in writing[131] to thank Rousseau for the book she tried to live up to his characterisation of herself as a philosopher—so very different from the usual picture of her as a scatterbrain—and she ventured a few critical comments, the main thrust of which was that Rousseau used intemperate language. Polemical literature was clearly not to her taste. Rousseau was too fond of her to take offence at her criticisms, but he was disturbed by a report in her letter that his pamphlet had been attacked as seditious by the Abbé de Mably.

It was a report he refused to believe. One can understand why. The Abbé de Mably was a man of the Left; he is remembered as an early theorist of socialism, even communism, one who carried to extremes some of the more radical ideas he took from Rousseau.[132] He had been on friendly terms with Rousseau in his early days in Lyons and Paris.[133] Why should he have attacked the *Letters from the Mountain*? Rousseau wrote[134] to him to express disbelief that he had done so. But the abbé admitted it: 'I pity you in your misfortunes, as I would pity Socrates,' he wrote[135] to Rousseau, 'but allow me to say to you that Socrates did not seek as revenge against his judges to excite sedition in Athens.'

In the *Confessions*[136] Rousseau ascribes Mably's unfriendly attitude to an ambitious author's jealousy of Rousseau's greater literary fame. However, in the state of mind provoked by *Le Sentiment des citoyens*, Rousseau was unwilling to entertain even friendly criticisms of the *Letters from the Mountain*. Leonhard Usteri, for example, coupled[137] detailed praise for the theological sections of the pamphlet with suggestions that the political arguments might be dangerous if employed by ill-intentioned revolutionaries. Rousseau was irritated by these remarks. He had considered Usteri to be his best friend in German Switzerland; he had entertained him and his bride at Môtiers when he had brought her there on their honeymoon the previous May; he had only recently★ congratulated him effusively on his election to a professorial chair; but after receiving this letter Rousseau never communicated with Usteri again.

One critic he handled more patiently. His village pastor, Montmollin, was naturally startled to receive the *Letters from the Mountain* after Rousseau had assured Montmollin that he was not writing any controversial material for publication. Moreover, the professor was shocked to find in its pages the most heterodox religious opinions of *Émile* reiterated, together with ungracious comments on the clergy of Geneva with whom his own Vénérable Classe of Neuchâtel was in fraternal union. He could be persuaded that the political disputes between the citizens and magistrates of Geneva were none of his concern, but he could not easily see how the author of this book could be a true believer in the Reformed religion. Nevertheless Rousseau continued for a time to charm his pastor. He spent many hours with him, listening attentively to his defence of revelation and miracles, and repeating as tactfully as he could his claim that belief in such things was not necessary for salvation.

When called upon by his imperious colleague in Geneva, Pastor Sarasin, to justify his tolerance of Rousseau, Montmollin explained[139] that while his 'heart had been sickened' by the *Letters from the Mountain*, he was obliged to acknowledge that the author had received his criticisms of the book in very good part, had showed him the utmost consideration and respect, and had always been most dutiful in performing religious duties, both in giving alms and in receiving the sacraments.

It was precisely this last exercise that Sarasin considered most offensive. He did not think that Rousseau should be admitted to communion, although it was only after several nagging letters that Sarasin asserted[140] bluntly to Montmollin his belief that 'a person who undermines the basis of religion cannot be left in peace in the bosom of the Church.'

★'There you are, my dear friend, Professor of Hebrew. I am overjoyed. I would still more happily see you Professor of Ethics: your teaching would be the more useful to mankind.'[138]

Montmollin did not enjoy being bullied by Sarasin, but he could not resist his arguments, especially as they came to be repeated by nearly all his fellow clergymen in Neuchâtel as soon as the *Letters from the Mountain* was read
in the principality. There was also the factor of the *Le Sentiment des citoyens*,
which, if seldom actually mentioned, contributed its share of poison to the
atmosphere. If Thérèse's homely appearance had hitherto warded off specu-
lation about the nature of her relationship with Rousseau, the allegations in
Voltaire's pamphlet led people to adopt different attitudes toward her,
whether of pity, disapproval, or contempt.

As for the allegations against himself, Rousseau could honestly dismiss
several of them as malicious lies, even allowing himself to hope that the
whole pamphlet was too grotesque to command belief. His first reaction was
to annotate[141] a copy with refutations of the main charges and send the copy
to Duchesne and Guy, asking them to reprint the pamphlet with his annotations. He then had second thoughts: He had to face the fact that the pamphlet was not entirely devoid of truth. While he could deny—as he did in
his annotations—that he had exposed his children at the gates of an orphanage, he could not honestly deny that he had them all handed over at the
office of an orphanage. This was the great secret of his life, which he had
confided[143] to Mme Francueil and which, through Mme d'Epinay, had
reached Théodore Tronchin, who circulated* the distorted version. Rousseau did not, however, choose at once to correct this distorted version with
a true account; he simply denied it categorically. Again, while it was false that
he had dragged a wretched girl from village to village and mountain to
mountain, he had undoubtedly exploited the devotion of an unpaid concu-
bine, nurse, and servant for many years without ever giving her the security
of marriage. He had not killed the girl's mother and he did not have a venereal disease, but neither was he guiltless. On reflection, he could not believe
that the publication of his denials as annotations to the pamphlet would re-
establish the purity of his public image. He would have to do something
more.

A fortnight after he had asked Duchesne and Guy to publish his response,
he wrote[145] to cancel his instructions, although he asked them to run off half
a dozen copies for his own use. By that time, however, they had already
printed a larger number of copies, one of which fell into the hands of Jacob
Vernes, who was understandably outraged to see himself named in print as
the author of *Le Sentiment des citoyens*. He sent[146] Rousseau a formal denial,
begging him to retract the accusations publicly. This Rousseau refused to
do. 'I must inform you,' he wrote[147] to his erstwhile friend, 'that I will not

---

*Dr Tronchin repeated the story to Voltaire and to others. James Boswell in his journal for 1 Jan-
uary 1765 reports Dr Tronchin's saying to him, 'When I found that [Rousseau] exposed his own infants, I did not wish to see him any more.'[144]

make the declaration you seem to hope and desire. I do not need to tell you why. Nobody in the world knows better than you. Since we can have no more to say to one another, please allow our correspondence to end here.'

Alexandre Du Peyrou encouraged[148] Rousseau's obstinacy by suggesting that anyone who wrote such an odious libel would be sure to deny it, although he regretted that Rousseau had named Vernes publicly: 'As an American,' he confessed, 'I would have preferred a more subtle vengeance.' Du Peyrou had by this time acquired such a measure of intimacy as to qualify as Rousseau's best friend, thus taking the place Moultou had once occupied and was never, despite his recent reconciliation, to regain.

In any case, Moultou's renewed devotion to Rousseau was less wholehearted than his letters to Rousseau suggest. Writing[149] to Jakob Meister before setting off with his sick and aged father to consult the noted physicians of Montpellier, Moultou expressed far more critical views about the *Letters from the Mountain* than he had expressed to the author: 'Why did he have to put so much ill-humour into a book dedicated to truth? And in dealing with religion, why was he not content simply to argue, without adding to the persuasiveness of his reasoning the mordant bitterness of an irony that can only support a charge of sophistry?' Moultou assured Meister that he admired Rousseau: 'I cherish his friendship; I count his esteem as an honour—but must I shed my blood for him?'

Du Peyrou took seriously his commission as Rousseau's literary agent in organising the financing and publication of Rousseau's *Complete Works*. He roped in François d'Ivernois, among other backers, and started looking for a publisher better than Fauche to produce Rousseau's books. He offered[150] Rousseau for the author's rights a lifetime annuity of one thousand six hundred francs together with a pension of four hundred francs for Thérèse on his death. This was rather less than Rousseau might have expected, since a 12 per cent annuity on his own estimate of an author's share of a quarter of profits of one hundred thousand francs would have produced three thousand francs a year. Rousseau, however, made no objection in his reply[151] to Du Peyrou's figures, saying only that his chief financial worry was for Thérèse's future welfare. He declared that as soon as Du Peyrou was formally established as his literary executor, his mind would be at rest. For once he did not speak of his impending death, but actually suggested that Du Peyrou and he might undertake a journey together the following summer.

Botany had become a bond of friendship between them. Even while shut up indoors for the winter, Rousseau continued to study. With the aid of a microscope, and watercolours he had ordered through François d'Ivernois, he made drawings and paintings of the wild flowers he had collected in the summer and autumn. The death in January of his instructor, Jean-Antoine d'Ivernois, did not interrupt the pursuit of his hobby, for his interest was aesthetic rather than scientific.★ Botany provided relaxation in a vegetable world that posed no threat to his tranquility.

The animal world, on the other hand, became increasingly menacing. While the *Sentiments des citoyens* did its harm by stealth, the *Letters from the Mountain* drew attacks that were open and official. Within a few weeks the book was banned and burned in turn by the governments at The Hague, Berne, and Paris. Rousseau made something of a joke of this in writing[153] to his 'daughter' Isabelle Guyenet, who was pregnant: 'They are burning my book everywhere. In this cold winter, people are being warmed by the flames. What bonfires burn in my honour throughout Europe!' He put on the same brave face in writing[154] to Lord Keith:

'You know, Milord, something of what is happening to me . . . but you do not know everything. Constant misfortunes and an almost universal hostility begin to overwhelm me completely. And yet while bad news multiplies daily . . . I am more at peace, even quite cheerful.' At the same time Rousseau admitted to Keith that he no longer felt safe in Môtiers and was thinking of seeking refuge in England or, better still, in Italy, 'where the climate and the Inquisition are both milder than in Switzerland.' Keith encouraged[155] neither project, preferring to pass on an invitation from King Frederick for Rousseau to come to Germany.

In his anxiety, Rousseau clung to friendships toward which in better times he had been rather nonchalant. He apologised[156] for the brevity of his letters to his 'beloved Marianne'. 'You have a very unfortunate friend,' he told Mme Alissan, 'but a very true one.' He explained that while he had to put on a show of strength in writing for publication, in writing to her 'I do not hide my weakness, and you will understand what that means.'

To Mme de Verdelin he reported[157] the burning of the *Letters from the Mountain* in Holland and Switzerland, saying 'since I am guilty of the unpardonable crime of being unjustly oppressed, I can only await the *coup de grâce.*' He said he could no longer believe he would be left in peace in Môtiers and began to feel his courage abandoning him. Even so, he continued to speak of her visiting him at Môtiers later in the year: 'The approach to our valley is awful, but staying here is not so bad as you perhaps might imagine.'

To Charles Duclos he revealed[158] his intention to answer the 'frightful libel' that had been published in Geneva with something more substantial than the annotations he had sent to Paris. He proposed to write the whole story of his life for publication after his death. He would not betray other people's secrets, but he would reveal all his own, 'not omitting a single one of my faults, not even my bad thoughts. I shall depict myself as I have been and as

★'Jean-Jacques was a collector, not a naturalist. Botany was an occupation for him, an amusement rather than a true activity. Again that activity was not an opening towards the world; he closed in on himself and drained his own inwardness.'[151]

I am. The bad usually hides the good, but I do not believe a single one of my readers will dare claim "I am a better man than he."'

Here, then, was an end to Rousseau's talk of retirement from authorship. He would write his autobiography, and in a rather different form from that suggested by Rey, not as reminiscences, but as confessions—and that purpose dictated at once the title he would give the book. Voltaire's libel can thus be seen as the stimulus that produced, at a time when Rousseau had written himself out as a philosopher, his greatest literary achievement.

For the first weeks of 1765, Rousseau derived some encouragement from events in Geneva. His liberal friends appeared to be doing well in their campaign, and he continued to advise them on their strategy. In letters to François d'Ivernois, he reminded[159] them of the importance of remaining united and acting peaceably; he warned[160] them against humiliating the Petit Conseil and against presenting their grievances in aggressive language, and he gave detailed suggestions[161] for the wording of their *représentation* on the subject of the *droit négatif*.

In early February, however, the Petit Conseil adopted a new policy. Nineteen of the twenty-five magistrates suddenly demanded a vote of confidence from the citizens, threatening if they did not receive one to resign en masse. To Rousseau's dismay, the citizens capitulated by a large majority. A numerous delegation went to the Hotel de Ville and made a slavish declaration of loyalty to the government. As Rousseau described[162] the situation to Lenieps:

Do you know the expedient the Petit Conseil has resorted to: It is one of the best of their tricks. To outwit the citizens, they complain more loudly than they do; and nineteen of the councillors, regarding themselves as dishonoured by my book and by the *Représentants* own reply to the *Letters from the Country*, threaten arrogantly to abdicate if the citizens do not go, with a rope around their necks, to beg for mercy. Can you not visualize our wretched burgesses on their knees, for they are too stupid to stand up and let the magistrates do what they threaten? It is Molière's George Dandin begging his wife to forgive him for objecting to her doing him the honour of making him a cuckold.

What made the pusillanimity of the Genevese the more nauseating to Rousseau was that they went on from their vote of confidence to accepting without demur a declaration[163] of the Petit Conseil condemning★ his *Letters from the Mountain* as a 'tissue of calumnies' and a 'false and unworthy attack on religion', because at the same time the declaration promised to concede 'any reasonable demands' that were made by the citizens 'whom the Petit Conseil always regards as its children'.

★Much to the continued irritation of Voltaire, the Petit Conseil still stopped short of actually burning the book.

It was all too clear to Rousseau that the citizens of Geneva had no further use for him. He had been of signal benefit to them as part of their campaign to restore the powers of their general assembly. His *Letters from the Mountain* had shaken the government out of its stubborn rigidity; but now that the citizens believed—however mistakenly—that there was a possibility of obtaining concessions, Rousseau's writings, and his name, were an embarrassment to their cause. Politics demanded that he be discarded.

Only Rousseau did not wait to be discarded; he withdrew. As he declared[164] to Lenieps: 'It is the end. Not only will I cease to meddle in the affairs of Geneva, I will not even listen to talk about them.' He expressed[165] the same resolve to the brothers Deluc: 'I have taken the only decision that remains to me, and I take it irrevocably. Since with all my pure intentions, all my love of justice and truth, I have done nothing but harm on this earth, I do not intend to do anything further. I shall retire within myself. I do not wish to hear any more about Geneva, or about what happens there. This is the end of our correspondence. I shall always keep you in my heart but I shall not write to you again.'

6

THE LAPIDATION

On 13 February 1765 the clergy of Neuchâtel, assembled in their Vénérable Classe, called on the government of the principality to suppress the *Letters from the Mountain* and forbid the projected publication of Rousseau's *Complete Works*. A few days later the Conseil d'État yielded to the extent of ordering, by a majority vote, the banning of the *Letters* and the suspension of the project for the *Complete Works*, pending a ruling from the King.[1] The municipal authorities of Neuchâtel went further and had the town crier proclaim, with the beating of his drum, that no book by Rousseau should henceforth be sold in the city.

Rousseau's reaction to these measures was mixed. He had already expressed[2] the intention of quitting Môtiers because of the harm done to Thérèse in the village by the pamphlet he attributed to Vernes: 'three years of irreproachable conduct has not been able to guarantee poor Mlle Levasseur from the effects of a libel coming from a country where neither of us has lived.' Now he yearned to leave the principality altogether. At the same time, he felt he ought to stay and fight for the rights that the King had conferred on him. His friends gave him conflicting advice. Lord Keith urged him to leave, believing that the King lacked the authority in Neuchâtel to ensure Rousseau's protection, however many royal orders were issued, and that Rousseau's only salvation lay in exile. Rousseau's supporters in Neuchâtel implored him to stay. Although Rousseau complained to Rey[3] that his enemies acted while his friends only talked, he listened to those friends rather than to Keith and settled down to do battle with the clergy. To a greater extent than he realised, Rousseau was being caught up in the *engrenage* of the politics of Neuchâtel, much as he had been in that of Geneva the year before. A faction in the principality wanted to use him for its own ends, to exploit the defence of his liberty as a means of advancing its own power.[4] It was a game with a different distribution of alliances from that played out in Geneva, where Rousseau was fielded by the bourgeois citizenry in a struggle against the government and the patrician élite; in Neuchâtel he was used by the King's officials and a significant section of the patrician élite in a struggle against the clergy and humble elements of the populace they called the rabble, or *canaille*.

The demand of the Vénérable Classe for action against Rousseau naturally called to mind the case of Petitpierre and the eternity of punishments in which the clergy had challenged the royal government and effectively won the battle. The supporters of secular authority were in no mood to allow the clergy a second victory in the case of Rousseau. This is not to say that Rousseau's champions were all committed royalists or that love of the sovereign in Berlin had become deeply ingrained in the hearts of his subjects in the half-century or so that Neuchâtel had been attached to the dynasty of Hohenzollern. As Prince of Neuchâtel the King of Prussia was a mere 'constitutional monarch', for in acceding to the title in 1707 Wilhelm I had agreed[5] to rule according to a Charter of Articles that, as Lord Keith discovered to his dismay, was held to include besides the known statutes 'unwritten laws' so indeterminate in their nature as to render the principality almost ungovernable.

The highest councillors of the principality, those on the Conseil d'État, were King's men to the extent that they were the King's nominees, but they all came from patrician families with political ambitions of their own. Those who held office in the state had their own obvious reasons for wishing to please the King, while others often veiled with protestations of loyalty a yearning for some other kind of régime: a principality under a French sovereign, an aristocratic republic on Bernese lines, or even a democratic republic like those of eastern Switzerland. While all such aspirations remained unsatisfied, the clergy had built up considerable political power for their Classe as an institution in the state and for themselves as leaders of the common people.

In such a situation, it is readily understandable that Rousseau's leading partisans should be of two kinds: the high officers of the state eager to prove themselves capable of enforcing the King's will and those members of the ruling élite most determined to thwart the ambitions of the clergy, that is, the free-thinking intellectuals. Monarchists and *philosophes*—the two sorts of men one would naturally think of as Voltairians—were thus, by the force of circumstance in Neuchâtel in 1765, Rousseau's backers in his struggle against the clergy, and his friends to the extent that he engaged in the struggle, if not friends in the sense that George Keith was a friend, solicitous only for Rousseau's welfare.

All the records[6] show that the high officers of the state were most assiduous in the defence of Rousseau's liberties. Whereas in Geneva the procurator-general Tronchin had led the prosecution, in Neuchâtel the procurator-general Meuron★ led the defence. In the Conseil d'État Meuron vigorously opposed all the clergy's demands for action against Rousseau, and when Rousseau thanked[7] him for his support of a 'pauvre opprimé', Meuron replied:[8] 'My way of thinking, Monsieur, conforms perfectly with my orders—which are as pleasing to me as they are noble—to provide for you all the security and support that depend on me and my office . . . I hate intolerance and persecution with all my heart, especially in those who ought to imitate the charity and goodness of their divine Master.'

Similar sentiments were expressed by several of Meuron's fellow magistrates. Charles-Guillaume d'Ivernois, the treasurer-general, voted with Meuron in the Conseil d'État against the resolution to ban the *Letters from the Mountain* and suspend the *Complete Works*, and he joined Meuron in sending to Potsdam a minority report defending Rousseau. In the Val de Travers, the intendant Martinet proved a stalwart champion of Rousseau, despite the fact that Rousseau had never wholly dissimulated his mistrust of him;[9] and in these efforts, Martinet had the eager collaboration of his lieutenant-civil, Guyenet.

Among the leaders of the anti-clerical faction who made Rousseau's cause their own, three were especially active. Jean-Frédéric Chaillet, a retired colonel who had not previously had much to do with Rousseau, was the most energetic. A politician noted for his tactless utterances, forced to resign from the Conseil d'État in 1763, Chaillet had conceived a bitter hatred of the Neuchâtel clergy because of their persecution of Pastor Petitpierre, who was his brother-in-law; and he saw in the defence of Rousseau an ideal opportunity to have his revenge.[10] He worked out the strategy of that defence in collaboration with that other retired colonel, Abraham de Pury, Rousseau's host at Monlési. Although de Pury had no part in the drama of Pastor Petitpierre, he had his own family grievance against the Vénérable Classe since it had dismissed his cousin Henry de Pury in 1727 for expressing doubts about the divinity of Scriptures. The third member of the *conseil de guerre* that directed the campaign against the clergy on behalf of Rousseau's rights was his friend Du Peyrou, a relative newcomer to Neuchâtel politics but as militant a free-thinker and freemason as the two colonels. In the spring of 1765 they moved the centre of their operations from the city of Neuchâtel to Môtiers, where Rousseau found himself confronted by a single chief adversary in the person of his parish pastor, Montmollin.

In the *Confessions*[11] Rousseau recalls how the professor, who had not previously expressed any disapproval of the *Letters from the Mountain*, 'came to see me towards Easter of 1765 and advised me not to take communion, as-

★Samuel Meuron (1703–1777) had succeeded Guillaume-Pierre d'Ivernois in this office less than twelve months previously.

suring me that he wanted nothing else of me and would leave me in peace.' Rousseau says he thought the request 'completely bizarre' and refused to accede to it: 'Montmollin went home displeased, giving me to understand that I should have reason to repent.'

This interview took place on Friday, 8 March. A letter[12] Rousseau wrote the day before to Du Peyrou shows that he was already in an angry mood: 'What do you say, Monsieur, about the stupidity of your clergy, who, considering their morals and their crass ignorance, ought to tremble at one even taking notice of their existence. You are the witness of my love of peace, but if they force me to take up arms again I shall do so, for I do not wish to be beaten into the ground . . . I hope not to have to seek vengeance, but if I do touch them, you can reckon them dead.'

Such fighting words were undoubtedly pleasing to Du Peyrou and the colonels, especially as Rousseau made it clear he would have no objection to their circulating the letter. The day after Montmollin's visit, Rousseau wrote[13] to Meuron, giving a fuller account of the episode than he does in the *Confessions*. He reported that Montmollin had warned him that excommunication by the Vénérable Classe was inevitable and urged him to abstain from Easter communion in order to avoid a scandal. Rousseau added that he had rejected this proposal and had offered instead to give an undertaking to publish nothing further on the subject of religion: 'M. de Montmollin protested that he was not master of the situation, and feared that the Classe had already made up its mind . . . On leaving he said he would do what he could. I said he should do what he liked, and so we parted.'

On the same day[14] Rousseau sent a copy of this letter to Moultou, expressing alarm at the developments: 'By subterranean manoeuvres unknown to me, the clergy, with Montmollin at their head, have suddenly unleashed their aggression against me, and with such violence that in spite of Lord Keith and the King himself I shall be chased from here without knowing where on earth to find a refuge.'

His fighting words notwithstanding, Rousseau still hoped to placate Montmollin, and shortly after the professor's departure Rousseau sent Montmollin the written declaration[15] he had suggested.

In deference to Monsieur le Professeur de Montmollin my Pastor, and from respect to the Vénérable Classe, I offer, if it is accepted, to undertake by a written declaration signed by my hand to refrain from publishing in my lifetime any new work on any matter touching religion, or to treat religion incidentally in any other new work I may publish on any other subject, and furthermore I undertake to continue to demonstrate by my sentiments and my conduct the value I attach to the happiness of being a member of the Church.

Meanwhile in Berlin Keith had failed to persuade the King's ministers to uphold Rousseau's rights by authorising the publication in Neuchâtel of his *Complete Works*, despite the lifting of the ban on the *Letters from the Mountain*, and he renewed[16] his advice to Rousseau to leave the principality as soon as possible: 'Go to Scotland or England and do not persist in living with those *enragés*. I take the liberty of offering you fifty louis in case you do not have the ready money for the journey.'

Keith also sought the help of the British *chargé d'affaires* in Potsdam, Alexander Burnett, in securing a refuge in Scotland for his friend, as we learn from a letter[17] written (in English) by Burnett to his father: 'The In-habitants of Neuchâtel, stirred up and excited by the Clergy, are persecuting the good innocent Jean Jacques Rousseau in such a cruel, barbarous and in-human manner that it is a shame to the Age we live in. Their minds are brought up to such a degree of Enthusiasm against him that his life is in the greatest danger; they talk of nothing but roasting, torturing him, and in short making an Auto-de-Fao of him.'

Rousseau's champions in Neuchâtel, however, refused to entertain such fears for his safety. 'I implore you *not* to follow the advice of Milord Keith,' wrote[18] Colonel Chaillet, sending a draft of a statement he thought Rousseau should submit to the Vénérable Classe. Colonel de Pury made the same appeal[19] to Rousseau to stay: 'At the time Milord Keith wrote to you, he was thinking only of your tranquillity . . . his character is well-known to be such that aversion for wrangling and trouble makes him throw in the towel without considering the longer-term consequences . . . If you emi-grate now you will give victory to the men of the Church and thus con-tribute to their insolence . . . and help undermine our liberty and happiness.' Du Peyrou had already made his plea:[20] 'Do not fulfil the hopes of the clergy by expatriating yourself.'

Rousseau's offer to give an undertaking to publish nothing further con-cerning religion failed to impress the Vénérable Classe, if only because in that offer he had promised to 'continue' in his dutiful ways when what they wanted was a retraction of his heresies. At its March assembly, the Classe re-solved that Rousseau should be summoned before the parish consistory of Môtiers to answer questions about his beliefs and be 'made to understand that he cannot be recognized as worthy of admission to the communion of the faithful while he fails to exhibit in every way the sentiments of a true Christian.'[21]

The menace of excommunication was explicit, and Rousseau could not fail to observe it. For Montmollin, the convocation of the consistory offered an escape from an embarrassing position; he could not on his own authority name Rousseau as a heretic without exposing himself to a reprimand for ad-mitting him to communion in the first place. In convoking a consistory, he could arrange for others to make the decision. Arrange it he did, by summoning lay elders he expected to be pliable and by bringing on to the bench a junior colleague he could count on, the deacon of the Val de Travers, Jean-Jacques Imer.

Du Peyrou accused[22] Montmollin of rigging the consistory, and Rousseau in the *Confessions*[23] accuses him of inviting the elders to drink wine at the parsonage and trying to persuade them 'with arguments drawn from his cellar.' On the other hand, Rousseau's champions were hardly less active in buttonholing the elders and pressing them to vote against their pastor.

The elders chosen to serve on the consistory were Jean-Henry Clerc, Abraham Jeanrenaud, and Daniel-François Jeanrenaud of Môtiers, together with Louis Barrelet, Abraham-Henry Bezencenet, and Abraham Favre from the neighbouring village of Boveresse, which formed part of Montmollin's parish. In calling these three elders from Boveresse on to his bench, the professor made an ill-judged move in view of the fact that he had also recruited Deacon Imer. The people of Boveresse disliked the deacon since he had persistently failed to provide Bible classes for their children as stipulated by the church authorities; thus Montmollin, with Imer at his side, could not count on the votes of the elders from Boveresse. Moreover, Rousseau's friends had been busy in both villages, suggesting to all the elders that according to law their consistory was a court of morals and not an inquisitorial tribunal entitled to examine a parishioner's beliefs. Since the intendant Martinet had the right to attend the consistory and could command the authority of a man of the law, he was well placed to keep this argument alive in the elders' minds. His plan was to save Rousseau from excommunication for heresy by a plea of *ultra vires*.

Rousseau was at first excited by the summons to the consistory. Writing[24] to Mme de Verdelin, he admitted that he had felt his courage failing in the week leading up to Montmollin's visit, but 'during the interview I recovered all the vigor I thought I had lost.' In the *Confessions*[25] he describes his reaction to the summons. Remembering how tongue-tied he had been in earlier public interrogations, he drafted a statement to read to the consistory:

I wrote the discourse, and began to memorize it. Thérèse laughed at me as she heard me muttering and repeating the same phrases over and over again as I tried to fix them in my head. I hoped at length that I had learned the words. I knew that the Intendant, as Officer of the Prince, would attend the consistory, and that notwithstanding the manoeuvres and the bottles of the Professor, most of the Elders were well-disposed towards me . . . I had reason, truth and justice in my favour . . . But when the time came to attend was almost at hand, my courage failed me totally. I absented myself, hastily stating my reasons and offering health as a pretext, and in truth, given the state I was in, my affliction would scarcely have allowed me to endure the whole proceedings.

Despite Rousseau's failure to attend the consistory, Montmollin was denied the success he hoped for. Only two* of the five elders voted with Montmollin on the resolution to decide whether Rousseau should be admitted to communion. Three elders voted with the intendant opposing that resolution on the grounds that a consistory had no powers to examine matters of faith. However, when the deacon used his vote to support the resolution, Montmollin astonished the company by declaring that there were now four votes against the resolution and four votes (including his own) in its favour, and that he would break the tie by using his chairman's casting vote in favour of the resolution. The intendant protested that the pastor had no right whatever to two votes and the deacon no right to a vote at all, and the consistory ended in disarray.[26]

The next day,[27] the three elders who had voted against Montmollin— Bezencenet, Barrelet, and Abraham Jeanrenaud—together with the absentee Favre—addressed a humble petition to the Conseil d'État, expressing their uneasiness 'at being required to deliberate on a case which exceeds our modest competence' and begging the Conseil d'État to rule on three questions: 'Should a consistory scrutinize men's belief and faith? Has the Pastor the right to two votes in his consistory and to reduce Elders to the status of "shadows"? Has a Deacon the right to attend sessions and vote?'[28]

This petition was submitted to the Conseil d'État by Martinet, and after a short discussion on 1 April the case of Rousseau was withdrawn from the jurisdiction of the consistory. The next day the Conseil d'État gave its rulings in response to two of the elders' questions: first, a consistory had authority only in matters of morals, not of belief; second, a pastor had no right to two votes in a consistory. The question of a deacon's rights was adjourned to a later meeting, on which occasion the Conseil d'État ruled that a deacon had a right to attend or vote in a consistory only as a deputy of an absent pastor.[29]

The outcome of these proceedings was thus a complete vindication of Rousseau's position and humiliating defeat for Montmollin. Rousseau showed his gratitude to Colonel de Pury by suggesting to Lord Keith that he should be made a Conseiller d'État. Since Keith had in the past mistrusted the colonel, knowing him to be one of those Neuchâtelois who objected to having a German as his prince, he was not predisposed to agree to this, but such was his affection for Rousseau that he did as he was asked, and Rousseau was able to boast in his *Confessions*[30] that 'while the populace was covering me with mud, I made a Conseiller d'État.'

---

*One of the elders known to be sympathetic to Rousseau, Abraham Favre, was absent.

1. Rousseau botanising

eighteenth-century engraving by an unknown artist

2. Yverdon (1765)
by Hershberger

3. Daniel Roguin
eighteenth-century engraving by an unknown artist

4. Thérèse Levasseur at Ermenonville
by Naudet

5. Mme Boy de La Tour
after Nonette

6. George Keith, Earl Marischal of Scotland
unknown artist

7. Louis François de Bourbon, Prince de Conti
unknown artist

8. David Hume
by Ramsay (1766)

9. Rousseau and Voltaire quarrelling
fanciful engraving by an unknown artist (c. 1760–70)

10. James Boswell
by Willison

11. Village of
Môtiers-Travers,
Neuchâtel
*eighteenth-century
engraving by an
unknown artist*

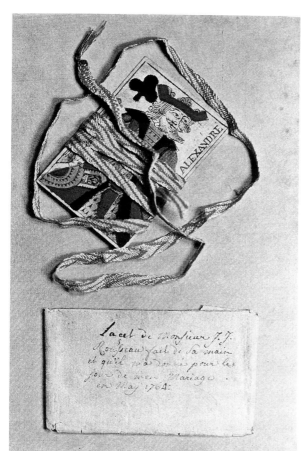

12. Ribbon and wedding message sent by Rousseau (1764)

13. P.-A. Du Peyrou
unknown artist

14. Rousseau stoned at Môtiers
unknown artist

15. Rousseau embarking with rabbits
late-eighteenth-century engraving by Monsiaux

16. Death mask of Rousseau
by Houdon (1778)

In fact, in the late spring and early summer of 1765, the populace had not yet started throwing mud at Rousseau. There was a lull in the conflict between his champions and the clergy, and Rousseau was allowed for a time to think of other matters and worry over other problems. One problem that troubled him sorely was the continued ill health of his beloved Isabelle. On her marriage to Guyenet she had moved from her father's fine new Louis XV mansion in Môtiers to the Old Priory, the lieutenant-civil's somewhat gloomy medieval residence near the parish church, and she was evidently none too happy there. In giving birth to her first child at the beginning of March she fell sick in mind and body. Rousseau thought at once of seeking the help of Dr Tissot, and knowing Prince Louis to be in contact with him, Rousseau implored[31] the Prince to ask 'that virtuous physician' to give an opinion on a memorandum about Isabelle's case that Rousseau proposed to send. A story[32] told in family history is that Rousseau crossed mountains on foot to bring Dr Tissot to Môtiers to attend to Isabelle, but Rousseau was far too poorly himself at the time to undertake any such journey. Moreover, Rousseau wrote again to Prince Louis on 11 March,[33] saying that his young friend was much better and that he would not, after all, be sending the memorandum for Dr Tissot. The Prince, however, had already approached the doctor, who had set off at once for Môtiers to attend to Isabelle in person, a kindness for which Rousseau wrote[34] 'on my knees' to thank him. A week later[35] Dr Tissot sent Rousseau his opinion of the case: the patient should leave Môtiers for a time 'not in search of better air but to distance herself from the objects which provoked her illness and the people who nursed her'. Rousseau himself expressed the belief, in writing[36] to Isabelle's cousin Marianne d'Ivernois, that Isabelle's trouble was sickness of the heart and that friendship itself would do little where medicine failed. Dr Tissot's advice was followed nonetheless, and Isabelle left Môtiers to stay with her cousin Marianne in Neuchâtel city, in which place she found the strength to write[37] to Dr Tissot to thank him for taking care of her: 'You came and I am cured.' She also wrote[38] to Rousseau, urging him to join her there 'before the city air loses its April salubrity.'

Fond as he was of Isabelle, Rousseau felt too unwell to contemplate any such visit. He may also have been deterred by the knowledge that Marianne's mother was a sister of Professor de Montmollin. When he thought of travelling it was of leaving Môtiers for good, without, however, knowing where to go. One by one the more pleasing prospects disappeared. From Les Charmettes, Conzié renewed[39] the offer of a farmhouse in the Duchy of Savoy but warned Rousseau that he would have to discard his Armenian costume if he went there and would also have to remain incognito. Prince Louis, through his contacts in Vienna, ascertained that Rousseau would not be afforded asylum in Austrian territories in Italy, and advised[40] him to 'turn your sights elsewhere.' Germany seemed to offer possibilities of asylum, but even there doubts existed. When Prince Louis informed Rousseau that two members of the Prussian royal family, Prince Henry and Crown Prince Frederick, were fervent admirers of his writings, Rousseau ventured to enquire[41] whether they would be willing to intervene with the King on his behalf, but the Crown Prince excused himself on the grounds that his name would do Rousseau more harm than good at Potsdam, and Prince Louis advised[42] Rousseau against using Prince Henry as an intermediary 'because of the jealousy which exists between him and the King'. Prince Louis suggested that Rousseau was more usefully served at Potsdam by the friendship of Lord Keith. Unfortunately, at Potsdam Lord Keith had found the King's ministers less sympathetic to Rousseau's predicament than was the King himself, and even if a refuge in Germany could be arranged, he did not believe Rousseau would be able to endure the climate. So Keith continued to press the idea of the British Isles as the right place of refuge, without being able to produce a concrete invitation.

In any case, Rousseau was under constant pressure from his friends at Monlési to stay in Môtiers, or at any rate in the principality, to continue the struggle against Montmollin and the Vénérable Classe. The stress under which he felt himself at this time is apparent from the sharp tone of his letters to several correspondents in Paris. When Marianne Alissan scolded[43] him gently for publishing controversial material that was bound to have unhappy consequences for him, he protested[44] bitterly that while he loved candour, he felt that a real friend, knowing 'the state I am in', would rather tell a consoling lie than a painful truth, and he ended his letter: 'Adieu, Madame.' Lenieps was dealt with no less harshly: their correspondence was broken off because of what Rousseau called[45] Lenieps's indiscretion in circulating to strangers letters he had written 'frankly in the bosom of our friendship'.

François d'Escherny chose this inauspicious season to try to bring about a reconciliation with Diderot. He informed[46] Rousseau that Diderot had written to him from Paris for news of his old friend's welfare: 'Dare I tell you that M. Diderot misses you? . . . Can you refuse to forget what is past?' Rousseau declined the olive branch. 'I do not understand,' he replied[47] to d'Escherny, 'why after seven years of silence, M. Diderot should suddenly ask anything of me. I ask nothing of him . . . I am far from wishing him ill and even farther from doing him ill or speaking ill of him. I know how to respect the rights of friendship until the end, even after the death of friendship. But I do not revive friendships. That is my most sacred rule.' D'Escherny was wise enough to let the matter drop* and busied himself henceforth in cementing his own friendship with Rousseau.

One friendship that grew noticeably warm at this period was between

*After Rousseau's death, Diderot wrote: 'I resisted all the repeated advances he made to be reconciled with me: the confidence was no longer there.'[48]

Rousseau and Mme de Verdelin. She continued[49] to urge him to seek refuge in England, although she was no more able than Lord Keith to offer him shelter there. What she was able to promise was a *laissez-passer* to see him through France on his way to England, and again she proposed—despite his earlier rebuffs—to subsidize his fare. His reply[50] to this was unusually gracious. He did not mention the fare but accepted the offer of the *laissez-passer* with a sigh: 'Ah, if only you could do more and *bring* it to me and then perhaps take me back with you . . . What a journey that would be, my beloved neighbour![†] How I should bless my misfortunes! Alas, such consolation is not for me.'

In the same letter, he asked Mme de Verdelin if she would take care of Thérèse in Paris if he decided to go to England. She responded[51] at once with a promise to find Thérèse an apartment in the convent where she now lived. Only Mme de Verdelin was far from well at the time; she had what she called a feverish colic, and her eldest daughter had developed an abscess on the knee as well as a deformity of the leg. In her next letter[52] she reported that she had called in no fewer than three celebrated consultants, the surgeons Jean-Nicolas Moreau and Pierre Dufouart and the physician Michel-Philippe Bouvart, to advise on her daughter's treatment. Rousseau's scorn for all medical practitioners was somewhat allayed when he learned that the only treatment they advised was taking the girl once more to the spa at Bourbonne; a harmless remedy, in his eyes, and one with the added advantage of enabling the mother to visit him that summer in Môtiers, if he was still there.

When Mme de Verdelin heard that the Conseil d'État was supporting Rousseau against the attempts of the clergy to excommunicate him, she withdrew[53] her plea to him to leave for England. She admitted she did not much care for the British people, not even for David Hume: 'He is the darling of all the pretty women here, which is probably why he is not mine.' By this time the thousand francs she had sent to pay for his fare to England reached Rousseau. He returned[54] it without the usual biting of the giver's hand: 'I am sending it back pending the moment when I may need it.'

Her daughter's health continued to cause Mme de Verdelin much anxiety, but the girl was strong enough by mid-May for her mother to be able to plan to take her to Bourbonne in the summer and to promise[55] Rousseau to visit him while the girl was receiving treatment.

But would he still be in Môtiers that summer? Even Rousseau's champions who begged him to remain in the principality did not expect him to stay in the village. Colonel Chaillet[56] suggested he should move to the neighbouring parish of Couvet, where Rousseau had been elected a burgess in January and where there was a sympathetic pastor in Simon Petitpierre,

---

[†]From the time they had been neighbours at Montmorency, Rousseau and Mme de Verdelin had addressed each other as 'Mon Voisin' and 'Ma Voisine'.

brother of that other victim of clerical intolerance, Ferdinand Petitpierre, and brother-in-law of Colonel Chaillet himself. Colonel de Pury proposed[57] part of a house at Le Chanet on the periphery of Neuchâtel city with access to a garden and a pretty orchard. Du Peyrou offered[58] something better still—an old house he was having restored at Cressier, which had the particular advantage of being in one of the two Catholic parishes in the principality and thus affording Rousseau shelter from the jurisdiction of the Vénérable Classe and Thérèse the possibility of attending mass.

Rousseau accepted[59] in principle the house at Cressier, on condition that Du Peyrou would let him pay rent for it, but as the building works there were far from complete, and as he did not wish to leave Môtiers in circumstances 'which would look like flight', he was unwilling to make an immediate move.

Another invitation he rejected was from Rodolphe de Vautravers, who offered Rousseau refuge on the handsome estate known as 'Rockhall' on the Lake of Bienne. The English name was part of Vautravers's display of his adoptive nationality as a British subject. By birth Bernese, the son of a tailor named Walltravers, he had changed the spelling of his name to that of the noble Vaudois family of de Vautravers before emigrating to England as a private tutor in a succession of aristocratic households. Like several other men who won Rousseau's friendship, Vautravers was something of a charlatan. He had somehow secured election to the Royal Society in London on the strength of an article about earthquakes,[60] and by selling antiques and antiquities to various noble and royal acquaintances in England, he had amassed a sizeable fortune. He had nevertheless a genuine enthusiasm for botany and the Alps that endeared him to Rousseau instantly. He also made liberal use of flattery, even in the direction of Thérèse, 'whose intelligence', he once declared[61] to Rousseau, 'shines in her eyes with fire and feeling'. When Rousseau spoke of disposing of the books he had accumulated at Môtiers, Vautravers promptly offered[62] to buy them, while expressing dismay that Rousseau should wish—or need—to sell them.

By the month of May Rousseau's health was so well restored that he set out on a series of mountain excursions and visits to friends. He went first to Neuchâtel city, where he put up at the inn La Couronne and at last met in person his most ardent Swiss fan, Julie von Bondeli. According to her testimony, Rousseau paid her two visits. She described[63] the first in a letter to Usteri, in which she confessed that she had allowed her feelings to overcome propriety to such an extent that she had 'kissed him at once in the face of heaven and earth'. At the same time, she admitted that she had not been greatly flattered by this first visit since she believed that it had been 'contrived by M. Du Peyrou'; the second visit pleased her more, since 'M. Rousseau had obviously made it of his own free will.' She told Usteri that

she had reproached Rousseau for cutting Usteri from his list of correspondents, and that he had defended himself by saying he had too much to think
about to write anything but absolutely necessary letters. Julie von Bondeli
told another friend[64] that Rousseau was 'making *Émiles* out of men aged 36
to 40, who had never walked two leagues in their lives', by 'having them run
like hares for hours through the countryside'.

Among the 'hares' was Du Peyrou, whose gout made him a reluctant run-
ner, and Erasme Ritter, his architect, who took Rousseau to see the house
that was being restored at Cressier. Rousseau assured[65] Du Peyrou that 'even
though it is too big for me, I want the whole house, equipped and furnished
and shuttered, with its little garden.' He liked the rustic situation of the place,
and while he was there he came across a flower that carried his mind back
to Les Charmettes and Mme de Warens—a periwinkle. From Cressier, they
walked on toward Bienne, where Rousseau was once again offered hospitality by Vautravers at Rockhall near Bienne. Bienne, he was reminded, was one
of the enclaves within Bernese borders that were subject to the Prince
Bishop of Basle, a sovereign notably more enlightened than those Excellencies of Berne who had banished Rousseau from their territories, so he might
expect to live there in safety. Rousseau took a liking to Rockhall and an even
greater liking to the little island of St-Pierre across the lake—but that was
subject to the government of Berne and therefore, Rousseau assumed, out
of bounds for more than a short visit.

From Rockhall, Rousseau returned on foot to Môtiers accompanied only
by his dog Sultan, who was run over by a carriage and badly hurt in the foot.
Rousseau was naturally distressed, but within a week he was able to report[66]
to Du Peyrou that Sultan's wound had been healed by the application of
thericca. Du Peyrou had in the meantime taken to his bed with a severe attack of gout, while still believing—or pretending to believe—that the exer-
tion of walking long distances with Rousseau was doing him good.

Rousseau, for his part, felt fitter than ever. 'The trip to Bienne was so ben-
eficial to body and soul that I am impatient to have more of the same treatment,' he declared[67] in writing to Du Peyrou. He had already told[68] Du
Peyrou that Môtiers had become 'uninhabitable', and that he was unwilling
to wait for the house at Cressier to be ready before leaving. He wanted a
temporary refuge and asked Du Peyrou to inspect Le Chanet, which had
been recommended by Colonel de Pury, near Neuchâtel city. In writing to
his Paris publishers, however, Rousseau said[69] he intended to spend the rest
of the summer at Môtiers.

The main subject of his correspondence with Duchesne and Guy at this
stage was his *Dictionary of Music*. The payment of the fee—an annuity of
three hundred francs—had been settled, and Rousseau was starting to receive
proofs of the text and the plates. As with all his publications, he was exces-

sively anxious to have it well and accurately printed, and the one consideration that made him hesitate to change his address was the fear that proofs sent him for correction might go astray.

Even so, a flood of visitors at Môtiers—among them a party of Englishmen including his translator, William Kenrick—increased his urge to escape. François d'Escherny at this stage proposed[70] to Rousseau a rustic retreat at Cornaux, a little hamlet on the way to Cressier, and warned him not to accept Le Chanet on the grounds that it was hot in summer and cold in winter and, in any case, 'a ruin'. At Cornaux, he promised Rousseau, he would find tranquillity and the society of simple agricultural folk.

Rousseau thanked[71] d'Escherny for the offer and promised to investigate it together with Du Peyrou as soon as that friend was well enough to make the trip. He added that he so much enjoyed wandering around the countryside looking for somewhere 'to pitch my camp' that he was in no hurry to reach a decision. While he was in the mood, Rousseau journeyed across the mountains to Yverdon, to visit both Daniel Roguin and his niece Mme Boy, who was far from well. On the way he stopped at Pierrenod to meet François d'Ivernois, who was hoping[72] that Rousseau—by way of return for his many kindnesses—would intervene with Lord Keith at Potsdam to secure him letters of nobility from the Prussian King just as he had secured the rank of Conseiller d'État for Colonel de Pury. On the same occasion François d'Ivernois reported that Voltaire was circulating in Geneva the story that Rousseau as a young man had been the ambassador's valet at Venice and not, as he claimed, the embassy secretary. After some discussion of this latest manifestation of Voltaire's petty malice, Rousseau decided to send the following note[73] to Ferney: 'If M. de Voltaire has asserted that instead of being the French Ambassador's secretary in Venice I was his valet, M. de Voltaire has lied without shame.' Voltaire did not answer this note, nor retract the accusation; he simply circulated it together with renewed allegations that Rousseau had been the ambassador's domestic servant.

After a few days at Yverdon, Rousseau returned to Môtiers on 9 June to face more trouble with the clergy. He had assumed that after the King had issued a rescript affirming his protection, and the Venerable Classe, following a further vote in the consistory in his favour, had decided to drop the case against him, the battle was ended. But it was not, for neither Montmollin nor Rousseau's partisans wished it to be ended. Already in April the professor started preaching sermons aimed at exciting the indignation of his parishioners against unbelievers in their midst, even against 'Anti-christ', although Montmollin afterward denied that he had Rousseau in mind in speaking of 'Anti-christ'. Despite the fact that Frederick issued on 22 May[74] a further rescript expressing his displeasure at sermons that disturbed the peace, Montmollin did not moderate his utterances from the pulpit. He was provoked to further activity by a pamphlet, published anonymously at the beginning of June, containing a full account of his dispute with Rousseau and the various documents on the case. It was entitled *Lettre à Monsieur . . . relative à Monsieur J.-J. Rousseau*. The author was Du Peyrou, who had originally asked Rousseau to write it, but had decided to write it himself when Rousseau explained that he felt constrained by his offer not to publish material on religious subjects. Even so Rousseau helped Du Peyrou collect the materials and suggested 'Goa' as its place of publication, since that city was fixed in the public mind as a centre of the Inquisition.

The *Lettre de Goa*, as it came to be known, is not an immoderate pamphlet. Its main charge against Montmollin is that he had acted illogically in having first admitted to communion the author of *Émile* and then denied communion to the author of the *Letters from the Mountain*. Montmollin was angered to see this charge reiterated. He did not know that Du Peyrou was the author of the *Lettre de Goa*, and, suspecting Rousseau himself, promptly sat down to write a reply.[75] In it he sought to rebut the charge of inconsistency by arguing that Rousseau himself had changed his position and that the *Letters from the Mountain* contained heretical opinions and offensive assertions (notably about the clergy of Geneva) that were absent from *Émile*. Montmollin claimed that he had himself, by contrast, been unchanging in charitable stance toward his parishioner. He repudiated the accusation of 'persecution'; his conduct, he protested, had always been that of a pastor animated by true Christian zeal and the love of order.

Montmollin was refused permission to have the pamphlet printed in Neuchâtel, on the grounds that it 'named certain personalities';[76] although he had no difficulty in finding a publisher in Yverdon, where it was printed in July as *Réfutation de la Lettre à Monsieur . . . relative à Monsieur J.J. Rousseau*, he resented the censor's rebuff, and his sermons became more belligerent than ever. Rousseau's friends at Monlési were equally inflamed, planning to use Montmollin's sermons as evidence against him.

Colonel Chaillet, on a visit to the city of Berne, had witnessed the hurried departure of a pastor who was known to be one of Rousseau's worst enemies—Elie Bertrand, chaplain to the French-speaking community. The circumstances governing Bertrand's removal are obscure, but Chaillet believed he had been effectively dismissed, and Rousseau believed that Chaillet had had some share in that dismissal. Whatever the truth, Chaillet returned to Môtiers with the idea of having the same fate inflicted on its pastor. Chaillet wrote[77] to Lord Keith, seeking Potsdam's support for the scheme: 'It would be very sweet to force the Professor to imitate his friend Bertrand.' Keith detested Montmollin as keenly as did Chaillet—indeed he invented for him the soubriquet 'Sacragorgon'—but it was beyond his powers to have any pastor removed from his benefice.

Besides, Montmollin was well able to defend himself. He belonged to one of the leading patrician families of the principality; two of his cousins* were members of the Conseil d'État, and he was related by marriage to several other legislators and state officials. His private school at Môtiers attracted the sons of distinguished Protestant families; and while it is true that his parish, as administrative centre of the region, was home to such hostile royal officers as the Martinets, d'Ivernois, and Guyenets, and that even worse enemies looked down on the village from the *jardin des philosophes* at Monlési, Professor de Montmollin had many friends and admirers throughout the Val de Travers and elsewhere.

Although Rousseau sometimes spoke as if Montmollin had no support beyond his uneducated parishioners, he took the professor's *Réfutation* of the *Lettre de Goa* seriously enough to write, in the form of a letter[78] to Du Peyrou, a rejoinder that, forgetting all promises, made or implied, to publish no more about religion, he expected Du Peyrou to print. This rejoinder, published as part of the *Seconde Lettre relative à Monsieur J.J. Rousseau*, is couched in Rousseau's sharpest polemical style. Recalling his first meeting with Montmollin, Rousseau describes him as 'a man of repellent aspect—I was surprised to see so much sweetness, humanity and virtue hidden by such grim physiognomy.' In those early days, Rousseau declares, the professor had shown such tolerance in matters of religious faith 'that I became worried sometimes on his behalf'. And indeed this tolerance, Rousseau continues, did attract the hostility of other clergymen, but 'instead of defending himself with the true Christian arms of truth, Monsieur de Montmollin chose the arms of his trade, and attacked me instead.'

Rousseau then goes on to recall how Montmollin had praised his *Letter to Archbishop Beaumont* when it was published, how he had at one stage wanted to invest in the project for his *Complete Works* to be published at Neuchâtel, how Montmollin had asked him to intervene at Potsdam for an augmentation of his prebend from the Crown; and how his attitude had changed when this favour was denied him. 'I always sought to show my gratitude to M. de Montmollin both privately and publicly, but he wanted to know all my business, meet all my correspondents, dictate my Will, govern my little household. This is what I could not bear. M. de Montmollin liked to sit for ages at the table, which for me is a real torture. He dined with me very seldom; I with him never. I have always resisted the intimacy he tried to force on me.'

Rousseau renewed the charge against the professor of stirring up the parishioners of Môtiers against Rousseau by his inflammatory sermons, although when he came to rewrite[79] the letter in his careful calligraphy for the

---

*Emer de Montmollin (1706–1774), intendant of Landeron, and George de Montmollin (1710–1786), mayor of Valangin.

attention of the printers, Rousseau deleted several undemocratic references to those villagers as *la canaille* and their womenfolk as *les caillettes*. It so happened that by the time the letter was published—in October—Rousseau ceased to have any motive for such tenderness toward their sensibilities. He had started to speak of them as 'wild beasts'.

He spent as little time as possible in Môtiers that summer. After the trip to Yverdon, he set out for La Ferrière to botanise with an instructor he hoped would take the place of the late Dr d'Ivernois—one Abraham Gagnebin. Rousseau travelled the twenty-odd miles to La Ferrière, as usual, on foot, and was accompanied, as he recalls[80] in the *Confessions*, by a French cavalry officer named Feins, 'who led his horse all the way by the bridle to adjust his pace to mine'. As soon as they arrived, however, Rousseau had to take to his bed with a feverish cold and did little botanising during the week he spent there. Besides, he was disappointed in Dr Gagnebin, who, as he reported[81] to Du Peyrou, taught him only that he had got the names wrong of the plants he believed he could identify: 'so I shall leave here more ignorant than when I arrived.'

After this ill-fated expedition, Rousseau set off once more to visit the Isle de St-Pierre on the lake of Bienne. Du Peyrou, still suffering from gout, did not accompany him this time, but Rousseau wrote[82] to him from there to tell him how much he liked the place and to report that he was employing his leisure hours to review the events of his life and 'prepare my confessions'—the first indication we have that he had started work on that *chef-d'oeuvre*.

Rousseau addressed this letter to 'My dear Host'—for such was the salutation he now proposed to use in letters to Du Peyrou after they had agreed to drop the formal 'Monsieur'; in return, he invited Du Peyrou to address him as 'My dear Citizen', despite the fact that he was no longer a citizen of Geneva and, as a naturalised subject of the Prince of Neuchâtel, was something less than a true citizen in the classical sense.

In a letter[83] to François d'Ivernois, Rousseau spoke of spending eight or ten delightful days on the Isle de St-Pierre, despite being surrounded by importunate visitors. 'I except from their number,' he added, 'M. de Graffenried,* Prefect of Nidau, who came to dine with me. He is a man full of wit and knowledge, titled and very rich, and yet in spite of all that, he strikes me as right-minded and sincere in saying what he thinks.' This estimable prefect belonged to the same noble Bernese family as the young lady with whom Rousseau, as a youth, had spent a memorable day picking cherries at Thônes.[84] He not only welcomed Rousseau to the territory of Berne, in which the island was situated, but assured him that he might safely reside

*Karl Emmanuel von Graffenried (1732–1780).

there if he chose. Rousseau, overestimating the extent of a prefect's authority, believed him.

In the summer of 1765, Rousseau's publisher in Paris, Nicolas-Bonaven-
ture Duchesne, died. The business, however, went on as usual, since it had
long been conducted by Duchesne's manager, Pierre Guy, and Guy continued to run it in the name of his widow, la Veuve Duchesne.[85] Guy was an
ex-artillery officer and, without being a chartered *libraire*, was as professional,
capable, and cunning as any Paris publisher. He profited from Rousseau's
work, and while paying the author decently for *Émile* and the *Dictionary of
Music*, Duchesne was far from giving Rousseau his due for other published
works—in several cases, not even letting Rousseau know what Duchesne
was doing with them. He started collecting Rousseau's letters[86] with a view
to publication, and he commissioned La Porte to put together a collection
of miscellaneous excerpts from Rousseau's writings to be published under
the title *Esprit, Maximes et Principes de M. Jean-Jacques Rousseau de Genève*. Nor
was this all. Progressively he added to the five volumes of the *Collected Works*
edited by La Porte books that had been banned in France. These Guy had
printed in Holland and shipped by devious channels, usually in bales dis-
guised as general merchandise, to a warehouse he maintained at St-
Denis, from which place they were smuggled in small packets into Paris.

Rey was well aware of all this. Indeed, after Guy had failed in May 1765[87]
to persuade the Amsterdam firm of Arkstée and Merkus to print pirate editions of *The Social Contract* and the *Letter to Archbishop Beaumont* for him, Guy
invited Rey to undertake the job, notwithstanding the fact that Rey was his
chief competitor as Rousseau's publisher. Moreover, Rey accepted without
hesitation.★ Since there was an enormous demand for Rousseau's forbidden
works in France—as many as thirteen pirated editions of *The Social Contract*
are now known to have appeared in the two years which followed
Rousseau's departure in 1762—the arrangement promised to be profitable.
Rey disappointed Guy by supplying books that were poorly printed, and relations between the two publishers deteriorated, although they continued to
do business together.

Unaware of these goings-on, Rousseau concentrated in his correspondence with Guy on ensuring that his *Dictionary of Music* was worthily
printed. In mid-August[89] he went so far as to promise to Guy that he would
forsake his search for a new home and stay on in Môtiers simply to correct
the proofs of the dictionary, although he made it clear that 'being here is
cruel in all sorts of ways.' At the same time Rousseau suggested to Guy that

★As Leigh remarks, 'the legitimate Dutch proprietor of two important works [agreed] to produce
a *contrefaçon* of them for a detested Paris rival, even though he was still carrying stocks of the
genuine article. Business is business.'[88]

he reprint Du Peyrou's *Lettre de Goa*, together with the letter Rousseau himself had written as a rejoinder to Montmollin's *Réfutation*.

Guy in his reply[90] said he would be glad to print anything Rousseau wished about the quarrels in Neuchâtel, and while he expressed gratitude for Rousseau's willingness to remain in Môtiers to correct the proofs of the dictionary, he begged him not to sacrifice his health or his tranquillity. Again he pressed Rousseau to allow him to offer a present to Thérèse, and, in his capacity as a bookseller, he sent Rousseau a further supply of works on botany. He did all he could to ingratiate himself with the exile, while shamelessly exploiting his work behind his back.

Guy's procedures were not entirely unpunished, for after he had sold some three thousand copies of his illegal imports of *The Social Contract* and the *Letter to Archbishop Beaumont*, his stocks at St-Denis were discovered by the police, and he was duly imprisoned in the Bastille for six months, although he was able to continue to run from there, with little change of policy, the business of La Veuve Duchesne.[91]

One request from Rousseau that Guy was unable to satisfy was for more engravings of the La Tour portrait, modified to show him in Armenian costume. Guy had to report[92] that 'there is hardly a passable copy left.'

It so happened that Rousseau was at just this time sitting for another portrait. He mentioned it in a letter to Du Peyrou:[93] 'The portrait is done and seems to be a rather good likeness, but the painter is not satisfied with it.' The 'painter', on this occasion, was a Milanese miniaturist named Ignazio Valaperta, who went on from Môtiers to Neuchâtel to visit Du Peyrou, probably with the aim of selling him the portrait. A letter[94] from Du Peyrou to Rousseau, however, mentions only a likeness *en crayon*, which shows that the portrait was not a painting, nor is any painting by Valaperta known to have survived. According to d'Escherny,[95] who claims to have introduced Valaperta to Rousseau, the artist gave him the original portrait 'of which he had already made several copies with the idea of selling in Italy.' D'Escherny further alleges—for what his word is worth—that Du Peyrou pilfered the original portrait from him and substituted the copy he had bought from Valaperta.

Another artist who wanted to paint Rousseau's portrait that summer was the celebrated Jean-Etienne Liotard. At first Rousseau welcomed the idea: 'Great talents demand consideration,' he declared[96] to Liotard's friend François d'Ivernois; 'He will not find me fit to be painted but he will be pleased by the reception I shall give him.' But when d'Ivernois informed[97] Rousseau that Liotard wanted to bring the English radical John Wilkes with him, Rousseau begged[98] d'Ivernois to ask Liotard to come alone and to postpone the visit until October.

Liotard himself wrote[99] to Rousseau to agree to this arrangement, expressing the hope that 'you will give me a few moments to capture your likeness' and offering to give Rousseau some instruction in drawing and painting if he would like to have it for his botanical studies. Unfortunately for Liotard, Rousseau was no longer in Môtiers by the month of October, and the visit did not take place. Liotard, however, seems to have made a pastel portrait of Rousseau without having the philosopher pose for him, and some years later Rey suggested to Rousseau that he might have it engraved for publication. It represented Rousseau in a very fanciful version of Armenian dress of the kind Liotard had doubtless seen in his years in the Orient,[100] and Rousseau disliked it: 'I am not at all of your opinion that my portrait made by M. Liotard is a perfect likeness,' he informed[101] Rey. 'It certainly will not be with my consent that you have it engraved. M. de La Tour is the only artist who has painted a good likeness of me.' For the rest of his life, no other portrait ever satisfied Rousseau.

Another visitor to Môtiers in August 1765 was Mme Boy, accompanied by her daughter Madelon. At the time of Rousseau's trip to Yverdon, Mme Boy had been unable to leave her sickroom, but Madelon informed Rousseau on 20 July[102] that her mother was now convalescent, and planned to visit Môtiers after spending a fortnight at Colombier with Colonel Chaillet and his family. The colonel himself promised[103] to bring Mme Boy to Môtiers after their stay with him. Rousseau urged[104] Mme Boy to take the utmost care of herself during her convalescence, and be 'guided by the admirable Madelon'. Evidently Mme Boy's health was good enough for her to spend the promised fortnight with the Chaillets and then to travel with the colonel and her two daughters to Môtiers, where she stayed for the last two weeks of August. While they were there, Rousseau invited the colonel to dine with him and play chess; and once again he discussed marriage plans with Madelon and her mother. Daniel Roguin was still eager to have the girl—now 18—married to his cousin Georges Roguin; but Rousseau helped Madelon persuade her uncle to allow her to marry a suitor of her choice, one Etienne Delessert. A letter[105] from Roguin to Rousseau, written in early September, when he speaks of Delessert as being reportedly a very handsome boy, indicates a willingness to yield to Rousseau's advice in the matter; and indeed Madelon was married to Delessert in October of the following year. It proved to be an altogether happier marriage than that of Rousseau's other protégée, Isabelle, to Frédéric Guyenet.

At the beginning of September, Mme de Verdelin paid her long-awaited visit to Môtiers. She made the uncomfortable journey from Pontarlier in one of the narrow carriages adapted to the roads through the Val de Travers, installed her daughter and servants at the local inn, and accepted for herself the spartan hospitality of the bed in Rousseau's *salon*. Here was a real testimony of friendship, for there cannot have been another marchioness who would cross mountains to stay with an unmarried man and his mistress in a three-room flat in a Swiss *chaumière*. Rousseau was decently grateful to her, and showed it. Only the timing was unfortunate.

Mme de Verdelin was there on the Sunday when Montmollin preached one of his more inflammatory sermons.[106] Taking as his text Proverbs 15, verse 8, the professor warned his congregation that the participation of the wicked in the worship of the church is an abomination to God. The simplest parishioner cannot have failed to understand that by the wicked their pastor was referring to the man he tried unsuccessfully to excommunicate. Meeting Rousseau in the street after church the villagers jeered at him, despite the fact that they saw him accompanied by a lady of obvious distinction. As he puts it in the *Confessions*,[107] 'although the presence of Mme de Verdelin was some check upon the insolent populace on our walks, she saw enough of their brutality to judge of what happened when I was alone.'

That same Sunday night, stones were thrown at Rousseau's windows, without on that occasion breaking them. Mme de Verdelin's maid found the stones on the gallery next morning. A plant was taken from the street and put against his front door with a stone on top in such a manner that if it had not been spotted from the window, it would have knocked down the first person who opened the door to go out. The next night, someone tried to force the door.

To Rousseau's admitted disappointment, Mme de Verdelin failed to comment on these events. Possibly she felt that politeness dictated silence, or simply assumed, in the manner of the Parisian *beau monde*, that mountain folk, being brutish, could only be expected to act brutishly. In any case, Rousseau says,[108] 'she seemed not to pay the least attention to what was happening to me.' Instead, she repeatedly urged him to accept David Hume's invitation to go to England.

The visit was a short one, but Rousseau found an opportunity to take his guest to the one *gentilhommière* in the village and introduce her to the d'Ivernois family. In a letter[109] she wrote immediately after her departure, Mme de Verdelin expressed her regret at not having been able to prolong her acquaintance with the former procurator-general, Guillaume-Pierre d'Ivernois. Ironically, this was the one member of the d'Ivernois family who was entirely on the side of Montmollin in the quarrel and, behind a mask of friendship, Rousseau's enemy.★

Mme de Verdelin and her daughters left Môtiers on Tuesday, 3 September,

---

★When Rousseau discovered Guillaume-Pierre's true attitude he came mistakenly to believe, and to assert in the *Confessions*, that both he and his son Charles-Guillaume d'Ivernois and their family 'joined the league of my persecutors'.[110] The son remained a friend of Rousseau as, even more ardently, did the daughter, Isabelle Guyenet.

to return to the spa at Bourbonne. Later in the day, while taking a walk in the direction of Fleurier, Rousseau was abused verbally by a group of farm workers and then threatened with a gun.

This was not the first time he had heard such threats. In the *Confessions*[111] he says that his Armenian costume made him a conspicuous target for a hostile populace: 'I was treated like a mad wolf as I walked in my caftan and fur hat amid the insults of the *canaille* and sometimes their stones. Sometimes as I passed their cottages I heard a cottager exclaim "Bring me my gun and I'll shoot him."'

On that Tuesday afternoon a gun was actually produced. Intendant Martinet took the matter seriously enough to hold a public enquiry two days later. He had already heard that Montmollin had decided to make a last desperate appeal for public sympathy by announcing from the pulpit next Sunday his resignation from the parish. Martinet wrote[112] to warn him against taking such a step, 'which can only increase the agitation and bitterness in certain minds and excite new disorders with regard to Monsieur Rousseau'. Martinet was anxious, above all, to calm things down. The enquiry he held that Thursday was plainly designed less to identify the guilty than to diffuse the hostility.[113] The findings were of a reassuring nature in that the workers who had raised a gun at Rousseau were proved to be not Môtisans at all, but strangers from the canton of Berne.

Calm, however, was by no means restored. The next day, Friday, 6 September, a fair was held at Môtiers. Much drinking and festivity took place in the village, and during the night Rousseau's house was attacked again—this time more dramatically. 'Rioting by the *canaille* has reached a point here,' Rousseau wrote[114] the next morning to Pierre Guy, 'that during the night the door of my house was forced, my windows broken and a stone as big as a head came close to landing on my bed . . . All this has reached a degree of violence that cannot go on.' In the *Confessions*[115] he gives a further account of the incident:

At midnight I heard a great noise in the gallery which runs along the back of the house. A shower of stones was thrown against the window and the door which opens on to the gallery and they fell on to it with so much force that my dog, who usually slept there and had started to bark, fell silent with fright and escaped to a corner, gnawing and scratching at the floorboards in an effort to escape. I got up at once and was going from my bedroom into the kitchen when a stone thrown by a powerful arm broke the window, crossed the kitchen, forced open the door of my bedroom and fell at the foot of my bed so that if I had been at the door a moment earlier I should have receive the full impact of the stone on my stomach. I judged that the noise had been made to attract me to the window and the stone thrown so as to hit me when I reached it. I ran into the kitchen where I found Thérèse, who had also risen, and was running towards me trembling. We placed ourselves against the wall away from the window to shelter from the stones and deliberated our next move, for going outside to seek help was a sure means of being knocked to the ground. Fortunately the servant of the old gentleman who lived under me was awakened by the noise and ran to call the Intendant whose house was next to mine. He jumped out of bed and throwing on his dressing gown came at once to me, accompanied by the guard who was making a round that night because of the fair and happened to arrive at that moment. The Intendant contemplated the damage with so much alarm that he turned pale and indicating the stones piled up on the gallery exclaimed 'My God. It's a quarry!' Downstairs the door of the courtyard had been forced, and it looked as if an attempt had been made to enter the house through the gallery.

Since Rousseau prefaces this account of the lapidation in the *Confessions* by saying[116] that he could 'not clearly recollect the circumstances of that very disagreeable period', several commentators have challenged its veracity. Contemporary records, however, confirm his later testimony.

The report Rousseau drew up on the morning[117] following the incident for the Conseil d'État varies in only one detail from that given in the *Confessions*. Instead of naming midnight as the hour of the attack, he says 'Having neither watch nor clock I asked my neighbour's servant, who had one, what time it was and she replied "Eleven o'clock".' On the same day Thérèse dictated a deposition,[118] stating that she had been awakened by the noise of the sawing of a plank and then heard a pane of glass smashed. Terrified, she was summoned by Rousseau, saw that a stone had been thrown through the kitchen window into his bedroom, and then ran to a window overlooking the neighbour's house and cried for help. Her statement mentions, as Rousseau's does not, that the guard, led by the Grand Sautier Clerc, arrived a moment before Martinet the intendant.

The Grand Sautier himself made a declaration[119] certifying that he had seen the broken windows, the stone behind the door of Rousseau's bedroom, and the pile of stones that had been thrown on the gallery. He added that he had been instructed by the intendant to remain at the house, with four guards, for the rest of the night.

The intendant took longer to prepare a full report,[120] adding to his own testimony the evidence he was able to collect into enquiries he held both publicly and *in camera*. This begins with an account of Professor de Montmollin's efforts to have Rousseau excommunicated; his failure to persuade the consistory to do so, and his subsequent inflammatory sermons, notably one on the first Sunday of September that was filled with remarks 'so violent and so pointed that one could not fail to see at whom they were directed'. Martinet then records the attack on Rousseau's house while Mme de Verdelin was visiting him, the insults and threats addressed to him while out walking, then the lapidation itself. He recalls how he was summoned and what he had seen. He describes the stone—weighing between three and four pounds—that had been thrown through the kitchen window with such force that it reached as far as Rousseau's bedroom, and speaks of the gallery's being filled with stones 'in a way to make one tremble'. He describes the 'inexpressible alarm' of Thérèse. Finally Martinet explains the steps he has taken to protect the house, trace the aggressors, and restore order in the village.

Despite the compelling evidence in support of the story told in the *Confessions*, a legend has developed according to which the whole drama was contrived by Thérèse in an effort to force Rousseau to leave a village she had come to hate. She is alleged to have herself broken the window, piled up the stones found on the gallery, and thrown the larger stone that penetrated Rousseau's bedroom.

The legend appears to have originated already at the time of Martinet's enquiry. A man named Clerc—not David-François Clerc, the Grand Sautier, or Jean Clerc the surgeon who sometimes went botanising with Rousseau, but Joseph Clerc, one of the two mayors of Môtiers—is reported at the intendant's secret enquiry on 13 September[121] to have suggested 'that it could well have been Mlle Levasseur who threw the stones, she having spoken a fortnight earlier about wanting to go away.'

A more important source of the legend was none other than Isabelle's father, who, as a friend of Montmollin, sent his own report[122] to Potsdam, seeking to refute the findings of the intendant. He stated that he had inspected Rousseau's house on 7 September and seen only a small, star-shaped hole in the kitchen window, and that he could find no stone that could have produced the effect. The stones in the gallery had every appearance of being put there, not thrown there. He had also noticed a plank near the door, not a heavy one, but a simple board that a child could easily lift. As for the sermons of the pastor, the former procurator-general declared that there was no seditious element in them and that it was ridiculous to pretend that those sermons had provoked the parishioners to riot. Furthermore, d'Ivernois *père* affirmed, as someone who had been living in Môtiers for some time, that he had never seen any local person show lack of respect toward Rousseau. The accusations against the people of the village, he argued, were prompted by panic and fear and had no foundation in truth.

Although d'Ivernois's testimony is contradicted by every other witness, the legend that 'Thérèse did it' was published by several Swiss authors[123] in the 1780s and often repeated thereafter. It is still taken seriously by writers sympathetic to Montmollin.[124]

One claim that cannot be sustained is that Rousseau was frightened away from Môtiers by the incident. In the letter[125] he wrote to Pierre Guy on the day after the lapidation, he spoke only of 'making a little journey tomorrow'. It was Martinet and the others who implored him to leave Môtiers immediately. As he puts it in the *Confessions*,[126] 'Colonel de Pury, the Procurator-General Meuron, the Lieutenant-civil Guyenet, the Treasurer d'Ivernois and his father—in a word all the dignitaries of the place—came to see me, united in their solicitude for me to yield to the storm and leave, at least for a time, a village where I could no longer live in safety.' He noticed that Martinet was the most insistent that he should go, and go at once. 'He was frightened,' Rousseau suggests, 'that the fury of the frantic people might extend to himself.'

It was agreed that Thérèse should stay to take care of Rousseau's possessions, and Martinet promised that the guard he had put on the house would remain as long as Thérèse did. Emissaries from the neighbouring village of Couvet came to offer Rousseau refuge as they had already offered him the status of a burgess, but Couvet was considered too near to be advisable. Rousseau was dispatched to Neuchâtel city and the welcoming arms of Du Peyrou. Martinet, failing to quell the disturbances even after Rousseau's departure, soon chose Couvet as a place of refuge for himself.

The city of Neuchâtel, however, had little to recommend it as a refuge for Rousseau. The Vénérable Classe was established there; the municipal council, having already voted to ban the sale of all his books, was ill disposed toward him. Du Peyrou, accepted only for his money, mistrusted as an immigrant, an 'American', a free-thinker, and freemason, and already facing litigation for defamation by Professor de Montmollin, was not well placed to protect his friend. Rousseau decided to spend only one night under his roof. He left Neuchâtel for a place with which he had fallen in love, the Isle de St-Pierre, and arrived there on Monday, 9 September, accompanied by Sultan, his dog.

The island has not greatly changed since Rousseau was there and as he described it both in his *Confessions*, on which he was already working, and in the *Reveries of the Solitary Walker*, which he wrote toward the end of his life. Set in the middle of Lake Bienne, the Isle de St-Pierre had once been the home of monks. It had in Rousseau's time—as now—only one house on it, but as Rousseau noted[127] the island provided all the necessities of life in fields, orchards, meadows, vineyards, woods and farmlands, all of which 'make it seem larger than it actually is'—some two miles in circumference.

In the *Reveries*[128] he speaks of Lake Bienne as being 'wilder and more romantic' than Lake Geneva—one of his rare uses of the word 'romantic' (*romantique*) so often associated with his name. He explains that nature there was less disturbed by the presence of towns and houses around the shores. Moreover, being some distance from main thoroughfares, Lake Bienne was 'little known to travellers and seldom visited'. Navigation on the lake was 'irregular and costly'.[129]

The Isle de St-Pierre—silent, remote, and beautiful—belonged to the Hospital of Berne, and the single dwelling on it was occupied by one of its officials, a custodian named Engel, whose acquaintance Rousseau had made on a previous visit. Engel offered him board and lodging on advantageous terms and installed him in a spacious room that can still be seen. Although it was a fortnight before Thérèse was able to join him and bring his baggage, Rousseau was well cared for by Engel's family and servants. 'By the grace of heaven,' Rousseau wrote[130] to Mme Boy, 'I am in peace and security on this island.'

He rejoiced in the isolation of his refuge. Not only was he pleased by the natural rustic beauty of the place, but he felt beyond the reach of his adversaries. To be separated from other people, as he puts it in the *Confessions*,[131] 'was to be better sheltered from their outrages, more forgotten by them—in a word, allowed to enjoy the sweetness of leisure and a contemplative life.' At that moment he decided that he would settle on the island for good. And why not? He calculated[132] that at last he had an income adequate to live on: he had accepted a pension of six hundred francs a year from Lord Keith, he had three hundred francs a year from Guy for the *Dictionary of Music*, and he had agreed with Du Peyrou to accept a further annuity in return for assigning editorial control after his death over all his published and unpublished work. With his financial problems thus settled, Rousseau adds,[133] 'I bade farewell to the world.'

In letters he wrote at the time, he shows no such expectation of settling down in his island refuge. Writing[134] to express his thanks to Mme de Verdelin for visiting him in Môtiers—'the memory of you effaces that of my disgrace and consoles me in an endless succession of adversities'—Rousseau said, 'I still do not know if I shall be allowed to inhabit this retreat.' In a letter[135] to Rey, in which he described how 'the Pastor of Môtiers, having failed to have me excommunicated, took the promptest and best means to have me assassinated,' Rousseau explained, 'I do not yet know where I shall settle . . . I am ill, overwhelmed with worries, and I need to breathe.'

Looking back later on the experience he depicted it in brighter colours. In the *Reveries*[136] he devotes a whole chapter—the Fifth Walk—to an evocation of the Isle de St-Pierre: 'Of all the places where I have lived . . . none has made me so truly happy.' He puts to himself the question: 'What was the nature of that happiness?' and he answers[137] 'idleness—that precious *far niente* and solitude.' However, it is clear, even from the account he gives in the *Reveries* and *Confessions* . . . that his 'idleness' was that of a very busy man and his 'solitude' that of a man who was seldom alone.

Botany, which he calls a 'lazy study', was his favourite occupation. He recalls in the *Reveries*[138] how he would set out every morning after breakfast, 'magnifying glass in my hand and my *Systema naturae*★ under my arm', to visit several areas of the island that he had carefully divided up on a map in order to study the vegetation of each in turn. Groping around on his belly, he would examine the various flowers and plants for two or three hours, and then 'go back laden with an ample harvest to amuse myself after dinner in my lodging if it rained'. His aim was no less than to make a complete record of all the plants on the island, a *Flora Petrinsularis*.

On some days he says he would go with Engel to visit the workers on the farm adjacent to the house and sometimes even lend a hand with the harvesting. In the *Confessions*[139] he recalls an occasion when his young Bernese friend Nicolas-Antoine Kirchberger came to visit him on the island and found him up a large tree, a sack tied to his belt, picking apples: 'I was not displeased by this encounter,' he adds. 'I hoped that the Bernese, seeing how I used my leisure, would not want to disturb my peace.'

The apples Rousseau picked were evidently given him by the custodian, because he sent a barrel of them to Du Peyrou's mother in Neuchâtel—'not as a present', he assured[140] his friend, 'but in exchange for the coffee sent to me'.

Rousseau kept in constant touch with Du Peyrou from his refuge. He arranged to have his friends correspond with him through Du Peyrou's address, marking letters destined for him with a cross, and he also found some means of having the French postmaster at Pontarlier forward his mail. Indeed he held out to Pierre Guy the hope that it might not be impossible for him to receive and return proofs from the island, as he explained in a letter[141] dated 1 October:

The little island where I am seems to me the right choice for my place of refuge. It is very pleasing. There are no clergy and no riotous brigands. The entire population consists of one household, which is composed of very decent people, very cheerful, very good company; and they supply all the necessities of life. The great difficulty is that the island and the house belong to the Noblemen of Berne, who are both proprietors and sovereigns, and you know that Their Excellencies forbade me three years ago to reside in their territories . . . It remains to be seen whether after chasing me from their country they will chase me from their house.

Rousseau had by this time been joined on the island by Thérèse. She arrived on Monday, 23 September, accompanied by a heavy load of boxes and trunks from Môtiers. In the *Reveries*[142] Rousseau says he left all this baggage

★The standard work by Carolus Linnaeus on the classification of plants.

packed 'and lived in what I hoped would be my settled home as at an inn
... Instead of books and papers, I filled my room with flowers and dried
plants.' When he had—reluctantly—to take up his pen to write, he says he
borrowed a table from the custodian.

In the *Reveries*[143] he also gives a lyrical account of idle afternoons spent
alone in a boat on the lake, describing how he would escape from the dinner table and row out to a place where he could ship the oars and simply
drift back and forth with currents—'sometimes for several hours, plunged
into a thousand confused and delightful reveries'. In the *Confessions*[144] he
suggests that he put these idle moments to more pious use, not only dream-
ing as the boat floated along but also praying—'lifting my soul to God, the
author of all the beauties around me'. The account he gives in the *Confessions* also suggests that the reveries were shorter: he mentions[145] there—as
he does not in the *Reveries*—that he had Sultan with him, and that as the dog
'did not enjoy lingering for a long time on the water as I did', he would take
him ashore for a walk 'on the smaller island'.

This second island on Lake Bienne, uninhabited and uncultivated, possessed a special charm for Rousseau; he even fancied building a hut for himself and living there like Robinson Crusoe.* He enjoyed exploring it alone
with his dog, but he also took Thérèse and others for walks there and tried
to persuade the custodian to make better use of it, not simply to strip it of
soil to replace that lost to erosion on the larger island. 'How the poor are always robbed to supply the needs of the rich,' he noted bitterly. He suggested
that a colony of rabbits be introduced to the smaller island, and although it
is not evident that Engel shared Rousseau's enthusiasm for the idea, he accepted the suggestion and imported a male and female rabbit from Neuchâtel to breed there.

Rousseau recalls[146] crossing the lake with Engel, together with his wife
and sister and Thérèse, to make a ceremonial installation of the rabbits: 'The
foundation of that little colony was a festive occasion. The pilot of the Arg-
onauts was no prouder than I, leading the company and the rabbits from the
larger island to the smaller.'

When the waters of the lake were calm, Rousseau liked to bathe; when
they were rough, he made a habit of sitting on the sandy bank of an evening
to watch the waves break at his feet. 'I saw in them,' he writes in the *Confessions*,[147] 'an image of the tumult of the world ending in the peace of my
habitation; and sometimes that sweet thought brought tears to my eyes.' In
the *Reveries*[148] he says that the rhythm of waves on the lake extinguished his
daydreams and 'made me find joy in the sense of my own existence without
even making the effort to think'.

*Readers will remember that *Robinson Crusoe* was the only book Émile was allowed to read: the
more Rousseau saw of the world, the more he envied the situation of Defoe's hero.

This last feeling, as Rousseau came to look back on it, was the closest he believed he ever got to happiness: 'not an imperfect happiness, poor and relative, such as one finds in the pleasures of life, but a sufficient happiness, perfect and full, which leaves in the soul no void it feels the need to fill. Such is the state in which I often★ found myself in my solitary reveries on the isle de St. Pierre.'[149]

Even on that island he found solitude only by escaping in his boat or hiding in a nook beside the shore. Despite his claim in the *Reveries*[150] that he had 'no company there except that of the custodian, his wife and his servants—very good souls but no more', all the evidence shows that he had a constant stream of visitors. Rousseau was on the island at the season of the harvests, when it was crowded with people of every description from Bienne and the neighbourhood. Others came from Berne. In the room he occupied at the custodian's house there can still be seen the trapdoor he used to evade the importunate. But he did not escape all his visitors, or even try to.

One visitor he took care to welcome was Friedrich Zehender, director of the Hospital of Berne, to which the island belonged. 'I grovelled to make myself agreeable to him,' Rousseau reported to Du Peyrou on 15 October.[151] 'I do not think I had much success, but fortunately my being here does not depend on him.' Rousseau still believed that the authorities in Berne would tolerate his presence, and he knew that the prefect Graffenried was well disposed. Indeed, in his confidence of remaining on the island, he asked Du Peyrou to send him supplies of paper for his *herbarium*, new razors ('not too fine for I have a very tough beard'), newspapers, and a present to give to his landlady, Mme Salomé Engel.

Rousseau's hopes were promptly dashed. On 16 October—the day after Zehender's visit—the prefect Graffenried informed[152] the philosopher that he had been instructed by their Excellencies of Berne to order Rousseau 'to quit the solitary refuge that you have chosen and the territories under their sovereignty.' Graffenried added, in a feeble effort to soften the blow, the suggestion that philosophy would console the refugee: '*l'univers entier est la Patrie de l'honnête homme.*'

Startled to receive this order, Rousseau wrote[153] back at once to enquire whether he was expected to leave immediately or could be granted some weeks' respite to make arrangements for his future. Autumn was nearly over, and he dreaded the prospect of travelling across Europe in winter.

'They are chasing me out of here, my dear host,' he wrote[154] on the same day—17 October—to Du Peyrou. 'The climate of Berlin is too harsh for me. I have resolved to go to England, where I ought to have gone in the first place.'

★In an earlier version of the *Reveries* Rousseau wrote 'quelquefois' (sometimes), before changing the word to 'souvent' (often).

Rousseau had heard by this time from Mme de Verdelin[155] that David Hume—then living in Paris as *chargé d'affaires* at the British Embassy—was able to promise him refuge in England, where his friend Horace Walpole had considerable estates in the country. Alternatively she reported[156] later, Hume could secure accommodation for Rousseau and Thérèse as boarders on a farm near London. Mme de Verdelin had by this time overcome her early suspicions of Hume—'he is the sweetest, the most sensible and the most cheerful of creatures.' She urged Rousseau not to linger in Switzerland until the weather worsened: 'Monsieur Hume wants you to leave at once.'

Her letters reached the Isle de St-Pierre at an opportune moment. Rousseau wrote to her on 18 October,[157] telling her of his expulsion and his decision to go to England, 'the only country where some liberty remains', and asking her to send to him the *laissez-passer* she had promised so that he could travel through France. He said the order to expel him had caused great indignation among the Bernese and had only been passed in the council because the majority of senators were absent attending to the harvest, and 'the few remaining were ruled by my enemies.'

In this belief Rousseau was sadly misinformed. The Conseil Secret of Berne had resolved unanimously to expel him, and the plenary council, attended by nineteen of the twenty-seven senators, confirmed the order without a dissenting vote.[158] Moreover, Graffenried's request that the expulsion be delayed to give Rousseau time to plan his departure was peremptorily refused. A further order dated Monday, 21 October,[159] stipulated that Rousseau be out of Bernese territory by the following Saturday.

Rousseau's bizarre response[160] to this order was to propose to their Excellencies of Berne that they imprison him on the island for the rest of his life. If they did so, he promised to write no more for publication; he would even consent to be forbidden the use of pen or paper and all communication with the outside world. He made several copies of this letter and encouraged its publication.* Predictably it made no impression on the authorities in Berne, and Rousseau was forced to leave.

In the meantime David Hume had been active on Rousseau's behalf. He had asked a distant relation, John Stewart, who had a house in Buckingham Street† near the Strand in London, to find a farmer outside the city who would provide board for Rousseau and his *gouvernante* for twenty or twenty-five pounds a year to be paid by Rousseau, plus a subsidy of twenty-five or thirty pounds to be paid without Rousseau's knowledge. Hume had been made well aware of Rousseau's fierce resistance to receiving charity. Stewart, a prosperous wine merchant and future MP, looked in vain for a suitable farm and ended up by offering Rousseau rooms in his own house near the Strand.

*It was published in the *Journal Encyclopédique* in December 1765.
†The house now known as 10 Buckingham Street.

While Rousseau was packing his bags to leave the Isle de St-Pierre, David Hume wrote[161]—this time in French—to assure him that a welcome would await him in England and that he would find there 'an absolute security against all persecution, not only from the tolerating spirit of our laws but from the respect that every one there bears to your character.' Hume also told Rousseau that the English publishers paid better fees to authors than did those of Paris, so he would 'have no difficulty to live frugally in that country on the fruits of your labour.' Hume expressed his regret at not being able to come to Switzerland to accompany Rousseau to London, but explained that his diplomatic duties prevented his doing so. He had, however, arranged for his friend Sir Gilbert Elliot to 'meet you on your arrival and conduct you to your retreat.'

One of Rousseau's chief worries as he prepared his departure concerned all the manuscripts, letters, and papers that Thérèse had brought from Môtiers and which he had still packed in cases and trunks. Seeing no prospect of bringing so much baggage to England, he decided to entrust the lot to Du Peyrou. One of his first moves on receiving the order to leave was to beg[162] his 'host' to come to the island to help him sort through his papers. Among other manuscripts was the first draft of the early chapters of his *Confessions*. After Du Peyrou had taken charge of his papers,[163] Rousseau sent him a note[164] saying, 'It would be impossible for anyone except myself to decipher this draft which contains the history of my youth up to my departure for Paris in 1741.[165] Take care of it always—if ever we meet again, I shall be able to revise it. If not you may still find in it here and there some anecdotes that will explain many things that no one knows about the character of your friend.'

Rousseau's last few days on the island were among the most hectic. As he recalls in the *Confessions*,[166] 'as soon as it became known that I was to be banished a crowd of visitors, especially Bernese, came to flatter me and assure me that only a minority of Senators had voted to expel me.'

Among these visitors was, once again, Kirchberger, who brought with him this time two official persons who urged Rousseau to go no farther than the little city that gave the lake its name, Bienne. The first was Alexander Wildremet, a prominent Biennois who implored Rousseau 'in the name of his co-citizens' to choose his refuge among them. The other was Antoine Barthes, secretary of the French Embassy in Switzerland, who pressed the idea upon him with a warmth and zeal that surprised and baffled Rousseau. Baffle him it well might, considering the manner in which he had been treated by the French government. The only explanation he could think of was that the French ambassador to Switzerland, Pierre de Beauteville, who had met him years before with M. de Luxembourg and shown him some goodwill, had persuaded the 'free city of Bienne' to offer refuge.

In fact, Bienne was not, as Rousseau believed, a free city, and the French had no particular influence there. It was in principle one of the domains of the Prince Bishop of Basle, in practice subject to the hegemony of Berne. Neither Wildremet nor Barthes had any real authority to invite Rousseau to settle there.

However, a number of prominent citizens of Bienne gave a dinner of welcome to Rousseau at the Croix Blanche inn on the day of his arrival, and Rousseau installed himself in lodgings that he described as 'rather agreeable' in a letter[167] to Du Peyrou but as 'hideous' and 'stinking' in his *Confessions*.[168] Writing to Du Peyrou he also said 'I have ceded, my dear Host, to caresses and solicitations. I shall remain in Bienne. I have decided to spend the winter here, and I have reason to believe I shall spend it peacefully.'

That letter was written on Sunday, 27 October, the third day of his presence in Bienne. The next day, when Rousseau was dining with Vautravers at Rockhall, Kirchberger appeared with the news that several magistrates of the city were opposed to Rousseau's being authorised to remain in their territory. It was therefore agreed among them that in order to avoid being expelled in midwinter, he should leave at once. 'I have been deceived, my dear Host,' Rousseau wrote[169] to Du Peyrou. 'I shall leave Bienne tomorrow morning before they throw me out. Send me your news to Basle.'

From Basle Rousseau wrote[170] to Thérèse, who was still on the island, to say that he had arrived without mishap but 'with a sore throat, fever, and death in the heart.' He told her he had brought Sultan with him—'he ran in front of the carriage like a courier for thirty miles and now he is sleeping on my overcoat under the table where I write . . . he is one of a kind.' He added that if he could arrange transportation he would resume his journey the next day. He did so. His friend Jean-Jacques de Luze, of the merchant family, found a carriage for him and, on Thursday, 31 October, Rousseau left Basle with his dog for Strasbourg. He was never to see Switzerland again.

It is at this point in his life that the story told in the *Confessions* ends. The last anecdote related there is of the prefect Graffenried's coming to him in Bienne in full official dress (*in fiocchi*) to present him with the passport he needed for the journey. The passport was marked 'Pour aller en Allemagne'. But Germany was not Rousseau's destination. 'It would be totally impossible for me at present to sustain a journey to Berlin,' he wrote[172] from Basle to Du Peyrou. As for what to do next, he would make up his mind in Strasbourg.

A CELEBRITY ACCLAIMED

Among the things on which Rousseau worked in his 'idle' hours on the Isle de St-Pierre was the *Project for a Constitution for Corsica* that he had promised to draft for Captain Buttafoco and General Paoli. Paradoxically, in view of his recent experiences, the central argument of the scheme is that the Corsicans should imitate the Swiss. Not, assuredly, the Swiss of Geneva, under their twenty-five despots, nor the *canaille* of Neuchâtel, nor again the rich, aristocratic cantons of Fribourg and Berne. It is the undeveloped, rustic, democratic cantons farther east to which Rousseau points: 'Look Corsicans, there is the model you should follow if you are to recover and preserve your primitive condition.'[1]

Rousseau does not deny that there is a great difference between Corsica, a Mediterranean island, and such landlocked Alpine fortresses as Glarus, Appenzell, Uri, Schwyz, and Unterwalden. The essential similarity is that they are all simple agricultural societies, and Rousseau asserts—wholly in conformity with what is said in his first *Discourse on the Sciences and the Arts* and often repeated—that a primitive rural economy is the only basis for a free, good life.

His *Project* is not a constitution in the more familiar sense of a system of fundamental laws, but rather a sketch of a civil association in its most general political, economic, and social structure. He insists, first, on its being rural in a sense that is sharply antagonistic to industry and towns. Everyone should live on the land, cultivate it, and 'love country life'.[2] Agriculture must be so organised that the island is fully self-supporting. Different areas should be assigned to different crops according to the distinctive natural character of each, and the produce exchanged at markets. At those markets, however, barter should replace cash transactions. Rousseau thus goes beyond the model of Swiss experience to envisage a society where money would have little, if any, place and wealth could not divide men into rich and poor. Even the magistrates and public officers should be paid in kind—in 'wheat, wine,

forage and wood'.³ Taxation would take the form of national service—the
corvée—rather than that of monetary imposts.

Looking once more to the Swiss of the less-developed cantons, Rousseau
urges the Corsicans to institute universal conscription and make themselves
a nation of citizen-soldiers as well as of peasants: 'Trained militias are the best
troops and the most reliable: the best education for a soldier is that of a
labourer.'⁴ Life on the land, he argues, breeds patriots: 'peasants are attached
to the soil far more closely than townspeople are attached to their towns.'

Next, Rousseau urges the Corsicans to imitate the Swiss of the eastern
cantons in adopting democratic rule. A pastoral and agricultural economy
'favours a democratic state',⁵ provided there are no marked inequalities of
wealth among the people. He advises limitations on the accumulation of private fortunes: 'Everyone must have enough to live on, but no one must en-
rich himself.' Private property is authorised, for Rousseau is no communist;
indeed he suggests that full citizenship be accorded only to those who possess a dwelling of their own, with land enough to sustain themselves and a
family of two children. What he seeks to eliminate is the kind of private
wealth that is incorporated in money and thus veiled from public inspection.
He would like to see Corsica rich: 'Far from wishing the state to be poor, I
would wish it, on the contrary, to have everything and for each person to
have his share in the common wealth in proportion to his services . . . In a
word, I would like the property of the state to be as great and strong and that
of the citizens to be as small and weak as possible.'⁶

He advises the Corsicans to adopt the direct democracy of the eastern
Swiss cantons, which hold regular meetings of all the adult male citizens in
Landesgemeinden to make the laws they live under and to elect their public
officers. At the same time, Rousseau recognizes that the population of Corsica is already too numerous for its citizens to be accommodated in a single
assembly, so he proposes yet another solution based on Swiss experience: a
confederal system. Corsica, he proposes, should be divided into twelve *pièves*,
or cantons, each with its own *Landesgemeinde*. The cantons should be sub-
stantially autonomous—he speaks of them as 'little states'⁷ united in a loose
confederation for common purposes and governed by a rotating presidency.
Rousseau warns the Corsicans against establishing a capital in a large city
such as Bastia; they would be better off, he suggests, with a simple *chef-lieu*,
or administrative centre, set in a small town such as Corte in the middle of
the island, where there would be fewer people and little opportunity for
metropolitan politics to vitiate direct democracy.

Rousseau adamantly opposes establishment of an hereditary nobility, despite Captain Buttafoco's hope that it be restored in Corsica:⁸

Democracy knows no other nobility besides virtue and liberty . . . but other
states have all the titles of marquis and count . . . The fundamental law of your

institution should be equality. Everything should reflect equality, including the authority itself, which is established only to defend equality. Everyone should be equal by right of birth. The state should award distinctions only to merit, to virtue, to public service, and those distinctions should be no more hereditary than the qualities for which they are awarded . . . All fiefs, vassalages, feudal rights and seigneurial privileges should be extinguished and suppressed throughout the island.'[9]

Rousseau never completed his *Project for Corsica*, never published it, never even showed it to Buttafoco. Events in Corsica nullified his efforts, for the French government, having successfully encouraged the Corsicans to repudiate the rule of Genoa, promptly annexed the island to France. Rousseau gave the unfinished manuscript[10] of the *Project* to Moultou shortly before his death, but it was not published until 1861.[11] Had it been published before 1789 it would undoubtedly have entered the literature of the French Revolution. As it was, Rousseau, being known mainly as the author of *The Social Contract*, could be invoked by the Jacobins as a champion of the unitary state they imposed so brutally on the *fédérés*; the exponent of federalism we find in the *Project for Corsica* was unknown.

Rousseau himself, when he arrived at Strasbourg on Saturday, 2 November 1765, was only too pleased to be out of the land of federalism. Among the marquises and counts of that French garrison town he was soon made to feel at home. The journey from Basle, he informed[12] Thérèse, had been 'the most detestable I have made in my whole life', but he was also to reassure her that he was comfortable in his room at the inn—the La Fleur—eating alone with his dog and looking forward to a walk on the ramparts. On the same day he thanked[13] Jean-Jacques de Luze for finding the room for him 'in a house where I can recover my strength and get back my breath at ease'.

He only dreaded the thought of having to move on. To several correspondents he protested that he could not face the ordeal of a journey in winter across Germany to Berlin, and he was hardly more reconciled to the prospect of travelling through Holland if he had to take that route to England. His hope, as he explained[14] to Guy, would be to travel through France and be allowed two months' rest in Paris on the way. In the meantime, he was in no hurry to leave Strasbourg and under no pressure to go.

At first he tried to preserve his incognito, but this did not last, and within a few days he was almost overwhelmed with friendly messages, visits, invitations, and offers of hospitality: 'not only welcomed but fêted'.[15] It was a great change from Môtiers. 'After having lived so long among mad wolves,' he wrote[16] to Colonel Chaillet, 'it is sweet to find myself among men.' To Du Peyrou he reported,[17] 'I receive nothing here but marks of goodwill and all the authorities of the province and the city are disposed in my favour: they make me realise very agreeably that I am no longer in Switzerland.'

Among those who welcomed him was the commandant of the province, the Maréchal-Duc de Contades, to whom Rousseau was presented a few days after his arrival, and who gave him to understand that he was 'as safe in Strasbourg as in Berlin'.[18] The commandant of the city, the Marquis de Nanclas, was no less cordial. Mme de Verdelin, who was a relation of his, wrote[19] to urge him to take an interest in her friend and protégé, but he seems to have needed no prompting. The Lord Lieutenant, M. de Saint-Victor, introduced Rousseau to the intendant M. Blair de Boisement, and the treasurer M. de Chastel invited him to concerts he gave every Saturday at his *hôtel particulier*. 'I receive more offers of service than I can possibly accept in this city of kindness and goodwill,' Rousseau reported to Coindet in a letter[20] of more than usual warmth when the eager young friend proposed[21] sending Rousseau a letter of credit for six hundred francs. Coindet did not name the benefactor, but Rousseau knew that Mme de Verdelin must have provided it, and he refused to accept it. 'I swear to you, Madame,' he wrote[22] to her, 'I protest that I have more than enough money for my needs, and if ever I do need money no one will be told before you are.'

One of his first letters from Strasbourg bespeaks an almost carefree mood: 'I feel very far from Switzerland amidst all the attentions and kindnesses I receive from everyone from the Commandant downwards,' he declared[23] to Colonel de Pury. But after three weeks of being lionized, he began to feel he had had too much of it—or so he claimed in writing[24] to Du Peyrou. 'The frequent dinners in town and social life with the ladies and men of fashion to which I yielded at first in return for all their goodwill to me has now become a burden and such a threat to my health that I must cut it out and become a bear once more.'

He did nothing of the kind. One thing that kept him from hibernating was theatrical activity. A few days after Rousseau's arrival, the director of the Théâtre Français, Villeneuve, asked his permission to stage a production of *Le Devin du village*. The work was being performed just then at the Paris Opera—much to the irritation of Rousseau, who had tried to withdraw it from the repertoire in his dispute with the directors over copyright. But the idea of seeing it put on in Strasbourg attracted him, especially as Villeneuve persuaded him that the first night would be a gala occasion in the presence of the Maréchal de Contades and other dignitaries.

The Paris production of *Le Devin du village* was a considerable artistic success, as Lenieps reported[25]* to Rousseau: 'Your *Devin du village* is so well performed here that it is the only thing people want to see: without it, the Opera would be dead.'

Rousseau did not expect to hear a performance of the same quality in

*There were nineteen performances of *Le Devin du village* in the Paris Opera during the month of November.

Strasbourg. He confided[26] to Colonel de Pury: 'The Director of the Theatre here wants to do me an honour by staging *Le Devin du village*. I am going this afternoon to the first rehearsal. I expect it all to be detestable,
although the actors are full of good will and the orchestra is fairly decent but
that is not enough. Do you see I have passed from the clutches of theologians into those of thespians?' At rehearsal, however, Rousseau became more
optimistic, especially when Villeneuve encouraged him to take charge of the
proceedings. The journal[27] of an anonymous witness for 9 November 1765
reads:

J.-J. Rousseau came today at 2 o'clock in the afternoon to the Theatre to see the
dress rehearsal of his opera, and to give his opinion. I saw him at close range and
at leisure for the two hours and a half of the rehearsal. He talked a lot, and
seemed at ease in the theatre, where he directed the actors himself and made
them rehearse the whole opera, very often making them repeat their parts. He
did not let the smallest fault pass, in the acting or in the musical score which was
complete, and which he had played very sweetly and very simply—the songs
too. I heard him say that village people speak simply, so they must sing simply.

The diarist added the next day:

Le Devin du village was performed today to all possible applause—except for
Colin, who was worth nothing, but the little soprano was marvellous . . . The
music could not have been better played. The theatre was already full at half-past
four: the box office had to give back money to people who could not find a seat.
Jean-Jacques had asked the Director to keep a *loge grillée* for four people, for
whose tickets he had paid as well as his own: and it proved impossible for the Director to refuse his money.

Rousseau himself was more than satisfied with the performance, and no
less pleased when Villeneuve asked if he might stage some of his plays, beginning with *Narcisse*. Rousseau wrote[28] to Du Peyrou, asking him to look
through the papers he had left with him to find the texts of *Pygmalion* and
L'Engagement téméraire: 'The Director of the Theatre,' he explained, 'has
shown me a thousand kindnesses. He has given me for my use a little *loge
grillée*, and had a key made to a side door so that I can enter incognito. He is
producing the plays that he thinks might please me. I would like to acknowledge his friendliness to me, and I believe that some of my scribblings,
good or bad, would be useful to him, seeing the public good will towards
me that was shown when he put on *Le Devin du village*.' Rousseau suggested
that Du Peyrou bring the plays to Strasbourg in person so that 'we might
amuse ourselves by having them rehearsed,' and also urged him that if he

came, 'to allow Mlle Levasseur to come with you.' He knew her to be languishing miserably on the Isle de St-Pierre.

Du Peyrou, who had a limited enthusiasm for Thérèse,* pleaded[30] that he could not leave Neuchâtel because of his aged mother and the need to supervise work on his new house. He sent Rousseau the plays by mail, together with some of his music. He dealt with Thérèse by sending her a few presents and 'tranquilising' her concerns about Rousseau's situation.

While waiting for further scripts to arrive, Villeneuve put into rehearsal Rousseau's *Narcisse*. This was the play Rousseau had robbed of success in Paris thirteen years earlier by running from the Comédie Française to the Café de Procope proclaiming, 'It's a bad play and I'm the author of it,'[31] embarrassed perhaps at coming before the public as a dramatist after his wholesale attack on the drama in the *Letter to M. d'Alembert*. In his preface[32] to the published version of *Narcisse*, Rousseau had justified his position by restating his thesis, explaining that whereas theatres were injurious for simple, uncorrupt people, such as the Swiss, for sophisticated people, such as the Parisians, theatres were useful in keeping them out of greater mischief. Hence his collaboration with the theatre at Strasbourg implied a judgement—flattering or otherwise—of the inhabitants that put them in the same moral category as Parisians. In fact, the audiences for Villeneuve's productions were mainly drawn from the upper classes—army officers and their families, and French government officials. The humbler ranks of the Alsatian populace spoke German and did not attend the Théâtre Français. In any case, Rousseau's experiences of the past few months had somewhat diminished his earlier faith in the innocence of the unworldly.

In the principality of Neuchâtel, his enemies turned his departure to their advantage. 'The Professor is on the warpath again,' Du Peyrou reported[33] in early November. Frederick's demand for action against persons who had incited his subjects to riot fell on deaf ears. Montmollin, together with his relations and the clergy generally, regained control of the Conseil d'État, and the restoration of the old order became the first priority even of those royal officials who had previously battled for Rousseau's rights. His cause was a lost one.

In Geneva, by contrast, there was at just this time a dramatic change in the political situation, in favour of Rousseau's friends. The majority of the citizen body, which had so disgusted Rousseau by bending slavishly to the demands of their patrician rulers a few months earlier, refused in the November elec-

---

*When Rousseau left the island for Bienne, Du Peyrou had complained to him about Thérèse's indiscreet gossiping: 'Yet again I implore Mlle Levasseur to avoid all commerce with women, . . . *entre nous* I am dismayed to hear that she is reported, in Brôt, to have spoken ungraciously about the conduct of the Intendant Martinet.'[29]

tions of 1765 to accept the candidates nominated by the Petit Conseil for the office of procurator-general and lieutenant-civil. At Strasbourg Rousseau received from the veteran citizens' leader Guillaume-Antoine Deluc[34] the wholly unexpected news that the citizens had expressed their displeasure by voting 833 to 465 for a 'nouvelle élection' to the office of procurator-general, and 746 to 549 to the office of lieutenant-civil. Alternative candidates nominated by the Petit Conseil a week later were rejected even more decisively: 838 to 321 for the office of procurator-general and 854 to 401 for the office of lieutenant-civil. Reporting these last figures to Rousseau, François d'Ivernois declared[35] that the philosopher had inspired the citizens' resistance: 'You see us united thanks to the *Letters from the Mountain* and the worthy author.'

Two more elections were held in December, and again the official candidates for the vacancies were rejected by even larger majorities. A further surprising development was that Voltaire transferred his support from the magistrates to the citizens. Du Peyrou suggested[36] that this arose because the Petit Conseil had antagonised Voltaire 'by burning his *Dictionnaire philosophique*.' Whatever the motive, Voltaire entertained the leading *Représentants* at Ferney and advised them on their strategy. Deluc and Vieusseux and other friends of Rousseau took part in these conversations. Only François d'Ivernois, knowing Voltaire to be Rousseau's implacable enemy, refused to join in even though, as he explained[37] to Rousseau, he believed that Voltaire was genuinely eager to help them. Rousseau wanted no such testimony of loyalty; he simply reproached d'Ivernois for missing an opportunity to further the citizens' cause: 'I am cross that you did not see M. de Voltaire. Could you think that such a step would upset me? How little you understand my heart . . . Whatever the man who restores your place and freedom, he will always be cherished and esteemed by me. If that man is Voltaire, then he can do me all the harm he chooses and still my constant wish until I draw my last breath will be for his happiness and glory.'

The developments at Geneva prompted Rousseau to modify his resolution to think no more about the political situation of his native city. He allowed himself to discuss it in his letters and was soon being asked to intervene again. 'After having pointed out the evil,' Lenieps pleaded,[38] 'you are needed now to point out the remedy . . . and restore the government of Geneva to its first principles.' But Rousseau was in no situation to run the risk of further penalties by public political utterances. Already, the crisis in Geneva had revived suspicions about him at Versailles, where his writings were believed to have been responsible for stirring up trouble in a place the French government desired to remain peaceful and neutral. Mme de Verdelin's friend the Duc d'Aumont did not easily obtain from the Duc de

Praslin* the passport for Rousseau to travel to France; and even though that document eventually reached him at Strasbourg, he could not afford to regard it as more than a transit visa that would rapidly expire.

He was fortunate in that another benefactress, Mme de Boufflers, had been as active on his behalf as Mme de Verdelin. She had persuaded the Prince de Conti to offer him hospitality in Paris at the Temple, a place where he would be completely safe since it was outside the jurisdiction of both the Versailles government and the Paris *parlement*. Somehow she failed to get this invitation to Rousseau while he was still in Strasbourg, and Rousseau accepted instead an invitation[39] from Pierre Guy to lodge in Paris with the nominal head of his publishing house, the widow Duchesne.

Guy's rival Rey also offered accommodation to their illustrious author and actually sent his clerk Potinus to Strasbourg to bring Rousseau back to Amsterdam with a promise of refuge there. It was a fruitless mission. 'Your emissary will return as he came,' Rousseau wrote to Guy.[40] 'I am in no state to travel, and if I were, I doubt whether my destination would be Amsterdam. The cold this winter is the worst I have known for years, and I hardly dare set my foot outside the door.' He offered Rey the modest consolation of a manuscript to publish: *La Reine fantasque*.

On 30 November Rousseau informed[41] Du Peyrou that he had definitely decided to go to England, and on 4 December[42] he wrote to David Hume: 'I shall leave here in five or six days' time to throw myself into your arms. It is the counsel of Lord Keith, my protector, my friend, my father; it is the counsel of Mme de Verdelin, whose enlightened kindness guides me even as it consoles me; and I will make bold to say that it is the counsel of my own heart, which is happy to be indebted to the most illustrious of my contemporaries.'

Rousseau asked Du Peyrou to have his papers and other belongs sent by riverboat up the Rhine to Rotterdam and then across the North Sea to England; and to François d'Ivernois, who had offered to put up Thérèse in Geneva,† he suggested[43] that she might take the same route to join him in the spring: 'I really cannot drag her with me at this season until I have found a refuge.' He added that he would be sorry to leave Strasbourg: 'I have rested my head here with the sort of pleasure one finds in the company of human beings after leaving that of wild beasts . . . everyone here would like me to stay for the rest of my days, but such is not my vocation.'

During his last week in Strasbourg, Rousseau fell ill for a day or two, al-

---

*He did so by appealing to the foreign minister's compassion for a persecuted man. Neither the King nor the Duc de Choiseul, the first minister, would authorise the passport. The Dauphin was known to be well disposed toward Rousseau, but he was on his deathbed.

†Vautravers also offered to put her up at Rockhall. Du Peyrou did *not* offer to put her up in Neuchâtel. She remained on the island.

though, as he wrote[44] to Mme Boy, he 'had the consolation of knowing that you are on the way to a complete recovery . . . Your best doctor is your beloved daughter—I have a great need for her equal to restore health to my poor heart and my poor sick body.' Despite these lamentations, he seems not to have suffered unduly from the lack of Thérèse's care, and seems even to have put on weight, to judge from a remark in the same letter to Mme Boy: 'The last belts I received are as narrow, short and thin as the others. I have to extend them with pins which is inconvenient and ruins them. Is there no way of having one, my dear friend, at least more ample and stronger?'

On 5 December Mme de Verdelin wrote[45] to tell Rousseau about the Prince de Conti's invitation to the Temple—'He cannot imagine how you even obtained a passport'—but Rousseau did not receive her letter in time, and confirmed[46] to Guy his intention to lodge—he hoped incognito—with Mme Duchesne. He refused all offers of transport to Paris in a private carriage and secured for himself, his dog, and a part of his luggage a passage in a post-chaise that was scheduled to leave Strasbourg at 7 A.M. on Monday, 9 December. Having to rise early, he excused himself from attending on Sunday the dress rehearsal of his play *Narcisse*, for which Villeneuve had hoped once again to have his collaboration. Rousseau begged[47] Villeneuve to express his apologies to the company: 'Do tell the actresses that the old greybeard I am cannot repent a youthful indiscretion which can command such adorable accomplices and tell the actors that it will be a real proof of their talents to revive a play that has flopped and to make something out of nothing.' Again, he thanked Villeneuve for all he had done 'to make my stay in Strasbourg agreeable.'

The journey took seven days; despite the fact that he 'nearly died during a sleepless night at Eperney',[48] Rousseau arrived in Paris in what he called 'un état assez passable'[49] on the evening of Monday, 16 December. As he had still not received the invitation from the Prince de Conti, he installed himself and Sultan at the house of the widow Duchesne. He wrote[50] at once a note to Jean-Jacques de Luze—the friend who arranged rooms for him in Basle and Switzerland, and who had preceded him to Paris—begging him to come to the rue St-Jacques as soon as possible to discuss their onward journey to London. He added that as he wished to keep his presence in Paris a secret, he did not 'dare to parade my fur hat in the streets'. Despite this assertion, and a further remark[51] to Mme de Verdelin that he needed two or three days' rest before going out of the house, he took Sultan the next day for a walk in the Luxembourg gardens, where the fur hat—and more especially the Armenian caftan—betrayed his presence to a curious public.

One reason why he wanted to preserve his incognito was, as he explained[52] to Du Peyrou, to 'avoid the dinners and fatigue of Strasbourg' and to husband his strength for England. On his third day in Paris he received

the Prince's invitation, and after that there was no avoiding dinners and fatigue. Jean-Jacques de Luze was his first visitor, but Mme de Verdelin and
Mme de Boufflers arrived on his heels, and Rousseau was promptly swept
from the bourgeois comfort of the rue St-Jacques to the royal splendour of
the Hôtel de St-Simon, one of the elegant modern buildings attached to the
grim medieval fortress of the Temple. There was, as Rousseau explained[53] to
Du Peyrou, no resisting the hospitality of the Prince de Conti: 'He wanted
me housed and served with a magnificence he knew was not to my taste, because, as I well understand, he intended by these means to offer a public testimony of his esteem for me.' The Prince also offered Rousseau a more
permanent refuge in his château at Trye, but this offer Rousseau declined because of an 'unacceptable condition' attached to it—probably that he should
live there under a false name.

At this stage Rousseau was resolved to accept Hume's offer of refuge and
was impatient to meet his benefactor. While still at Mme Duchesne's, he had
begged Mme de Verdelin to introduce him at once to 'that sublime genius'.
The genius was no less eager to meet him.

In December 1765, David Hume was far from certain about his own future. After several months as *chargé d'affaires* at the British Embassy, he had
been replaced and was unemployed. He had arrived in Paris more than two
years earlier as private secretary to Lord Hertford, the first ambassador appointed by London after the end of the Seven Years War. In a situation rem-
iniscent of Rousseau's at the French Embassy in Venice, Hume was
employed by the ambassador personally and did not become official Embassy
secretary until the summer of 1765, barely in time to take over the function
of *chargé d'affaires*. He was nonetheless from the start a busy and effective
diplomat and an enormously popular figure in Parisian society.

'It is difficult to imagine,' he recalled[54] soon after his arrival, 'the caresses,
civilities and panegyrics which pourd on me from all sides.' His books—or
at least his history books, and especially his *History of England*—were universally admired in France, and Hume was delighted to find that the French,
unlike the English, held writers in high esteem. Literary society and fashionable society embraced him with equal fervour. Even the royal family paid
homage. Presented at Versailles to the three sons of the Dauphin, he was congratulated on his books by each prince in turn; by the future Louis XVI,
aged ten, who quoted passages he had learned; by the future Louis XVIII,
aged eight; and even the future Charles X, aged five, who mumbled an encomium that Hume realised he had learned from his father, 'who is not, on
any occasion, sparing in my praise.'[55]

Only the few English noblemen living in Paris stood aloof from the cult;
they could not understand how this fat, untidy, ungainly Scotsman, who
spoke French with a heavy accent, was, as Horace Walpole put it[56] with un-

mistakable envy,★ 'treated here with perfect veneration'. Being a Scotsman was perhaps one secret of Hume's success, for after the loss of Canada and India to England in the Seven Years War, French Anglomania was no longer what it had been. In any case, the French found Hume's personal charm and quick wit irresistible; if he was clumsy, unceremonious, or *gauche*, they saw that as evidence of his sincerity. He was always cheerful, generous, good tempered, and good natured—he was *le bon David* to one and all.

Even those hostesses who loathed one another in their rivalry to rule *le monde* were united in their adoration of Hume: Mme Geoffrin, who treated him like a son, Mlle de Lespinasse, who treated him like a father, and even Mme Du Deffand, until jealousy extinguished her love for him. The one whose love he returned, to the extent that his repressed emotions allowed him to experience sexual love, was Mme de Boufflers, who chased him even more shamelessly than she had once chased Rousseau. Her attitude only changed when her husband died and she began her futile campaign to make the Prince de Conti marry her. Whereupon Hume, realising 'that she would have no further use for a lover',[58] descended gracefully to the status of a confidant, a status he already enjoyed with the Prince. The Prince gave him the thankless task of persuading Mme de Boufflers to forget her dream of marrying into the royal family. Mme de Boufflers—together with Mme de Verdelin—gave him the task of taking care of Rousseau in his hour of need.

Hume found no corresponding sympathy for Rousseau among the *philosophes*, with most of whom he had made friends soon after his arrival in Paris. 'Those whose persons and conversations I like best,' he wrote[59] in 1763, 'are d'Alembert, Buffon, Marmontel, Diderot, Duclos, Helvétius and old Président Hénault.' He also knew—but does not name—Rousseau's two great enemies, Grimm and Holbach. What others said against Rousseau he did not listen to, for Hume was far from sharing the outlook of the *philosophes*—even of d'Alembert, his favourite among them. He considered them altogether too dogmatic—in their atheism, in their materialist philosophy, in their radical politics, and in their physiocratic economics. Hume's own attitude in all these fields was one of scepticism. There was, he maintained, no basis for certain knowledge of either the physical or the metaphysical worlds, let alone of the social. All one could rely on was habit, custom, and tradition. Like Montaigne, Hume believed one could only rest one's head on the pillow of ignorance and incuriosity.

In several important ways, Hume had more in common with Rousseau than with the *philosophes*. Like Rousseau he had had a Calvinist upbringing, and like him reacted against it. Both rejected the rationalism of the Enlightenment. Neither had any faith in the gospel of progress or the salvation of

★Walpole, whose own command of French was dismal, said of the French ladies who idolized Hume, 'I defy them to understand any language which he speaks.'[57]

mankind through science. Each felt himself to be alienated from his contemporaries. Hume, however, flattered by the praise he received as a historian, was wounded by the total neglect of his work as a philosopher and by the hostility of the English toward his receiving any public office. A short while before Rousseau's arrival in Paris, Hume's job at the British Embassy had ended with the appointment of a new ambassador, and a promised opening in Dublin with his former employer Lord Hertford had been withdrawn.

Rousseau and Hume each possessed a sense of his own genius and a respect for the other's. And yet they cannot be thought of as being *made* to be friends. Rousseau was intensely emotional; he wept freely, and he embraced his friends, when the spirit moved him, with unrestrained ardour. He promised, and exacted, absolute commitment and devotion. He was brutally honest, tactless, and demanding. Hume, in a lifetime of self-discipline, did not admit intense feelings and could not easily articulate even moderate feelings—at least in speech, though he might in writing. Friendship, which for Rousseau was an *épanouissement* of the heart, a form of love, was for Hume a matter of cheerful good companionship and mutual usefulness.

In the spirit of this understanding that a good friend is a man who does you good turns, *le bon David* sent Jean-Jacques through Mme de Verdelin[60] not only a renewed promise to find him a refuge in England but an offer to accompany him to London in person. Hume had to go there to make a report to the Foreign Office on his Paris mission. Since Rousseau had already planned to travel with de Luze, who owned a private coach of superior quality and held out the promise of a more comfortable journey to Calais than those he had experienced from Basle to Strasbourg or Strasbourg to Paris, he hesitated. When Hume met Rousseau, however, it was happily agreed that all three would travel together. Hume's first impression of Rousseau was entirely favourable. He described[61] Rousseau in a letter to his friend Hugh Blair, professor of philosophy at Edinburgh:

I find him mild, and gentle and modest and good humourd; and he has more the behaviour of a man of the world than any of the learned here, except M. de Buffon who in his figure and air and deportment answers your idea of a Mareschal of France rather than that of a philosopher. M. Rousseau is of small stature, and wou'd rather be ugly, had he not the finest physiognomony [sic] in the world, I mean, the most expressive countenance. His modesty seems not to be good manners; but ignorance of his own excellence: As he writes and speaks and acts from the impulse of genius, more than from the use of his ordinary faculties, it is very likely that he forgets its force, whenever it is laid asleep. I am well assurd, that at times he believes he has inspirations from an immediate communication with the divinity. He falls sometimes into ecstacies which retain him in the same posture for hours together. Does not this example solve the difficulty of

Socrates's genius and of his ecstacies? I think Rousseau in many things very much resembles Socrates: . . . I wish he may live unmolested in England. I dread the bigotry and barbarism which prevail there.

Once he moved to the Temple, Rousseau seldom left his quarters, less from fear of arrest by the *parlement*'s agents* than to avoid being mobbed by admirers. People who wished to see him had to visit him at the Hôtel de St-Simon, where he held audience like a king under the watchful eye of Mme de Boufflers, who lived next door. If Rousseau seldom went out to dine, the Prince ensured that he could entertain his friends in style. The Prince even arranged a production of Rousseau's little opera *Les Muses galantes* at his private theatre, and there were other musical evenings at the Temple in the sumptuous 'hall of four mirrors', although Rousseau had left before the child Mozart arrived a few weeks later to perform on a high stool at the harpsichord, as depicted in the famous painting by Ollivier. On the Mondays of Rousseau's presence the Prince gave his usual weekly dinners in the grande salle for up to a hundred guests, and on Fridays Mme de Boufflers presided over her own more intimate salon. As the day of Rousseau's arrival at the Temple was a Friday, she was able at once to display him proudly together with David Hume, like two great wonders of nature, to her bemused, admiring friends.

In his letter to Hugh Blair, Hume spoke of Rousseau's popularity in Paris:

I am perswaded, that were I to open here a subscription with his consent, I shoud receive 50,000 pounds in a fortnight. The second day after his arrival, he slipt out early in the morning to take a walk in the Luxembourg gardens. The thing was known soon after: I am strongly sollicited to prevail on him to take another walk, and then to give warning to my friends: Were the public to be informd, he could not failt to have many thousand spectators. People may talk of antient Greece as they please, but no nation was ever so fond of genius as this; and no person ever so much engag'd their attention as Rousseau. Voltaire and every body else, are quite eclipsd by him. I am sensible, that my connexions with him, add to my importance at present. Even his maid, La Vasseur, who is very homely and very awkward, is more talkd of than the Princess of Monaco or the Countess of Egmont, on account of her fidelity and attachment towards him. His very dog, who is no better than a coly, has a name and reputation in the world.

The talk about Thérèse prompted Rousseau to urge her to join him as soon as possible. When he first arrived in Paris he sent Du Peyrou a letter[63] 'for the poor girl who is on the island' suggesting that while she should pre-

---

*'It seems that the *Parlement* wishes to close its eyes to his presence here.'[62]

pare to come to England she should 'do nothing hastily'. A week later, he
wrote[64] again to Du Peyrou asking him to speed Thérèse's departure: 'Everyone here urges me to have her come immediately.'

By 'everyone' Rousseau probably meant the two ladies who liked Thérèse
best, Mme de Luxembourg and Mme de Verdelin, for Mme de Boufflers
considered Thérèse an unworthy companion for him.* Mme de Luxembourg visited Rousseau at the Temple with the Duchesse de Montmorency,
the Duchesse de Boufflers, and other members of her family whom
Rousseau had known in his years at Montlouis. She was said to have been
overcome with afflictions after the death of her husband, and Rousseau
found her in poor health. He had tried to restore his friendship with her after the unkind things he had written in some of his letters; he had sent her
a copy of the *Letters from the Mountain* and even sent her a present of Swiss
cheese—both of which she praised eagerly—but the old intimacy between
them could not be renewed. Even so, the Maréchale urged Rousseau to
arrange for Thérèse to stay with her at the Hôtel de Luxembourg on her way
from Switzerland to join him in England.

Mme de Verdelin was the friend to whom Rousseau's heart was closest at
this time. As soon as he reached Paris, he had assured[65] her that 'my first and
perhaps unique outing will be to visit you,' and indeed he was about to go
to her convent when she appeared at the rue St-Jacques. He was worried
about her rattling across Paris in a perilous kind of rickshaw known as a
brouette, for she was the kind of woman who economised on herself while
giving generously to others—including, if only he would accept it, her 'cher
Voisin'. Like Mme de Luxembourg—with whom she remained on distant
terms—Mme de Verdelin was in far from robust health. Moreover, a few days
after Rousseau arrived in Paris, her father, the Comte Brémond d'Ars, died
in his eightieth year. Rousseau hurried to the convent to express his condo-
lences and cancelled a concert that had been planned at the Temple. Since
Mme de Verdelin was both unwell and in mourning, Rousseau saw less of
her than he had hoped in the three weeks he spent in Paris.

Mme de Boufflers, on the other hand, was constantly in his company, offi-
ciating over the busy social life he was forced to lead at the Temple. She did
little to discourage visitors, but seemed rather to glory in showing him off.
An English acquaintance of Hume named Robert Liston recalled[66] going to
the Temple simply to 'stare' at Rousseau when 'the Countess of Boufflers
came out . . . and insisted on introducing me to Jean-Jacques.'

The most assiduous of Rousseau's visitors at the Temple were ladies of
fashion. He remarked once in conversation with Mme de Boufflers and
Hume (as Hume reported[67] to Hugh Blair): 'Is it not strange that I, who have

*It was probably she who told Hume, who had never met Thérèse, that Thérèse was 'very homely
and very awkward'.

wrote so much to decry the morals and conduct of the Parisian ladies should yet be beloved by them—while the Swiss women, whom I have so much extolled, would willingly cut my throat?' Mme de Boufflers then replied to Rousseau: 'We are fond of you because we know that however you might rail, you are at bottom fond of us to distraction: but the Swiss women hate you because they are conscious that they have not merit to deserve your attention.'

In this same letter to Hugh Blair, Hume reported that Rousseau was beginning to be worn out with all visits he had to receive at the Temple:

The concourse about him gives him so much uneasiness, that he expresses the utmost impatience to be gone. Many people here will have it, that this solitary humour is all affectation, in order to be more sought after; but I am sure that it is natural and unsurmountable. I know, that two very agreeable ladies breaking in upon him, discomposed him so much, that he was not able to eat his dinner afterwards. He is short sighted; and I have often observed, that while he was conversing with me in the outmost good humour (for he is naturally gay) if he heard the door open, the greatest agony appeard on his countenance, from the apprehension of a visit, and his distress did not leave him, unless the person was a particular friend.

Who were his particular friends? One who claimed that privilege was Marianne Alissan. She learned of his presence in Paris from the public gazettes, and was deeply hurt that he had not informed her of his arrival. She wrote[68] to reproach him for ignoring her: 'Do you think me capable of betraying your secret? Have you forgotten how much I value you?' After more in this vein, she added, paradoxically, 'the illustrious friend whose genius exalts my soul . . . shall never be the object of my reproaches. I have loved you, I love you, I shall love you.' Two days later, she wrote him another letter[69] filled with even more bitter reproaches, accusing him of treating her, the one who loved him most, as if she were his greatest enemy.

'Toujours des reproches!' Rousseau exclaimed in his reply.[70] 'I have not been to see you because I have not gone to see anyone.' He could not upset old friends, he added, by giving preference to a new one. Evidently wounded at being thus considered a new friend, Marianne protested,[71] 'I thought you loved me because you said you did . . . Adieu, <u>Monsieur</u> [she underlined the word] I use that form because I am made to adopt the tone you impose on me . . . I hope you keep all your friends, that you acquire many more, and that they are happier than I, and above all that your misfortunes, your sorrows and your coldness will not cost them so many tears.'

Having written these bitter words, she carried the letter to the Hôtel de St-Simon and had it delivered to Rousseau by a footman while she waited in an antechamber in the hope of being admitted. In due course, he sent a note[72] back, saying, 'I am not alone, Madame, but that will not prevent my receiving you with the greatest pleasure if you care to enter.' So at last she saw her idol face to face, and was soon addressing him in her letters as '*Mon cher* Jean-Jacques'. He in turn resumed the habit of writing to '*chère* Marianne' and assured[73] her that 'I desire exceedingly that you should love me, that you should not reproach me and even more that I should not deserve your reproaches.'

It is not recorded who was with Rousseau when Marianne called—it could as easily have been one of the *philosophes* as a woman of fashion. Malesherbes, Morellet, Turgot were among those who hurried to the Temple to proclaim their friendship. Madame de Buffon persuaded[74] Hume to bring Rousseau to dine with her illustrious husband; Mme Helvétius tried, with less success, to do the same; Mme Trudaine de Montigny is said[75] to have bullied Rousseau to dine among the *philosophes* at her house. There was even talk of a reconciliation between Rousseau and Diderot. In a letter[76] to Sophie Volland, Diderot wrote on 20 December: 'Rousseau has been in Paris for three days. I do not expect him to visit me, but I do not hide the fact that it would give me great pleasure if he did and that I should be happy to see him. How would he justify his behaviour towards me? I do not give easy access to my heart, but one who is accepted cannot leave without breaking it; there is a wound that does not heal.'

Diderot made no approach to Rousseau, nor can one believe that Rousseau would have welcomed one from a former friend who expected him 'to justify his behaviour'. In any case, as he had reminded d'Escherny, a friendship once ended with him was ended forever. Nevertheless, Rousseau at the Temple was in an expansive mood, and even gave ready assent when Hume asked him to sit for a portrait bust by the sculptor Jean-Baptiste Lemoyne. Hume recommended[77] the sculptor as a man of 'singular vivacity and original mind', promising Rousseau that he would need only two sittings. There were rather more sittings than that. At one of them an admirer from Nîmes named Laliaud★ appeared and, according to his testimony,[79] was so impressed by the likeness that he took the bust in his arms and embraced it: 'Then I looked at Monsieur Rousseau who was sitting in a chair with his eyes modestly lowered and his face covered with tears. I went over to him, took his hands and shook them . . . then we all three embraced in silence.'

Unfortunately, Rousseau did not share the same enthusiasm for Lemoyne's work. The sculptor eventually produced two busts,[80] one in marble and an-

---

★In the *Confessions* Rousseau says that Laliaud 'was very eager to render me little services and to meddle in my little affairs.' Laliaud said he wanted Rousseau's bust to ornament a library stuffed with Rousseau's books, but Rousseau came to doubt 'whether any of my books figured among the few he had ever read.'[78]

other in plaster, which Rousseau described[81] as 'une mauvaise esquisse en terre, sur laquelle il a fait graver un portrait hideux'. The engraving was by Samuel-Charles Miger and shows Rousseau full face, bare-headed, with an open shirt and fur-collared robe. In the *Dialogues*[82] he claims that copies, further distorted to make him look a criminal, were circulated by his enemies to further their vilification of him. To the impartial observer the portrait looks inoffensive, the expression anxious rather than vicious; but Rousseau hated all the portraits made of him, other than La Tour's.

Among the visitors to the Temple, one who could surely have claimed the status of a 'particular friend' was Lenieps. Naturally excited by the political developments in Geneva, he was eager to discuss them with Rousseau and to recruit Rousseau's polemical skills once more for the citizens' cause. A hardened radical, Lenieps was pressing the *Représentant* party in Geneva to carry their opposition to further extremes by resisting the Petit Conseil's call for the intervention of the French as mediating power. Since Rousseau had expressed equally radical views in the *Letters from the Mountain*, the Genevese authorities assumed he was in cahoots with Lenieps. In fact, it is clear from the letters Rousseau wrote to François d'Ivernois that he advocated moderation, urging the citizens to seek peace as well as liberty and to accept the good offices of the French mediators to restore order in the city. He urged[83] d'Ivernois not to be led by the extremists:

My good Friend, let your friends do as they will and stay calm. I give you my word that if the Mediation takes place the wretches who threaten you will do you no harm by such means. That is something you can count on. However, do not fail to take the opportunity of seeing the French Resident in order to counter any efforts that may have been made to prejudice him against you. For the rest, I repeat, stay calm. The Mediation will do you no harm.

Time was to prove this judgement overconfident. The French resident, Pierre-Michel Hennin, was no friend of the citizens' cause. He had surveillance extended even to Genevese radicals in exile, including Lenieps, who within a matter of months was to be imprisoned in the Bastille. Rousseau was also targeted, but he did not risk arrest by lingering in France.

On New Year's Day, 1766, he wrote[84] to Du Peyrou, saying, 'I am here in my hotel like Sancho Panza on the island of Barataria on display all day. I have a crowd of all ranks from the moment I wake up until the moment I go to bed. I am even forced to dress in public. I have never suffered so much, but it will soon be over.'

There were people who were equally impatient to see him go. Apart from his actual enemies, there were those who, without setting eyes on him, or even reading his books, mocked him. One such was Horace Walpole. He picked up the idea, perhaps from Holbach, that Rousseau really enjoyed being persecuted, and one evening in December he drafted, for fun, an imaginary letter[85] from Frederick II to Rousseau, offering to persecute the philosopher at his pleasure.

My dear Jean-Jacques.

You have renounced Geneva, your homeland; you have had yourself driven out of Switzerland, a place much praised in your writings; the French have issued a warrant for your arrest; so come to me. I admire your talents; I am amused by your reveries, on which, incidentally, you dwell too much and too long. In the end, you must be wise and happy. You have excited enough talk by singularities that hardly become a truly great man. Show your enemies that you sometimes have common sense. That will annoy them and do you no harm. My states offer you a peaceful refuge. I wish you well and will treat you well if you wish me to. But if you persist in rejecting my help, believe me, I shall tell no one. If you go racking your brains to find new misfortunes, choose what you will. I am a King and can provide you with as much suffering as you desire and—something you will not obtain from your enemies—I shall cease persecuting you when you cease to seek glory in being persecuted.

Your good friend
Frederick.

According to his own recollections[86] Walpole showed the first draft of this letter to Helvétius and the Duc de Nivernais, who both suggested improvements to the French, and urged the author to circulate it. He then read it in the *salons* first of Mme de Rochefort and then of Mme Du Deffand, who sent a copy to Voltaire and passed another to President Hénault for further stylistic *retouches*. Mme de Mirepoix also distributed copies to all her smart friends. These events added to the mirth of the festive season in Paris between late December and early January, when Rousseau left the city. He did not see a copy of Walpole's letter until several weeks later.

He had never met Walpole, but assumed him to be well disposed since Hume had reported from him an offer of a refuge in England. And although he had never liked Mme Du Deffand, Mme de Mirepoix, or President Henault, none of the participants in Walpole's *facétie* was thought of by Rousseau as an enemy. Indeed, Helvétius, whose wife was pressing him to dine, he counted as a friend. The Duc de Nivernais★ had been reported[87] by Mme de Verdelin to be willing to put at his disposal his knowledge of

★Louis Mancini, Duc de Nivernais, a prominent diplomatist and academician, was known to Rousseau chiefly as the friend and protector of Alexandre Deleyre, who continued to send Rousseau long letters from Parma full of lamentations about Catholic intolerance and the tedium of provincial life in Italy.

England. Rousseau can hardly have expected to be attacked by these people. In any case, there was probably no real malice behind the 'letter'; it was just a joke. It was not, however, a joke that Rousseau would laugh at, and those who understood his nature best—the Prince de Conti, Mme de Boufflers, and Mme de Luxembourg—reproached Walpole angrily for something they considered more cruel than funny.[88]

Since Hume was then living in the same house as Walpole—the Hôtel du Parc Royal[89]—he might be expected to have had some knowledge of the 'letter'; but it seems he only heard about it when he reached London. Later Rousseau came to suspect that Hume not only knew about it but had had a hand in its composition. No suspicions, however, clouded his relationship with Hume during their time together in Paris.

On Friday, 3 January, Hume spent two hours in the company of Rousseau and Mme de Boufflers, making plans for their departure the following day. Afterward Hume went to take leave of Holbach, full of enthusiasm about his forthcoming trip to England with his 'pupil', as he had started to call Rousseau, although he was only one year older. According to Morellet,[90] who was present, the Baron said: 'I am sorry to dispel the hopes and illusions that flatter you, but I tell you that it will not be long before you are unde-ceived. You do not know your man. I tell you plainly that you are nursing a viper in your bosom.'

Hume also visited Mme de Verdelin; her message was very different. In writing to bid farewell to Rousseau, she said,[91] 'I have just seen Mr. Hume. I commended your welfare to him. He is worthy of the trust; the more I lis-ten to him the more I admire his candour. His soul is made for yours.'

Plans were made for Rousseau. Hume, de Luze, and the dog Sultan were to travel with him in two carriages from the Temple at 11 A.M. on Saturday, 4 January.* The weather was bitterly cold, for this was one of the most se-vere winters France had experienced for many years; but Rousseau's spirits were high, almost euphoric, as the party set out for Calais. During their first night's stopover, variously remembered as Senlis and Roye—an odd thing happened, or was imagined to have happened. Rousseau recalled it in a let-ter he wrote[93] some months later:

We slept in the same room, and several times during the night Hume cried out in French with extreme vehemence 'I've got hold of Jean-Jacques Rousseau.'† I

---

*On 3 January, Rousseau wrote a note to his old friend, Mme de Créqui, apologising for failing to visit her. The desire to see her, he protested politely, had been one of his motives for coming to Paris, only 'necessity, that cruel necessity which always governs any life, forbids the satisfaction of that desire . . . I leave with the bitter certainty of never seeing you again.' His bitter certainty was re-futed by experience. Mme de Créqui lived to be nearly ninety, and in the fulness of time Rousseau was able once more to enjoy her company and her pious conversation.[92]

†'Je tiens Jean-Jacques Rousseau.'

do not know if he was awake or asleep. The expression is remarkable in the mouth of a man who knows French too well to be mistaken about the power and choice of words . . . Every time he spoke those words I felt a shudder of fear which I could not control, but it only took a moment for me to pull myself together and laugh at my terror. Next day everything was so completely forgotten that I did not think about it again until later events revived the memory.

The travellers moved on through Arras and St-Omer to Calais, where they were held up by bad weather for two days. It was still stormy on the night of their crossing, and Hume was impressed by Rousseau's fortitude, as he revealed in a letter[94] to Mme de Boufflers: 'He believes himself very infirm. He is one of the most robust men I have ever known. He passed ten hours above deck during the most severe weather, when all the seamen were almost frozen to death, and he caught no harm.' When they landed in Dover, Rousseau threw his arms round Hume's neck and covered Hume's face with kisses and tears. 'That was not the only time,' Rousseau noted[95] later, 'that Monsieur Hume saw in me the transports of a pierced heart.'

One might surmise that Hume was simply embarrassed. In his letter to Mme de Boufflers, however, Hume wrote, 'My pupil has an excellent warm heart; and in conversation kindles often to a degree of heat which looks like inspiration. I love him much, and hope I may have some share in his affections.'

In the hours they had spent waiting for the boat at Calais, Hume raised the possibility of seeking a pension for Rousseau from King George III; for although Hume had few friends in England, those few included one well placed to help, namely, General Seymour Conway, Secretary of State and brother of Lord Hertford, the ambassador under whom Hume had served in Paris. Hume asked if Rousseau would accept. Rousseau hesitated. Dreading the high cost of living in England, and conscious of the modesty of his resources, he was prompted to agree; but having already rejected offers of a pension from the King of France and the King of Prussia, could he, without offence to both, accept one from the King of England? He told Hume that if his 'father', Lord Keith, approved, his answer would be yes.

Hume reported[96] this conversation to Mme de Boufflers. He also informed her that he had 'exhorted [Rousseau] on the road to write his memoirs. He told me that he had already done it . . . "At present," says he, "it may be affirmed that nobody knows me perfectly any more than himself, but I shall describe myself in such plain colours that henceforth everyone may boast that he knows himself and Jean-Jacques Rousseau." I believe that he intends seriously to draw his own picture in its true colours: but I believe at the same time that nobody knows himself less.'

REVERSAL OF FORTUNE

On Monday, 13 January 1766, Rousseau and his travelling companions arrived in London. Several newspapers reported the event, the *Public Advertiser*, on the Wednesday, announcing[1] that ''tis with pleasure we find he has chosen an asylum amongst a people who know how to respect one of his distinguished talents.'

Rousseau and Hume went straight to the house of John Stewart in Buckingham Street and were put up in rooms next door with a Mrs Adams. Hume decided not to go to his usual pied-à-terre in the house in Lisle Street of a fellow Scotsman, William Rouet, a former professor at Glasgow University, who had been expecting him.[2] One unpleasant discovery Rousseau made soon after his arrival was that Louis-François Tronchin, son of his great enemy Dr Théodore Tronchin, 'the Juggler', also had rooms in the same Lisle Street house.

Crowds gathered whenever Rousseau appeared in the street, startled by his Armenian outfit. Hume thought the costume a 'whim', but as Rousseau had confided that he needed a chamber pot every minute, Hume recognised[3] that the dress was not altogether an affectation: 'He has an infirmity from his infancy which makes breeches uncomfortable for him.'

The first four days were unclouded. Rousseau paid no visits, but many important persons came to his rooms to visit him. They included the Duke of York, incognito; Charles William Ferdinand of Brunswick, the Prince Héritier; Viscount Nuneham; Colonel Richmond Webb; Lord Keith's friend the Rev. Richard Penneck, director of the reading room in the British Museum; and Rousseau's cousin Jean Rousseau. The eccentric French *chargé d'affaires*, the Chevalier d'Eon, sent Rousseau a fervent fan letter but did not appear in person; had he done so the public would have been still more startled, since the chevalier dressed as a woman. After the splendour of the Temple, Rousseau pronounced himself relieved to be in the more modest environment of Buckingham Street. He also praised London: 'From the wide pavements in the street,' he remarked[4] to a journalist, 'it is apparent that you respect the people.'

David Garrick was another visitor. He invited Rousseau to attend a gala performance at Drury Lane in the presence of King George III and the Queen. Rousseau accepted but almost missed the performance when his dog Sultan started howling and, he told Hume, he could not bear to leave the animal unattended lest it run away.[5] Hume insisted that they could not disappoint Mrs Garrick, who was expecting them in her box. He persuaded Rousseau to lock the dog in his bedroom and pocket the key, then took his 'pupil' to Drury Lane. According to a newspaper,[6] 'the crowd was so great at getting into Drury-Lane theatre . . . that a great number of gentlemen lost their hats and wigs, and ladies their cloaks, bonnets, etc.' Mrs Garrick's box was opposite that of the King and Queen, who were said by Hume to have 'looked more at Rousseau than at the players'.[7]

Two plays were performed that evening, the tragedy *Zara*, by Aaron Hill, and the comedy *Lethe*, by Garrick himself. Although he did not understand the words, Rousseau wept at the tragedy and laughed at the comedy, becoming so excited at one point that Mrs Garrick had to hold the skirt of his caftan to prevent his falling out of the box.[8] After supper Rousseau and Hume went to a reception at Garrick's house, where Rousseau was introduced to Oliver Goldsmith and other English writers.

Despite all these attentions, Rousseau was restless in London and impatient to go to a country retreat. The refuge at Fulham that John Stewart found for him proved quite unsuitable: the house was dirty, and the room Rousseau was offered already had a sick man in the second bed. Hume spent a good deal of time looking for another place but could not come up with an immediate solution. Meanwhile, Rousseau retired to the village of Chiswick on the outskirts of London to await developments, lodging there with a grocer and causing something of a commotion whenever he appeared in the shop.

The delay in finding permanent lodgings made Rousseau uneasy, and several things happened to alarm him. One day he was botanising with Professor John Walker beside the Thames when a jolly party of young sailors disembarked nearby. Convinced they had come to arrest and deport him, Rousseau took to his heels and fled in panic. Professor Walker had the greatest difficulty in catching him and putting his mind to rest. Rousseau also suspected that some hostility towards him was growing in literary quarters, and in this matter he was not mistaken. Edmund Burke was cultivating a dislike that was to culminate in an attack on Rousseau, in his *Reflections on the Revolution in France* (1790), as the 'founder of the philosophy of vanity'. Dr Johnson told Boswell[9] that in his opinion Rousseau should not be allowed to remain in England: 'Sir, if you mean to be serious, I think him one of the worst of men: a rascal who ought to be hunted out of society, as he has been. Three or four nations have expelled him and it is a shame he is protected in this country . . . Rousseau, Sir, is a very bad man. I would sooner sign a sentence for his transportation than that of any felon who has gone from Old Bailey these many years.'

With London becoming so uncongenial, Rousseau was ever more eager to settle in the countryside. The chief difficulty Hume encountered in trying to find a suitable venue was presented by Thérèse. Wherever he was to board, Rousseau wished to have Thérèse take her meals with him, and since Hume described her to potential hosts as Rousseau's 'maid', the proposal was resisted. Good manners in England allowed a gentleman to dine with a mistress but not with a servant.

Hume, of course, had never met Thérèse, but he had heard more than enough from those who had. In a letter to Mme de Boufflers,[10] Hume wrote concerning Rousseau that 'we shall have many ways of settling him to his satisfaction' but that his *gouvernante*, Thérèse, posed the chief obstacle. Evidently unaware that the Countess already knew Thérèse, he went on to observe that 'M. de Luze, our companion, says that she passes for wicked, and quarrelsome, and tattling, and is thought to be the chief cause of his quitting Neufchâtel.' Rousseau himself, Hume added, 'owns her to be so dull, that she never knows in what year of the Lord she is, nor in what month of the year, nor in what day of the month or week; and that she can never learn the different value of the pieces of money in any country. Yet she governs him as absolutely as a nurse does a child. In her absence his dog has acquired that ascendant. His affection for that creature is beyond all expression or conception.'

Soon Hume reported[11] to Mme de Boufflers that he had persuaded Rousseau to accept a pension of one hundred pounds a year from King George III. He explained that the King was 'extremely prudent and decent, and careful not to give offence. For which reason, he requires that this act of generosity shall be an entire secret'. It turned out that Rousseau disliked the idea of the royal pension being an 'entire secret', and Hume had next to find some means of having that condition waived. At the same time he had to persuade Rousseau, who vacillated between wanting the pension and insisting on being dependent upon no one, to indicate he would accept it. Hume accomplished the first of these delicate tasks more successfully than the second. In May he was informed that the royal pension would be granted. By then, however, Rousseau was reluctant to express his willingness to accept it.

Persuading Rousseau where to settle was also proving difficult. There was a scheme for him to go to Wales, another to the Isle of Wight, others to Plymouth and Surrey, but all were rejected. Thérèse came to join him, after her eventful journey in the all-too-solicitous company of Boswell. At the time they were living as guests in the country home in Dorking of Daniel Malthus, an English friend they had met in Switzerland who was the father of Thomas Robert Malthus, later to become famous for his *Essay on Population*. One afternoon Rousseau was in Harley Street having his portrait painted, in full Armenian costume, by the celebrated Allan Ramsay—a portrait he afterward came to dislike intensely because he claimed it made him look like a 'Cyclops'. There he was introduced to an elderly, cultured gentleman of considerable means, Richard Davenport.

Hearing that Rousseau was looking for somewhere to live, Davenport offered him the use of Wootton Hall, a mansion he owned on the borders of Staffordshire and Derbyshire. Although its architecture was nothing to boast about, he said (too modestly, for it was an impressive building), it was set in a park and he thought Rousseau might like the surrounding countryside, which was wild and hilly and unspoiled—in fact, almost Swiss. Davenport explained that he himself disliked the climate, which was too severe for him, and that he never spent more than one month in twelve at the house; but he kept it open and was very willing to put it at Rousseau's disposal if he wished to use it. Warned by Hume not to offend Rousseau by offering it to him for nothing, Davenport agreed to name a very low rent of thirty pounds a year. The terms were accepted, and Rousseau and Thérèse prepared to leave for the north. Davenport generously made his coach available for their journey, pretending that it was 'returning empty' to Wootton.

On 17 March, two days before they were to go, Hume invited Rousseau to bring Thérèse to dine at his rooms in Lisle Street with General Seymour Conway, the Secretary of State through whom Hume was negotiating the royal pension, and Lady Aylesbury. Rousseau asked to be excused. He explained,[12] 'I am not well, and in no state to come, and Mademoiselle Levasseur, good and estimable a person as she is, is not made to appear in high society.'

On the eve of the departure for Wootton, Rousseau went to Lisle Street to thank Hume but also to reproach him. Rousseau suspected that he had not been told the truth about the coach being made available for the journey. He saw Davenport's white lie as an attempt to disguise a gift that would impair his independence by putting him under an obligation to a would-be benefactor. Insisting that he would rather live like a beggar than be treated as a child, he berated Hume for his apparent complicity in the deception. When Hume answered the accusation evasively, Rousseau sat down in what Hume described as a very sullen humour. Hume recounted[13] what happened next in a letter to his old Scots friend Dr Hugh Blair:

After passing near an hour in this ill humour, he rose up and took a turn about the room: but judge of my surprize, when he sat down suddenly on my knee,

threw his hands about my neck, kiss'd me with the greatest warmth, and be-
dewing all my face with tears, exclaim'd, *'Is it possible you can ever forgive me, my
dear friend: After all the testimonies of affection I have received from you, I reward you
at last with this folly & ill behaviour: but I have notwithstanding a heart worthy of
your friendship; I love you, I esteem you; and not an instant of your kindness is thrown
away upon me.'*

Hume returned the embrace, he told Blair, remarking that 'no scene of my
life was ever more affecting.'

When Rousseau reached Wootton, he was delighted with what he found
there. The weather was bad, but Nature was magnificently present. The servants gave him and Thérèse a cordial welcome, and a few agreeable neighbours came to visit them. Rousseau took long walks each day, collecting
botanical specimens as he had done at Montmorency. He continued writing
his *Confessions*, begun at Môtiers, and kept up a large correspondence. Davenport made the correspondence considerably less expensive than it would
otherwise have been by collecting the letters addressed to Rousseau in London and bringing them to Wootton, saving him the cost of forwarding them
by post. Rousseau, now settled comfortably, wrote[14] to Hume on 22 March
to express his appreciation: 'If I live in this pleasing house of refuge as happily as I hope, one of the sweet joys of my life will be the thought that I owe
it to you.'

Soon afterward Rousseau's attitude to Hume underwent an abrupt
change. The occasion of this was the appearance in the *St James Chronicle*,
the issue dated 1 April 1767, in the original French, and a day later in English translation, of the jesting letter written by Walpole purportedly from
King Frederick II inviting Rousseau to Prussia, and promising to use his
royal authority to make him there 'as miserable as you could possibly wish'.

Rousseau already knew of the existence of this poor, rather laboured joke
at his expense, and that Walpole was at any rate a part-author of it, but its appearance in the *St James Chronicle* made him think of another name. He remembered that Walpole was a friend of David Hume's. He also remembered
that the editor of this journal was William Strahan, an even closer friend of
Hume's. Was it merely a coincidence that Louis-François Tronchin, the son
of one of his greatest enemies in Geneva, was already living in the same
lodging house in Lisle Street to which he had been brought by the same
Hume?

There was also the matter of Rousseau's correspondence. To avoid paying
what he considered excessive postage, Rousseau thought of not accepting
letters addressed to him. Hume warned him that if he did so his letters would
be opened at the postal office and all his affairs known by the authorities. He
offered to arrange some accommodation in the matter of franking. This so-

licitude now struck Rousseau as a sign of an altogether sinister curiosity on Hume's part about his correspondence.

Never one to keep black thoughts buried in his bosom, Rousseau wrote[15] to Hume, sarcastically accusing him of seeking to dishonour him and curtly breaking off their friendship:

Knowing me only by my literary reputation, you were eager to place at my disposal your friends and your services; touched by your generosity I threw myself in your arms, and you brought me to England, ostensibly to find me asylum, but in fact to dishonour me. You have applied yourself to this noble task with a zeal worthy of your heart and with a success worthy of your abilities . . . I leave the field open to the manoeuvres of your friends and yourself, and surrender my reputation to you with but little regret . . . I wish you, Monsieur Hume, the truest happiness, but as we can have nothing more to say to each other, this is the last letter you will ever receive from me.

Hume replied[16] at once, expressing shock at the accusations and demanding they be made specific:

As I am conscious of having ever acted towards you in the most friendly part, of having ever given you the most tender, the most active proofs of sincere affection, you may judge of my extreme surprize on perusing your epistle: Such violent accusations, confined altogether to generals, it is as impossible to answer as to comprehend them. But affairs cannot, must not remain on that footing. I shall charitably suppose, that some infamous calumniator has belied me to you. But in that case, it is your duty, and I am persuaded it will be your inclination, to give me an opportunity of detecting him, and of justifying myself, which can only be done by your mentioning the particulars, of which I am accused . . . As an innocent man; I will not say, as your friend; I will not say, as your benefactor; but I repeat it, as an innocent man, I claim the privilege of proving my innocence and of refuting any scandalous lie which may have been invented against me.

Rousseau's lengthy answer[17] exceeded seventy-five hundred words. In it he did not so much provide a bill of particulars as express his intuitive suspicions:

I am ill, Monsieur Hume, and little disposed for writing, but as you ask for an explanation it should be given you . . . I live outside the world, and am ignorant of much that goes on in it. I belong to no party, I am involved in no intrigues. Nothing is told me, I only know what I feel. But since good care is taken to make me feel very forcibly, I know well what I feel. Naturally, the first precaution taken by people who plot is to hide all legally actionable proofs . . . but there are other sorts of proofs which can bring inner conviction to an honest man . . .

You ask, with great confidence, who is your accuser? Your accuser is yourself, your accuser is David Hume.

Rousseau then recalled how he had been introduced to London by Hume, who had arranged for many services to be done for him by his friends. In the beginning, all had been pleasant. Then he had noticed a change of attitude, 'at first vague, but soon obvious'. Abruptly, the tone of the newspapers changed from one of effusive friendship to one of malevolent derision. Even stranger was the fact that the attitude of David Hume's friends changed simultaneously with that of the public. He recounted the signs that he now recognised all pointed to Hume's hostility, accusing him of having been a party to the forged letter from Frederick—that 'most cruel malignity'. It could hardly have been coincidence that Hume shared lodgings with Tronchin *fils*. Now he understood why at the inn on the road to Calais Hume had cried out in the night, 'I've got hold of Jean-Jacques Rousseau. I've got hold of Jean-Jacques Rousseau.' 'Yes,' the letter continued,

you do hold me, but only by circumstances which are external to me. You hold me, by the control of the opinions and judgements passed on me by other men; you hold my reputation, even perhaps my safety . . . It is easy for you to pass me off, as you have begun to do, as a monster . . . The general public will not show me any more sympathy . . . Yes, Monsieur Hume, you hold me, and by all the ties of the world, but you have no hold on my virtue or my courage, they remain my own . . . I am surprised I have had the strength to write this letter. If one died of grief, I should have died at every line . . .

Hume was taken aback by the tone and ferocity of the accusations and recognised that there was no way he could hope to dispel such delusionary fantasies of persecution. In his response he said[18] the only thing he was guilty of was entering into a good-natured artifice with Davenport to make Rousseau believe that an empty *retour chaise* was available. As for the rest,

I shall only add in general that I enjoyed about a month ago an uncommon pleasure, when I reflected, that . . . I had . . . provided for your repose, honour and fortune by means of a pension from the King. But I soon felt a very sensible uneasiness, when I found that you had, wantonly and voluntarily, thrown away all these advantages, and [were] the declared enemy of your own repose, fortune and honour. I cannot be surprised after this, that you are my enemy. Adieu, and for ever.

Hume is revealed by this exchange to have been much the more temperate and injured party, and his willingness to continue to pursue a royal pension for Rousseau even after the breach in their friendship shows exceptional magnanimity. But the next scene in the drama does not display him in so favourable a light. Hume decided to print and publish the correspondence which had passed between Rousseau and himself. This was an extraordinary step, since the correspondence had nothing to do with ideological questions, or any public controversy. What Hume had decided to do was simply to wash his dirty linen in public.

Hume was strongly advised against this drastic course. Adam Smith, writing[19] from Paris, tried to dissuade him by arguing that to publish against Rousseau would only call attention to him, just when he was in danger of falling into obscurity. 'Your whole friends here wish you not to write, the Baron [d'Holbach], d'Alembert, Madame Riccaboni, Mademoiselle Riancourt, Mr. Turgot, etc., etc.' Mme de Boufflers wrote[20] in a similar vein, expressing distress that the most enlightened people in Europe should thus tear each other to shreds. Acknowledging that Rousseau's 'atrocious' letter was evidence of gross ingratitude and 'the most complete insanity', she urged Hume to show forbearance and put compassion ahead of a wish for vindication.

Hume would not listen to such counsels of restraint. Quite convinced that Rousseau would not have written to him at such length if he had not intended to publish the letter, Hume thought it desirable to get into print first. In fact, there is no evidence whatever for thinking that Rousseau intended to publish their exchanges or to determine what should be published. As for Hume, he was anxious to do both. Writing[21] to Dr Blair before replying to Rousseau, he took care to cover his tracks, lest his previously effusive praise for Rousseau now make him appear foolish: 'You will be surprised, dear Doctor, when I desire you most earnestly never in your life to show to any mortal creature the letters I wrote you with regard to Rousseau: He is surely the blackest and most atrocious villain, beyond comparison, that now exists in the world; and I am heartily ashamed of anything I wrote in his favour . . . I am afraid I must publish this to the world in a pamphlet . . .'

The pamphlet, entitled 'A Concise And Genuine Account of the dispute between Mr. Hume and Mr. Rousseau', included their exchange of letters and was printed on Hume's instruction first in French in October and then in English in November; its contents became a favourite topic of gossip and controversy in both London and Paris. Before having the correspondence printed, Hume wrote to his friends in Paris, many of whom were predisposed against Rousseau, to assure himself of their support. Having failed to dissuade him from making the controversy public, they rallied to his side. Voltaire, informed by a Parisian ally that Rousseau had been 'unmasked' and was an object of derision on both sides of the Channel, declared that it was high time every intellectual who had been taken in by him joined in the denunciation.[12] Some of Rousseau's friends, including Mme Boy de La Tour and the painter Fuseli, defended him, but Rousseau himself maintained a pained and dignified silence.

Throughout this contretemps, in fact, everybody at Wootton thought him remarkably happy. He had taken a liking to a French-speaking neighbour, Bernard Granville, who lived at Calwich, about two miles away, and became especially fond of Granville's twenty-year-old niece, Mary Dewes. A number of other sympathetic ladies stayed at Granville's house during the summer, including the Duchess of Portland, the Countess Cowper, Viscountess Andover, and Lady Kildare. Rousseau, as one might expect, was a great success with them all, especially with the Duchess, who joined him on many of his botanising rambles. At other times Rousseau wandered alone about the district. At first, because of his strange dress and taciturn ways, he alarmed the local cottagers, but Thérèse and he were so generous to the poor that they soon became very popular figures. The local people called him 'Mr Ross Hall', and her 'Madam Zell', a corruption of 'Mademoiselle'.[23]

Meanwhile, in London his friends encouraged Dr Charles Burney to adapt Rousseau's *Le Devin du village* for the English stage. Dr Burney did so, and it was performed to Rousseau's music, under the title *The Cunning-Man,* at Garrick's theatre, Drury Lane, on 31 November. The first half of the piece was very warmly received, but for some reason there broke out toward the end what one witness described[24] as 'the buzz of hissing followed by the shrill horror of the catcall'. Several people wrote to the press complaining of what seemed to be senseless objection to the piece. One correspondent noted[25] that 'a great deal of the opposition to *The Cunning-Man* came from the other side of the Tweed.'*

Rousseau, who had the newspapers sent to him at Wootton, was well informed about its reception. The implication that Hume was responsible for the catcalls was not lost on Rousseau. Indeed it is hardly surprising that he should have taken it as a positive documentary evidence that his suspicions were justified. Hume certainly did not hire a claque of fellow Scotsmen to go to Drury Lane and boo, but there was an element of reality in the charge

---

*Rousseau did not altogether lack for British sympathizers, one of whom offered encouragement in the *St James Chronicle* (9–11 December 1766) in rhyming verse:

> Rousseau be firm! tho' Malice, like Voltaire,
> And supercilious Pride, like d'Alembert,
> Though mad Presumption W[alpo]le's form assume,
> And base born Treachery appear like H[um]e,
> Yet droop not thou, these Spectres gathering round,
> These night-drawn Phantoms want the power to wound:
> Fair truth shall chase th' unreal Forms away;
> And Reason's piercing Beam restore the Day;
> Britain shall snatch the Exile to her Breast,
> And conscious Virtue soothe his Soul to rest.

nevertheless. Hume had appropriated and exploited Rousseau's private correspondence in order, as he thought, to defend his own reputation by making Rousseau look ridiculous. He had, in fact, turned the public against Rousseau by publishing those letters. By making him a laughing-stock he created a situation in which people were disposed to go to the theatre and jeer at Rousseau's work.

Towards the end of the year things began to go bad at Wootton. Thérèse, getting rather bored, started to quarrel with the servants. She was not the kind of woman to get on well with servants at the best of times: she was too plebeian herself. Servants, not unnaturally, resented being given orders by a woman they regarded as no better—in fact, a good deal worse—than themselves. It would not have been any easier if she had been married to Rousseau. In the eighteenth century, domestic servants did not expect a very high standard of chastity in their employers; but they did expect manners and breeding, and Thérèse was as coarse as she was uneducated.

Rousseau sensed the change in the atmosphere and came to the conclusion—rightly in her case, but wrongly in his own—that Thérèse and he were no longer welcome at Wootton. He therefore wrote to Davenport, seeking reassurance. When no answer came (for the post had been, by ill chance, delayed) Rousseau wrote[26] again: 'Every man has his own character. Mine is open and trusting, more open and trusting than it should be, perhaps. I do not ask you to be like me, but it is making too much of a mystery to refuse to say precisely on what footing I am in your house, and whether I am in the way or not.'

In the early spring of 1767, Davenport had been surprised to hear that Rousseau expected to be paid the pension King George had granted him the year before. Everyone had assumed that Rousseau was refusing the pension when he said that he would accept no service with which David Hume was concerned. In fact, Rousseau felt himself on the horns of a dilemma. He did not wish to accept a benefit arranged by someone he regarded as a traitor who had dishonoured him, but neither did he wish to appear ungrateful to the King. Davenport approached General Conway on Rousseau's behalf, but the general refused to re-open the question without Hume's consent. Hume gave his consent, though he wrote to Dr Blair,[28] saying: 'This step of my old friend confirms the suspicion which I always entertained, that he thought he had interest enough to obtain the pension of himself, and that he had only picked a quarrel with me in order to free himself from the humiliating burden of gratitude towards me. His motives, therefore, were much blacker than many seem to apprehend them.'

Davenport's representations were successful, and he was soon able to inform Rousseau[29] that the King himself had personally authorised the payment of the pension. Rousseau was warned, however, that he must not offend his patron by hesitating a second time to accept it, and gave appropriate assurances. Pleased at having been of service to his honoured guest, Davenport wrote: 'I heartily wish you joy.'

Joy was not the emotion Rousseau was at that time experiencing. In April, his thirteenth month at Wootton, tension in the house reached breaking point. After a quarrel with Thérèse, the housekeeper put cinders and ashes in the soup. Rousseau took up his pen and wrote[30] indignantly to Davenport to announce that he was leaving Wootton:

The master of a house should know what is going on in it, particularly with regard to strangers whom he entertains. If you do not know what has been happening to me in your house since Christmas, you are to blame: if you do know, and allow it, you are still more to blame . . . Tomorrow, Monsieur, I leave your house. I shall leave behind my small effects and those of Mademoiselle le Vasseur and also the proceeds of my collection of engravings and books to meet the costs of my supplies since Christmas. I am not unaware of the dangers that await me, or of my impotence to protect myself against them . . . Receive once more my warm and sincere thanks for the lavish hospitality you have accorded me. If it had finished as it began, I should carry away from you tender memories which could never be effaced from my heart. Adieu, Monsieur. I shall often regret the house I am leaving: but I shall regret still more having failed to make so amiable a host my friend.

Rousseau left this letter for Davenport in a guest room at Wootton, where it escaped the notice of the servants for some weeks. Davenport was in Cheshire and therefore had no knowledge of Rousseau's departure until the third week of May. Rousseau had in the meantime gone to Spalding in Lincolnshire, a destination a hundred miles distant. His purpose in going there remains something of a mystery. One possible explanation is that he was on his way to the residence in Louth of Jean-François Maximilien Cerjat, a Swiss married to an Englishwoman, and a friend of Rousseau's own friend and patron, Pierre-Alexandre Du Peyrou. But although Rousseau had corresponded with Cerjat and may have been en route to see him, possibly to deposit for safe keeping the manuscript of the chapters of the *Confessions* he had then completed, there is no documentary evidence of this. What is abundantly clear from the written evidence is that Rousseau was by this time in a state of acute anxiety and that he felt himself to be in real danger. He wrote[31] from Spalding on 5 May to the Lord Chancellor of England, Camden, asking for a bodyguard to conduct him to Dover:

My Lord,
Will you allow a poor foreigner, who must be under the protection of the law here, to put himself also under your protection? My situation, which is strange and little known, compels me to take this unusual and perhaps indiscreet liberty,

but it is my only resource. Since I have been in this district, by the impossibility of going further alone and without danger, I thought that the first minister of the law must also be the first minister of public hospitality, and I venture to ask you to be good enough to find, at my expense, an authorized guide to conduct me immediately, and in safety, to Dover, where I propose to embark without bringing any complaint against anyone.

Davenport had in the meantime found a letter from Rousseau and replied[32] in the most earnest terms: 'I never was at Spalding, but I have always understood it to be one of the most cursed and disagreeable places in England. I can't conceive what motive could possibly make you go there, and all that flat country is reckoned very unwholesome, especially for those, who are not natives: for God's sake return out of it as soon as you can.'

Rousseau remained determined to leave England. A letter from Lord Camden[33] assured him that he would be as safe with any postboy as with any guide he, Camden, should choose. A few days later, Rousseau was in Dover. While there he wrote General Conway a letter that Hume saw and described[34] to Turgot:

Nothing could be more frenzical than this letter. He supposes himself to be a prisoner of state in the hands of the general at my suggestion, entreats for leave to depart the kingdom, represents the danger of assassinating him in private, and while he owns that he has been infamous in England during his life, he foretells that his memory will be justified after his death. He says that he has composed a volume of memoirs, chiefly with regard to the treatment he has met with in England, and the state of captivity, in which he has been detained, and if the General will give him permission to depart, this volume, which is deposited in safe hands, shall be delivered to him, and nothing ever can appear to the disgrace of the nation or its ministers.

Hume went on to say that Rousseau was 'absolutely lunatic' and that the kindest thing would be to put him in quiet retreat under 'a discreet keeper' in France.

Whatever the significance of Rousseau's promise to Conway, there is no trace of any volume of memoirs dealing with his visit to England. One of the final paragraphs of the twelfth and last book of the *Confessions*, thought to have been written in 1771, notes[35] the omission:

In the third part of my memoirs, if ever I am able to write them, I shall relate in what manner, thinking of going to Berlin, I actually set forth for England, and how the two ladies who wished to dispose of my person [the reference is clearly to Mme de Boufflers and Mme de Verdelin], after having by their manoeuvres driven me from Switzerland, where I was not sufficiently in their power, at last delivered me into the hands of their friend [Hume].'

Whatever Rousseau wrote after this, no account by him of his experiences in England is known to exist.

Rousseau's departure from England attracted some notice. A little news item, signed 'Rusticus', appeared[36] in the *European Magazine* in London, describing his last days in England and his eagerness to depart: 'On his arrival at Dover, in Kent, as the wind or tide did not serve for the passage-boats to sail immediately, Rousseau received an invitation to dine with P____ F____, a respectable character of that place. Whilst at table he expressed the greatest impatience to be at sea, and could not be persuaded but Mr. F____ had been requested by General Conway, then Secretary of State, to detain him. In this belief he arose from the table repeatedly, ran to the window, and eagerly looked if the wind was fair.' The writer then describes how Rousseau became so alarmed that he hurried on board the boat, locked himself in his cabin, and was brought out by the insistence of Thérèse, who is not very politely referred to as 'an elderly lady who resided with Rousseau under the appellation of his *gouvernante*'. Yielding to her rage and abuse, Rousseau 'returned to Mr F____'s house, and conversed sociably with that gentleman and his family till late in the evening'.

The boat finally set sail for Calais on 21 May 1767. Rousseau's spirits were restored by a festive reception at Amiens four days later. He put aside his Armenian garb and went about under his own name, in defiance of the authorities. Warned by the Prince de Conti that he was risking arrest, Rousseau left Amiens secretly at night on 3 June and settled down as the Prince's guest at the château de Trye in Normandy, where he would remain for about a year.

At Trye Rousseau hoped to find tranquillity but soon suffered a full recurrence of his fears of persecution. The servants were as unpleasant to him and Thérèse as Davenport's seem to have been at Wootton. He thought himself surrounded by spies and enemies; he interpreted anything unusual, however accidental it might appear to others, as evidence of sinister plotting. Writing[37] plaintively to Mme de Verdelin, he claimed he could discern his enemies' hidden hand behind the insults and hostile actions of the staff. He thought of surrendering to the authorities; either he would be exonerated and set free or imprisoned in the Bastille, where he would at least be safer than he was at the château.[38] The Prince tried to calm his fears, but to no avail.

In November Du Peyrou came to visit him, and Rousseau was momentarily relieved. But his calm did not last. Du Peyrou was seriously ill with gout, an affliction he had suffered from early youth. He became feverish and in his delirium cried out that he must have been poisoned. Rousseau, fearing that if Du Peyrou died he might be accused of having been the poisoner, wrote out a declaration renouncing any share in his wealthy friend's estate, thereby removing any possible motive. Du Peyrou recovered and sent Rousseau a letter of apology. Rousseau forgave him and Du Peyrou remained at the château until January.[39] Their friendship was saved but it was strained by the episode.

Rousseau's determination to leave the château became ever more intense. Late in 1767 his *Dictionary of Music*, which he had been completing for several years, was published in Paris. He was pleased at its appearance because he thought of it as a fundamental contribution to musical theory, but even this consideration only caused him worry because he feared that it might serve as a pretext for trouble of the sort his earlier writings on music had provoked. Increasingly agitated, he wrote to Mme de Boufflers for help in finding a new domicile and violated the Prince's instructions by also writing in March to the King's minister, the Duc de Choiseul, begging to be allowed to live under his protection. De Choiseul replied, but what he said is not known.

Finally, in May, the Prince agreed to allow Rousseau to leave Trye, provided he remained outside the jurisdiction of the Paris *parlement* and agreed to live under his newly assigned pseudonym of Renou. Until a new refuge was found, Thérèse was to remain at Trye and Rousseau, alias 'M. Renou', was to go first to the Temple in Paris, which he reached 12 June. From there he went on to stay briefly at Lyons and Grenoble. While in Grenoble in July he made a nostalgic visit to Chambéry, where he paid tearful homage at the grave of Mme de Warens. On 12 August he fled Grenoble, possibly because he feared that an attack was about to be mounted there on his writings.[40]

Rousseau went next to the nearby town of Bourgoin, where he resolved to marry Thérèse so as to make her situation more respectable in the eyes of any neighbours and dispel doubts about his claim that she was his wife. She arrived 26 August pretending to be Mlle Renou, his sister. On 30 August, without telling her of his intention in advance, he asked the mayor of the town and an artillery captain to come to the inn where they were staying and witness their marriage, which took the form of a declaration of mutual consent; legal marriage between a Protestant and a Catholic was forbidden. Following the exchange of vows, he made so impassioned a speech about the duties of marriage that his listeners shed tears.[41]

Rousseau explained[42] his decision to marry Thérèse as a dutiful gesture in appreciation of her devotion: 'I have never carried out any duty more cheerfully or freely, since I had never given her any hope of it and she had no idea of what I wanted to do two minutes before . . . Since she will not leave me, at least I want her to follow me with honour.'

In late August, before the marriage took place, Rousseau became embroiled in yet another controversy, this one altogether out of the blue and involving such a patently invalid allegation as to confirm further his suspicions of persecution. He was undoubtedly suffering from paranoia, but in this instance, as in some of the others, he had some cause to feel that he was being persecuted. A certain Nicolas-Élie Thévenin, a chamois worker, demanded to be reimbursed nine francs he claimed to have lent Rousseau years before. Rousseau, whose memory was exceptionally keen, knew that he had never met such a person. Although initially he balked at returning to Grenoble to confront his accuser, he finally did so on 14 September. Questioning Thévenin effectively, he showed that there were contradictions and absurdities in the man's account. But he was not satisfied that his accuser be punished for mendacity. He saw the false accusation as further proof that there was a plot against him and demanded that the instigators be found and punished. And even though he had been vindicated, he felt that the populace was against him.[43]

Frustrated at having to remain in Grenoble for the trial, he amused himself by composing some 'scribblings' and posting them on the wall of his room. They show that while he had certainly fallen victim to delusions of persecution, he could still describe his imagined predicament with wit and insight. In a letter to Madelon Delessert he enclosed[44] a copy of what he had written, to be shared with her family:

Attitudes of the various orders of the public towards me:
   Kings and great aristocrats do not say what they think, but they always treat me magnanimously.
   The true nobility, which loves glory and knows that I understand it, honour me and are silent.
   The magistrates hate me because of the wrong they have done me.
   The *philosophes*, whom I have unmasked, want at all costs to ruin me and they will succeed.
   The bishops, proud of their birth and status, esteem me without fearing me and honour themselves by showing me respect.
   The lower clergy, owned by the *philosophes*, hound me in order to court their favour.
   The wits take revenge on me by insulting the superiority they sense in me.
   The people, whom I have idolised, see in me only an unkempt old fogey and a wanted man.
   Women, dupes of two cold fish who despise them [Voltaire and d'Alembert?], betray the one man who deserves the best of them.
   The Swiss will never forgive me for the evil they have done to me.
   The Magistrates of Geneva understand these wrongs, know that I forgive them, and would make amends if they dared.

The champions of the people, having climbed up on my shoulders, would like to hide me so well that only they could be seen.

Writers plagiarize me and accuse me; scoundrels curse me, the rabble boo me.

Decent people, if they still exist, decry my fate, and I for my part am blessed if one day it will be a lesson to humanity.

Voltaire, whom I keep from sleeping, will parody these lines. His coarse insults are a tribute he is forced to pay me in spite of himself.

Despite the successful outcome of the legal case, Rousseau remained apprehensive about his safety. Seeking to escape from France altogether, he wrote again to de Choiseul, who sent him a passport. He thought of going to Minorca or to Cyprus, even to America. Finally he decided to go back to Wootton and wrote asking Davenport's permission. But fearing that Walpole was plotting with the English ambassador, he concluded reluctantly that he must remain in France. On 30 January 1769 he moved to the village of Monquin, near Bourgoin but at a higher elevation, facing the Alps, where he hoped the air would be better for him. In July he went to Pougues, near the Loire, to see the Prince de Conti at his summer residence, hoping to persuade his protector to arrange for him to move elsewhere in France. The Prince evidently failed, and warned him that if he moved he would forfeit protection.[45]

On 24 June 1770 Rousseau nevertheless went back to Paris using his own name, despite the Prince's warning, stopping first for two months at Lyons, where he was entertained by Mme Boy de La Tour and other friends and where his *Pygmalion* and *Le Devin du village* were performed in his honour. En route to Paris Rousseau also stopped at Dijon, where he discussed botany with the celebrated naturalist the Comte de Buffon and his assistant L.J.M. Daubenton. It was reported[46] that Rousseau had been given permission to live in Paris on two conditions: he must not call attention to himself by wearing his Armenian garb, and he must refrain from any form of publishing—a restriction he was able to evade only by writing books that would be published posthumously. Constraining and threatening though the formal terms may have been, he was let alone by the authorities. He earned a living once again by copying music, had many visitors, and was often invited to dine at fashionable houses.

It was in Paris that Rousseau wrote the last pages of the *Confessions*, part of which he read in salons in presentations lasting from fifteen to seventeen hours at a stretch. But in his hope of responding to the attacks of his enemies among the *philosophes*, he realised that he was not succeeding. On the contrary, now that he had revealed so much of himself, including his weaknesses, he saw that they would only have new ammunition to fire against him.

His efforts at self-exoneration were interrupted in 1770 by a request for constitutional advice from Polish noblemen. Count Michel-Joseph Wielhorski had been sent to Paris by the members of the Confederation of Bar, an alliance of Catholic aristocrats who had risen in revolt in 1768 after Empress Catherine II of Russia had sent troops to help Stanislaw II, August Poniatowski, become king four years earlier. He had then imposed a constitution on the Polish parliament, the sejm. The confederates were interested in winning support for Polish independence and wanted advice on how to set up a new constitution once they achieved it. Although Rousseau knew little about Polish conditions, he knew enough to recognise that the Poles were at the mercy not only of the Russians but of other neighbouring powers as well, notably Prussia and Austria, and that the barriers preventing their winning national independence were virtually insuperable. In this he proved prescient: in 1772, the revolt was crushed and Poland suffered the first of several partitions that put its territory directly under foreign control.

Pleased nevertheless to be asked for his advice, Rousseau set about studying the complex social and political history of the country as best he could, from documents Wielhorski made available, devoting six months to the task. As with the inquiry from Corsica, he took advantage of the opportunity to restate the general theory he had advanced in *The Social Contract* and to show how it did and did not apply to conditions other than those for which it was intended.

In his *Considerations on the Government of Poland* Rousseau gave very different advice from that he had given the Corsicans. He made clear that the freedom that could in theory be achieved through the social contract was not a practical objective in all circumstances. He also used the Polish case as an occasion to indict all modern Europeans, who he said lacked the patriotic spirit and the institutions that had made possible the great political achievements of the ancient Greeks, Romans, and Israelites.

As to Poland itself, he pointed out first of all that it was a large and populous country—its population at the time numbering over 11 million—and a landlocked kingdom with a long tradition of feudal government and politics. Republican constitutions, he had always said, were suited only to small states, so there was no question of his advising the Poles to try to set up a republic. 'Large populations, vast territories! There you have the first and foremost reason for the misfortunes of mankind . . .'[47] The best he could suggest for the Poles was to nurture a spirit of patriotism and modify their social and political system.

Poland's constitutional monarchy was at the time one of the most confused in Europe, as well as one of the weakest and most corrupt. The sejm had become the oligarchic instrument of the three hundred noble families who controlled the suffrages of their propertyless dependents. Each of its members had a right of veto—the notorious *liberum veto*—and the right to elect successors to the monarchy. Because all Polish gentlemen were held to be of equal rank, each was given the right to block any piece of legislation merely by uttering the words 'Nie pozwalan' (I disapprove). This right, first used in 1652, had been so extended before the end of the seventeenth century that the exercise of a single veto by a deputy—who might easily be bribed by foreign diplomats or wealthy magnates—could at any time dissolve the session of the sejm. As a result, parliamentary activity had come to a standstill. To make matters still worse, success in election to the monarchy was determined both by the willingness of candidates to allow the nobles their traditional prerogative and by their ability to invoke outside assistance, guaranteeing that a weak monarchy would be incapable of making up for a hamstrung Diet.

Rousseau congratulated the confederates on their patriotic feelings but did not encourage their uprising. Mixing praise with counsels of prudence, he told the Poles as politely as possible that in view of their circumstances freedom was simply not a realistic option for them. Poland, he said admiringly, 'depopulated, devastated, and oppressed, wide open to its aggressors, in the depths of misfortune and anarchy, still shows the fires of youth'[48] in demanding new government and laws. But the Poles must not expect the impossible and risk forfeiting an opportunity for future independence by expecting to achieve it under present conditions. On the one hand, there was the 'self-interest and prejudice' of noblemen; on the other, the 'vice and laziness' of the serfs.[49] Such people would not even know the price of liberty, let alone be able to pay for it. 'Liberty is a food easy to eat, but hard to digest; it takes very strong stomachs to digest it.'[50] The best that could be hoped for was that all Poles would take inspiration from the Confederation of Bar and establish the republic in their hearts[51] by cultivating and preserving a distinctive and vibrant national culture. If they could keep themselves from being absorbed by a conqueror they could achieve 'stability' and might eventually hope to gain and keep their political independence. The Poles could not prevent the Russians from swallowing them, he said bluntly, but they might be able to keep from being digested.[52]

Far from endorsing the Polish social system, which conferred all authority on the nobility, Rousseau described it in terms as acid as any he had used in his *Discourse on the Origin of Inequality*. 'The Polish nation,' he observed, 'consists of the nobles who are everything, the bourgeoisie who are nothing, the peasants who are "less than nothing." '*[53] Invoking the law of na-

---

*Rousseau's language prefigures the revolutionary catechism of the famous pamphlet of 1789 written by his admirer, the Abbé Emmanuel Joseph Sieyès: 'What is the third estate? Nothing. What should it be? Everything.'

ture, which he had not done explicitly in *The Social Contract*, Rousseau insisted that laws cannot be binding on anyone who has not cast his vote on them in person or through freely chosen representatives.[54]

Having reaffirmed the principle, however, he did not counsel social revolution or radical political change. He would lift the burden of taxation from the poor by taxing only the proceeds of landed property, but proportionately, not progressively. He would change the social structure by degrees, ennobling some members of the bourgeoisie and enfranchising a legally specified number of peasants 'who have distinguished themselves by their good behaviour, their husbandry, their manners, their devotion to their families, and their faithful discharge of the duties of their station'.[55] A special popular assembly might be convened every two years to invite discussion of social problems and proposals for reform, but these assemblies would have no power to enact laws or elect a government. The *liberum veto* should be retained, he suggested artfully, but restricted to matters of fundamental law, in keeping with the principle of *The Social Contract* that virtual unanimity is required for ascertaining the general will. As to the monarchy, he would keep it elective but open candidacy beyond the ranks of princes to anyone who showed distinction, perhaps even choosing by lot among a group of the most distinguished citizens who would be appointed for life to a senate that would serve as an upper chamber above the chamber of deputies. There should be no standing army, which might become too powerful, but only local militias, as in Switzerland.

To deal with the problem posed by Poland's large size, Rousseau proposed a solution he had already suggested in his unfinished work on Corsica: 'extend and perfect the federal system, which is the only system that can meet your needs'.[56]

In this work, which Rousseau laboured over diligently and earnestly, he gave expression to the conservative element in his political thinking. He believed that people could never have a good government unless they already had some experience of it, and a civic spirit inbred in the people. He did not believe in revolution. All popular revolutions, he wrote, bring terrible disputes and infinite disorders. Once the dismemberment of common life begins, greater slavery is inevitable, and greater evils are introduced, on the pretext of improving things. Reforms, he urged the Poles to remember, must be piecemeal and judicious 'without any perceptible revolution'.[57]

Apart from this one venture into political writing, and his much-admired *Lettres sur la botanique*, written in 1772 for Mme Madelon Delessert, his favourite among the daughters of Mme Boy, and published posthumously, Rousseau's last years were preoccupied with self-examination. In addition to the *Confessions*, it was during these final years that he wrote *Rousseau Juge de*

Jean-Jacques (1772–76), also known as his *Dialogues*, and his final work, *The Reveries of the Solitary Walker* (1776–78).

Rousseau's autobiographical writings are of several different kinds. He had already produced an early manuscript entitled *Mon portrait*[58] and the well-known letters to Malesherbes of 1762,[59] in which he told the magistrate about the experiences that lay behind his philosophical writings. The *Confessions*, according to Rousseau himself, was suggested to him by the publisher Rey,[60] who 'for some strange reason had been urging me to write my memoirs. Although they were not up to that time particularly interesting in terms of events, I realized that they could become interesting through the frankness which I was capable of contributing to the task'. Thus, from the beginning Rousseau intended his *Confessions* to be something other than mere memoirs. He would do what he believed no author had done before: to lay bare his soul with utter truthfulness. He had at least two motives for doing this: he wished to unburden his conscience and he wished to enlarge human knowledge by describing in candid detail one man's experience of life on this earth.

The title itself suggests that the first motive may be seen as the primary aim. This is a deliberate echo of St Augustine's *Confessions* of A.D. 397, in which the author first recounts his earlier sinful life and then describes his conversion through God's grace, the narrative of past sins being clearly subordinate to the testimony to salvation. But the writing of Rousseau that corresponds in a certain sense to St Augustine's testimony of saving faith is the *Profession du foi du vicaire savoyard,* which appears in *Émile* and which he puts in the mouth of a Savoyard curate to distance it from himself, thus separating it from his autobiographical writings. It is the second motive, the unburdening of the soul, rather than the unburdening of conscience, which gives Rousseau's *Confessions* its importance in the history of literature. It has sometimes been described as the first true autobiography ever written.

The unveiling of the soul is undertaken for the benefit of two audiences—for the author himself and for mankind in general. St Augustine and others who had published *Confessions* addressed themselves to God. Rousseau addressed himself to the public, and in doing so he proposed to be as open to them as he was to himself. Rousseau's emphasis is rather on the narrative—indeed there is no testimony of salvation, since Rousseau, unlike St Augustine, did not consider himself to have been originally bad, but rather to have been throughout his life singularly good—and he looks back on his past sins as the occasional rare failings of an essentially innocent being. Nevertheless these occasional rare failings have always tormented him, and he feels the need to confess them.

In revealing the shameful and mean as well as the really bad things he had done, Rousseau may well have hoped, but not expected, that he might receive, as a reward for his candour, some sort of absolution. He knew that public confession has no such outcome: the penitent is punished just as ferociously as if he had been caught by others in the sins he himself reveals. The world, Rousseau came to reflect with bitterness, rewards discretion, not truth, which is certainly one reason he came to detest 'polite society' with its hypocrisy and lack of compassion. He criticized[61] such earlier autobiographical writers as Montaigne for being 'falsely sincere': measuring their disclosures so as to make themselves attractive to readers. He intended to exclude nothing. He had long taken as his motto a modification of a verse by Juvenal: *vitam impendere vero*, 'to consecrate one's life to truth'. In the *Reveries* he was to remark[62] that 'know thyself' is 'not so easy a maxim to follow as I had believed in my *Confessions*'. He set out on the enterprise in the belief that by looking inward he could discover himself, though he did not rely entirely on introspection. From about 1762 onward, he started to copy out all his important letters to provide 'empirical data', so to speak, for his record of past experiences.

To these purposes of self-knowledge and public edification, Rousseau added another at a critical stage in the composition of the *Confessions*—a process that took several years. That purpose is self-justification. Voltaire's anonymous pamphlet of 1764, *Le Sentiment des citoyens*, had blackened Rousseau's character, by revealing for the first time in public that he had 'abandoned' his five illegitimate children at the door of an orphanage at their birth. Rousseau denounced the accusation as false but did not explain that his reason for denying it was that he had not 'abandoned' his children but had put them up for adoption—in accordance with what was then a common practice among those who for whatever reason did not wish to raise their own infants. But until Voltaire forced his hand, Rousseau did not publicly acknowledge his behaviour toward his children. Earlier, in June 1761, when he fell so ill that he thought himself on the verge of death, he had written[63] to Mme de Luxembourg to admit that he had lived with Thérèse and that they had had offspring:

From these liaisons were born five children, all of whom were placed in the Foundling Hospital, and with so little thought of the possibility of their later identification that I did not even keep a record of their dates of birth. For several years now, remorse over my neglectful behaviour has disturbed my peace of mind and I am about to die without being able to remedy it, much to the mother's and my regret. All I did was to have a mark put on the clothes of the eldest child, and I have kept a duplicate of it . . . If there was some means of tracing the child, it would give great happiness to his loving mother; I, however, have no hope of this, and cannot take this consolation with me when I die.

The 'ideas with which my mind was filled as a result of this error', Rousseau added, 'were to a large extent responsible for my writing the *Traité de l'éducation* [*Émile*] . . . and you will find there a passage which indicates this disposition.'*

But apart from this veiled allusion, Rousseau's reflections on his behaviour towards his children were to remain unpublished until the *Confessions*. There he tries to justify his conduct by offering several different explanations. With respect to the first two children he asserts[64] that he had no hesitation in following the custom of his social circle. The main difficulty he had was in persuading Thérèse that this was the best way to save her honour. He succeeded with the help of her mother, who was anxious to save her family from the scandal of illegitimate births. When Thérèse became pregnant for the third time, he took the same decision but after more careful consideration. He considered his obligations towards his children in the light of the laws of nature and the precepts of true religion. The conclusion he came to[65] was not in the least hard-hearted. How could anyone suppose that he could be so lacking in compassion, so capable of 'trampling underfoot, without the least scruple, the sweetest of obligations', in view of all that is so plain about his true character: 'my natural good will towards all my fellow-creatures, my ardent love of the great, the true, the beautiful, the just; my horror of evil of every kind, my utter inability to hate or injure, or even to think of it; the compassion, the sweet and lively emotion which I feel at the sight of all that is virtuous, generous, and amiable . . .'

The decision to give his children up for adoption, he insists, was one of principle, even though he now sees that he was mistaken. His error, he claims rather lamely, was in thinking that he was performing the act of a father and citizen of Plato's Republic. But he continues to think[66] that he was not altogether wrong, given the alternatives:

I have often blessed heaven for having preserved them from their father's lot, and from the lot which threatened them as soon as I should have been obliged to abandon them. If I had left them to Madame d'Épinay or Madame de Luxembourg, who, out of friendship, generosity or whatever other motive, were willing to take charge of them, would they have been brought up at least as honest men? I do not know; but I am sure they would have been brought up to hate, perhaps to betray, their parents; it is a hundred times better that they have never known them.

---

*This passage, added after the first version of *Émile* (where the duties of paternity go unremarked) was completed, appears in Book I: 'Anyone who cannot fulfill the duties of a father has no right to become one. Neither poverty nor the pressure of work nor social prejudice excuses him from the duty of rearing his children. Readers, believe me: whoever has natural feelings and neglects his sacred duties will long shed bitter tears and be inconsolable.'

In the *Reveries* he reflects[67] that if he had been indifferent to his offspring, he would have allowed them to be raised by their mother, who would have spoiled them, and by her family, who would have 'made monsters of them'. In putting them in an orphanage, he claims, he saved them from a fate a thousand times worse.*

The most plausible explanation of Rousseau's behaviour toward his offspring is that when he gave them up, he knew he could not both earn a decent living for a family as a music copyist and write the books he had to write, so rather than watch his children grow up hungry, he let them find better luck elsewhere.† Whatever one makes of his varying explanations, however, they belie the simplistic view of him as someone who blames all vices on social institutions rather than on personal irresponsibility. On the contrary, his continual unburdening of conscience and his expressions of regret for failures to live up to his own professions indicate that he recognised a need to take moral responsibility for his own conduct. But for him the most important form of contrition is self-revelation. He acknowledges the force of circumstances and of erroneous views in shaping behaviour and does not propose making intentions rather than actions the test of virtue. But he insists upon the goodness of his natural feelings and implores the reader to accept the sincerity of his remorse. Self-exposure, even at the cost of revealing contradictory reasoning, self-delusion, and second thoughts, becomes its own justification.

If self-justification was thus a subsidiary motive in the writing of the *Confessions*, it was clearly the primary motive for the writing of the *Dialogues*. This work is cast in the form of a conversation between Rousseau and 'a Frenchman' about a personality that has come to exist in popular mythology called 'Jean-Jacques' that is not Rousseau as he really is, and knows himself to be, but the image of Rousseau that hostile publicists and *philosophes* have instilled in people's minds. Rousseau adopts this unusual formula in the hope of demonstrating that the 'Jean-Jacques' of mythology is totally fictitious and false, and that the real Rousseau is a good man.

The writing of the *Dialogues* is highly polemical and altogether too shrill to be wholly effective: it dates from a period when Rousseau's mind was disturbed. It is this book he tried to place on the altar of Notre Dame in the hope that it would come to the attention of the King. (When he was pre-

---

*Unlike Karl Marx, who kept his children but gave them so little nourishment and medical attention that he had to watch his favourite son die as a result of neglect.

†Jean Starobinski suggests a different, more psychological explanation: Rousseau 'never agreed to recognise the long-term effects of what he did. He pursued only immediate goals, hence he never wished for all the embarrassing repercussions and dishonourable aftermath. He put his children in a public orphanage, but only because they were unwanted consequences of immediate pleasures savoured in all innocence with Thérèse.'[68]

vented from doing so because the gates to the altar were locked, he drew up a broadsheet entitled 'To All Frenchmen who Still Love Justice and Truth' and handed out copies in the streets of Paris.) It is not a very pleasing book. But Rousseau was correct in believing that libels and falsehoods about him were in circulation and were sabotaging his enterprise of making himself known to the world in clear and naked truth.

The *Dialogues* were intended to set the record straight by showing that anyone who would read his works carefully would find that they were consistent in their essential themes. Throughout them runs the principle that 'nature made man happy and good but society depraves him and makes him miserable.' From this it does not follow that society as it is now must be rejected in favour of a 'return to nature'; for 'human nature does not go backward, and it is never possible to return to the times of innocence and equality once they have been left behind.'[69] Rather than a preacher of revolution, which can only invite chaos and false hopes, then, the 'real Rousseau' is a meliorist who favours reforms within particular frameworks, constitutional and conventional, that have arisen through social evolution. In this assertion, Rousseau was indeed being consistent with his earlier work: he had dedicated *The Social Contract* to Geneva, for which it was appropriate, while explicitly warning that it would not be appropriate for large countries; he had given very different advice to the Corsicans and Poles.

Rousseau's last autobiographical work, *The Reveries of the Solitary Walker*, ends with a last entry written in 1778, the year he died. Here again he turns his attention inward, this time producing a book that is wholly delightful to read. The work is cast in the form of Ten Walks, during which the author explores his own soul in a spirit of resignation. The Tenth Walk, begun on Palm Sunday in 1778, was left incomplete. No longer, as in the *Dialogues*, is Rousseau bothered about what other people think or say about him: he accepts his destiny as an outcast from society, and even welcomes the total solitude in which he can make his inward journey undisturbed. Whereas the *Confessions* is about Rousseau's experience of the world, the *Reveries* is about Rousseau's contemplation of himself. Having found how difficult it is to achieve self-knowledge, he decides to concentrate on the search for that alone—discarding the aim of instructing or edifying the public or refuting the libels of his enemies.

The First Walk of the *Reveries* begins[70] with a stark and plaintive *cri de coeur*, marking Rousseau's resigned acceptance of his isolation: 'So here I am, alone on the earth, with no longer a brother, neighbour, friend or society other than myself.' It is not a condition he has sought or that he welcomes. Despite all his efforts to reach out to humanity, 'the most sociable and the most loving of human beings' has been cast out of society. Those who hate him have contrived to inflict the worst punishment that could possibly be suffered by one like himself, who craves intimacy and a sense of belonging.

Although he has been in this condition for some fifteen years, it still seems like a dream he cannot begin to understand.

But now he is ready, he continues, to accept his fate. When he had written his *Dialogues*, Rousseau still hoped to escape his fate by persuading the public that it had been deceived into accepting a false image of him. This hope, he now realises, was mistaken. Fortunately, he came to this realisation in time to enjoy an interlude of calm before his final hour. He feels now as if he were 'on a foreign planet onto which I have fallen from the one I inhabited'. The consolation is that he can now give himself up to the 'sweetness of conversing with my soul'.[71] His enterprise will be the same as Montaigne's, except that 'he wrote his essays only for others, whereas I write my reveries only for myself.'[72]

On the remaining walks, Rousseau mixes ruminations about many things: his botanical excursions, his recollections of traumatic events such as his injury by a Great Dane, and his great happiness on the Isle de St-Pierre—later to be called the 'Isle de Rousseau'—in the middle of Lake Bienne. On one walk, but only on this one, he brings up his quarrels with the *philosophes*, reaffirming his innocence in the face of their calumnies and reminding himself that he invited the wrath of these 'ardent missionaries of atheism and very imperious dogmatists' by refusing to allow them to make him doubt the truths of the heart that are most important to human life.[73]

During the Eighth Walk he makes a striking observation[74] that could well serve as an epigram for the experience of what has been called 'romantic agony':

The several short intervals of prosperity in my life have left me with virtually no pleasant memory of the way in which they affected me. Conversely, during all the most miserable moments of my life, I always felt myself filled with tender, sweet and delightful sentiments which, in pouring a healing balm over the wounds of my broken heart, seemed to transform suffering into pleasure.

The Tenth, unfinished, Walk consists of a single long paragraph[75] devoted entirely to Mme de Warens, the *maman* and mistress of his youth, who first awakened his heart—a heart 'naturally full of life'—and inspired him with tenderness. He remembers the bliss of their times together: 'No day passes but what I recall with joy and tenderness this unique brief time of my life when I was myself, fully, without admixture and without obstacle, and when I can truly say I lived.' In his later years he was at least fortunate to be loved by Thérèse, a 'woman full of desire to please and of gentleness', who enabled him to do what he wanted, to be what he wanted. He had longed for the country and obtained it. He needed a friend suited to his heart, and he found her. His solitary self had found enough peace to shield and console him.

In May of 1778, Rousseau and Thérèse retired to a cottage provided by an admirer, René-Louis, Marquis de Girardin, at Ermenonville, about thirty miles from Paris on the road to Soissons. There, after a brief illness, Rousseau died of a stroke on 2 July, aged sixty-six. Shortly after his death, his widow became the mistress of a groom in the employ of the marquis; she would outlive Rousseau by twenty-two years.

Rousseau was laid to rest at Ermenonville on the Isle des Peupliers, a small island in the middle of a lake so named because of its poplar trees. In the aftermath of the French Revolution, the National Assembly called for the transfer of Rousseau's remains to a suitable place of honour in Paris. The Marquis was able to resist the demand at first, but after he had been under arrest for sixteen months for the crime of being an aristocrat, the decision was finally implemented. On the morning of 9 October 1794, as musicians played tunes composed by Rousseau, the triple casket of lead encased in oak and again in lead in which he had been buried was unearthed and carried in a cortège to Paris. At each village on the route—including Montmorency, which had been renamed 'Émile'—crowds gathered to render homage, covering the coffin with garlands of flowers and foliage. Some onlookers stood in respectful silence, others are reported to have shouted, 'Vive la République! Vive la mémoire de Jean-Jacques Rousseau!'[76]

On the evening of 10 October the cortège was met at the Tuileries by an immense crowd bearing torches. The casket was covered with a woodwork frame adorned with painted emblems of the Revolution and installed on a temporary bier encircled by willows, in imitation of the setting at Ermenonville. The following morning, a formal ceremony was held at the site, after which the cortège resumed its journey, ending at the Panthéon, the converted Church of Ste Geneviève.

There Rousseau was united in death with his old adversary Voltaire, who had expired a month before him and had been installed in the Panthéon three years earlier. The procession escorting Rousseau's remains was led by a captain of the United States Navy carrying the stars and stripes, along with others bearing the tricolour and the flag of republican Geneva. At the end came members of the national legislature, preceded by their 'beacon', *The Social Contract*.[77] The American Minister in Paris, James Monroe, accompanied by his staff, was the only foreign guest invited to witness the ceremony inside the Panthéon.[78]

In 1821, when religious services were resumed in the building after the Bourbon Restoration, the coffins of both Rousseau and Voltaire were removed from the consecrated ground beneath the dome where they had been placed. A rumour arose and came to be widely credited that the coffins were then desecrated and the bones within them removed and scattered. To scotch the rumour once and for all, a commission of distinguished citizens was appointed in 1897 by the Minister of Instruction and Fine Arts and charged with determining the truth. The commission found that both coffins were still in an underground vault of the Panthéon, now again a secular building, and that their contents had been undisturbed. Rousseau's skeleton, the commission reported, 'was perfectly preserved, the arms crossed on the chest, the head slightly bent to the left, like a man asleep'.[79]

EPILOGUE: ROUSSEAU THEN AND NOW

In the more than two hundred years since Rousseau's death, readers have disagreed sharply in their understanding of what he intended to say. Liberals, socialists, conservatives, anarchists, even the 'Greens' of recent years, have all found footing on his literary landscape, either on the crags or in the crevices. He himself admitted there were contradictions in his writings; but he felt that what he had to say could not be expressed according to the rules of clear and witty exposition as practised by the *philosophes*. Rousseau had complex attitudes to what he considered, not unjustifiably, to be complex problems.

The difficulty of achieving a consistent and faithful rendering of his views is compounded by the altogether extraordinary apotheosis that transformed Rousseau's reputation in the years immediately following his death. In later life an outcast, in death he became a legend. The process of canonization began almost immediately when his tomb on the Isle des Peupliers became a place of pilgrimage. It reached its zenith when his remains were ceremonially deposited in the Pantheon.

The maudlin Marquis de Girardin lost no time setting the stage. At Rousseau's death, he invited the sculptor Jean Antoine Houdon to come quickly and make a death mask that was to serve as the basis of a bust. On the tomb on the tiny island Girardin ordered inscribed the simple epitaph, *Ici repose L'homme de La Nature et de la Vérité*. In a letter he wrote,[1] prophetically as it turned out: 'Men honour him, women weep for him.'

What happened next has been well described[2] by a modern critic, nonplussed that a mere man of letters, especially one so given to bouts of paranoia, should have been elevated to secular sainthood. Among the early visitors to the grave was the ill-fated Marie Antoinette, who came with an entourage of princes and princesses and spent more than an hour under the canopy of poplars in soulful contemplation. One visitor came to commit suicide in the hope of being buried alongside the tomb. Another left a prayer comparing its occupant with Jesus Christ. A poet felt his heart 'filled with religious mourning' as he came to 'meditate in this pious temple'. A husband recounted that his wife 'pressed her bosom against the sacred marble'.

And there was more, much more, to come. In 1794, when Rousseau's remains were transferred to the Pantheon, the governing council of Geneva, whose predecessors had banned *The Social Contract*, organized a procession in honour of the birthday of its author and erected monuments to memorialize this illustrious son of the *patrie*. As the cortège passed his birthplace a chorus sang,[3] to the tune of a well-known air, *C'est un enfant*:

> Amis, saluons d'âge en âge
> La maison de cette Cité,
> Où naquit Rousseau, ce vrai sage,
> Bienfaiteur de l'humanité.
> Cette simple pierre
> Fait un sanctuaire
> Du lieu qui servit de berceau
> Au grand Rousseau.*

In Paris, where he and his books had been proscribed by the pre-Revolutionary *parlement*, a statue of him was placed on the Champs Elysées. Other monuments went up to mark his periods of residence at Montmorency, Môtiers, and Wootton. In Lyons the local Jacobins held a ceremony of remembrance. At several revolutionary *fêtes* in Paris, Robespierre offered fulsome eulogies of Rousseau, on one occasion praising him[4] especially because he made enemies of other intellectuals who defended monarchy and espoused atheism:

He attacked tyranny candidly, he spoke of the divinity with enthusiasm; his virile eloquence painted in flaming colours the charms of virtue . . . the purity of his teaching, drawn from nature, was profoundly opposed to vice, as much as his contempt for the conniving sophists who usurped the name of philosophers brought down upon him the hatred and persecution of his rivals and false friends. Ah! If he had witnessed this revolution of which he was the precursor and which has carried him to the Pantheon, who can doubt that his generous soul would have embraced with rapture the cause of justice and equality?

In the face of such passionate claims and of the many conflicting interpretations that have arisen since in the scholarly literature, it would be foolhardy to suppose that any single interpretation of 'what Rousseau really

*'Friends, salute from age to age / The house in this city / Birthplace of Rousseau, this true sage, / Benefactor of humanity. / This simple stone / Makes a sanctuary / Of the place which served as cradle / To the great Rousseau.'

meant to say' could command universal assent. But the empirical approach to his biography can at least offer some chastening guidance as to what he did not mean to say. Together with an examination of the major texts and the influence they exerted, reflection upon the interplay of his life and work suggests a way to think about his central preoccupations.

Nature, Self, and Society

Rousseau believed more than most philosophers in the radical individualism of natural man; yet he also believed that man was, as Aristotle put it, a political animal, a *zoon politikon*. How can these beliefs be reconciled? The answer lies perhaps in the ambiguity of a word that figures prominently in all eighteenth century thought: 'nature'. Nature, for Rousseau, stood opposed to culture; natural man was original man as he lived in the savage state under the rule of nature alone. But nature was also a force that demanded the attention of man in the civilised state. There its commands were of a different order, and were often unheeded; unheeded to such an extent that Rousseau could even claim that modern man was alienated from nature and, as a result of this, that man had lost both his happiness and his freedom.

When in the autumn of 1753 the Academy of Dijon announced an essay competition on the question 'What is the origin of inequality among men, and is it authorized by natural law?', Rousseau answered promptly. 'If the Academy has the courage to raise such a question,' he said to himself, 'I will have the courage to respond.'[5] Rousseau did not in his final treatment of the subject have much to say about the second part of the question—as to whether inequality was authorized by natural law; what interested him was the problem of origins. He tells us that he went for long walks in the forest of Saint-Germain to reflect on the life of man as it must have been before civilizations began: 'I dared to strip man's nature naked, to follow the evolution of those times and things which have disfigured him; I compared man as he made himself with man as nature made him, and I discovered that his supposed improvement had generated all his miseries.'[6]

The theme of apparent progress concealing actual regression was not a new one for Rousseau. He had expounded it in the earlier, prize-winning essay he had written for the Academy of Dijon, his *Discourse on the Sciences and the Arts* of 1749. There Rousseau had argued that the more science, industry, technology, and culture became developed and sophisticated, the more they carried human societies away from decent simplicity toward moral corruption. Paradoxically, this discourse was a great success among the very people Rousseau attacked: the fashionable salons and scientific circles of Paris, in which he himself moved at that time. What Rousseau said in his first discourse was not particularly original, for similar attacks on modern culture had been made by reactionary writers, both Catholic and Puritan. Rousseau's argument amazed the public because it came from a supposedly progressive author, one of the leading collaborators of Diderot's great *Ency-clopédie*, an enterprise dedicated to the ideals of scientific progress and the improvement of knowledge. Some readers were left in doubt about the author's sincerity, but time was to prove that he really meant what he said. Progress, Rousseau insisted, was an illusion. The human race had taken a wrong turning, or more than one wrong turning. In the second discourse Rousseau wrote for the Academy of Dijon, he carried his analysis much further back in time.

On this occasion, Rousseau did not succeed at Dijon, but the work was altogether more original and remarkable than the earlier discourse that won the prize. In less than a hundred pages Rousseau outlined a theory of human evolution that prefigured the discoveries of Darwin;*[7] he revolutionized the study of anthropology and linguistics,[9] and he made a seminal contribution to political philosophy.[10] Even if his argument was distorted by his critics, and perhaps not always well understood by his readers, it altered people's way of thinking about themselves and their world, and even changed their ways of feeling.

Apart from distortions, Rousseau's ideas became such a subject of contro-versy and conflicting interpretation because they helped foster two very dif-ferent tendencies in European thought. One tendency came to be called romanticism because it emphasized sentiment rather than reason; originality, spontaneity, and diversity over convention, artifice, and conformity; the in-nocence and purity of the self against the corruptions of society; nostalgia for a natural paradise instead of confidence in progress and perfectibility; and not uncommonly the 'romantic agony' that Rousseau himself came to ex-perience. The other tendency sought to achieve civil freedom by political re-forms based upon the republican principles of the social contract but taking account of particular conditions. Nature is the shared premise animating both tendencies. Ironically, the variability Rousseau admired in nature is what has allowed his influence to become so ubiquitous yet so divergent.

Rousseau and Romanticism

The romanticism of the Romantic Movement is a product of modernity; it begins in the eighteenth century Age of Reason, and it is in part a reaction against that age. Historians, whether sympathetic or hostile, are agreed about

---

*Although Rousseau did not advance the view later put forward by Darwin that man evolved from a cousin of the apes, he did suggest that man developed from a primitive biped, related to the orang-utan, into the sophisticated creature of modern times, and that this evolution could be un-derstood largely as a process of adaptation and struggle.[8]

one thing: Rousseau is the first of the Romantics. He introduced the movement—or the 'moment'—in the cultural history of Europe with the publication in 1761 of *Julie, ou La Nouvelle Héloïse*, the original romantic novel.
Even before that date, however, Rousseau had adumbrated a philosophy of
romanticism in his writings on music, in the course of controversy with
Jean-Philippe Rameau.[11] The pamphlets with which these two writers battled are nowadays neglected, virtually forgotten, but when they were first
published their impact was dramatic. In those pages Rameau outlines a systematic rationalistic theory to justify conservative French aesthetic taste, and
Rousseau opposes him with an argument for the radical alternative we now
call romanticism.

Their controversy was the sequel to the *querelle des Bouffons*, a dispute that
had broken out in Paris between supporters of the traditional French opera
and supporters of the new Italian opera, the most eloquent champions of
Italian music being the young intellectuals attached to the *Encyclopédie* of
Diderot and d'Alembert and the defenders of French music being the academic allies of the church and crown. Music in mid-eighteenth century
Paris was still much as it had been in the time of Lully and Louis XIV; it asserted the same Bourbon myths of majesty and *gloire*, proclaiming the splendour of kings, the supremacy of France, and the triumph of order over
chaos. At the opera houses, earthly princes were represented on the stage in
the image of gods; patriotic sentiments were stirred by the sound of trum-
pets and drums; and the words, as monotonous as the score, were declaimed
with pomp and solemnity. French music spoke to the ear much as the architecture of Versailles addressed the eye.

In the summer of 1752, a company of Italian musicians led by Eustachio
Bambini brought to Paris a very different kind of music, works of opera
buffa by Scarlatti, Leo, Jommelli, Vinci, and, above all, Pergolesi. The *Ency-
clopédistes* promptly made themselves the unpaid publicists of Bambini's
troupe. Rousseau, still an active collaborator of the *Encyclopédie*, edited Pergolesi's opera *La serva padrona* for publication in Paris; Frédéric-Melchior
Grimm, then a friend of Rousseau, wrote a series of pamphlets arguing that
French music had become so lifeless, stale, and provincial that its only hope
lay in reforming itself on the model of the Italian composers, who aimed to
please rather than elevate the listener, who were satisfied with small orches-
tras and modest productions, who banished declamation, and whose *libretti*
were simple and scored to melodic music of which the *aria*, or song, was the
most distinctive feature.

Rousseau attacked Rameau in print as a representative of all that was bad
in French music, a composer 'with more knowledge than genius', 'with
more cleverness than creativeness', the 'fabricator of over-elaborate coun-
terpoints and harmonies that ought to be relegated to the cloister as their last

resting-place'. As for Rameau's theoretical writings, Rousseau went so far as to assert that 'they had acquired their great reputation without ever being actually read'.

There is no mistaking the personal hostility behind these words. Rousseau and Rameau had known each other, and disliked each other, for several years. They had first met in 1745 on decidedly unequal terms. Rameau was then already over sixty years old and at the height of his fame. Rousseau was thirty years younger, an unknown fellow who had come to Paris from Geneva with a project for a new musical notation and the score of an operatic ballet in his pocket. Rousseau's project was politely rejected by the Academy, and when his ballet was given a private performance, Rameau, who was present, rudely and angrily declared it a mixture of plagiarism and bad composition. Eight years later Rousseau's situation was much improved. His *Discourse on the Sciences and the Arts* won the essay prize at Dijon, and its publication in Paris was one of the most talked-about literary events of 1751. His portrait by Maurice-Quentin de La Tour was exhibited at the Paris salon together with those of d'Alembert, Duclos, La Condamine, and other leading writers of the time. Moreover, Rousseau had established himself almost overnight as an authority on music. He accepted the job—that Rameau had refused—of writing the articles on musical subjects for the *Encyclopédie*; at Fontainebleau he enjoyed an enormous fashionable success as a composer with the performance of his opera *Le Devin du village*, in which he developed the techniques of Pergolesi into a more lyrical pastoral style. It would be foolish to suggest that Rousseau was as good a musician as Rameau, but the dispute between them soon became a dispute about philosophy, and in that field Rousseau was Rameau's match.

It was a dispute that continued long after Bambini's Italian musicians had left Paris, and although it arose from the *querelle des Bouffons*, Rousseau soon distanced himself from the ideological stance of those *Encyclopédistes* who supported Italian music because it was progressive. He had already made clear in his *Discourses on the Sciences and the Arts* that he had no faith in progress, and although he had already started to write his *Discourse on the Origin of Inequality*, he was no egalitarian. It is instructive to compare the libretto of his *Le Devin du village* with that of Pergolesi's *La serva padrona*. Rousseau's opera introduces a shepherdess who is distressed because her sweetheart has gone off with an aristocratic lady. In the end, love prevails as the village soothsayer helps to restore the shepherd to the shepherdess, and the two are happily and properly united—a very different tale from that of Pergolesi's opera, where a servant is shown to be the right bride for the master. If the message of *La serva padrona* is egalitarian, the argument of Rousseau's opera is that people should find love and happiness in their own station in society, and not try to trespass the barriers of class.

It is hardly surprising that *Le Devin du village* should have given such plea-sure to the King at Fontainebleau, for, however 'radical' the music, the li-bretto is plainly conservative, and although the King felt duty-bound to protect French music against Italian competition, he could hardly conceal the fact that he personally enjoyed Rousseau's Italian-style music more than that of the French composers. Indeed, after the success of *Le Devin du village* Rousseau could have received a royal pension if only he had had the grace to pay his respects to the King. He had decided, however, to resist all temp-tations of worldly glory as a musician in order to preserve his integrity as a philosopher; and it was as a philosopher that he resumed his attack on the principles of Rameau.

Reality for Rousseau is visible, palpable nature; music, he says, can conjure up that nature. It can also express human feeling, which is nature, so to speak, within us; the expression of feeling, he claims, is achieved through melody. Thus, when Rousseau and Rameau quarrelled over melody and harmony they were concerned with something more than music; their dispute was about reality itself. For Rameau, reality was the Newtonian universe acces-sible to reason; for Rousseau it was the concrete world of perception and ex-perience.

Where Rameau, in his Cartesian manner, demanded unity, Rousseau was content with variety; where Rameau looked for fixed rules in music as in mathematics, Rousseau insisted that music was logically different from math-ematics and that musical styles must vary as nature varied. The marvellous gift of melody was that it could express what was natural, whereas harmony was essentially artificial, an invention of the mind.

Rousseau felt persecuted, even as Rameau felt betrayed by the *Ency-clopédistes*, who refused to accept Rameau's theory of the superiority of har-mony over melody. But in a very important sense Rousseau succeeded where Rameau failed. Rousseau had propelled French music into a new di-rection, away from the artificial constraints of the seventeenth century to-ward the creative freedom of the future. By the example of *Le Devin du village* and his doctrine of the supremacy of melody over harmony, Rousseau introduced a new development in the history of western culture. On the musical stage he prepared the way for Mozart, whose opera *Bastien und Basti-enne* is based on *Le Devin du village*, and for the operas of Gluck, who brought new life to the French opera after the death of Rameau. Gluck once wrote:

All I have tried to accomplish as a musician is to produce the kind of work which Jean-Jacques Rousseau would have produced if he had not forsaken com-position in order to write books.

Gluck and his successors developed as composers the full potentialities of ro-mantic music envisaged in Rousseau's theory; Rousseau himself went on to

produce a model of totally romantic art in another medium, that of literature, with his novel *La Nouvelle Héloïse*. Its appearance in 1761 turned
Rousseau from a celebrity into an object of a cult. *La Nouvelle Héloïse* was a
universal best seller, devoured by readers, and not least by the ladies of fashion about whom Rousseau had written so many ungracious words. Julie, the
heroine of *La Nouvelle Héloïse*, was hailed as a perfect woman; and Rousseau
received a constant flow of letters asking him for more information about
her and even for her portrait. As for Julie's lover, female readers yearned to
meet him. The message of the novel was seen as a liberating one: that the
imagination need no longer be the slave of reason; that feelings should not
be suppressed, denied in the name of decorum; that if one could only strip
away the falseness and pretence by which modern society was dominated,
there was goodness to be discovered in the human heart.

   La Nouvelle Héloïse changed lives and fashions. Buffon once remarked,
'Others write, but Monsieur Rousseau commands.' The romanticism that
was adumbrated in his theories of music was now exemplified in Rousseau's
imaginary persons, and French readers were so thrilled by what they saw that
they began to forsake the rigid mores of a neoclassical, Gallican, and Cartesian tradition to think and feel in new ways. The Enlightenment had already
poured scorn on religion and traditional political beliefs, but its Baconian
empiricism was too dry and utilitarian to offer a satisfying alternative to
Catholic spirituality. Rousseau's romanticism, by contrast, was rich enough
in emotional intensity to replace lost faith with new excitements.

   The form Rousseau chose for his novel was one that Richardson and others had made popular in the eighteenth century—the *roman épistolaire*, a series of letters in which fiction could be given the appearance of fact.
Rousseau presented himself to the public not as the author but as the 'editor' of the letters in the book, and even carried this platonic 'noble lie' to the
point of assuring his friends that he had discovered what were described in
the original title as *Lettres de deux amants*. However contrived this procedure,
the aim was to achieve the effect of authenticity as opposed to the manifest
artificiality of neoclassical literature. Rousseau's fiction was dressed up as fact
to serve, like melody in music, as 'the true voice of feeling', to communicate
an understanding of human experience in all its immediacy and intensity.

   Rousseau also intended *La Nouvelle Héloïse* to be a moral tale, and he was
particularly gratified when readers recognized it as such, for not all readers
did. The novel does not preach conventional morality as does, for example,
Richardson's *Pamela*, which had been highly esteemed in France since its appearance in 1740. Richardson's heroine is a girl who cherishes her virginity
as a capital that she will exchange for nothing less than a marriage contract,
a bargain she triumphantly affects after many trials and temptations. *Pamela*
provides a lesson in bourgeois prudence. *La Nouvelle Héloïse* is a moral tale
in a very different sense. The central conflict of the story is not between rea-

son and passion, for one principle of the romanticism introduced by Rousseau is that human beings are not governed by reason; rather, the conflict in *La Nouvelle Héloïse* is between one passion and another. Rousseau's ideal woman—Julie—is the daughter of a Vaudois baron who employs as her tutor a young man of bourgeois origins named St-Preux. St-Preux falls in love with Julie and she with him; she encourages him to make love to her and promises to be his forever. Her father, horrified at the idea of his daughter marrying a bourgeois, tells her that she must marry into her own class and to a man of his choosing. The chosen bridegroom is an upright and coolly estimable atheist, the Baron de Wolmar. Julie, who adores her father and dreads the consequences of breaking his heart, asks St-Preux to release her from her pledge. St-Preux nobly acquiesces; and Julie goes on to atone for her youthful misdemeanour by becoming in Wolmar's model feudal household the perfect Christian wife and mother. Some years later St-Preux returns from a wandering life to the Wolmars' estate at Clarens on the shores of Lake Geneva as a tutor to their children; but as he goes on excursions with Julie around the lake against a background of alpine scenery it becomes agonizingly clear that she has never ceased to love him, and death itself has to intervene to keep her from returning once more into his arms.

In correspondence with readers of the novel, Rousseau explained clearly that Julie's motive for rejecting St-Preux was not one of duty, but of love for her father, who would, she believed, die if she disobeyed him. To a friend who protested that Julie was doubly unfaithful in first repudiating her pledge to St-Preux and then marrying a man she did not love, Rousseau argued that the novelist's task was not to show people acting as they ought to act (as conventional novelists such as Richardson might chose to do) but to show people acting according to their character, as they would in real life. The novelist should be a truthful chronicler of human behaviour.

Rousseau's belief that such human behaviour is governed by passion rather than reason was not new. Pascal had asserted no less in his critique of Cartesian rationalism, but Pascal was a pious Jansenist, to whom the self, *le moi*, was hateful, whereas to Rousseau, and the Romantics who came after him, the self was the object of the highest and most enduring interest. Many readers assumed that St-Preux was based on the author himself; Voltaire declared that the novel was nothing other than Rousseau's autobiography. But insofar as *La Nouvelle Héloïse* is autobiographical, it is only indirectly so. Some years later Rousseau produced a book that was directly autobiographical, to an extent unprecedented in European literature: the *Confessions*, in which all the restraint demanded by traditional culture was thrown to the winds as Rousseau stripped bare his soul and his past. His autobiography was an innovation in literature, no less revolutionary than *La Nouvelle Héloïse*: the novel introduced serious romantic fiction to French literature, the *Confes-*

sions introduced the romantic personality—Jean-Jacques himself, the virtuous exemplar. While he asserted his individuality and uniqueness, he also
claimed to be somehow representative of everyone. Rousseau believed that
all members of the human race had, at the deepest level, some things in common. He once told his beloved Sophie d'Houdetot that he could learn about
her soul by looking into his own. He discovered the secrets of humanity by
means of introspection.

His attachment to Sophie was itself one of the outcomes of *La Nouvelle
Héloïse*. Having created his ideal woman—Julie—in imagination, Rousseau
afterward recognized her in reality in the person of the Comtesse
d'Houdetot, who encouraged him to flirt with her and with whom he fell
in love. Alas, his affair with her proved no more enduring than St-Preux's
affair with Julie. After a summer in Rousseau's arms, Sophie rejected him in
favour of the Marquis de St-Lambert, just as Julie had rejected St-Preux in
favor of the Baron de Wolmar. Nature imitated art.

In the *Confessions* Rousseau recalls Sophie's saying to him, 'No lover loved
as you loved'; in the novel St-Preux tells Julie that, for him, love is an all-con-
suming feeling—it is his life. Romantic love surpasses the sexual, not by sub-
limating it in the platonic matter, but by assimilating the sexual to a total
passion that is as much metaphysical as physical, and that tends to be inten-
sified rather than modified by frustration. At the same time Rousseau suggests that love purifies sexual congress and carries it into an altogether
different realm from that of lust. The Romantic Byron eulogized Rousseau's
view of love in 'Childe Harold':

> His love was passion's essence—as a tree
>   On fire by lightning: with ethereal flame
> Kindled he was, and blasted: for to be
>   Thus, and enamour'd, were in him the same.
> But his was not the love of living dame,
>   Nor of the dead who rise upon our dreams.
> But of ideal beauty, which became
>   In him existence, and o'erflowing teems
> Along his burning page, distemper'd though it seems.

In this 'o'erflowing', Rousseau's romanticism does not judge in terms of
rules and precepts. It has much in common with the morality of earlier German pietists, who argued that the Christian life should be guided by Christ's
example of charity in all things rather than by adherence to a code of Old
Testament commandments and interdictions. Rousseau himself made the
acquaintance of German pietism through his first mistress, Mme de Warens,
who did much to educate him when he lived with her in his later adoles-

cence. Although she converted to Catholicism after she left Switzerland, Mme de Warens had herself been educated by a Swiss adherent of German pietism, François Magny, and absorbed much of his teaching. If she did not live according to conventional rules of chastity and thrift, she felt that she was a better Christian for always following the impulses of a generous heart.

Pietism also authorized what Pascal forbade: the contemplation of the self, albeit the self understood as the soul. But for pietism to be developed into romanticism, it had to be purged of its Lutheran obsession with salvation and the doctrine of original sin, and to recognize the soul as a thing of beauty. Rousseau, with his supreme assurance of the purity of his own soul, felt well placed to accomplish this. His religious creed was minimal: belief in the benevolence of Providence and in life after death was all that remained of Christianity in his system. But to that minimum he clung with a humble and reverent devotion.

He had the temperament of a worshipper, and the object of his veneration—which was to take the place of God for many Romantics—was nature, in those forms least touched by the hand of man: high mountains, dense forests, windswept lakes. In the alpine scenery of Switzerland, St-Preux comes close to having a mystical experience, and it is against a background of the rocks and gorges of the southern shore of Lake Geneva, where St-Preux and Julie are trapped by a storm, that their love comes closest to overcoming their moral scruples. The Alps, an object of horror for the Age of Reason, became for Romantics of the succeeding generations a place of pilgrimage. People lost the taste for formal gardens and artificial lakes, favouring instead nature, as Rousseau had described it, in its wildest and most savage forms. He taught his readers to see the world with new eyes.

This element of romanticism was to prove a source of inspiration and renewal in painting. Fragonard, Watteau, Boucher, Chardin, and the other leading painters of the age of Louis XV domesticated nature by depicting orchards, meadows, gardens, and elegant *fêtes champêtres*. For Fuseli and Courbet, nature was represented as Rousseau had seen it, in all its unkempt grandeur, although fully romantic painting took longer to manifest itself than romantic literature, if only because revolutionary France favoured neoclassical art in its attempt to restore the ideals of ancient Rome.

Romantics who came after Rousseau sought inspiration in the arts and lifestyles of the Middle Ages, but he himself had no share in this. Although he was profoundly critical of modernity, he always insisted that there was no going back in time, either to the state of nature he described in his political writings or to the period of nascent society he called the golden age of humanity. The only escape from the sophisticated world he envisaged was found in the villages and country places that had not been corrupted by the industries, luxuries, and cultural institutions of cities. This is another aspect of his cult of nature: the retreat to rusticity.

Rousseau claimed to be a Christian, indeed a better Christian than most adherents of established churches, but Christ was not seen by him as the redeemer, not even as the object of adoration and prayer. Christ was rather a being in whom he saw himself prefigured, a good man ill used, a victim of society's hostility. St-Preux, who loses Julie to Wolmar, is hardly the hero of *La Nouvelle Héloïse*, and Rousseau himself, chased from one refuge to another, vilified and mocked, depicts himself in the *Confessions* as another loser. Even so, he establishes for such victims a place in romantic mythology as compelling as that of the hero. After St-Preux comes the Werther of Goethe, the René of Chateaubriand, and all the wounded and defeated warriors who figured in the paintings of Géricault. Romanticism was to have its heroes, its conquerors, even as classicism had; but what is distinctive is the 'anti-hero', the victim, the man of sorrows like Rousseau himself. Poets, claimed a later Romantic Shelley, are

> cradled into poetry by wrong;
> They learn in suffering what they teach in song . . .

Byron too saw Rousseau as a kindred spirit, describing him as 'the apostle of affliction'.

Rousseau and Civil Freedom

Individualism, if not logically implied, seems at any rate to be suggested by the romantic cult of creativity, originality, and variety, and its pleas for liberation from external, universal, artificial rules. In later writings such as *La Nouvelle Héloïse*, the *Confessions*, and the *Reveries*, Rousseau makes even more of the priority of the self, the solitary, alienated ego. But there is also the Rousseau of *The Social Contract* and *Letter to M. d'Alembert*: Rousseau the Citizen—or perhaps the Citizen *manqué*—whose great yearning is for the integration of free individuals with the political group or city or republic, acquiring there full dignity as men in membership of a political community.

It is this Rousseau, of course, who has been linked to the rise of modern democracy. But he did not have what might be called a democratic temperament. In one of his early poems he wrote:

> Il ne serait pas bon dans la société
> Qu'il fût entre les rangs moins d'inégalité.*[12]

He took pride in the fact that he was born to a family whose manners distinguished it from the people. He says in the *Confessions* that he was never

*It would not be good in society / If there were less class inequality.

attracted to working-class girls, or even to daughters of the bourgeoisie; he responded only to the elegant and delicate looks of the nobly born; the only two women he fell in love with were titled ladies.

In *The Social Contract* he feels the need to introduce a lawgiver to design a legal code for the people because they are too ignorant to devise one for themselves; indeed they are so stupid that the lawgiver will have to pretend that God himself has drawn up the tables of the law that they must adopt. When Rousseau gave up city life at the age of forty-five for what he called solitude in the country, he simply exchanged the society of bourgeois intellectuals in Paris for that of the landed aristocracy of the Isle de France. But if Rousseau had no desire for social equality, he did favour equality of rights.

In dedicating his *Discourse on Inequality* to the citizens of Geneva he congratulates them on being 'that people which, among all others, seems to me to possess the greatest advantages of society and to have guarded most successfully against the abuses of society'.[13] Rousseau is proud to number himself among those citizens:

Having had the good fortune to be born among you, how could I reflect on the equality which nature established among men and the inequality which they have instituted among themselves, without thinking of the profound wisdom with which the one and the other, happily combined in this Republic, contribute in the manner closest to natural law and most favourable to society, to the maintenance of public order and the wellbeing of individuals.[14]

The Republic of Geneva was undoubtedly a state unlike others, and Rousseau, who was born there in 1712, had been brought up to be an eager and uncritical patriot. Geneva had been an independent city-state since the middle years of the sixteenth century, when its constitution was, in a manner of speaking, founded by a legislator of genius, Jean Calvin. At first the Genevese had not intended to proclaim themselves a republic; they aspired only to seek incorporation as a canton in the Swiss confederation. This purpose was thwarted as a result of the Reformation, which divided the Swiss among themselves: the Genevans had counted on joining the confederation on the basis of an existing alliance with Fribourg and Berne, but as Fribourg remained Catholic and Berne turned Protestant, Geneva could not please one without antagonising the other. In the event Berne proved more useful to the Genevans in turning out the Savoyard rulers, so the Genevans chose to become Protestant. By this step they so alienated Fribourg and the other Catholic Swiss cantons that Geneva's entry into the Swiss confederation was vetoed until the nineteenth century.

Calvin enabled the Genevans to make a virtue of a necessity; denied membership of a larger nation, they learned from him how to construct a peaceful little nation of their own. They instituted an autonomous, independent city, where the people themselves were sovereign. Administration was placed in the hands of elected elders, and the guidance of the people was entrusted to the clergy of the national Calvinist Church. The republican constitution was a skillful mixture of democratic, aristocratic, and theocratic elements. Almost by a miracle, it survived as an independent city-state in an age of expanding kingdoms and empires. But not entirely by a miracle. In Calvin's lifetime, Swiss troops from the friendly Protestant canton of Berne surrounded Geneva's frontiers, and after Calvin's death, when Geneva became a centre of international banking, the rulers of Europe's larger powers preserved Geneva's neutrality in order to protect their own financial interests. And so, despite having no natural defences whatever, the city-state of Geneva kept its autonomy at a time when other small republics of Europe— Florence, Siena, and Lucca, for example—fell into the hands of monarchs.

Rousseau had been brought up by his ardently patriotic father to think of Geneva as the one state in the modern world which had recovered the glory of the ancient republics. As a child he read the works of Plutarch, and could later boast, 'I was a Roman at the age of twelve.'[15] In his *Confessions* Rousseau says that admiration for ancient Rome 'helped to create in me that free and republican spirit, that proud and strong character, impatient of any yoke or servitude, which has tormented me all my life in situations where it has been least appropriate'.[16]

In the dedication of his *Discourse on Inequality*, Rousseau explains why he considers Geneva the nearest to an ideal state to be found on this earth. It is small; with a population of only several thousand, every citizen can be acquainted with every other citizen, and everyone's life is open to the gaze of others; it is a state where everyone's private interest coincides with the public interest; where no one is subject to any law except the law he has made and imposed on himself; where the constitution has stood the test of time; where military virtues are cultivated but wars are not engaged in; where the magistrates are chosen by all but vested with undisputed authority so that democracy is wisely tempered.

This is not at all an accurate description of Geneva as it had become in the middle of the eighteenth century, but it is what Calvin had designed Geneva to be, what Geneva should have been, and what the rulers of Geneva in all their public pronouncements claimed that Geneva was. To the author of the *Discourse on Inequality* the myth of Geneva was more important than the reality of Geneva. For it is that myth which holds out the possibility of what might be called the renegotiation of the social contract. The old fraudulent social contract that had marked the introduction of government into human experience could be reenacted as a genuine social contract. Such a contract could end the centuries of servitude; and men could come together, as the Genevans had come together under the guidance of Calvin in the sixteenth century, to make a civil covenant that would not be the device by which the rich would cheat the poor, but a means of combining liberty and law.

Geneva, which Rousseau visited for several months after he had written the *Discourse on Inequality*, was something of a disappointment to him. He came to realise that it was far from being the 'wisely tempered democracy' he had described in his dedication. But he did not forsake the idea of an authentic social contract as a means of reconciling liberty and law. He did not falter in his republicanism. This is what inspired his next most important essay in political theory, the book he called *The Social Contract*, which was published in 1762, some seven years after the *Discourse on Inequality*.

The *Discourse on Inequality* was coldly received by the authorities of Geneva; *The Social Contract* was actually banned, burned on the orders of the censors, and a warrant was issued for the author's arrest. And yet Rousseau could say, with complete sincerity, that in *The Social Contract* he had presented Geneva as an example to all governments. 'People were pleased to relegate *The Social Contract* with the *Republic* of Plato to the realm of illusions: but I depicted an existing object . . . My book proposed one state as a model, and in just that one state it is burned!'[17]

The ideas of Thomas Hobbes were in Rousseau's mind when he wrote *The Social Contract*, just as they were when he wrote the *Discourse on Inequality*. His knowledge of Hobbes was imperfect, for Rousseau could not read English, and probably did not read more than fragments of Hobbes's Latin works. But Rousseau read enough of Hobbes to be excited by him, and to regard his theory as a challenge that must be answered.

Hobbes, as Rousseau understood him, argued that men had to choose between law and liberty, between being governed and being free. For Hobbes freedom meant the absence of constraint: 'the liberty of subjects is the silence of the law.' Freedom went with anarchy: law entailed the rule of an absolute and individual sovereign. Men loved freedom, but the consequences of anarchy were so appalling that any sort of government was better than no government at all. Hobbes's social contract was a covenant made between men to surrender collectively their natural rights to a sovereign in return for the peace and security of a civil order the sovereign could impose, by holding all men in awe.

Rousseau did not agree that freedom stood thus opposed to law. Freedom was not the absence of constraint, but the exercise of ruling oneself. He believed it was possible to combine liberty and law by instituting a regime that enabled men to rule themselves. It would entail, as Hobbes's system did, a covenant made between individuals to surrender their natural rights to a sovereign; but that sovereign should be none other than the people themselves, united in one legislative corps.

Rousseau not only rejects Hobbes's idea that men must choose between being free and being ruled, he asserts that it is only through living in society that men can experience their fullest freedom. In the *Discourse on Inequality* Rousseau speaks of the three kinds of freedom men enjoy in the state of nature, one and perhaps two of which they lose upon entering society. In *The Social Contract* he speaks of another kind of freedom, one they can experience only in a well-ordered society: political freedom. And this is something altogether superior to mere independence.

In *The Social Contract* Rousseau speaks less of the innocence of savage man and more of his brutishness. Man in the state of nature is described as a 'stupid and unimaginative animal' who becomes 'an intelligent being and a man' only as a result of entering civil society. Assuredly, as a result of the impact of passions and sophistry, which society breeds, men have generally grown worse with the passage of time; but that is because culture, instead of improving men, has corrupted them—the theme of Rousseau's early *Discourse on the Sciences and the Arts*, to which he returned again and again. Culture is bound to change men, and if it does not make them better it will make them worse.

In the state of nature, a man cannot, by definition, be a citizen. But once he has quit the state of nature and entered society, man's nature can be realised only if he becomes a citizen. In this sense Rousseau accepts Aristotle's definition of man as a *zoon politikon*. Here, as in the *Discourse on Inequality*, we meet the two senses of 'nature' in Rousseau's argument. Just as the family, unnatural in the state of nature, becomes natural in society, so does political freedom, totally alien to the savage, become natural for the civilised man.

In a way, Rousseau's response to the challenge of Hobbes is wonderfully simple. Clearly, men can be at the same time ruled and free if they rule themselves. For them the obligation to obey will combine with the desire to obey; everyone in obeying the law will be acting only in obedience to his own will. In saying this, Rousseau was going a good deal further than liberal theorists such as John Locke, who associated freedom with the people's consent to obey a constitutional monarch in whom they invested sovereignty. For Rousseau there is no investment or transfer of sovereignty: sovereignty not only originates in the people, it stays there.

One must note, in *The Social Contract*, the particular use Rousseau makes of the word 'government'. He carefully separates government, as administration, from sovereignty, as legislation. He maintains that legislation must be democratic, in the sense that every citizen should participate in it, and participate in person. This is the democratic element in the constitution of

Geneva Rousseau has in mind when he speaks of that state as democracy 'wisely tempered'. At the same time, Rousseau rejects—as unsuited to men—democratic administration. The participation by all the citizens in the administration, or executive government, of the state, Rousseau considers altogether impractical and utopian an arrangement. Executive government, he argues, must be entrusted to duly elected magistrates or ministers.

In the Dedication to Geneva of his *Discourse on Inequality*, Rousseau declares, 'I would have fled from a republic, as necessarily ill-governed, where the people . . . foolishly kept in their own hands the administration of civil affairs and the execution of their laws.'[18] He stresses the need for a state to have 'chiefs' (*chefs*). 'I would have chosen a republic where the individuals, content with sanctioning the laws and making decisions in assemblies on proposals from the chiefs on the most important public business . . . elected year by year the most capable and upright of their fellow citizens to administer justice and govern the state.'[19]

The point Rousseau dwells on is that superiority in public office shall correspond to superiority of capability and rectitude. Such a system he can call 'aristocratic' in the true, classical sense of the word: government by the best. This is clearly the sense he has in mind when he speaks in *The Social Contract* of an elective aristocracy as 'the best form of government';[20] and in doing so he does not contradict the preference expressed in the *Discourse on Inequality* for 'democratic government, wisely tempered'—for what he means there is democratic legislation, wisely tempered by an aristocratic administration, democratically elected. He contrasts this sort of aristocracy with an aristocracy based on heredity, characteristic of feudal regimes: 'the worst form of government'.[21]

In *The Social Contract* he draws attention to the dangers inherent in a system that separates the executive, the aristocratic body, from the legislative, the democratic body. He points out that while it is desirable for the business of administration to be entrusted to magistrates or chiefs, those magistrates will naturally tend with the passage of time to encroach on the sacred territory of legislation, and thus to invade the sovereignty of the people, and finally to destroy the republican nature of the state. 'This is the inherent and inescapable vice which, from the birth of the body politic, tends relentlessly to destroy it, just as old age and death destroy the body of a man.'[22]

Rousseau said nothing about this 'vice' in his dedication of the *Discourse on Inequality*. One can suggest a reason for this. Rousseau did not realise, when he wrote that dedication, the extent to which the magistrates of Geneva had invaded the sphere of democratic sovereignty; but by the time he wrote *The Social Contract* he was aware of the reality of the political situation of his supposedly ideal city-state.

In the two hundred years since Calvin had designed these arrangements, the Council of Twenty-Five had progressively taken over control of the state, dominating the Council of Two Hundred and summoning the General Council as seldom as possible—and then only to give mute assent to the magistrates' proposals for legislation and their list of candidates for executive office. What is more, the members of the Council of Twenty-Five were drawn from an even narrower circle of Genevese society, a group of patrician families who contrived to keep all the offices of state for themselves and their nominees. In fact an hereditary nobility had grown up in Geneva—not an open, avowed patriciate like that of Berne, but one that clothed itself in all the forms and rhetoric of classical republican ideology.

At the same time the citizen class shrank progressively. In the sixteenth century the vast majority of adult men in Geneva were enrolled as burgesses and citizens. By the end of the seventeenth century those citizens constituted a middle class of about fifteen hundred men in a population of twenty-five thousand. Below that was a disfranchised lower class, not only excluded from the voting register but denied access to the more lucrative trades of the city.

Rousseau was born into a family of equivocal social standing. His paternal grandfather was a superior artisan and burgess who had been engaged in political activity on behalf of citizens' rights against the patrician magistrates—a 'liberal' we might call him, anachronistically. Rousseau's father seems to have been more of a 'conservative'. He had married a woman of superior social status: not quite in the patrician class, but in the upper academic class, and living among the élites at the fashionable centre of town. Rousseau was born in one of the smartest houses. When his mother died soon after his birth, Rousseau and his father had to move down the hill to humble quarters, but the young Rousseau was brought up by his father to take an uncritical view of the political arrangements of his native city-state. Writing about Geneva many years later, Rousseau recalled a military festivity he had witnessed as a child with his father: 'My father, embracing me, was thrilled in a way that I can still feel and share. "Jean-Jacques," he said to me, "love your country. Look at these good Genevans: they are all friends; they are all brothers. Joy and harmony reign among them. You are a Genevan. One day you will see other nations . . . but you will never find any people to match your own." '

Rousseau ran away from Geneva when he was sixteen because he was unhappy in his work as an engraver's apprentice, and he did not return to the city for any length of time until the age of forty-two—just after he wrote the *Discourse on Inequality*. When he wrote *The Social Contract* he had learned rather more about the way things were in Geneva, and one cannot doubt that his warnings about the tendency of the executive government to invade the rights of the legislative were based on this newly acquired awareness of what had happened over several generations of Genevan history.

Perhaps we should not be surprised that *The Social Contract* was banned and burned in Geneva. Rousseau could well have protested that he had provided in his pages an advertisement for the republic: 'I took your constitution as my model for political institutions.'[23] But at the same time he showed how such a constitution came to be undermined. Moreover, other features of Rousseau's argument were bound to offend people who proclaimed themselves not only good republicans but good Christians.

For although Rousseau distanced himself from that universally detested atheist and materialist Thomas Hobbes, he did so only to align himself with a political philosopher of equally ill repute, Niccolò Machiavelli. For Rousseau saw in Machiavelli, not the supposed champion of monarchy who wrote *Il Principe*, but the ideologue of republicanism who wrote the *Discorsi*. Like Machiavelli, Rousseau was in love with the political systems of antiquity: that is what he meant when he said, 'I was a Roman at the age of twelve.' In time he came to prefer Sparta to Rome, but only because it remained more perfectly republican.

Rousseau does not tell the whole truth when he says that in writing *The Social Contract*, 'I took your constitution [of Geneva] as my model'; for he took another constitution as his model as well. At the end of his exploration of the idea of what a civil society must look like if it is successfully to combine liberty and law, what we can find is Calvin's Geneva fortified with further institutions and practises derived from Sparta.

Rousseau insists that citizens can be free—can be citizens in the true sense of the word—only if they make in person the rules under which they live. The idea of representation or delegation is wholly unacceptable to him. He writes very critically of the parliamentary system of elected deputies: 'The English people believes itself to be free; it is gravely mistaken; it is free only during the election of Members of Parliament; as soon as the Members are elected, the people are enslaved; it is nothing.'[24]

The Social Contract begins with a sensational opening sentence: 'Man was born free, but he is everywhere in chains.'[25] But the argument of the book is that men need not be in chains. When a state is based on a genuine social contract (as opposed to the fraudulent social contract depicted in the *Discourse on Inequality*), men receive in exchange for their independence a better kind of freedom, true political or republican freedom. In altering the kind of social contract, man loses his 'natural liberty and his unqualified right to lay hands on all that tempts him', but he gains 'civil liberty and the rightful ownership of what belongs to him';[26] to this is added the moral liberty that makes man master of himself, 'for subjugation to appetite alone is slavery, while obedience to a law one has prescribed for oneself is liberty.'[27]

In this formulation of Rousseau's argument we confront a serious problem. It is easy to understand that an individual can be said to be free if he prescribes to himself rules he obeys in his life; but how can a group of people be said to be free in prescribing for themselves the rules they obey? An individual is a person with a single will; but a group of people is a number of persons each with his own will. How can a group of persons have *a* will, in obedience to which all its members will be free? For it clearly must have such a single will, if any sense is to be made of Rousseau's proposition.

Rousseau's response to the problem is to define his civil society as an 'artificial person' with a single will, which he calls *la volonté générale*, or general will. The social contract that brings the civil society into being is itself a pledge, and that civil society remains in being. Ernest Renan defined the nation as a 'plebiscite renewed every day'; and this is exactly Rousseau's conception: the republic is the creation of will, of a will that never falters, in each and every member, to further the public, the common, the national interest—even though it might sometimes compete with personal interest. Of course, no one would cease to desire his own good; but as each individual is transformed into a citizen, he acquires besides his private will a general will.

Rousseau sounds very much like Hobbes when he says that under the pact by which men enter into civil society, everyone makes a 'total alienation of himself and all his rights to the whole community'.[28] It must be understood, however, that Rousseau represents this alienation as a form of exchange: men give up natural rights in return for civil rights. The total alienation is followed by a total restitution, and the bargain is a good one because what men surrender are rights of dubious value, motivated by nothing but an individual's own powers, rights that are precarious and without a moral basis, while what they receive in return are rights that are legitimate and enforced. The rights they alienate are based on might; the rights they acquire are based on law.

When Rousseau speaks of forcing a man to be free,[29] he is thinking of the occasional individual who, as a result of being enslaved by his passions, disobeys the voice of law, or the general will, within him. The general will is something inside each man as well as in society generally, so the man who is coerced by the community for a breach of the law is, in Rousseau's view of things, being brought back to an awareness of his own true will.

Thus in penalizing a lawbreaker, society is literally correcting him, restoring him to his own true purposes. Legal penalties are a device for helping the individual in his struggle against his own passions, as well as a device for protecting society against the anti-social depredations of lawbreakers. Political freedom and moral freedom come together in Rousseau: both consist of doing what one wants to do and doing what is right.

Rousseau and Nationalism

When the two tendencies Rousseau helped foster—romanticism and the quest for liberty in community—are combined, the result is modern nationalism. The alternation between a concentration on the self and a yearning for a larger community is more pronounced in the German successors of Rousseau and the other early Romantics (notably Diderot and Burke). In the 1760s and 1770s it is especially marked in the work of Johann Gottfried von Herder. Not satisfied with the theoretical exposition of romanticism, Herder published what was in effect a call to action to the poets and artists of Germany to enlarge the culture of the nation by new German creations and to stimulate people's feeling of nationhood by recovering the half-forgotten achievements of the German past. He viewed adherence to the canons of classicism or neoclassicism as a form of constraint that he urged German artists to throw off. He also sought to revalorise, as Rousseau had done before him, demotic, folkloric arts as proof that German literature had its own distinctive history, and he edited a two-volume edition of *Volkslieder* to reinforce his argument.

This fusion of romanticism and nationalism had varying appeal. Thanks to the efforts of Herder and his followers, it soon became an immensely powerful force in Germany. It made very little headway in the England of Sir Joshua Reynolds, Alexander Pope, Berkeley, and Hume, and still less in France, where Rousseau and Diderot were simply oddities in a massively Cartesian and neoclassicist culture. The dominant themes in France were modified by Baconian empiricism but essentially perpetuated by the Enlightenment. The French Revolution was inspired not by the romantic Rousseau of *La Nouvelle Héloïse* and the *Confessions* but by Montesquieu's celebration of British constitutionalism and Rousseau's neoclassical revival, in his political writings, of the republican institutions of ancient Rome and the republican virtues of ancient Sparta.

Napoleon also sought legitimation from classical models, notably Roman imperialism. Seeing himself as the Caesar of the modern world, he was fortunate in having at least in the visual arts outstanding talents at his disposal. In such paintings as that by Jacques David representing the Emperor crowning himself, or that by Ingres showing the Emperor enthroned, art and propaganda were magnificently fused. Napoleon was doubly fortunate in the fact that despite his hostility to romanticism, romantic artists often admired him and saw him as at long last a romantic hero. Some of them even tried to win his friendship and patronage, but for the most part French romanticism was cultivated only by those who were banished from France by the revolution, by Mme de Staël, for example, by Benjamin Constant, and above all by the greatest French writer of that time, Chateaubriand.

Thus, while Rousseau's romanticism cannot be blamed for producing the

French Revolution or its illiberal and violent aspects, one may say that romanticism, allied with the longing for political community, shaped modern
nationalism by introducing the idea of the nation as a cultural entity. Some
manifestations of cultural nationalism have certainly been extremely malevolent, but Rousseau is at most only very indirectly responsible for inciting
the chauvinistic and xenophobic form of nationalism.

Rousseau's Legacy

In trying to discern Rousseau's influence over others and in later times, we
should not lose sight of what he himself thought and sought to teach. He
believed that people ought to live, as far as possible, in harmony with nature,
admiring its beauty and respecting it as the very source of all being and all
possibility. He was as convinced as Locke and Jefferson that nature made all
human beings free and capable of associating peacefully with one another.
He did not suppose that the natural liberty lost because of the advance of
civilisation could be restored by revolution or that a reformed society would
subordinate the individual to the community, let alone to some dictator. His
hope was rather that if people were brought up to make fundamental moral
decisions by and for themselves by listening to the inner voice of natural
compassion, they would want to form communities in which they could all
enjoy the freedom to exercise moral will. This freedom, or autonomy, would
enable them to regulate their own lives in self-regarding matters and to participate as equal citizens in the exercise of constitutional sovereignty.

Rousseau is therefore rightly considered a champion of the belief in universal human rights, though he thinks of these rights as civil rather than natural, arising out of the conversion of natural into civil liberty by the social
compact. He also thought that communities so constituted might be linked
in federations like that of the Swiss. It was Rousseau's formulation of this
principle of autonomy that led Immanuel Kant to think of him as the New-
ton of the moral world; Kant also followed Rousseau and the Abbé de St-
Pierre in championing a federation of republics as the path to a more
peaceful world.

Rousseau's ideas may seem to have been unrealistic for an age marked by
the rise of populous imperial states and the manipulation of nature by science and technology in the industrial revolution. But some of the consequences of modernization—impersonal bureaucracy, insensitivity to human
suffering, the erosion of family ties and social loyalties, the follies of acquis-
itiveness, expansionism, and over-centralization, disregard for other species
and for the natural environment—all tell a different story. They suggest that
Rousseau's legacy may be more profound and worth heeding than critics in
his own day and since would have us believe.

CHRONOLOGY OF ROUSSEAU'S LIFE AND WORK

1712	Born Geneva 28 June.
1722	Entrusted to care of a country pastor.
1728	Runs off to Savoy, agrees to study Catholicism with a recent convert, Mme de Warens. Baptized a Catholic in Turin.
1729	Studies for priesthood at a seminary but leaves to enroll in choir school.
1733	Mme de Warens decides to terminate his virginity, seduces him.
1742	Academy of Sciences in Paris rejects his proposal to replace musical notation with numbering. Thérèse Levasseur becomes his companion and lover.
1743–44	Begins work on his opera, *Les Muses galantes* (The Amorous Poets). Employed as secretary to the French ambassador to Venice.
1747–49	Writes a play, *L'Engagement téméraire* (The Rash Commitment), and articles, mainly on music, for the *Encyclopédie* of Diderot and d'Alembert. Earns a living copying music.
1751	His *Discourse on the Sciences and the Arts* wins prize offered by Academy of Dijon.
1752-53	His opera, *Le Devin du village* (The Village Soothsayer) is performed and well received. His comic play, *Narcisse,* is also staged but fares badly. His *Letter on French Music* entangles him in a fierce quarrel with the composer Rameau.
1753	Writes *Discourse on the Origin of Inequality.*
1754	Repudiates his youthful apostasy, is accepted back into the Calvinist Church.
1754–55	Settles in Paris, writes entry on 'Political Economy' in *Encyclopédie.*
1756	Moves to the Hermitage in Montmorency. Writes *La Reine fantasque* (The Capricious Queen), a fairy tale. His *Letter on*

Providence defends benevolence of God against Voltaire, who replies by writing *Candide*.

1757   Falls in love with Sophie d'Houdetot.

1758   His *Letter to Monsieur d'Alembert on the Theatre* rejects proposal of a theatre for Geneva, infuriating Voltaire.

1761   *Julie*, or *Lettres de deux amans*, afterwards known as *La Nouvelle Héloïse*, appears and is a huge success.

1762   *Émile* and *The Social Contract* both published and make him an outcast. Ordered arrested, flees to Switzerland. Expelled from Yverdon, moves to Môtiers, in Neuchâtel, is granted asylum. Drafts *Émile et Sophie, ou les solitaires*, intended as a sequel to *Émile*.

1763   Defends his religious views in *Letter to Christophe de Beaumont, Archbishop of Paris*. When this letter is banned by the Petit Conseil, renounces his Genevan citizenship.

1764   Attacks Genevan Petit Conseil in his *Letters from the Mountain*. Agrees to draft constitution for Corsica.

1765   When Genevans capitulate to the Petit Conseil, declares he will have nothing further to do with Genevan affairs. Moves to the Isle de St-Pierre in Lake Bienne. Ordered out, agrees to seek refuge in England.

1766   Accompanied to London by David Hume. Turns on Hume, returns to France.

1767   Takes refuge in the Château de Trye in Normandy under protection of Prince de Conti.

1768   His *Dictionary of Music* is published in Paris.

1769   Leaves for Bourgoin, near Grenoble, moves to nearby village of Monquin, marries Thérèse.

1770   Permitted to return to Paris on condition he publish no writings on politics or religion. His play *Pygmalion* is set to music and performed en route in Lyons. Completes the *Confessions* in Paris.

1771   At the behest of the Confederation of Bar, completes the *Considerations on the Government of Poland*.

1772   Takes long walks in the countryside collecting specimens and making notes. Composes *Elementary Letters on Botany* for the young daughter of a friend.

1776   Completes *Rousseau Juge de Jean-Jacques*, also known as his *Dialogues*.

1778   In April makes last entry in final work, *The Reveries of the Solitary Walker*. Retires with Thérèse to a cottage in Ermenonville, succumbs to a stroke on 2 July, aged 66.

LIST OF PRINCIPAL
ABBREVIATIONS USED IN
THE NOTES

AEG	Archives d'État, Geneva
AEN	Archives d'État, Neuchâtel
Annales	*Annales de la Société Jean-Jacques Rousseau*, Geneva, 1905–
Bachaumont	L.P. de Bachaumont, *Mémoires secrets pour servir à l'histoire de la république des lettres en France, depuis 1762 jusqu'a nos jours*, London, 1777–89, four volumes
Berthoud (1881)	F. Berthoud, *Jean-Jacques Rousseau au Val de Travers, 1762–1765*, Paris, 1881
Berthoud (1884)	F. Berthoud, *J.-J. Rousseau et le pasteur de Montmollin, 1762–1765*, Fleurier, 1884
Besterman	T. Besterman, ed., *The Correspondence of Voltaire: Definitive Edition* (The Complete Works of Voltaire), Geneva, Banbury, and Oxford, 1960–80, thirteen volumes
BL	British Library, London
BN	Bibliothèque Nationale, Paris
Bodemann	E. Bodemann, *Julie von Bondeli und ihr Freundeskreis*, Hannover, 1874
BPUG	Bibliothèque Publique et Universitaire, Geneva
BPUN	Bibliothèque Publique et Universitaire, Neuchâtel
Buffenoir	H. Buffenoir, *Les Portraits de Jean-Jacques Rousseau*, Paris, 1913
BVN	Bibliothèque de la Ville, Neuchâtel
CC	R.A. Leigh, ed., *Correspondance complète de Jean-Jacques Rousseau*, Geneva, Banbury, and Oxford, 1965–95, fifty-one volumes
Creighton	D.G. Creighton, *Jacques-François Deluc of Geneva and His Friendship with Jean-Jacques Rousseau*, University, Mississippi, 1982
Crocker	L.G. Crocker, *Jean-Jacques Rousseau*, New York, 1968–73, two volumes

De Crue	F. de Crue, *L'Ami de Rousseau et des Necker, Paul Moultou*, Paris, 1926
D'Escherny	F.-L. d'Escherny, *Oeuvres philosophique, littéraires, historiques et morales*, Paris, 1814, three volumes
Dutch Royal Library	The Library of HM The Queen of the Netherlands, the Hague
Eigeldinger	F.S. Eigeldinger, *'Des Pierres dans mon jardin,' les années neuchâtelois de Jean-Jacques Rousseau et la crise de 1765*, Paris-Geneva, 1992
Finlayson	I. Finlayson, *The Moth and the Candle*, London, 1984
François	A. François, *Jean-Jacques Rousseau et Leurs Excellences*, Lausanne, 1924
G	The 'Geneva' manuscript of Rousseau's *Confessions* (in BPUG)
Gagnebin	B. Gagnebin, *Album Rousseau*, Paris, 1976
Guyot (1936)	C. Guyot, *Pèlerins de Môtiers*, Neuchâtel, 1936
Guyot (1958)	C. Guyot, *Un Ami et defenseur de Rousseau*, Neuchâtel, 1958
Guyot (1962)	C. Guyot, *Plaidoyer pour Thérèse Levasseur*, Neuchâtel, 1962
HL	J.Y.T. Greig, ed., *The Letters of David Hume*, Oxford, 1932, two volumes
Hume (1820)	*Private correspondence of David Hume with several distinguished persons between the years of 1761 and 1766*, London, 1820
J.-J.	M. Cranston, *Jean-Jacques: the Early Life and Work of Jean-Jacques Rousseau, 1712–1754*, London and New York, 1983
Jost	F. Jost, *Jean-Jacques Rousseau, Suisse*, Fribourg, Switzerland, 1961, two volumes
Kehl	Beaumarchais, Condorcet, and Decroix, eds., *Oeuvres complètes de Voltaire*, Kehl, 1785–89, seventy volumes
Leigh	R.A. Leigh, *Unsolved Problems in the Bibliography of Jean-Jacques Rousseau*, ed. J.T.A. Leigh, Cambridge, 1990
Lettre de Goa	A.-P. Du Peyrou, *Lettre à Monsieur . . . relative à Monsieur J.J. Rousseau*, Goa (Lyon), 1765
Matthey	F. Matthey, *Catalogue du Musée Rousseau à Môtiers*, Môtiers, 1968
MN	Musée Neuchâtelois
Mossner	E.C. Mossner, *The Life of David Hume*, New York, 1980
Musset-Pathay (1827)	V.-D. de Musset-Pathay, *Histoire de la vie et des ouvrages de J.-J. Rousseau*, Paris, 1827, two volumes
NS	M. Cranston, *The Noble Savage: Jean-Jacques Rousseau, 1754–1762*, Chicago and London, 1991
OC	*Oeuvres complètes de Jean-Jacques Rousseau*, edited for the Bib-

	liothèque de la Pléiade by B. Gagnebin, M. Raymond, J. Starobinski, et al., 1959–95, five volumes
P	The 'Paris' manuscript of Rousseau's *Confessions* (in Palais Bourbon)
Palais Bourbon	Bibliothèque de l'Assemblée Nationale, Palais Bourbon, Paris
Pottle	F.A. Pottle, *Boswell on the Grand Tour*, London, 1953
Rosselet	Claire Rosselet, *L'Affaire Rousseau-Montmollin*, Neuchâtel, 1934
RSE	Royal Society of Edinburgh
Saussure	H. de Saussure, *Rousseau et les manuscrits des 'Confessions'*, Paris, 1958
SC	J.-J. Rousseau, *The Social Contract*, ed. M. Cranston, Harmondsworth and Baltimore, 1968
Soc. J.-J.R.	Archives of the Société Jean-Jacques Rousseau (in BPUG)
Scott	G. Scott, ed., *Private Papers of James Boswell*, New York, 1928, eighteen volumes
Starobinski	J. Starobinski, *Jean-Jacques Rousseau, la transparence et l'obstacle*, Paris 1971
Tourneux	M. Tourneux, ed., *Correspondance littéraire, philosophique et critique par Grimm, Diderot, Reynal, Meister*, Paris, 1877, sixteen volumes
Walpole	W.S. Lewis, ed., *The Yale Edition of the Correspondence of Horace Walpole*, Oxford, 1937–83, forty-eight volumes

NOTES

CHAPTER 1: A MIXED WELCOME
(pages 1–15)

1. To Moultou, 15.6.1762. BPUN, MS R289, f.24 (*CC*, XI, 1873).
2. 17.6.1762. Palais Bourbon, P7074, ff.83–4 (*CC*, XI, 1882).
3. C. V. von Bonstetten, *Erinnerungen*, Zürich, 1827, p.249.
4. François, p.30.
5. Jost, I, p.343.
6. BPUN, MS R319, ff.26–7 (*CC*, XI, 1877).
7. 15.6.1762. BPUN, MS R292, f.9–10 (*CC*, XI, 1874).
8. P, II, p.130 (*OC*, I, p.574).
9. Ibid.
10. 17.6.1762. BPUN, MS R91, ff.4–5 (*CC*, XI, 1879).
11. 17.6.1762. BPUN, MS R91, ff.5–6 (*CC*, XI, 1880).
12. P, I, p.141 (*OC*, I, pp.594–5).
13. 23.6.1762. BPUN, MS R294, ff.124–5 (*CC*, XI, 1904).
14. 24.6.1762. BPUN, MS R308, ff.25–8 (*CC*, XI, 1910).
15. 17.6.1762. BPUN, MS R91, f.3 (*CC*, XI, 1881).
16. 4.7.1762. Montreal, McGill University Library (*CC*, XI, 1953).
17. De Crue, p.29.
18. 'La Condemnation du "Contrat Social" et d' "Émile", prononcée par le Conseil de Genève', *Annales*, XI, 1916–17, pp.201–8.
19. BPUG, Archives Tronchin, 291, no.9 (*CC*, XI, 1955).
20. BPUG, Archives Tronchin, MS Supp. 1036, ff.104–5 (*CC*, XI, 1867).
21. BN, n.a.f.24.330, ff.47–8 (*CC*, XI, 1887).
22. BPUN, MS R289, ff.25–6 (*CC*, XI, 1898).
23. 22.6.1762. BPUN, MS R319, ff.32–3 (*CC*, XI, 1899).
24. Lausanne, Archives Cantonales; Archives de La Sarraz C474 (*OC*, XI, 1894).
25. 24.6.1762. BPUN, MS R299, f.114 (*CC*, XI, 1911).
26. New Haven, Yale University, Beinecke Library, Boswell MS (Pottle, p.267).
27. 4.7.1762. Montreal, McGill University Library (*CC*, XI, 1953).
28. 7.7.1762. Zürich, Zentralbibliothek, MS Hirzel, 238, no.130, pp.1–3 (*CC*, XI, 1963).
29. Berne, Burgerbibliothek, MS Hist. Helvetica, XVIII, 21, no.74 (*CC*, XI, 1891).
30. Ibid. no.89 (*CC*, XII, 2006).
31. To David Hume, 24.10.1766. Besterman, XXXI, D13621. Voltaire later published the letter in *Notes sur la lettre de Monsieur de Voltaire à Monsieur Hume*, Paris, 1776.
32. *NS*, p.9.
33. AEG, Registres du P.C., vol.262 (*CC*, XI, 1901).

34. Tourneux, V, p.138.
35. BPUN, MS R289, ff.29–30 (CC, XI, 1958).
36. 5.7.1762. BPUN, MS R294, ff.5–6 (CC, XI, 1954).
37. 6.7.1762. BPUN, MS R301, ff.40–1 (CC, XI, 1960).
38. 7.7.1762. BPUN, MS R319, ff.38–9 (CC, XI, 1961).
39. 28.6.1762. BPUN, MS R292, ff.111–12 (CC, XI, 1920).
40. 2.7.1762. Hume (1820), pp.8–9.
41. 2.7.1762. BPUN, MS R307, ff.128–9 (CC, XI, 1944).
42. In her letter of 24.6.1762. BPUN, MS R308, ff.25–8 (CC, XI, 1910).
43. 9.7.1762. BPUN, MS R319, f.40 (CC, XI, 1974).
44. Undated, BPUN, MS R322, ff.37–8 (CC, XI, 1922).
45. 29.6.1762. BPUN, MS R328, ff.62–3 (CC, XI, 1925).
46. 8.7.1762. BPUN, MS R300, ff.44–5 (CC, XI, 1966).
47. L'Onanisme, Lausanne, 1760.
48. OC, VI, p.663.
49. François, p.60.
50. Berne State Archives, Ratsmanual no.361, 1762, pp.159–80.
51. Musset-Pathay (1827), I, p.194.
52. See NS, p.342.
53. 2.7.1762. BPUN, MS R321, ff.5–6 (CC, XI, 1945).
54. This letter cannot be traced.
55. 3.7.1762. Berne, Burgerbibliothek, MS Hist. Helvetica, XII, 92, no.88 (CC, XI, 1948).
56. Ibid. no.89 (CC, XI, 1949).
57. P, II, p.161 (OC, I, p.631).
58. Berne State Archives, Schulratsmanual no.9, pp.343–4.
59. 8.7.1762. Berne State Archives, Ratsmanual no.261, 1762, pp.233–234.
60. New Haven, Yale University, Beinecke Library, Boswell MS (Pottle, p.267).
61. 20.7.1762. Zürich, Zentralbibliothek, MS Hirzel, 238, no.160 (CC, XII, 2014).

62. P, II, p.140 (OC, I, p.592).
63. P, II, p.139 (OC, I, p.592).
64. P, II, p.140 (OC, I, p.593).
65. Ibid.

CHAPTER 2: MÔTIERS
(pages 16–40)

1. J. Courvoisier, 'Notes sur la "maison Rousseau" à Môtiers', MN, III, May 1968, pp.167–72.
2. J.-J. Rousseau, Politics and the Arts, ed. and trans. A. Bloom, Ithaca, N.Y., 1960.
3. 18.7.1762. BN, Collection Rothschild (CC, XII, 2007).
4. 20.7.1762. BPUN, MS R304, ff.16–17 (CC, XII, 2011).
5. 27.7.1762. BPUN, MS R283, f.158 (CC, XII, 2016). The letter was in fact printed in 1763 in a pirated edition of the Lettres de J.-J. Rousseau.
6. 10.7.1762. BPUN, MS R284, f.3 (CC, XII, 1978).
7. See E. E. Cuthell, The Scottish Friend of Frederic the Great, London, 1915.
8. 12.7.1762. BPUN, MS R316, ff.1–2 (CC, XII, 1985).
9. 11.7.1762. BPUN, MS R91, f.7 (CC, XII, 1976).
10. 29.7.1762. Merseburg, Zentralarchiv, Nachlass Keith, II, 2, f.211 (CC, XII, 2047).
11. 1.9.1762. Merseburg, Zentralarchiv, Nachlass Keith, II, 2, f.212 (CC, XIII, 2128).
12. P, II, p.143 (OC, I, p.599).
13. AEN, Fonds Sandoz, 51 (CC, XII, 1984).
14. P, II, p.142 (OC, I, p.597).
15. P, II, p.142 (OC, I, p.597).
16. MN, III, 1876, p.183.
17. J. H. Bonhôte, 'Un Gouverneur de Neuchâtel,' MN, I, 1864, pp.43–111.
18. MN, n.s., 1920, pp.7–9 (with a portrait of Emetulla).
19. Guyot (1958), pp.25–31.
20. Cited in Berthoud (1881), p.49.

21. 12.7.1762 (see note 20).

22. Berthoud (1884).

23. 11.7.1762. BPUN, MS R289, ff.31–2 (*CC*, XII, 1982).

24. 17.7.1762. BPUG, unclassified (*CC*, XII, 1992).

25. BPUN, MS R289, ff.33–4 (*CC*, XII, 1992).

26. 17.7.1762. BPUN, MS R319, ff.41–2 (*CC*, XII, 2003).

27. 17.7.1762. Zürich, State Archives, FAU 68, Nachlass Moultou, no.2 (*CC*, XII, 2005).

28. De Crue, p.19.

29. 21.7.1762(?). BPUN, MS R303, ff.76–7 (*CC*, XII, 2018).

30. BPUN, MS R291, f.32 (*CC*, XVIII, 3046).

31. 30.11.1762. BPUN, MS R291, f.32v (*CC*, XIV, 2354).

32. 21.7.1762. Palais Bourbon, P7074, ff.85–6 (*CC*, XII, 2017).

33. P, II, p.141 (*OC*, I, p.595).

34. Guyot (1962), p.85.

35. 21.7.1762. Palais Bourbon, P7074, ff.85–6 (*CC*, XI, 2017).

36. 21.7.1762. BPUN, MS R308, ff.29–32 (*CC*, XII, 2019).

37. 22.7.1762. Bordeaux, Archives de Luze (*CC*, XII, 2023).

38. 24.7.1762. Bordeaux, Archives de Luze (*CC*, XII, 2030).

39. Berthoud (1881), p.52.

40. 30.6.1764. BPUG, Soc. J-J.R., MS R105 (*CC*, XX, 3372).

41. See Matthey, p.11.

42. Cited in Guyot (1936), pp.16–17.

43. BPUN, MS R321, ff.12–13 (*CC*, XII, 2025).

44. François, p.89.

45. See Bodemann, pp.8–11, 86–121.

46. Jost, I, p.364.

47. 27.7.1762. Berne, Burgerbibliothek, Nachlass Fellenberg (*CC*, XII, 2039).

48. Bodemann, p.233.

49. Jost, I, p.352.

50. He lived from 1739 to 1800.

51. P, II, p.172 (*OC*, I, p.653).

52. Bodemann, p.244.

53. *Émile et Sophie, ou les solitaires* was still unpublished (see *NS*, pp.191–93). It was printed for the first time posthumously in the Moultou and Du Peyrou edition of the *Collection complète* (see *OC*, IV, pp.clxi–clxvii).

54. BPUN, MS R300, f.186 (*CC*, XII, 2024).

55. BPUN, MS R310, ff.124–5 (*CC*, XII, 2045).

56. 11.7.1762. BPUN, MS R310, ff.2–3 (*CC*, XII, 1980).

57. Leigh, p.14.

58. 25.8.1762. BPUN, MS R n.a.9, ff.16–17 (*CC*, XII, 2110).

59. 6.9.1762. BPUN, MS R306, ff.31–2 (*CC*, XIII, 2137).

60. 4.10.1762. BPUN, MS R306, ff.33–4 (*CC*, XIII, 2211).

61. L. F. Benedetto, *Madame de Warens*, Paris, 1914, pp.288–9.

62. P, II, p.154 (*OC*, I, p.620).

63. 3.12.1762. BPUN, MS R321, ff.16–17 (*CC*, XII, 2055).

64. BPUN, MS R321, ff.22–3 (*CC*, XII, 2095).

65. 4.9.1762. BPUN, MS R318, ff.70–1 (*CC*, XIII, 2132).

66. P, II, p.138 (*OC*, I, p.590).

67. BPUN, MS R8, ff.1–8v. (*OC*, II, pp.1290–98)

68. He named the *Lettres à Sara* in the list of writings to be included in volume 3 of the *Collected Works* that Du Peyrou proposed to sponsor in 1765 (Dutch Royal Library, G16-A434, no.127).

69. 10.8.1762. BPUN, MS R288, ff.116–17 (*CC*, XII, 2068).

70. 14.8.1762. BPUN, MS R284, f.95 (*CC*, XII, 2075).

71. 20.8.1762. BPUN, MS R288, ff.118–19 (*CC*, XII, 2094).

72. BPUN, MS R318, ff.160–61 (*CC*, XII, 2087).

73. BPUN, MS R316, ff.3–4 (*CC*, XII, 2079).

74. 10.8.1762. BPUG, MS Fr.203, no.108, ff.223–24 (*CC*, XII, 2067).

75. 13.8.1762. BPUN, MS R302, ff.7–8 (*CC*, XII, 2071).

76. BPUN, MS R302, ff.9–11 (*CC*, XII, 2082).

77. 20.8.1762. BPUG, MS Fr.203, ff.225–26 (*CC*, XII, 2092).

78. 3.8.1762. BPUN, MS R289, ff.37–8 (*CC*, XII, 2054).

79. 7.8.1762. BPUN, MS R319, ff.45–6 (*CC*, XII, 2064).

80. Cited in Berthoud (1881), p.141.

81. BPUN, MS R319, ff.47–8 (*CC*, XII, 2100).

82. 18.8.1762. BPUN, MS R91, ff.11–12 (*CC*, XII, 2086).

83. P, II, p.144 (*OC*, I, p.601).

84. 24.8.1762. BPUN, MS Rn.a.5, ff.3–5 (*CC*, XII, 2108).

85. F.-G. Montmollin, *Lettre . . . relative à J.-J. Rousseau*, Neuchâtel, 1765.

86. 10.9.1762. BPUN, MS R319, ff.50–1, (*CC*, XIII, 2149).

87. 8.9.1762. Kehl, LXVIII, p.211.

88. 10.10.1762. BPUN, MS R308, ff.37–38 (*CC*, XIII, 2223).

89. Manuscript not traced. (*CC*, XII, 2122).

90. Cited in R. A. Leigh, 'Avertissement de treziéme volume' (*CC*, XIII, p.xxv).

91. 4.9.1762. BPUG, Soc. J.-J. R., MS R105 (*CC*, XIII, 2131).

92. See *NS*, p.336.

93. 26.9.1762. BPUN, MS R322, ff.39–40 (*CC*, XIII, 2191).

94. See Berthoud (1881), p.47.

95. BPUN, MS R91, f.13 (*CC*, XIII, 2161).

96. P, II, p.145 (*OC*, I, p.602).

97. Jost, I, p.345.

98. 25.9.1762. Bordeaux, Archives de Luze (*CC*, XIII, 2189).

99. 12.10.1762. Bodemann, pp.239–40.

100. 9.9.1762. BPUN, MS R320, f.187 (*CC*, XIII, 2146).

101. 26.10.1762. BPUN, MS R310, ff.126–27 (*CC*, XIII, 2258).

102. 12.10.1762. Zürich, Zentralbiblio-thek, Hirzel, 238 no.157 (*CC*, XIII, 2227).

103. Jost, I, p.367.

104. *NS*, pp.323–27.

105. 28.10.1762. New York Public Library, Herter Collection (*CC*, XIII, 2253).

106. 13.11.1762. BPUN, MS R295, ff.49–50 (*CC*, XIII, 2298).

107. See *NS*, pp.248–49.

108. L. Witmer, 'Gessner et Watelet', *Revue de littérature comparée*, II, 1922, pp.553–4.

109. 5.12.1767. BPUG, MS Fr.203, f.135 (*CC*, XXXIV, 6147).

110. Jost, I, p.435.

111. 24.9.1762. BPUN, MS R299, ff.129–30 (*CC*, XIII, 2188).

112. 12.10.1762. Zürich, Zentralbibliothek, MS Hirzel, 238 no.157 (*CC*, XIII, 2227).

113. 24.9.1762. BPUN, MS R299, ff.129–30 (*CC*, XIII, 2188).

114. 23.7.1762. BPUN, MS R300, ff.82–3 (*CC*, XII, 2026).

115. 30.9.1762. BPUN, MS R302, ff.94–7 (*CC*, XIII, 2201).

116. 2.10.1762. BPUN, MS R316, ff.10–11 (*CC*, XIII, 2204).

117. 1.10.1762. RSE, Hume MS, vol.99 (Burton, II, 1846, pp.105–6).

118. 9.10.1762. BN, Collection Rothschild (*CC*, XIII, 2220).

119. 1.11.1762. BPUN, MS R91, f.13 (*CC*, XIV, 2275).

120. To Frederick II. *Annales*, IX, 1913, p.84.

121. 3.11.1762. BPUN, MS R316, ff.20–1 (*CC*, XIV, 2279).

122. 11.11.1762. BPUN, MS R316, ff.22–3 (*CC*, XIV, 2294).

123. 18.10.1762. BPUN, MS R316, ff.14–15 (*CC*, XIII, 2239).

124. 27.10.1762. BPUN, MS R321, ff.33–4 (*CC*, XIII, 2260).

125. 2.11.1762. BPUN, MS R321, ff.35–6 (*CC*, XIV, 2278).

126. A. Petitpierre, MN, XV, 1878, pp.145–74.

127. 6.11.1762. BN, Collection Roth-schild (*CC*, XIV, 2284).
128. 14.9.1782. BPUN, MS R321, ff.27–8 (*CC*, XIII, 2162).
129. 9.10.1782. BN, Collection Roth-schild (*CC*, XIII, 2220).
130. 8.10.1762. Dutch Royal Library, G16-A434, no.94 (*CC*, XIII, 2219).

CHAPTER 3:
A GOSPEL CHRISTIAN
(pages 41–56)

1. 10.9.1762. BPUN, MS R319, ff.50–1 (*CC*, XIII, 2149).
2. 12.9.1762. BPUN, MS R302, ff.44–5 (*CC*, XIII, 2155).
3. 23.9.1762. BPUN, MS R285, ff.9–10 (*CC*, XIII, 2186).
4. 14.9.1762. BPUN, R n.a.12, ff.2–3 (*CC*, XIII, 2163).
5. 1693–1760. See *J.-J*, p.334.
6. 25.9.1762. BPUN, MS R n.a.12, ff.4–4b (*CC*, XIII, 2191).
7. To Du Peyrou, 8.8.1765. BPUN, MS R286, ff.83–92 (*CC*, XXVI, 4573).
8. 20.9.1762. BPUN, MS R289, ff.44–5 (*CC*, XIII, 2175).
9. 22.9.1762. BPUN, MS R319, ff.52–4 (*CC*, XIII, 2182).
10. 18.6.1762. BPUN, MS R319, f.29 (*CC*, XI, 1888).
11. 23.6.1762. BPUN, MS R319, f.35 (*CC*, XI, 1903).
12. Creighton, p.42.
13. 2.7.1762. BPUN, MS R31, ff.36–7 (*CC*, XI, 1942).
14. 6.7.1762. BPUN, MS R289, ff.29–30 (*CC*, XI, 1958).
15. Creighton, p.45.
16. 24.9.1762. BPUN, MS R312, ff.1–4 (*CC*, XIII, 2187).
17. 10.10.1762. BPUG, MS Fr.248, ff.10–11 (*CC*, XIII, 2222).
18. 1.9.1762. BPUN, MS R289, ff.41–2 (*CC*, XIII, 2126).
19. 28.9.1762. BPUN, MS R319, ff.55–6 (*CC*, XIII, 2199).
20. 10.9.1762. BPUN, MS R303, f.22 (*CC*, XIII, 2150).
21. L. J. Courtois, 'Visiteurs Genevoises de Rousseau à Montmorency et à Môtiers', *Annales*, XVII, 1926, p.166.
22. 4.10.1762. BPUG, MS Fr.498, ff.71–2 (*CC*, XIII, 2212).
23. Courtois, *Annales*, XVII, 1926, p.169.
24. Musset-Pathay (1827), II, pp.501–2.
25. *OC*, II, pp.1177–92.
26. 3.3.1766. Dutch Royal Library, G16-A434, no.136 (*CC*, XXIX, 5089).
27. BPUN, MS R n.a.12 (*CC*, XIII, 2230).
28. 19.10.1762. BPUN, MS R n.a.12 (*CC*, XIII, 2243).
29. 12.10.1762. BPUN, MS R303, ff.23–4 (*CC*, XIII, 2229).
30. 20.10.1762. BPUN, MS R302, ff.21–2 (*CC*, XIII, 2244).
31. 13.10.1762. BPUN, MS R301, ff.1–2 (*CC*, XIII, 2232).
32. 13.10.1762. BPUN, MS R310, ff.37–8 (*CC*, XIII, 2231).
33. 21.10.1762. BPUN, MS R289, ff.49–50 (*CC*, XIII, 2245).
34. 16.10.1762. BPUN, MS R n.a.1 (*CC*, XIII, 2236).
35. 18.10.1762. Manuscript not traced (*CC*, XIII, 2238).
36. 21.10.1762. BPUN, MS R289, ff.49–50 (*CC*, XIII, 2245).
37. 13.9.1762. BPUN, MS R289, ff.53–4 (*CC*, XIV, 2296).
38. 9.11.1762. BPUN, MS R319, ff.59–60 (*CC*, XIV, 2289).
39. 13.11.1762. BPUN, MS R289, ff.53–4 (*CC*, XIV, 2296).
40. 19.10.1762. BPUN, MS R n.a.12, no.8 (*CC*, XIII, 2242).
41. 23.11.1762. BPUN, MS R n.a.12, no.19 (*CC*, XIV, 2332).
42. 4.11.1762. BPUN, MS R302, ff.46–7 (*CC*, XIII, 2209).
43. 30.10.1762. BPUN, MS R n.a.12, no.11 (*CC*, XIII, 2268).
44. BPUN, MS R n.a.1, ff.109–10 (*CC*, XIV, 2315).

45. 14.11.1762(?). BPUN, MS R92, ff.9–10 (*CC*, XIV, 2299).
46. BPUN, MS R91 (*OC*, IV, pp.925–1030).
47. *OC*, IV, p.927.
48. Ibid. p.929.
49. Ibid. p.931.
50. Ibid.
51. Ibid. p.933.
52. Ibid. pp.932–3.
53. Ibid. p.960.
54. Ibid. p.939.
55. Ibid. p.960.
56. Ibid.
57. Ibid. p.987.
58. Ibid. p.990.
59. Ibid. p.978.
60. Ibid. p.996.
61. Ibid. p.997.
62. Dutch Royal Library, G16-A434, no.95 (*CC*, XIV, 2306).
63. 1.12.1762. Dutch Royal Library, G16-A434, no.96 (*CC*, XIV, 2358).
64. Manuscript not traced (*CC*, XIV, 2390).
65. 26.12.1762. BPUN, MS R297, ff.56–7 (*CC*, XIV, 2408).
66. 14.12.1762. BPUN, MS R320, f.192 (*CC*, XIV, 2385).
67. This is what ultimately appeared in print as the false 'Neuchâtel Edition' of 1764–68.
68. 16.11.1762. BPUN, MS R317, f.4 (*CC*, XIV, 2308).
69. 25.12.1762. BPUN, MS R317, f.7 (*CC*, XIV, 2406).
70. See *NS*, pp.152–3.
71. 8.1.1763. BPUN, MS R310, ff.8–9 (*CC*, XV, 2429).
72. BPUN, MS R308, ff.39–40 (*CC*, XIV, 2292).
73. 26.11.1762. BPUG, MS Fr.232, ff.33–4 (*CC*, XIV, 2342).
74. 15.10.1762. BPUN, MS R288, ff.130–1 (*CC*, XIV, 2234).
75. 28.11.1762. BPUN, MS R288, ff.140–1 (*CC*, XIV, 2350).
76. 18.12.1762. BPUN, MS R288, ff.142–3 (*CC*, XIV, 2395).
77. 13.1.1763. BPUN, MS R288, ff.150–3 (*CC*, XV, 2431).
78. See *OC*, IV, p.714.
79. 24.12.1762. BPUN, MS R322, ff.41–2 (*CC*, XIV, 2403).
80. 19.12.1762. BPUN, MS R289, ff.59–60 (*CC*, XIV, 2396).
81. 19.12.1762. BPUN, MS R289, ff.59–60 (*CC*, XIV, 2396).
82. BPUN, MS R321, ff.46–7 (*CC*, XIV, 2399).
83. 9.12.1762. BPUN, MS R316, ff.32–4 (*CC*, XIV, 2377).
84. 9.12.1762. AEN, Fonds Sandoz, 51 (*CC*, XIV, 2378).
85. 24.12.1762. AEN, Fonds Sandoz, 51 (*CC*, XIV, 2403).
86. *Annales*, XXXIV, 1959, pp.29–30.
87. BPUN, MS R284, ff.71–3 (*CC*, XV, App. 289).
88. See *NS*, p.288.
89. Before he left the Val de Travers in 1765, Rousseau recovered the will from Martinet and subsequently gave it to Richard Davenport; thus the presence of a copy of the will in the Bromley-Davenport Collection at the John Rylands Library, Manchester.
90. 4.1.1763. BPUN, MS R319, ff.69–70 (*CC*, XV, 2423).
91. Besterman, XXV, D10789.
92. Besterman, XXV, D10857.
93. Besterman, XXV, D10877.
94. 9.1.1763. Besterman, XXV, D10897.
95. Besterman, XXV, D10953.
96. Besterman, XXV, D10971.
97. BPUN, MS R289, ff.62–3 (*CC*, XV, 2441).

CHAPTER 4: THE TOCSIN
OF SEDITION
(pages 57–79)

1. 4.1.1763. BPUN, MS R321, ff.48–9 (*CC*, XV, 2422).
2. 6.1.1763. Dutch Royal Library, G16-A434, no.98 (*CC*, XV, 2427).
3. 5.2.1763. Dutch Royal Library, G16-A434, no.100 (*CC*, XV, 2470).

4. 29.1.1763. Dutch Royal Library, G16-A434, no.99 (*CC*, XV, 2460).

5. 8.1.1763. BPUN, MS R310, ff.8–9 (*CC*, XV, 2429).

6. 27.1.1763. BPUN, MS R310, ff.10–11 (*CC*, XV, 2456).

7. 9.1.1763. BPUG, MS Fr.206, ff.24–5 (*CC*, XV, 2430).

8. To Deluc, 24.1.1763. BPUG, MS Fr.236, ff.109–10 (*CC*, XV, 2450).

9. 27.1.1763. BN, Collection Rothschild (*CC*, XV, 2454).

10. BN, Collection Rothschild (*CC*, XV, 2472).

11. 15.1.1763. BPUN, MS R321, ff.52–3 (*CC*, XV, 2484).

12. 20.1.1763 and 28.1.1763. BVN, MS R284, ff.76–93. Published in facsimile by F. S. Eigeldinger, ed., *Deux Lettres . . . [au] Duc de Luxembourg*, Neuchâtel, 1977.

13. 19.2.1763. RSE, Hume Archives, VII, nos.17 and 18 (*CC*, XV, 2491).

14. 27.1.1763. BPUN, MS R288, ff.154–5 (*CC*, XV, 2453).

15. 4.2.1763. BPUN, MS R288, ff.156–8 (*CC*, XV, 2467).

16. 20.2.1763. BPUN, MS R288, ff.161–2 (*CC*, XV, 2499).

17. 24.2.1763. BPUN, MS R288, ff.163–5 (*CC*, XV, 2508).

18. 7.4.1763. BPUN, MS R288, ff.166–7 (*CC*, XVI, 2599).

19. 16.4.1763. BPUN, MS R288, ff.168–9 (*CC*, XVI, 2627).

20. 14.5.1763. BPUN, MS R288, ff.170–1 (*CC*, XVI, 2691).

21. 19.5.1763. BPUN, MS R288, ff.172–3 (*CC*, XVI, 2711).

22. 17.7.1763. BPUN, MS R288, ff.176–7 (*CC*, XVII, 2824).

23. 13.2.1763. BPUN, MS R316, ff.36–40 (*CC*, XV, 2481).

24. 27.2.1763. BPUN, MS R289, ff.64–5 (*CC*, XV, 2489).

25. 19.2.1763. BPUN, MS R319, ff.75–6 (*CC*, XV, 2496).

26. 23.3.1763. BPUN, MS R319, ff.79–80 (*CC*, XV, 2560).

27. 30.3.1763. BPUN, MS R319, ff.81–2 (*CC*, XV, 2577).

28. 19.3.1763. BPUN, MS R319, ff.77–8 (*CC*, XV, 2548).

29. 21.3.1763. BPUN, MS R283, f.26 (*CC*, XV, 2558).

30. 21.3.1763. BPUN, MS R289, ff.70–1 (*CC*, XV, 2557).

31. 18.1.1763. Besterman, XXIV, D10107.

32. 30.3.1763. BPUN, MS R319, ff.81–2 (*CC*, XV, 2577).

33. P. Rabaut, *Lettres à divers*, Paris, 1892, I, p.334.

34. Besterman, XXVII, D11571.

35. Besterman, XXVII, D11608.

36. 19.2.1763. BPUN, MS R312, ff.11–12 (*CC*, XV, 2497).

37. 26.2.1763. BPUN, MS R283, ff.119–20 (*CC*, XV, 2511).

38. 27.4.1763. AEG, PH 4869 (*CC*, XVI, 2653).

39. Undated. BPUN, MS R316, ff.59–60 (*CC*, XVI, 2598).

40. P, II, p.155 (*OC*, I, p.621).

41. 7.5.1763. BN, Collection Rothschild (*CC*, XVI, 2678).

42. P, I, p.112 (*OC*, I, p.216).

43. 7.5.1763. Manuscript not traced (*CC*, XVI, 2677).

44. To Moultou, 26.2.1763. BPUN, MS R289, f.67 (*CC*, XV, 2512).

45. P, II, pp.152–3 (*OC*, I, p.616).

46. 9.4.1763. BPUN, MS R315, ff.3–4 (*CC*, XVI, 2606).

47. P, II, p.153 (*OC*, I, p.617).

48. 30.4.1763. Manuscript not traced (*CC*, XVI, 2662).

49. P, II, p.153 (*OC*, I, p.617).

50. Ibid.

51. BPUN, MS R316, ff.73–4 (*CC*, XVI, 2752).

52. A. François, *Correspondance de Rousseau et Coindet*, Geneva, 1922, p.vii.

53. P, II, p.153 (*OC*, I, p.616).

54. BPUG, MS Supp. 22, ff.2–3 (*CC*, XVI, 2705).

55. 26.5.1763. BPUN, MS R283, ff.59–60 (*CC*, XVI, 2726).

56. 31.5.1763. BPUN, MS R319, ff.95–6 (*CC*, XVI, 2735).

57. 7.6.1763. BPUN, MS R319, ff.97–8 (*CC*, XVI, 2746).

58. 5.5.1763. Manuscript not traced (*CC*, XVI, 2675).

59. 8.6.1763. BPUN, MS R319, ff.99–100 (*CC*, XVI, 2747).

60. 28.6.1763. BPUN, MS R321, ff.83–4 (*CC*, XVI, 2778).

61. 18.6.1763. BPUN, MS R312, ff.19–20 (*CC*, XVI, 2761).

62. 25.6.1762. Turin, Biblioteca Civica, Cosilla MS 33 (*CC*, XVI, 2770).

63. BPUN, MS R319, ff.101–2 (*CC*, XVI, 2772).

64. 29.6.1763. BPUN, MS R319, ff.103–4 (*CC*, XVI, 2784).

65. 7.7.1763. Manuscript not traced (*CC*, XVII, 2803).

66. 27.7.1763. BPUN, MS R283, ff.135–6 (*CC*, XVII, 2844).

67. 16.6.1763. BPUN, MS R311, ff.82–3 (*CC*, XVI, 2760).

68. 4.7.1762 and 9.9.1762. BPUN, MS R318, ff.86–9 (*CC*, XVII, 2795 and 2912).

69. 10.3.1763. BPUN, MS R322, ff.45–6 (*CC*, XV, 2533).

70. 27.3.1763. BPUN, MS R289, ff.65–6 (*CC*, XV, 2570).

71. 12.6.1763. BPUN, MS R322, ff.51–2 (*CC*, XVI, 2753).

72. BPUN, MS R292, ff.117–8 (*CC*, XVII, 2848).

73. 18.8.1763. Zürich, Zentralbibliothek, A167, no.6 (*CC*, XVII, 2878).

74. 25.5.1764. BPUN, MS R306, ff.85–6 (*CC*, XX, 3292).

75. P, II, p.153 (*OC*, I, p.617).

76. Ibid.

77. Published by Lajos Racz in *Rousseau és Sauttersheim*, Budapest, 1913. Until he learned enough French, Sauttern continued to write to Rousseau in Latin.

78. 1.8.1763. BPUN, MS R283, f.137 (*CC*, XVII, 2852).

79. *La Nouvelle Héloïse* (*OC*, II, p.389).

80. 14.8.1763. BN, Collection Rothschild (*CC*, XVII, 2872).

81. 23.8.1763. BPUN, MS R321, ff.92–3 (*CC*, XVII, 2890).

82. 25.8.1763. BPUN, MS R291, ff.32–3 (*CC*, XVII, 2895).

83. 31.8.1763. BPUN, MS R294, ff.17–18 (*CC*, XVII, 2905).

84. 27.8.1763. BPUN, MS R320, ff.204–5 (*CC*, XVII, 2897).

85. P, II, p.150 (*OC*, I, p.612).

86. Ibid.

87. 22.8.1763. BPUN, MS R293, ff.1–2 (*CC*, XVII, 2888).

88. 27.8.1763. BPUN, MS R312, ff.27–8 (*CC*, XVII, 2901).

89. Creighton, p.78.

90. 10.9.1763(?). Coppet, Archives of the Château (*CC*, XVI, 2914).

91. 13.8.1763. BPUN, MS R319, ff.115–6 (*CC*, XVII, 2869).

92. 6.10.1763. BPUN, MS R319, ff.117–8 (*CC*, XVIII, 2958).

93. 15.10.1763. BPUN, MS R289, ff.89–90 (*CC*, XVIII, 2969).

94. 30.11.1763. Zürich, State Archives, FAU 68, no.5 (*CC*, XVIII, 3043).

95. See Creighton, p.80.

96. 29.10.1763. Zürich, State Archives, FAU 68, no.4 (*CC*, XVIII, 2995).

97. 20.10.1763. BPUG, MS Fr.248, ff.27–8 (*CC*, XVIII, 2980).

98. 25.10.1763. BPUG, MS Fr.248, ff.29–30 (*CC*, XVIII, 2990).

99. 18.10.1763. BPUN, MS R317, ff.25–6 (*CC*, XVIII, 2979).

100. 12.12.1763. Dutch Royal Library, G16-A434, no.105 (*CC*, XVIII, 3083).

101. 29.11.1763. BPUN, MS R293, ff.3–4 (*CC*, XVIII, 3039).

102. 29.11.1763. BPUN, MS R293, ff.5–6 (*CC*, XVIII, 3040).

103. 30.10.1763. BPUG, Soc. J.-J. R., MS R105 (*CC*, XVIII, 2996).

104. BPUN, MS R322, ff.57–8 (*CC*, XVIII, 3033).

105. 25.12.1763. BPUG, Soc. J.-J.R., MS R105 (*CC*, XVIII, 3075).

106. 15.12.1763. BPUN, MS R308, ff.41–2 (*CC*, XVIII, 3068).
107. 28.12.1763. Montreal, McGill University Library (*CC*, XVIII, 3082).
108. 10.9.1763. BPUG, Soc. J-J.R., MS R115 (*CC*, XVII, 2913).
109. To Weguelin. Cited in H. F. Sturz, *Schriften*, Karlsruhe, 1784, p.185.
110. 20.8.1763. Palais Bourbon, P7073, p.300 (*CC*, XVII, 2879).
111. 21.8.1763. BPUN, MS R288, ff.182–3 (*CC*, XVII, 2881).
112. 15.9.1763. BPUN, MS R288, ff.186–7 (*CC*, XVII, 2922).
113. 16.10.1763. BPUN, MS R288, ff.194–6 (*CC*, XVIII, 2975).
114. 23.10.1763. BPUN, MS R288, ff.196–7 (*CC*, XVIII, 2987).
115. 21.8.1763. Manuscript not traced (*CC*, XVII, 2882).
116. 9.12.1763. Bibliothèque de Nantes, MS Fr.674 (*CC*, XVIII, 3058).
117. 27.12.1763. BPUN, MS R310, ff.41–2 (*CC*, XVIII, 3080).
118. 1.11.1763. BPUN, MS R288, ff.198–201 (*CC*, XVIII, 3002).
119. BPUN, MS R288, ff.202–4 (*CC*, XVIII, 3076).
120. 6.12.1763. BPUG, MS Cramer, 85, ff.309–310 (*CC*, XVIII, 3053).
121. *OC*, III, p.810.
122. *OC*, III, pp.cxcv–cxcviii.
123. Ibid. p.844.
124. Ibid. p.874.
125. Ibid. p.430.
126. Ibid. p.875.
127. Ibid. p.835.
128. Creighton, p.84

CHAPTER 5:
'MARMOT' AND 'BEAR'
(pages 80–109)

1. Besterman, XXVII, D11760.
2. 22.1.1764. Manuscript not traced (*CC*, XIX, 3120).
3. 30.1.1764. BPUN, MS R288, ff.204–5 (*CC*, XIX, 3127).
4. *OC*, I, p.601.
5. 23.9.1763. BPUN, MS R306, ff.123–4 (*CC*, XVII, 2935).
6. 4.10.1763. BPUN, MS R306, ff.125–8 (*CC*, XVIII, 2955).
7. 21.1.1764. BPUN, MS R285, ff.121–2 (*CC*, XIX, 3116).
8. 21.12.1764. New Haven, Yale University, Beinecke Library, Boswell MS (Scott, IV, p.124).
9. 16.3.1764. BPUN, MS R306, ff.146–7 (*CC*, XIX, 3181).
10. 15.4.1764. BPUN, MS R285, ff.124–5 (*CC*, XIX, 3220).
11. 18.4.1764. BPUN, MS R306, ff.150–1 (*CC*, XIX, 3222).
12. 5.8.1764. BPUN, MS R306, ff.156–7 (*CC*, XXI, 3441).
13. 3.9.1764. BPUN, MS R306, f.157 (*CC*, XXI, 3479).
14. 5.9.1764. BPUN, MS R306, ff.158–9 (*CC*, XXI, 3484).
15. 21.12.1764. New Haven, Yale University, Beinecke Library, Boswell MS (Scott, IV, p.124).
16. BPUN, MS R306, ff.164–5 (*CC*, XXII, 3652).
17. Undated. BPUG, Soc. J.-J.R., MS R18 (*CC*, XIX, 3150).
18. 20.4.1764. Lausanne, Bibliothèque Cantonale, MS 100 (*CC*, XIX, 3225).
19. April 1764. Coppet, Necker Archives (*CC*, XIX, 3223).
20. 25.4.1764(?). Coppet, Necker Archives (*CC*, XIX, 3235).
21. 14.3.1764. BPUN, MS R296, ff.167–8 (*CC*, XIX, 3176).
22. 17.3.1764. Dutch Royal Library, G16-A434, no. 106 (*CC*, XIX, 3187).
23. 6.4.1764. BPUN, MS R292, ff.9–10 (*CC*, XIX, 3208).
24. 11.5.1764. BPUN MS R293, ff.13–14 (*CC*, XX, 3266).
25. 3.6.1764. BPUN, MS R293, f.17 (*CC*, XX, 3316).
26. *OC*, III, p.702.
27. 9.6.1764. Dutch Royal Library, G16-A434, no. 109 (*CC*, XX, 3333).

28. 20.6.1764. BPUN, MS R320, ff.216–18 (*CC*, XX, 3355).

29. 2.2.1764. BPUN, MS R316, ff.87–8 (*CC*, XIX, 3132).

30. 31.3.1764. BPUN, MS R284, ff.5–6 (*CC*, XIX, 3198).

31. 28.1.1764. BPUN, MS R285, ff.67–8 (*CC*, XIX, 3125).

32. 10.5.1764. BPUN, MS R294, ff.19–20 (*CC*, XX, 3263).

33. 9.2.1764. BPUN, MS R322, ff.61–2 (*CC*, XIX, 3140).

34. 28.1.1764. BPUN, MS R285, ff.67–8 (*CC*, XIX, 3125).

35. 13.5.1764. BPUN, MS R285, ff.69–70 (*CC*, XX, 3271).

36. 1.6.1764. BPUN, MS R322, ff.65–7 (*CC*, XX, 3310).

37. 24.6.1764. BPUG, Soc. J.-J.R., MS R105 (*CC*, XX, 3361).

38. 2.7.1764. BPUN, MS R311, ff.90–1 (*CC*, XX, 3379).

39. 12.5.1764. Bachaumont, II, p.56.

40. 28.5.1764. BPUN, n.a.ff.91–2 (*CC*, XX, 3301).

41. Besterman, XXVII, D11963.

42. Guyot (1958), pp.37–40.

43. 2.2.1764. BPUG, Soc. J.-J.R., MS R170 (*CC*, XIX, 3131).

44. D'Escherny, III.

45. Ibid. p.11.

46. Conserved in the Collection Albert Reinhart at Winterthur, and published in the *Bibliothèque universelle de Genève*, I, 1836, pp.83–93.

47. 5.6.1764. BPUN, MS R284, f.96 (*CC*, XX, 3319).

48. 10.6.1764. BPUN, MS R318, ff.164–5 (*CC*, XX, 3337).

49. 17.6.1764. Palais Bourbon, P7074, ff.88–9 (*CC*, XX, 3350).

50. P, II, p.154 (*OC*, I, p.619).

51. *Reveries of the Solitary Walker* (*OC*, I, p.1042).

52. Guyot (1958), pp.9–24.

53. P, II, p.145 (*OC*, I, p.602).

54. Ibid.

55. Guyot (1958), pp.14–25.

56. P, II, p.145 (*OC*, I, p.602).

57. Guyot (1958), p.17.

58. *OC*, I, p.1072.

59. D'Escherny, III, pp.65–77.

60. 4.7.1764. Bordeaux, Archives de Luze (*CC*, XX, 3423).

61. P, II, p.152 (*OC*, I, p.615).

62. 20.7.1764. Moscow Historical Museum, Orlov Collection 15/110 (*CC*, XX, 3409).

63. 30.7.1764. BPUN, MS R309, ff.7–8 (*CC*, XX, 3433).

64. 15.9.1764. BPUG, MS Fr.203, f.77 (*CC*, XXI, 3503).

65. To Count K.J.C. von Zinzendorf, 20.10.1764. BPUN, MS R285, f.131 (*CC*, XXI, 3586).

66. 6.8.1764. BPUN, MS R311, f.92 (*CC*, XXI, 3443).

67. 17.10.1765. BPUN, MS R311, f.93 (*CC*, XXI, 3580).

68. 9.9.1764. BPUN, MS R288, ff.226–7 (*CC*, XXI, 3489).

69. 21.8.1764. BPUN, MS R284, f.9 (*CC*, XXI, 3459).

70. See BPUG, Archives Tronchin, 291, no.35 (*CC*, XXI, 3458).

71. To F. d'Ivernois, 1.8.1764. BPUN, MS R287, ff.15–16 (*CC*, XXI, 3436 bis).

72. 15.8.1764. BPUN MS R322, ff.72–3 (*CC*, XXI, 3453).

73. 19.8.1764. BPUG, Soc. J.-J.R., MS R115 (*CC*, XXI, 3455).

74. BPUN, MS R284, f.9 (*CC*, XXI, 3459).

75. 2.9.1764. BPUN, MS R322, ff.74–6 (*CC*, XXI, 3481).

76. 26.8.1764. Montreal, McGill University Library (*CC*, XXI, 3468).

77. See A. Dubois, 'Jean-Jacques Rousseau au Champ du Moulin', MN, XXXIV, 1897, pp.10–17.

78. 31.8.1764. BPUN, MS R306, ff.12–15 (*CC*, XXI, 3475).

79. *OC*, III, p.391.

80. See E. Dedeck-Héry, *J.-J. Rousseau et la Corse*, Philadelphia, 1932.

81. 22.9.1764. BPUN, MS R290, ff.197–9 (*CC*, XXI, 3523).

82. 3.10.1764. BPUN, MS R306, ff.16–18 (*CC*, XXI, 3542).
83. 20.9.1764. BPUN MS R288, ff.228–30 (*CC*, XXI, 3517).
84. 14.10.1764. Manuscript not traced (*CC*, XXI, 3571).
85. 21.10.1764. BPUN, MS R288, ff.231–2 (*CC*, XXI, 3590).
86. 26.10.1764. BPUN, MS R288, ff. 233–4 (*CC*, XXI, 3602).
87. 26.10.1764. BPUN, MS R288, ff.233–4 (*CC*, XXI, 3602).
88. 11.11.1764. BPUN, MS R283, f.1 (*CC*, XXII, 3636).
89. 17.11.1764. BPUN, MS R322, ff.82–3 (*CC*, XXII, 3653).
90. 25.11.1764. BPUG, Soc. J.-J.R., MS R105 (*CC*, XXII, 3673).
91. Guyot (1958), p.48.
92. 29.11.1764. BPUN MS R286, ff.14–15 (*CC*, XXII, 3682).
93. Matthey, p.9.
94. 2.12.1764. BPUN, MS R313, ff.17–18 (*CC*, XXII, 3693).
95. 8.12.1764. BPUN, MS R286, ff.16–17 (*CC*, XXII, 3712).
96. 20.12.1764. New Haven, Yale University, Beinecke Library, Boswell MS C.2716 (*CC*, XXII, 3753).
97. 18.11.1764. BPUN, MS R285, ff.109–10 (*CC*, XXII, 3657).
98. 10.12.1764. BPUN, MS R296, ff.169–70 (*CC*, XXII, 3729).
99. 30.12.1764. BPUN, MS R313, ff.21–2 (*CC*, XXII, 3808).
100. 31.12.1764. BPUN, MS R286, ff.22–3 (*CC*, XXII, 3812).
101. 2.12.1764. Manuscript not traced (*CC*, XXII, 3692).
102. See *NS*, p.291.
103. 18.11.1764. BPUN, MS R285, ff.109–10 (*CC*, XXII, 3657).
104. 2.12.1764. BPUN, MS R283, ff.138–9 (*CC*, XXII, 3691).
105. 2.12.1764. New Haven, Yale University, Beinecke Library, Boswell MS L.1104 (*CC*, XXII, 3694).
106. 3.12.1764. BPUN, MS R307, ff.3–4 (*CC*, XXII, 3694 bis).
107. See I. Finlayson, *The Moth and the Candle* , London, 1984, p.98.
108. 3.12.1764. New Haven, Yale University, Beinecke Library, Boswell MS L.418 (*CC*, XXII, 3695).
109. New Haven Yale University, Beinecke Library, Boswell MS J.6. English translations of the journal, different from mine, appear in Scott and Pottle.
110. Finlayson, pp.105–28.
111. 20.12.1764. New Haven, Yale University, Beinecke Library, Boswell MS C.2716 (*CC*, XXII, 3753).
112. 31.12.1764. New Haven, Yale University, Beinecke Library, Boswell MS L.860 (*CC*, XXII, 3819).
113. 31.12.1764. BPUN, MS R307, ff.7–8 (*CC*, XXII, 3818).
114. BPUN, MS R312, ff.45–6 (*CC*, XXII, 3663).
115. 21.12.1765. BPUN, MS R315, ff.60–1 (*CC*, XXII, 3759).
116. 27.12.1764. BPUG, Archives Tronchin, 170, ff.173–4 (*CC*, XXII, 3789).
117. 23.12.1764. BPUN, MS R319, ff.119–20 (*CC*, XXII, 3770).
118. To Mme de Boufflers, 21.1.1765. Manuscript not traced (*CC*, XXIII, 3935).
119. 7.2.1765. Winterthur, Collection Reinhart (*CC*, XXIII, 3995).
120. To Moultou, 16.1.1765. Winterthur, Collection Reinhart (*CC*, XXXIII, 3890).
121. 23.12.1764. BPUN, MS R319, ff.119–20 (*CC*, XXII, 3770).
122. 7.1.1765. BPUN, MS R289, ff.91–2 (*CC*, XXIII, 3845).
123. 8.1.1765. BPUN, MS R312, ff.49–50 (*CC*, XXIII, 2851).
124. *NS*, p.3.
125. To G. Cramer, 26.12.1764. BN, n.a.f.24.333, f.203 (*CC*, XXII, 3784).
126. 9.1.1765. Kehl, LXVIII, pp.336–7.
127. 9.1.1765. Kehl, LIX, pp.5–8.
128. 27.12.1764. BPUG, f.173–4 (*CC*, XXII, 3789).
129. 25.1.1765. Zürich, State Archives,

Usteri MS, 68, no.26 (CC, XXIII, 3928).

130. OC, III, p.783.
131. 11.2.1765. BPUN, MS R292, ff.133–4 (CC, XXIII, 4013).
132. Encyclopaedia Universalis, Paris, 1979, X, p.1158.
133. J.-J., pp.156ff.
134. 5.2.1765. BPUN, MS R92, f.26 (CC, XXIII, 3983).
135. 11.2.1765. BPUN, MS R294, ff.135–6 (CC, XXIII, 4014).
136. P, II, p.155 (OC, I, p.621).
137. 1.2.1765. BPUN, MS R300, ff.127–8 (CC, XXIII, 3959).
138. 14.12.1764 (CC, XXII, 3737).
139. 15.1.1765. BPUN, MS R n.a.12, no.30 (CC, XXIII, 3881).
140. 22.5.1765. BPUN, MS R n.a.12, no.38 (CC, XXV, 4430).
141. Reproduced in facsimile in CG, XII, pp.366–82.
142. 6.1.1765. BPUN, MS R283, ff.125–6 (CC, XXIII, 3843).
143. J.-J., pp.244–6.
144. New Haven, Yale University, Beinecke Library, Boswell MS (Scott, IV, p.144).
145. 20.1.1765. Bucharest, Rumanian Academy, MS no.108669 (CC, XXIII, 3906).
146. 2.2.1765. BPUN, MS R303, ff.78–9 (CC, XXIII, 3967).
147. 14.2.1765. BPUG, MS Fr.203, ff.263–4 (CC, XXIV, 4020).
148. 10.2.1765. BPUN, MS R313, ff.31–2 (CC, XXIII, 4009).
149. 25.2.1765(?). Winterthur, Collection Reinhart (CC, XXIV, 4078).
150. 20.1.1765. BPUN, MS R313, ff.25–6 (CC, XXIII, 3910).
151. 24.1.1765. BPUN, MS R286, ff.24–5 (CC, XXIII, 3921).
152. Starobinski, p.279.
153. 6.2.1765. BPUN, MS R n.a. no.1, ff.19–20 (CC, XXIII, 3987).
154. 11.2.1765. BPUN, MS R284, f.12 (CC, XXIII, 4011).

155. 11.4.1765. BPUN, MS R316, ff.121–2 (CC, XXV, 4270).
156. 10.2.1765. BPUN, MS R288, ff.241–2 (CC, XXIII, 4007).
157. 3.2.1765. BPUN, MS R n.a. no.17 (CC, XXIII, 3973).
158. 13.1.1765. BPUN, MS R283, ff.140–1 (CC, XXIII, 3875).
159. 7.1.1765. BPUN, MS R287, ff.38–9 (CC, XXIII, 3846).
160. 17.1.1765. BPUN, MS R287, ff.42–3 (CC, XXIII, 3892).
161. 21.1.1765. BPUN, MS R287, ff.44–5 (CC, XXIII, 3913).
162. 10.2.1765. BPUG, MS Fr.206, ff.30–2 (CC, XXIII, 4008).
163. 12.2.1765. AEG, Registres du P.C., vol.265, pp.69–74 (CC, XXIV, app.339).
164. 10.2.1765. BPUG, MS Fr.206, ff.30–2 (CC, XXIII, 4008).
165. 24.2.1765. BPUN, MS R92, f.39 (CC, XXIV, 4059).

CHAPTER 6: THE LAPIDATION
(pages 110–140)

1. Rosselet, p.148.
2. To Du Peyrou, 14.2.1765. BPUN MS R286, ff.34–5 (CC, XXIV, 4019).
3. 16.2.1765. Dutch Royal Library, G16-A434, no.126 (CC, XXIV, 4028).
4. Rosselet, p.200.
5. See L.-E. Roulet, Histoire du Conseil d'État neuchâtelois, Neuchâtel, 1987, pp.99ff.
6. See Eigeldinger, pp.95–157.
7. 25.2.1765. BPUN, MS R n.a.2, ff.6–7 (CC, XXIV, 4063).
8. 28.2.1765. BPUN, MS R305, ff.1–2 (CC, XXIV, 4076).
9. Eigeldinger, p.132.
10. Ibid. p.111.
11. P, II, p.157 (OC, I, pp.624–5).
12. 7.3.1765. BPUN, Salle Rousseau, no.69 (CC, XXIV, 4105).
13. 9.3.1765. BPUN, MS R n.a.2, ff.10–11 (CC, XXIV, 4119).

14. 9.3.1765. BPUN, MS R289, ff.98–9 (*CC*, XXIV, 4120). He also sent a copy of the letter to Mme de Verdelin.

15. AEN, Cultes 2/II (*CC*, XXIV, 4125).

16. 9.3.1765. BPUN, MS R316, f.112 (*CC*, XXIV, 4124).

17. 7.3.1765. BPUN, MS R316, ff.115–16 (*CC*, XXIV, 4113).

18. 20.3.1765. BPUN, MS R305, ff.53–6 (*CC*, XXIV, 4171).

19. 21.3.1765. BPUN, MS R305, ff.51–2 (*CC*, XXIV, 4176).

20. 12.3.1765. BPUN, MS R313, ff.40–1 (*CC*, XXIV, 4135).

21. AEN, Actes de la Classe, XII, pp.203–4.

22. *Lettre de Goa*, p.30.

23. P, II, p.158 (*OC*, I, p.627).

24. 8.3.1765. BPUN, MS R n.a. 17, no.24 (*CC*, XXIV, 4115).

25. P, II, p.158 (*OC*, I, pp.626–7).

26. *Lettre de Goa*, pp.42–4.

27. 30.3.1765. Eigeldinger, p.259.

28. Ibid. p.260.

29. Ibid.

30. P, II, p.159 (*OC*, I, p.629).

31. 7.3.1765. Manuscript not traced (*CC*, XXIV, 4108).

32. See C.-L. Borel (nephew of Isabelle Guyenet), *Pieces relatives à la persécution suscitée à Môtiers-Travers contre M. J.-J. Rousseau*, 1765, cited by R.A. Leigh (*CC*, XXIV, p.231).

33. BPUN, MS R285, f.130 (*CC*, XXIV, 4132).

34. BPUG, Soc. J.-J.R., MS R308 (*CC*, XXIV, 4153).

35. 23.3.1765. BPUN, MS R300, ff.48–51 (*CC*, XXIV, 4186).

36. 25.3.1765. BPUN, MS R287, ff.121–2 (*CC*, XXIV, 4195).

37. 16.4.1765. BPUG, MS Supp. 1908, f.124 (*CC*, XXV, 4297).

38. 18.4.1765. BPUN, MS R304, ff.105–6 (*CC*, XXV, 4306).

39. 15.3.1765. BPUN, MS R306, ff.42–3 (*CC*, XXIV, 4148).

40. 24.4.1765. BPUN, MS R306, ff.197–8 (*CC*, XXV, 4336).

41. 11.3.1765. BPUN, MS R285, f.130 (*CC*, XXIV, 4132).

42. 13.3.1765. BPUN, MS R306, ff.185–6 (*CC*, XXIV, 4140).

43. 25.2.1765. BPUN, MS R288, ff.243–4 (*CC*, XXIV, 4066).

44. 10.3.1763. BPUN, MS R288, ff.245–6 (*CC*, XXIV, 4126).

45. 28.4.1765. St. Petersburg National Library, MS 289, no.3 (*CC*, XXV, 4350).

46. 23.3.1765. BPUN, MS R304, ff.96–7 (*CC*, XXIV, 4185).

47. 6.4.1765. Somerville, New Jersey, Hyde Collection (*CC*, XXV, 4249).

48. Diderot, *Oeuvres complètes*, ed. Dieckmann et al., Paris, 1975–90, XXV, p.130.

49. 10.3.1765. BPUN, MS R322, ff.90–1 (*CC*, XXIV, 4161).

50. 24.3.1765. BPUN, MS R n.a.17, no.25 (*CC*, XXIV, 4191).

51. 31.3.1765. BPUN, MS R322, ff.92–3 (*CC*, XXIV, 4225).

52. 10.4.1765. BPUN, MS R322, ff.94–5 (*CC*, XXV, 4266).

53. 18.4.1765. BPUN, MS R322, ff.96–7 (*CC*, XXV, 4307).

54. 21.4.1765. BPUN, MS R n.a.17, no.28 (*CC*, XXV, 4322).

55. 15.5.1765. BPUN, MS R322, ff.100–1 (*CC*, XXV, 4403).

56. 2.4.1765. BPUN, MS R304, ff.64–5 (*CC*, XXV, 4233).

57. 26.5.1765. BPUN, MS R305, ff.65–6 (*CC*, XXV, 4443).

58. 30.4.1765. BPUN, MS R313, ff.65–8 (*CC*, XXV, 4359).

59. 2.5.1765. BPUN, MS R286, ff.59–60 (*CC*, XXV, 4368).

60. G. de Beer, *Notes and Records of the Royal Society*, London, 1946, pp.216–26.

61. 4.2.1765. BPUN, MS R305, ff.116–17 (*CC*, XXIII, 3979).

62. 22.5.1765. BPUN, MS R305, ff.122–3 (*CC*, XXV, 4428)

63. 19.6.1765. Zürich, State Archives, FAU 68, no.27 (*CC*, XXVI, 4494).
64. Dr J.G. Zimmermann. See Bodemann, pp.302–3.
65. 2.5.1765. BPUN, MS R286, ff.59–60 (*CC*, XXV, 4368).
66. 23.5.1765. BPUN, MS R286, ff.61–2 (*CC*, XXV, 4431).
67. 30.5.1765. BPUN, MS R286, ff.63–4 (*CC*, XXV, 4449).
68. 23.5.1765. BPUN, MS R286, ff.61–2 (*CC*, XXV, 4431).
69. 26.5.1765. BPUG, Soc. J.-J.R., MS R21 (*CC*, XXV, 4440).
70. 26.5.1765. BPUN, MS R304, ff.98–9 (*CC*, XXV, 4444).
71. 1.6.1765. BPUN, MS R n.a. 9, ff.10–11 (*CC*, XXVI, 4460).
72. François d'Ivernois supplied his genealogical data to Rousseau in a letter of 5 June. BPUN, MS R315, ff.108–9 (*CC*, XXVI, 4468).
73. 31.5.1765. BPUN, MS R285, ff.101–2 (*CC*, XXV, 4457).
74. AEN, B362–3 (*CC*, XXV, 4426).
75. Eigeldinger, p.275.
76. Guyot (1958) p.80.
77. 4.5.1765. Merseburg, Prussian Central State Archives, Rep. 64.IV.2 (*CC*, XXV, 4381 bis).
78. 8.8.1765. BPUN, MS R20, ff.1–18 (*CC*, XXVI, 4573 bis).
79. 8.8.1765. BPUN, MS R286, ff.83–92 (*CC*, XXVI, 4573).
80. P, II, p.150 (*OC*, I, p.611).
81. 16.6.1765. BPUN, MS R286, ff.67–8 (*CC*, XXVI, 4487).
82. 3.7.1765. BPUN, MS R286, ff.71–2 (*CC*, XXVI, 4507).
83. 20.7.1765. BPUN, MS R287, ff.54–5 (*CC*, XXVI, 4536).
84. See *J.-J*, pp.88–91.
85. Leigh, p.78.
86. Ibid. p.80.
87. 10.5.1764. BPUN, MS R320, f.218 (*CC*, XX, 3264).
88. Leigh, p.107.
89. 11.8.1762. New York, Morgan Library, Heinemann MS (*CC*, XXVI, 4577).
90. 17.8.1765. BPUN, MS R310, ff.76–7 (*CC*, XXVI, 4590.
91. Leigh, p.108.
92. 17.8.1765. BPUN, MS R310, ff.76–7 (*CC*, XXVI, 4590).
93. 18.8.1765(?). BPUN, MS R286, ff.81–2 (*CC*, XXVI, 4591).
94. 18.9.1765. BPUN, MS R313, ff.96–7 (*CC*, XXVII, 4670).
95. D'Escherny, III, p.159.
96. 15.8.1765. BPUN, MS R287, ff.58–9 (*CC*, XXVI, 4584).
97. 20.8.1765. BPUN, MS R315, ff.132–3 (*CC*, XXVI, 4597).
98. 25.8.1765. BPUN, MS R287, f.61 (*CC*, XXVI, 4607).
99. 2.9.1765. BPUN, MS R301, ff.149–50 (*CC*, XXVI, 4633).
100. Buffenoir, p.115.
101. 26.7.1770. Dutch Royal Library, G16-A434, no.147 (*CC*, XXXVIII, 6764).
102. BPUN, MS R304, ff.50–1 (*CC*, XXVI, 4537).
103. 23.7.1762. BPUN, MS R304, f.72 (*CC*, XXVI, 4542).
104. 3.8.1762. BN, Collection Rothschild (*CC*, XXVI, 4564).
105. 3.7.1765. BPUN, MS R321, ff.206–7 (*CC*, XXVI, 4635).
106. BPUN, MS R n.a.5, no.28 (*CC*, XXVII, app.383).
107. P, II, pp.159–60 (*OC*, I, p.629).
108. Ibid.
109. 4.9.1765. BPUN, MS R322, ff.112–13 (*CC*, XXVI, 4636).
110. P, II, p.161 (*OC*, I, p.631).
111. P, II, p.159 (*OC*, I, pp.627–8).
112. 4.9.1765. BPUN, MS R n.a.5, no.30 (*CC*, XXVI, 4637).
113. Eigeldinger, p.349.
114. 7.9.1765. Manuscript not traced (*CC*, XXVI, 4646).
115. P, II, p.163 (*OC*, I, pp.634–5).
116. P, II, p.163 (*OC*, I, p.634).
117. 7.9.1765. Merseburg, Prussian Cen-

tral State Archives, R64 (*CC*, XXVI, app.386).

118. 7.9.1765. Merseburg, Prussian Central State Archives, R64 (*CC*, XXVI, app.387).

119. 7.9.1765. Merseburg, Prussian Central State Archives R64 (*CC*, XXVI, app.388).

120. 12.10.1765. AEN, Série Cultes, 49/IV (*CC*, XXVI, app.400).

121. Merseburg, Prussian Central State Archives, R64 (*CC*, XXVI, app.390).

122. 19.12.1765. Merseburg, Prussian Central State Archives, R64 (*CC*, XXVI, app.401).

123. A. Servan, *Réflexions sur les Confessions* Lausanne, 1783; P.-C. Bridel, *Course de Bâle à Bienne*, Basle, 1789.

124. See, for example, H.C. Payne, 'Deciphering the Stones of Môtiers,' *Eighteenth Century Life*, II, no.2, 1987.

125. 7.9.1765. Manuscript not traced (*CC*, XXVI, 4646).

126. P, II, p.164 (*OC*, I, p.635).

127. P, II, p.165 (*OC*, I, p.637).

128. *OC*, I, p.1040.

129. To Guy. 1.10.1765. New York Public Library, Berg Collection (*CC*, XXVII, 4693).

130. 13.9.1764. BN, Collection Rothschild (*CC*, XXVII, 4723).

131. P, II, p.165 (*OC*, I, p.638).

132. P, II, p.166 (*OC*, I, p.639).

133. P, II, p.166 (*OC*, I, p.640).

134. 1.10.1765. BPUN, MS R n.a.17, no.31 (*CC*, XXVII, 4692).

135. 12.9.1765. Dutch Royal Library, G16-A434, no.130 (*CC*, XXVII, 4660).

136. *OC*, I, pp.1040-9.

137. Ibid. p.1042.

138. Ibid. p.1043.

139. P, II, p.169 (*OC*, I, p.644).

140. 6.10.1765. BPUN, MS R286, ff.106-7 (*CC*, XXVII, 4704).

141. New York Public Library, Berg Collection (*CC*, XXVII, 4693).

142. *OC*, I, p.1042.

143. Ibid. p.1044.

144. P, II, p.168 (*OC*, I, p.642).

145. P, II, p.168 (*OC*, I, p.644).

146. *Reveries* (*OC*, I, p.1044).

147. P, II, p.169 (*OC*, I, p.645).

148. *OC*, I, p.1045.

149. Ibid. p.1046.

150. *OC*, I, p.1041.

151. BPUN, MS R286, ff.110-11 (*CC*, XXVII, 4726).

152. BPUN, MS R299, ff.117-18 (*CC*, XXVII, 4727).

153. 17.10.1765. BPUN, MS R n.a.1, ff.103-4 (*CC*, XXVII, 4730).

154. BPUN, MS R286, ff.112-13 (*CC*, XXVII, 4731).

155. 10.10.1765. BPUN, MS R322, ff.114-15 (*CC*, XXVII, 4711).

156. 11.10.1765. BPUN, R322, ff.116-17 (*CC*, XXVII, 4717).

157. BPUN, MS R n.a.17, no.32 (*CC*, XXVII, 4735).

158. S. Wagner, *L'Île Saint-Pierre*, Lausanne, 1926, pp.18-23.

159. Berne State Archives, Ratsmanual no.277, pp.237-8 (*CC*, XXVII, 4743).

160. 20.10.1765. BPUN, MS R n.a.17, no.32 bis (*CC*, XXVII, 4740).

161. 22.10.1765. BPUN, MS R307, ff.130-1 (*CC*, XXVII, 4747).

162. 17.10.1765. BPUN, MS R286, ff.112-13 (*CC*, XXVII, 4731).

163. See Saussure, p.86.

164. 23.10.1765(?). BPUN, MS R286, f.113 bis (*CC*, XXVII, 4752).

165. In fact, Rousseau did not go to Paris until 1742. See *J.-J.*, p.154.

166. G, II, p.126 (*OC*, I, p.652).

167. 27.10.1765. BPUN, MS R286, ff.116-17 (*CC*, XXVII, 4766).

168. G, II, p.127 (*OC*, I, p.655).

169. 28.10.1765. BPUN, MS R286, ff.118-19 (*CC*, XXVII, 4772).

170. 30.10.1765. New Haven, Yale University, Beinecke Library, Boswell MS C2418 (*CC*, XXVII, 4777).

171. Related only in G. P ends with the departure from the island.

172. 30.10.1765. BPUN, MS R286, ff.120–1 (*CC*, XXVII, 4778).

CHAPTER 7:
A CELEBRITY ACCLAIMED
(pages 141–160)

1. *OC*, III, p.906.
2. Ibid. p.904.
3. Ibid. p.933.
4. Ibid. p.905.
5. Ibid. p.906.
6. Ibid. p.931.
7. Ibid. p.912.
8. See S. Stelling-Michaud, *OC*, III, p.ccvi.
9. *OC*, III, p.310.
10. It is now in Geneva: BPUG, MS Fr.229, nos.1 and 2.
11. See G. Streckheisen-Moultou, ed., *Oeuvres complètes de J.-J. Rousseau*, Paris, 1861.
12. 4.11.1765. New Haven, Yale University, Beinecke Library, Boswell MS (*CC*, XXVII, 4790).
13. 4.11.1765. Manuscript not traced (*CC*, XXVII, 4791).
14. 4.11.1765. New York, Morgan Library MA1041 (*CC*, XXVII, 4792).
15. 5.11.1765. BPUN, MS R286, ff.122–3 (*CC*, XXVII, 4796).
16. 12.11.1765. BPUN, MS R283, ff.55–6 (*CC*, XXVII, 4817).
17. 10.11.1765. BPUN, MS R286, ff.124–5 (*CC*, XXVI, 4812).
18. Ibid.
19. 9.11.1792. BPUN, MS R322, ff.120–1 (*CC*, XXVII, 4809).
20. 16.11.1792. BPUG, MS Fr.203, ff.86–7 (*CC*, XXVII, 4829).
21. 8.11.1765. BPUN, MS R309, ff.19–21 (*CC*, XXVII, 4805).
22. 14.11.1765. BPUN, MS R n.a.17, no.36 (*CC*, XXVII, 4823).
23. 8.11.1765. BPUN, MS R n.a.4, ff.20–1 (*CC*, XXVII, 4804).
24. 25.11.1765. BPUN, MS R286, ff.128–9 (*CC*, XXVII, 4847).

25. 25.11.1765. BPUN, MS R317, f.67 (*CC*, XXVII, 4849).
26. 8.11.1765. BPUN, MS R n.a.4, ff.20–1 (*CC*, XXVII, 4804).
27. Tourneux, VI, pp.434–6.
28. 17.11.1765. BPUN, MS R286, ff.126–7 (*CC*, XXVII, 4833).
29. 28.10.1765. BPUN, MS R313, f.116 (*CC*, XXVII, 4773).
30. 1.12.1765. BPUN, MS R313, ff.136–7 (*CC*, XXVIII, 4863).
31. See *J.-J.*, p.268.
32. *OC*, II, p.972.
33. 9.11.1765. BPUN, MS R313, ff.126–7 (*CC*, XXVII, 4807).
34. 19.11.1765. BPUN, MS R312, ff.63–4 (*CC*, XXVII, 4825).
35. 24.11.1765. BPUN, MS R315, ff.142–3 (*CC*, XXVII, 4853).
36. 18.11.1765. BPUN, MS R313, ff.130–1 (*CC*, XXVII, 4834).
37. 23.11.1765. BPUN, MS R315, ff.151–2 (*CC*, XXVII, 4921).
38. 2.12.1765. BPUN, MS R317, f.68 (*CC*, XXVIII, 4865).
39. 4.11.1765. New York, Morgan Library MA1041 (*CC*, XXVII, 4792).
40. 25.11.1765. Dutch Royal Library, G16-A434, no.133 (*CC*, XXVII, 4848).
41. BPUN, MS R286, ff.130–1 (*CC*, XXVII, 4857).
42. RSE, Hume Archives, VII, no.19 (*CC*, XXVIII, 4864).
43. 2.12.1765. BPUN, MS R287, ff.66–7 (*CC*, XXVIII, 4864).
44. 4.12.1765. BN, Collection Rothschild (*CC*, XXVIII, 4872).
45. BPUN, MS R322, ff.128–9 (*CC*, XXVIII, 4876).
46. 7.12.1765. Manuscript not traced (*CC*, XXVIII, 4877).
47. 8.12.1765. BPUN, MS R285, ff.76–7 (*CC*, XXVIII, 4880).
48. To Du Peyrou, 17.12.1765. BPUN, MS R286, ff.132–3 (*CC*, XXVIII, 4898).
49. Ibid.
50. 16.12.1765. BPUN, MS R283, ff.106–7 (*CC*, XXVIII, 4894).

51. 17.12.1765. BPUG, Soc. J.-J.R., MS R105 (*CC*, XXVIII, 4896).

52. 17.12.1765. BPUN, MS R286, ff.132–3 (*CC*, XXVIII, 4898).

53. 24.12.1765. BPUN, MS R286, ff.134–5 (*CC*, XXVIII, 4923).

54. *HL*, I, pp.437–8.

55. *New Letters of David Hume*, ed. R. Klibansky and E.C. Mossner, Oxford, 1954, p.76.

56. Walpole, VI, p.301.

57. *Memoirs of Horace Walpole*, ed. E. Warburton, London, 1851, II, p.263.

58. Mossner, p.470.

59. *HL*, I, pp.419–20.

60. 5.12.1765. BPUN, MS R322, ff.128–9 (*CC*, XXVIII, 4876).

61. 28.12.1765. RSE, Hume Archives, I, no.11 (*HL*, I, pp.297–303).

62. Bachaumont, II, p.302.

63. 17.12.1765. BPUN, MS R286, ff.132–4 (*CC*, XXVIII, 4898).

64. 24.12.1765. BPUN, MS R286, ff.134–5 (*CC*, XXVIII, 4923).

65. 17.12.1765. BPUG, Soc. J.-J.R., MS R103 (*CC*, XXVIII, 4896).

66. *Modern Language Notes*, LV (1940), p.451.

67. 28.12.1765. RSE, Hume Archives, I, no.11 (*HL*, I, p.527).

68. 21.12.1765. Palais Bourbon, P7073, p.441 (*CC*, XXVIII, 4914).

69. 23.12.1765. BPUN, MS R288, ff.263–4 (*CC*, XXVIII, 4919).

70. 24.12.1765. BPUN, MS R288, ff.265–6 (*CC*, XXVIII, 4922).

71. 24.12.1765. BPUN, MS R288, ff.267–8 (*CC*, XXVIII, 4924).

72. 28.12.1765. Palais Bourbon, P7073, p.451 (*CC*, XXVIII, 4936).

73. 2.1.1766. BPUN, MS R288, ff.273–4 (*CC*, XXVIII, 4957).

74. 24.12.1765. RSE, Hume Archives, IV, no.9 (*CC*, XXVIII, 4927).

75. A. Morellet, *Mémoires de l'abbé Morellet*, Paris, 1821, I, p.103.

76. D. Diderot, *Correspondance*, ed. G. Roth, Paris, 1955–70, V, p.226.

77. 22.12.1765. BPUN, MS R307, ff.132–3 (*CC*, XXVIII, 4917).

78. P, II, p.151 (*OC*, I, p.613).

79. Buffenoir, p.108.

80. See Gagnebin, p.165.

81. P, II, p.151 (*OC*, I, p.613).

82. Palais Bourbon, P1493, p.84 (*OC*, I, p.782).

83. 20.12.1765. BPUN, MS R287, ff.70–1 (*CC*, XXVIII, 4911).

84. BPUN, MS R286, ff.136–7 (*CC*, XXVIII, 4955).

85. Walpole, XXXI, pp.100–1 (French text).

86. Walpole, XXXIX, pp.42–3.

87. 10.4.1765. BPUN, MS R322, ff.94–5 (*CC*, XXV, 4266).

88. Walpole, VII, p.294, and VIII, pp.156–7.

89. Mossner, p.504.

90. Morellet, *Mémoires*, pp. 105–6.

91. 3.1.1766. BPUN, MS R322, ff.132–3 (*CC*, XXVIII, 4962).

92. BPUG, MS Fr.232 (*CC*, XXVIII, 4961).

93. To Hume, 10.7.1766. RSE, Hume Archives, VII, no.24 (*CC*, XXX, 5274).

94. 19.1.1766 (in English). Manuscript not traced (*CC*, XXVIII, 4990).

95. 10.7.1766. RSE, Hume Archives, VII, no.24 (*CC*, XXX, 5274).

96. 19.1.1766 (in English). Manuscript not traced (*CC*, XXVIII, 4990).

CHAPTER 8:
REVERSAL OF FORTUNE
(pages 161–187)

1. App. 436 (*CC*, XXIX, p.296).

2. W. Rouet to W. Mure, 10.1.1776. W. Mure, ed., *Selections from the Family Papers Preserved at Caldwell*, Glasgow, 1854, II, p.58.

3. To Hugh Blair, 1.1.1776. RSE, Hume Archives, I (*CC*, XVIII, 4938).

4. *European Magazine*, XIX, February 1791, p.96.

5. *Annales*, VI, 1910, p.18.

6. App. 436 (*CC*, XXIX, p.297).

7. To John Home, 2.2.1776. RSE, Hume Archives, I, no.47 (*CC*, XXVIII, 5031).

8. J. Cradock, *Literary and Miscellaneous Memoirs*, London, 1828, I, p.203.

9. J. Boswell, *Life of Johnson*, Oxford, 1887, p.11.

10. 19.1.1776. *HL*, II, 298.

11. 12.1.1766. *HL*, II, 302.

12. 17.3.1776. Hume (1820), p.305, n.2; reprinted in *Annales*, VI, 1910, p.33n.

13. 25.3.1776. *HL*, II, 314.

14. 22.3.1766. RSE, Hume Archives, VII, no.21 (*CC*, XXIX, 5188).

15. 23.6.1766. RSE, Hume Archives, VII, no.23 (*CC*, XXIX, 5242).

16. 26.6.1766. BPUN, MS R307, ff.163–4 (*CC*, XXIX, 5246).

17. 10.7.1766 RSE, Hume Archives, VII, no.24 (*CC*, XXX, 5274).

18. 22.7.1766. BPUN, MS R307, ff.165–6 (*CC*, XXX, 5303).

19. 6.7.1766. RSE, Hume Archives, VII, no.35 (*CC*, XXX, 5274).

20. 22.7.1766. RSE, Hume Archives, III, no.96 (*CC*, XXX, 5303).

21. 1.7.1776. RSE, Hume Archives, I, no.15 (*CC*, XXX, 5256).

22. R. Trouson, *Jean-Jacques Rousseau*, Paris, 1993, p.255.

23. W. Howitt, *Visits to Remarkable Places*, London, 1840, pp.507–14.

24. *CC*, XXXIII, p.281.

25. *St. James Chronicle*, 25–27 November 1776.

26. 22.12.1766. BL, 29626, f.56 (*CC*, XXI, 5636).

27. 24.3.1767. BPUN, MS R307, ff.67–8 (*CC*, XXXII, 5790).

28. 24.2.1767. RSE, Hume Archives, I, no.17 (*CC*, XXII, 5742).

29. 19.3.1767. BPUN, MS R307, ff.65–6 (*CC*, XXXII, 5782).

30. 30.4.1767. BL, 29626, ff.57–8 (*CC*, XXXIII, 5782).

31. 5.5.1767 Paris, Bibliothèque de l'Institut, MS 866, Fonds Condorcet, xix, no.22 (*CC*, XXXIII, 5844).

32. 18.5.1767. BL, 29626, ff.63–4 (*CC*, XXXIII, 5860).

33. R.B. Mowat, *Jean-Jacques Rousseau*, Bristol, 1938, p.285.

34. 22.5.1767. Chateâu de Lantheuil (*CC*, XXXIII, 5870).

35. *OC*, I, p.656. See ibid., p.1611, nn.2 and 3.

36. *European Magazine and London Review*, 10 January 1787, pp.295–6

37. 22.7.1767. BPUN, MS R n.a.17 (*CC*, XXXIII, 5985).

38. Crocker (1973), II, p.305.

39. Ibid. p.307.

40. Ibid. p.311.

41. Ibid. p.313.

42. To Madeleine-Catherine Delessert, MS private collection (*CC*, XXXVI, 6411).

43. *OC*, I, p.1638, n.2.

44. 3.19.1768. BPUN, MS 1598a (*CC*, XXXVI, 6419).

45. Crocker, II, pp.313–14.

46. Ibid. pp.314–5.

47. *OC*, III, p.970. For an English translation of the *Considerations* with commentary, see W. Kendall, trans., Indianapolis, 1985.

48. *OC*, III, p.954.

49. Ibid. p.974.

50. Ibid.

51. Ibid. p.959.

52. Ibid. p.960.

53. Ibid. p.972.

54. Ibid. p.973.

55. Ibid. pp.1024–6.

56. Ibid. p.971.

57. Ibid. p.1027.

58. *OC*, I, pp.1120–9.

59. Ibid. pp.1130–47.

60. Ibid. p.516.

61. Ibid.

62. Ibid. p.1024.

63. 12.6.1761. Manuscript not found (*CC*, IX, 1430).

64. *OC*, I, p.344.

65. Ibid. p.356.

66. Ibid. p.357.

67. Ibid. p.1087.

68. Starobinski, p.275; trans. A. Goldhammer, Chicago, 1988, p.231.

69. *OC.*, I, pp.934–5.
70. Ibid. p.995. For a sensitive English translation, see C.E. Butterworth, ed. and trans., *The Reveries of the Solitary Walker*, New York, 1979.
71. *OC*, I, p.999.
72. Ibid. p.1001.
73. Ibid. p.1016.
74. Ibid. p.1074.
75. Ibid. pp.1098–9.
76. 'The coffin of Rousseau transported to Paris', report of the commission (*CC*, XLVIII, 8217).
77. 'The Rousseau Fête at Paris', *Le Moniteur*, no.24, 15 October 1794 (*CC*, XLVIII, 8219).
78. G. de Beer, *Jean-Jacques Rousseau and His World*, London, 1972, p.115.
79. 'The Fate of the Mortal Remains of Rousseau and Voltaire', including the report of the commission (*CC*, XLVIII, 8224).

EPILOGUE:
ROUSSEAU THEN AND NOW
(pages 188–209)

1. Letter of René-Louis, Marquis de Girardin, to M.-M. Rey, 2.7.1778. Chaalis, Musée Jacquemont-André, Fonds Girardin D33 (*CC*, XL, 7178 bis).
2. J. H. Huizinga, *The Making of a Saint, The Tragi-Comedy of Jean-Jacques Rousseau*, London, 1976, pp.xv–xvi.
3. 24.6.1794. 'The Rousseau Fête at Geneva'. Report of François Vernes (*CC*, XLVII, 8179).
4. 'Robespierre Eulogises Rousseau', *Le Moniteur*, no.229, 8 May 1794 (*CC*, XLVII, 8169).
5. *OC*, I, p.388.
6. Ibid. p.389.
7. See B. Glass, ed., *Forerunners of Darwin*, Baltimore, 1968; E. Guyénot, *Les sciences de la vie au XVIIe et XVIIIe siècles*, Paris, 1941.

8. See A. O. Lovejoy, 'Monboddo and Rousseau', in *Essays on the History of Ideas*, Baltimore, 1948; R. Wokler, 'The Ape Debates in Enlightenment Anthropology', in *Studies in Voltaire and the Eighteenth Century*, ed. H. Mason, Geneva and Oxford, 1980, CXII, pp.1164–75.
9. See C. Lévi-Strauss, 'J.J. Rousseau, fondateur des sciences de l'homme', in *J.J. Rousseau*, Neuchâtel, 1962, pp.240ff.; J. Derrida, *De la Grammatologie*, Paris, 1967, pp.194–202; M. Duchet, *Anthropologie et histoire au siècle des lumières*, Paris, 1971; R. Wokler, 'Le *Discours sur les sciences et les arts* and Its Offspring', *Reappraisals of Rousseau*, ed. S. Harvey et al., Manchester, 1980.
10. See R. Masters, *The Political Philosophy of Rousseau*, Princeton, 1968; Starobinski; J. Charvet, *The Social Problem in the Philosophy of Rousseau*, Cambridge, 1974; R. Polin, *La Politique de la solitude*, Paris, 1971; the special number of *Daedalus* magazine, CVII, no.3 (Summer 1978), 'Rousseau for Our Time'.
11. For a detailed account of the controversy, see *J.-J.*, pp.275–91.
12. *OC*, II, p.1140.
13. *OC*, III, p.111.
14. Ibid.
15. *CC*, V, p.242.
16. *OC*, I, p.17.
17. *OC*, III, p.810.
18. Ibid. p.114.
19. Ibid.
20. Ibid. p.406.
21. Ibid.
22. Ibid. p.421.
23. Ibid. p.1661.
24. *SC*, p.141.
25. *OC*, III, p.351.
26. Ibid. p.364.
27. Ibid. p.365.
28. *SC*, p.60.
29. Ibid. p.64.

INDEX

Letters from the Country, 74, 77

Letters from the Mountain: the writing of, 74, 76; compared with *The Social Contract*, 77–78; arrangements for publishing, 83–84; role of d'Ivernois in, 90; needed for Geneva elections, 92; R. correcting, 95; presentation copies of, 96; reception in Geneva, 100–109; banned in Neuchâtel, 110; lifting of the ban on, 114; Montmollin compares with *Émile*, 123; d'Ivernois on inspiration of, 147

Letter to Archbishop Beaumont, 48–51, 57, 64, 124, 126

Letter to M. d'Alembert, 17, 49, 59, 80, 146, 199

Lettre à l'Archevèque d'Auch de J.-J. Rousseau, Citoyen de Genève, 84–85, 91

Lettre à Monsieur . . . relative à Monsieur J.-J. Rousseau, 123, 127

Lettres sur la botanique, 2, 179

Levasseur, Thérèse: does not accompany R. to Yverdon, 1; declares her love for R., 3–4; R. ceases to sleep with, 4; prepares to leave for Yverdon, 12; with R. at Môtiers, 17, 23–24; room at Môtiers, 25; her cooking praised, 25; Mme de Luxembourg's praise of, 30; nursing Deluc, 47; annuity for 1763 paid, 51; R. concerned for her should anything happen to him, 53–54; as sole heir in R.'s will, 54; Moultou thanks for her kindness, 68; Mme de Verdelin visits mother of, 70; retrieves Sauttern's things after his departure, 70; R. on her fidelity and affection, 71; R.'s continuing concern for, 72; Keith gives annuity to, 84; d'Escherny's praise of, 85–86; as fed up with Môtiers, 90; with R. at Champ-de-Moulin, 93; Boswell's interest in, 97, 98, 99, 100; allegations against in *Le Sentiment des citoyens*, 105, 110; Du Peyrou offers pension for, 106; Mme de Verdelin promises to take care of, 119; Vautravers flatters, 120; deposition on lapidation of R.'s house, 131; accused of faking the lapidation, 132; remains in Môtiers after R. leaves, 133; joins R. on St-Pierre, 134, 135; remains on St-Pierre after R.'s departure, 140; R. writes from Strasbourg, 143; De Peyrou's opinion of, 146; remains on St-Pierre while R. goes to England, 148; R. urges her to go to England, 153–54; as obstacle to lodging in England, 163; invited to dine by Hume, 164; at Wootton, 165, 169, 170, 171; at Trye, 173; R. resolves to marry, 174; children of R. and, 181, 182; retirement with R. to Ermenonville, 185–86

Linnaueus, Carol, 135n

Liotard, Jean-Étienne, 127–28

Liston, Robert, 154

Littret, M., 86

Locke, John, 209

Louis of Wurttemberg, Prince, 81–82, 103, 117, 118

Lully, Jean Baptiste, 192

Luxembourg, Charles-François-Frédéric de Montmorency-Luxembourg, Maréchal-Duc de: R. reports arrival at Yverdon to, 1; suspected of hiding R., 5; sends R.'s things to Yverdon, 12; informs R. of his financial situation, 28–29; R. describes Val de Travers to, 59; R. considers him one of his few French friends, 69; death of, 87–88

Luxembourg, Madeleine-Angélique, Maréchale-Duchesse de: R. tells he wants his presence at Yverdon kept secret, 2; R. fears d'Alembert's interest in, 3; sends Judgement on *Émile* to R., 5; R. thanks for her friendship to Thérèse and himself, 23; R. complains of his persecutions to, 24; R. corresponds with from Môtiers, 30; pleased with R.'s profession of Protestantism, 33; favors publishing *Complete Works*, 51, 58; R. accuses her of forsaking him, 69; R.'s correspondence with on death of her husband, 87–88; presentation copy of *Letters from the Mountain*, 96; Voltaire tells her he has defended R., 102; with R. in Paris, 154; reproaching Walpole, 159; R. writes of his children, 181; as willing to take care of R.'s children, 182

Luze, Jean-Jacques de, 140, 143, 149, 150, 159, 163

Luze, Marianne-Françoise de, 24–25, 35n, 85, 90, 93, 152

Mably, Gabriel Bonnot, Abbé de, 103–4

Machiavelli, Niccolò, 206

Magny, François, 198

Malesherbes, Chrétien-Guillaume de Lamoignon de, 36, 51, 57, 180

Malthus, Daniel, 164

Malthus, Thomas Robert, 164

Marcet de Mézières, Isaac-Ami, 31

Margency, Adrien Cuyret, Seigneur de, 53, 84

Marie Antoinette, 188

Marmontel, Jean-François, 151

Martinet, Jacques-Frédéric, 19, 54, 55, 112, 115, 116, 130, 131–32, 133

Marx, Karl, 183n

Meister, Jakob-Heinrich, 86–87, 106

Meuron, Samuel, 112, 113, 133